THE BEHAVIORAL BASIS OF PERCEPTION

THE BEHAVIORAL BASIS OF PERCEPTION

by James G. Taylor

With a Mathematical Appendix to Chapter 8
by Seymour Papert

GREENWOOD PRESS, PUBLISHERS
WESTPORT, CONNECTICUT

Library of Congress Cataloging in Publication Data

Taylor, James Garden, 1897-
The behavioral basis of perception.

Bibliography: p.
Includes index.
1. Perception. I. Title.
BF311.T35 1975 153.7 73-8151
ISBN 0-8371-6957-7

Originally published in 1962 by Yale University Press, New Haven

Reprinted with the permission of Yale University Press

Reprinted in 1975 by Greenwood Press,
a division of Williamhouse-Regency Inc.

Library of Congress Catalog Card Number 73-8151

ISBN 0-8371-6957-7

Printed in the United States of America

TO
THE MEMORY OF
CLARK L. HULL,
WHO LAID THE FOUNDATIONS;
TO
THEODOR ERISMANN AND IVO KOHLER,
WHO PROVIDED MOST OF THE
EXPERIMENTAL EVIDENCE;
AND TO
W. ROSS ASHBY,
WHO SUPPLIED THE LOGICAL FRAMEWORK,
THIS BOOK IS
GRATEFULLY AND AFFECTIONATELY
DEDICATED

Preface

THE THESIS of this book is that all conscious experience is a function of learned behavior, although the detailed exposition is confined to a relatively restricted sector of that experience—the visual perception of the material environment. If circumstances permit, I hope to follow this with a work on auditory perception, but if that should prove impossible, I trust that others will take up the task, and that ultimately the whole range of conscious phenomena will prove to be explainable in terms of natural scientific principles.

The behavioral theory of consciousness is by no means new. It has been formulated by several authors, both philosophers and psychologists, but never in such a way that it could be subjected to a critical test and either proved or disproved. The reason for this failure is not that the theory is false, but that there are formidable difficulties in the way of making it testable. To test a theory it is not enough to state it in general terms; it is also necessary to substitute specific values for the general terms and calculate the results that must follow if the theory is true. Then, if the specific values are drawn from a real system and not from an abstract mathematical or logical system, the calculated results can be compared with observation, and preferably with observation resulting from experimental manipulation of the independent variables.

The obstacles that have hitherto prevented the behavioral theory from being adequately tested are of two main kinds. First, the independent variables are multidimensional. For example, as I sit at my desk writing these lines, the stimulus that evokes the response of picking up my pen must be defined as a region within an 11-dimensional afferent space. Previous exponents of the theory have not recognized this complexity, and in consequence have not been able to calculate results with any measure of accuracy, but have had to express their deductions in the form of probabilities and test them by statistical methods.

Second, if the theory is true it follows that consciousness is built up stage by stage as the individual acquires appropriate responses to more and more aspects of his environment. Consequently the theory cannot be fully tested unless we begin at the earliest stage of life at which learning can occur. But at this stage the subject cannot report his conscious experiences, so that no direct testing of deductions is possible. In face of this difficulty writers who favor the behavioral theory have tended to choose aspects of conscious experience that may be assumed to have been acquired relatively late and are still subject to modification by changing some pattern of behavior. The results of such manipulation are revealed in the subjects' reports, but there is no means of determining how far they are attributable to other forms of behavior that have not been controlled, and particularly those acquired at the earliest stages of life. Thus once more results cannot be calculated and statistical methods must be used for the testing of deductions. If, in addition, the multidimensional character of the stimulus is not recognized, the possibility of exact calculation is even more remote.

In this book an attempt is made to overcome these difficulties. I have tried to include all the dimensions that are necessary and sufficient for calculation of results rather than estimation of probabilities. At first I tried to define in ordinary language the complex functions that this entailed, but as the work progressed the expressions became intolerably cumbersome, and before the penultimate draft of the book had been completed I decided that a compact notation was required. The notation I have adopted is derived from mathematical set theory, but the reader needs no preliminary training in mathematics. All that is demanded is enough patience to become familiar with the definitions of the symbols. Most of the basic symbols are defined in Chapter 2 and the first three sections of Chapter 3. These definitions are repeated in section 3.4, and the reader is advised to become thoroughly familiar with them before continuing. As a further aid to memory there are numerous cross references to the definitions.

The reader is further advised to beware of imposing his own definitions on the symbols. For example the symbol Π derives its meaning from a long chain of preceding definitions; and when I state the hypothesis that what Π represents is equivalent to a strictly limited form of perception, the reader must not assume that henceforth Π may be read as a symbol for what he understands as perception. If the hypothesis should be disproved, Π will continue to have the meaning I have assigned to it but it will not be legitimate to use it as a symbol for perception. Since the hypothesis is herewith placed on trial the duty of an impartial judge is to read the symbol as carrying the meaning I have given it.

To meet the second difficulty I have tried to trace the development of visual perception from the beginning of life. Here the procedure must of necessity be speculative, since deductions about conscious experience cannot be tested. However it is not entirely speculative, for if the behavioral theory is true the infant's acquired responses to his environment must continue to be valid when he comes to maturity. Hence, although his perception is enormously enriched by that time it must still display those properties that were acquired early in life, and a test of the speculative hypothesis is thus available.

My procedure here is the reverse of that adopted by a developmental psychologist such as Gesell. He first made detailed observations of the behavior of children and then derived a series of empirical generalizations from his findings, whereas I have begun by writing a theory, which must stand or fall by the results of observations. His method may be described as Baconian induction, mine as the Galileian hypothetico-deductive procedure.

The solution of these problems was reached as a result of a process of trial and error lasting over a period of more than fifteen years, in the course of which I came to the painful conclusion that psychology, considered as the science of conscious phenomena, is the most undisciplined of all the scientific disciplines. I found that my own thinking on the subject had hitherto been disgracefully loose and disorderly. Although my aim was to construct a theory of perception within the framework of the natural sciences, there were numerous relics of earlier modes of thinking that had to be rooted out before I could complete my task. The usual way in which this happened was that some train of reasoning led to absurd results, and when I examined the steps I invariably found that one of them involved an untenable assumption. When this error was eliminated the conclusion was no longer absurd. Frequent experiences of this kind ultimately purged my thinking of all the relics of a philosophy I had decided to abandon.

At the same time it became clear that it was not only my own thinking that was confused. The faults I found in myself were manifest in other writers as well, and particularly in those whose philosophical outlook was nearest to my own. I therefore took the deliberate decision to read no more of the current literature on perception, since it only served to deflect me from the task of constructing an internally consistent theory. No doubt this policy has caused me to miss many studies that could have strengthened my argument, and others that would have demanded revision. But scientific investigation is essentially a communal enterprise, and my errors will be corrected by others.

My major debts are already acknowledged in the dedication. Clark L. Hull's *Principles of Behavior* was largely responsible for prompting me to undertake the work, and I received a great deal of encouragement from him in correspondence. It was he who first convinced me of the possibility of turning the study of conscious phenomena into an exact science.

My debt to Professor Theodor Erismann and Professor Ivo Kohler is equally great. Their brilliant researches on visual perception provided me with a wealth of material for the testing of my theory. During two visits to Innsbruck they generously put at my disposal the detailed records of several of their experiments, and gave me permission to use as much of their material as I needed. I have availed myself of this permission to include in Chapter 10 a translation of several passages from Professor Kohler's monograph, *Ueber Aufbau und Wandlungen der Wahrnehmungswelt*, but my most important borrowings are invisible. It was their carefully recorded results, presented in their published works, in the protocols of experiments, and in numerous face-to-face discussions that compelled me to examine the unformulated assumptions at the root of my thinking, and enabled me to eliminate many crudities and errors in the theory as originally formulated. An example of this is presented at the end of Chapter 10.

My debt to Dr. W. Ross Ashby is more obvious, since I have freely used his theory of the multistable system. I have also derived much encouragement and enlightenment from personal discussions with him.

I am indebted to Dr. Seymour Papert, and not only for the mathematical argument presented in the Appendix to Chapter 8. He read the first draft of the book, and as a result of discussions with him I decided to rewrite it, aiming at a higher level of precision. He volunteered to act as subject in the first of the three experiments described in Chapter 9. His contributions to this experiment, as well as those of my colleague Mrs. A. Schermann, are recorded in the appropriate place.

The second experiment was performed in Innsbruck, with the collaboration of Dr. Kohler, whose assistance I gratefully acknowledge.

The third experiment, involving the wearing of a distorting contact lens, was made possible by the generous collaboration of a number of people in Johannesburg. I have to thank Dr. Graham Scott for making the optometric measurements, Dr. H. A. Beiles for making a mold of my eye and fitting the lens, the Obrig Contact Lens Laboratories for constructing the lens, and Dr. A. Adelstein, Dr. J. Wolpe, and Dr. S. Biesheuvel for helping me in various ways during the course of the experiment.

I have to thank my colleagues, past and present, in the University of Cape Town, who have patiently listened to my arguments and by their criticism have helped me to clarify my ideas and express them in a more intelligible and unambiguous form. I have received similar help from numerous psychologists in other countries, and more particularly from Professor F. V. Smith and his colleagues in the University of Durham, England. I am grateful to them all.

I have to thank certain publishers for permission to quote: Routledge and Kegan Paul for Piaget's *The Child's Construction of Reality* and Hayek's *The Sensory Order*, Macmillan and the University of Manchester for Alexander's *Space, Time and Deity*, and George Allen and Unwin for Janet's *Principles of Psychotherapy*.

I am grateful to Mrs. R. de Kock for undertaking the laborious and often exasperating task of typing the manuscript.

I have to thank Mr. Arnold Abramovitz for invaluable assistance in the preparation of the index.

I cannot sufficiently express my debt to my wife for her unfailing patience and encouragement during the preparation of the work.

J. G. T.

Cape Town
March 1962

Contents

	Preface	vii
1.	Introduction	1
2.	The Beginnings of Adaptation to the Environment	14
3.	The Beginnings of Space Perception	36
4.	Further Development of Space Perception	53
5.	Gravity	70
6.	Expanding the Visual Field	98
7.	Parallax	134
8.	Experimental Evidence	163
	Mathematical Appendix, by Seymour Papert	189
9.	Three Experiments	194
10.	The Perception of Color	232
11.	The Modalities	270
12.	Other Theories	298
13.	Philosophical Implications	338
	References	365
	Index	367

Im Anfang war die That.

GOETHE. *Faust*

Ascent takes place, it would seem, through complexity. But at each change of quality the complexity as it were gathers itself together and is expressed in a new simplicity. . . .

We do not do because we know; but we know because we do, and we end by knowing without doing. Yet our mental action, whether speculative or not, remains to the end a doing.

SAMUEL ALEXANDER. *Space, Time and Deity*, 1920

We shall some day describe mental disorders solely in terms of action and conduct. The psychology of behaviour so useful in the study of animals should be applied to men also by describing even the higher psychic phenomena in terms of conduct.

PIERRE JANET. *Principles of Psychotherapy*, 1924

CHAPTER 1

Introduction

1.1. In the twentieth century a great deal of attention has been devoted to the study of perception, and a bewildering variety of theories have been proposed to account for the facts. Those theories cannot all be true, and it seems unlikely that a viable theory can be constructed by borrowing a bit from this one and a bit from that. An eclectic theory must by its very nature generate mutually incompatible deductions and thereby prove itself false. Accordingly, the most promising procedure is to start from basic principles and neglect, without exception, all current theories. If perception is a genuine natural phenomenon and not an illusion or an artifact generated by man's use of language, it should be possible to fit it into the conceptual framework of general scientific theory and to demonstrate that it is a necessary and predictable consequence of the properties of the living organism. As argument about current theories would only retard the progress of the project, no reference will be made to any of them.

1.2. Since the time of Newton it has been a basic assumption of scientific thought that all events are determined and that the function of science is to discover what determines what. This is not an easy task, and in psychology it is made much harder by the fact that the events to be explained occur within the scientist himself, where they are directly observable, but are open to observation in others only through their verbal reports. This inaccessibility led the early behaviorists to maintain that mental experience could never be a fit subject for scientific investigation.

This assertion seemed to imply either that mental events do

not exist or that they are not determined. If they do not exist there is of course no possibility of a science of mind. If we say that they exist but are undetermined, we assert the existence of a realm of nature that is not subject to natural law. But that is a conclusion that is completely repugnant to the spirit of science. Existence implies lawfulness, and if we are unwilling to accept the latter we must logically deny the former. This book starts from the assumption that mental phenomena are both real and lawful, and therefore a legitimate subject for scientific inquiry.

1.3. There has been a great deal of argument on the question whether the inaccessibility of mental events to independent observation constitutes an insuperable barrier to scientific investigation; and it would seem that any writer who maintains the scientific respectability of such events is in duty bound to take a stand on this question and to justify his position. That is precisely what I do not propose to do, and for a very simple reason. Inaccessibility is a universally recognized property of the phenomena in question and is therefore one of the facts that have to be explained. If a scientific theory of mind can be formulated, the fact of inaccessibility should be directly deducible from it. The question whether it constitutes a barrier to scientific investigation then ceases to have any meaning.

There are, however, two related questions that call for some discussion. The first concerns the reliability of reports on perceptual experience. Can we accept without question a subject's reports on what he has perceived? The answer is that we have no alternative. The facts as he reports them *are* the facts that stand in need of explanation, and if we refuse to accept them we might as well retire at once from the field of science. Of course we do not choose as subjects people whose reliability as witnesses is questionable, but having chosen them we cannot do otherwise than accept their reports as true statements of fact.

The second question is whether differences between the reports of two subjects who have gone through the same experimental routine justify a suspicion that either of them is unreliable. The answer is that having decided that the reports of our subjects are a true reflection of the facts to be explained, we cannot logically accept one and reject the other, no matter how disparate or even contradictory they may be. This implies that any theory of perception we may construct must be such that it can account exactly for all types of results. That is to say, it must be so general that when two sets of values, derived from two subjects, are assigned to the parameters and variables of the theoretical system, it must generate different results that will be in accord with the reports of the subjects.

1.4. As a preliminary to constructing such a theory I propose to follow the example of Descartes and to doubt all current beliefs about perception, and in particular those that appear to be justified by everyday experience. For example, a great many human actions are preceded by perception, and it is commonly believed that such actions are, by virtue of the preceding perception, essentially different from others, the so-called "unconsciously motivated" actions. It is assumed that the former are "guided" by perception while the latter are not. Indeed the truth of this proposition appears to be self-evident.

Nevertheless I propose to doubt it. This does not mean that I deny its truth outright. It is not impossible that it may turn out to be true in some way. My doubt merely means that I shall not use it as an explanatory principle or as a postulate or axiom of the theoretical system I propose to build. And the same applies to any other "self-evident truth" about perception, as well as to the more sophisticated theories that have been proposed by psychologists. In short, the basic postulates out of which the theory of perception is to be constructed will include none in which any statement is made about perception.

There is of course nothing novel about such a proposal. In other scientific disciplines it is a commonplace that it is impossible to explain any natural phenomenon by merely postulating the properties of the phenomenon as primary principles. Thus we cannot explain the viscosity of oil or the toughness of iron by appealing to a principle of viscosity or a principle of toughness. We must look for an explanation in the geometrical structure of the molecules of oil and iron. Similarly, we do not try to explain the elliptical motion of the planets round the sun by postulating ellipticity as a primary principle of planetary motion; we explain it by reference to principles that contain not the slightest hint of ellipticity.

1.5. The next step is to state the basic principles on which the theory of perception is to be built. The first is that the living organism in its environment constitutes what Ashby (1952) has called a *multistable system*. As Ashby's theory has received less attention from psychologists than its importance merits, I shall summarize it briefly.

A *system* is any set of variables that an investigator chooses to record. A *state* of the system is an ordered set of numbers specifying the values taken by the several variables at a given moment of time. A system changes from one state to another when a *primary operation* is applied to one or another of its variables. A system having the property that when it is in state A and a given primary operation is applied it always changes to state B is a *regular* system. If a system is irregular, no scientific laws can be deduced from it, and the scientist must then choose another system. As a rule this will involve the addition of fresh variables, and occasionally the elimination of irrelevant variables. Thus when the system refers to the behavior of an organism it will usually be necessary to include variables descriptive of the environment. A system is said to be *absolute* or *state determined* if, when it starts from state A, it always moves to another specific state B, no matter how it arrives at A. A change from one state to another, whether directly or through a series of intermediate states, is a *line of behavior*, and the totality of the lines of behavior of a system is its behavioral *field*. We shall subsequently develop a notation for the exact specification of both lines and fields of behavior.

A *critical state* is defined as a state that tends to the disruption or even disintegration of the system if it is maintained beyond a limited period of time. Ashby is chiefly concerned with systems in which a critical state is equivalent to what other writers have called *drive*. A system is said to be *stable* or to have a stable field if, whenever it enters a critical state, it changes to a noncritical state. A system may be initially unstable, but if it has the property of *ultrastability* it develops a stable field. An ultrastable system is one that contains certain *step-functions* that change their values in a random manner whenever the system enters a critical state. Each value of a step-function changes the behavior of the system in a determinate manner, and if such a change takes the system out of the critical state, the relevant value of the step-function is retained; it becomes a constant of the system. The process of transforming an initially unstable into a stable system is called *adaptation*.

A *multistable* system is a large system containing many subsystems, each of which is ultrastable. A large multistable system cannot adapt in a reasonable period of time if all its step-functions have to arrive simultaneously at the appropriate values, but if one of the subsystems can be isolated from the rest for a time, it can adapt as if it were completely independent. Ashby envisages two types of relationship between the subsystems, which we may call the *parallel* and *serial* arrangements. In the first the subsystems can adapt independently of one another and in any order, including simultaneity. In the second arrangement adaptation of the first subsystem is a prerequisite for adaptation of the second one.

1.6. Ashby's theory is a logically worked out statement of the properties that an organic system must possess if it is to be at the same time determinate and adaptable. It is a general theory in the true sense of the term. That is, its validity can be tested by substituting for the general system a specific system derived from a real organism and deducing what its behavior must be. If the behavior of the real system is found to be in agreement with the deductions, the validity of the theory is confirmed.

In the following chapters we shall describe selected subsystems abstracted from the larger system of the human organism in its environment and try to deduce the properties that the system must acquire through the process of adaptation. As it happens, the initial helplessness of the human infant provides exactly the conditions postulated by Ashby as being necessary for the serial adaptation of subsystems. For example, stimulation of the retina by fixed features of the environment is unaffected by movements of the legs, and it is therefore possible for adaptation to take place in a subsystem containing retinal variables but excluding all functions of leg movements. When the infant begins to sit without support, to stand, and ultimately to walk, fresh variables are thereby added to the active system, but if at every stage some measure of adaptation is achieved, the addition of these variables does not make the task of further adaptation impossibly difficult. We shall try to trace this serial development in some detail.

1.7. In addition to substituting specific systems for the general system we must also substitute specific mechanisms of adaptation for the general mechanism described by Ashby in terms of step-functions that change their values whenever the system enters a critical state and retain permanently the values that result in the termination of the critical state. The mechanism that most obviously meets the requirements of the theoretical system is conditioning in conjunction with the Hullian principle of unlearned behavior. According to Hull (1943) a drive stimulus, S_D, in conjunction with a stimulus, S, determined by some feature of the environment, gives rise to a succession of unlearned responses that goes on until one response results in a diminution of the drive. The reduction of the drive has the effect of establishing a relatively permanent neural connection such that when the same S and S_D occur again, the response that led to the reduction of S_D is more likely to be evoked than any other response.

This means that we shall give to Ashby's "critical state" the specific interpretation of a need-state of the organism giving rise to a drive. His "step-functions" will be given the specific interpretation of the mechanisms that are responsible for unlearned reactions; and his concept of the retention of those values of the step-functions that end the critical state will be interpreted as the neural connections that are formed through the process of conditioning.

We shall not be concerned here with the question whether classical and instrumental conditioning can be regarded as variants of a single process. Both are well authenticated by experimental evidence, and when conditioning is postulated, it is to be understood that the type appropriate to the system under examination is intended. No further reference to the distinction will be made. The essence of the matter is that conditioning will be treated in this book not as a subject for inquiry or argument but as an explanatory principle.

1.8. The systems to be discussed in the following chapters are among the most complex to be found in nature, and if we are to talk about them unambiguously and at the same time without being intolerably long-winded, it will be necessary to adopt some kind of notation that is both concise and precise. Fortunately a notation exactly suited to our purpose already exists in modern mathematics. It is the notation of *set theory*. The remainder of this chapter will be devoted to an explanation of the principal conventions of this notation. The reader who wishes to know more about it may profitably consult *The Anatomy of Mathematics*, by Kershner and Wilcox (1950), which can be read even by one who has no prior knowledge of mathematics. As the authors say in their preface: "The only prerequisites for reading this book are the desire to start and the perseverance to finish."

1.9. A *set*, usually represented by a capital letter, is defined as a collection of *elements*. The elements may be anything we choose, from simple things such as the pieces in a set of chessmen, positive integers, or galvanometer readings, through rather more complex things such as intelligence quotients, or the moves a knight may make on the chessboard, to the most complicated of abstractions that would require hundreds of words to define them. For some purposes a subset of the set may be considered as an element of the set. For example, the elements of the set of white chessmen may be taken either as the sixteen separate pieces or as the king, the queen, and the subsets of bishops, knights, rooks, and pawns. In the former case we would write

(1.9.1) $W \equiv [w; w \text{ is a white chessman}]$

and in the latter

(1.9.2) $W = [k, q, B, Kt, R, P]$.

Several conventions are incorporated in these two statements. In (1.9.1) the symbol $\equiv$ means that the statement following it is a definition of the term preceding it. In ordinary language (1.9.1) would read: we define W as the set of elements, w, satisfying the condition that each w is a white chessman. The square brackets enclose either a complete list of the elements included in the set, as in (1.9.2), or, as in (1.9.1), a sample element followed by a semicolon and a statement of the conditions that have to be satisfied for an element to be included in the set.

It is frequently necessary to make statements that refer not to all the elements of a set but to certain selected elements. Such a selection is known as a *subset*. Thus in (1.9.2) the set, P, of pawns is a subset of W. We indicate this relation by $P \subset W$ or by $W \supset P$. There are many ways of forming subsets. For example, one way that is relevant to statistics may be illustrated. Suppose that a set, A, has five elements. There is one way of forming a subset that has no elements at all; this empty subset is represented by the symbol Θ. There are five ways of selecting subsets each of which has only one element of A; there are ten subsets each containing two elements, ten that contain three elements, five that have four elements, and one that contains all the elements of A. The reader who is familiar with the binomial theorem will recognize that these numbers are the coefficients of the powers of x from 0 to 5 in the expansion of $(1 + x)^5$. In this context it is logically convenient to think of the set A as being a subset of itself. Subsets that do not contain all the elements are known as *proper subsets.* Thus in (1.9.2) P is a proper subset of W. This statement is abbreviated to $P \subsetneqq W$, which simply combines the two statements, $P \neq W$ and $P \subset W$.

In our work we shall be concerned exclusively with proper subsets, since the selection of subsets will in general be determined by physical or physiological limitations. For example, if we define H as the set of all horizontal deviations of the left eye from the median plane of the head, and we assign a fixed direction to the right eye, then the directions that the left eye can take constitute a proper subset of H. Again, if V is the set of vertical deviations of the left eye, assigning a fixed direction to the right eye means that the directions that can be taken by the left eye constitute a proper subset of V. In this case the physiological limitations have the effect that the subset has only one element, whereas the corresponding subset of H has several elements.

To indicate the set to which a particular element belongs we use the Greek letter epsilon, ε. Thus, $p \,\varepsilon\, P$ means that p is an element of P. If P is the set of white pawns, then, since $P \subset W$, it follows that $p \,\varepsilon\, W$. The negation of this statement is represented by ε′. Thus, if *p* is a black pawn, $p \,\varepsilon'\, W$.

1.10. Sets may be combined in a variety of ways, and some of these may be conveniently illustrated by reference to the game of chess. Let

$$(1.10.1)\ X = [1, 2, \ldots 8]$$

be defined as the set of the 8 columns of the chessboard, and

$$(1.10.2)\ Y = [1, 2, \ldots 8]$$

be the set of the 8 rows. The position of any square on the board may be represented by specifying an element of X and an element of Y, in that order. A pair of elements, (x,y), formed in this way is an *ordered pair*. It is ordered in the sense that the first of the pair is always an element of X and the second is always an element of Y. Adherence to the order serves to avoid ambiguity. If it were not enforced, a pair such as (3, 5) might refer to either of two squares. The set of the positions of the 64 squares can then be represented by

$$Z = [(x,y); x \in X, y \in Y].$$

It will be seen that an element of Z is analogous to the specification of the position of a point on a plane by reference to Cartesian coordinates. This analogy has in fact given rise to the convention that Z is described as the *Cartesian product* of X and Y. This is expressed in the notation by

$$(1.10.3)\ Z = X \times Y$$

where the symbol $\times$ is to be understood not as an instruction to multiply, as in arithmetic, but as an instruction to pair the first element of X with all the elements of Y in turn and to do the same with all the other elements of X. The list of ordered pairs thus assembled is the set Z.

There is no limit to the number of sets that can be combined to form a Cartesian product. Thus

$$E = A \times B \times C \times D = [(a,b,c,d); a \in A, b \in B, c \in C, d \in D].$$

An element, (a,b,c,d), of E is an ordered 4-tuple.

1.11. The game of chess is played by making moves. A move is defined by specifying the position, z_i, from which the piece starts, and its terminal position, z_j; and it is at once obvious that the set of all possible moves can be represented by

$$(1.11.1)\ M = Z \times Z.$$

An element of M is an ordered pair, (z,z), in which the first of the pair is the initial position of the piece and the second is its terminal position. It should be noted that M includes zero moves. As these are of no importance in the game it is desirable to exclude them from the definition. This can be done by

$$(1.11.2)\ M \equiv [(z_i, z_j); z_i, z_j \in Z, z_i \neq z_j].$$

This implies that $M \subset Z \times Z$. Another way of stating this is to say that M is a *relation* on $Z \times Z$.

M includes all moves that are physically possible, but many of these are excluded by the rules of the game. To express those rules in terms of the notation we must remember that each $m \in M$ is an ordered pair of ordered pairs, which we may write in full as $((x_1,y_1), (x_2,y_2))$. The set of moves that can be made by the knight is

$$(1.11.3)\ Kt \equiv [kt \in M; x_2 = x_1 \pm 2 \textit{ and } y_2 = y_1 \pm 1, \textit{ or } x_2 = x_1 \pm 1 \textit{ and } y_2 = y_1 \pm 2].$$

Note that the condition that $kt \in M$ prevents the knight from jumping off the board. For if $x_2 = x_1 \pm 2 = -1$ or 0 or 9 or 10, then $x_2 \varepsilon' X$ and consequently, by (1.10.3) $z_2 \varepsilon' Z$, and by (1.11.2) kt ε' M. There is no square from which a knight may not start; this is expressed by saying that the *domain* of Kt is Z. Similarly, there is no square to which it may not move. The *range* of Kt is Z.

The moves open to the bishop are

(1.11.4) $B \equiv [b \ \varepsilon \ M; x_2 = x_1 \pm \alpha, y_2 = y_1 \pm \beta, \alpha = \beta]$.

It is clear the B includes all diagonal moves within the area of the board, but the domain of B is a subset of Z, and its range is the same subset.

The set of the rook's moves is

(1.11.5) $R \equiv [r \ \varepsilon \ M; x_2 = x_1 \pm \alpha$ *and* $y_2 = y_1$, *or* $x_2 = x_1$ *and* $y_2 = y_1 \pm \alpha]$.

The domain of R is Z, and so is its range.

The queen can make any move that a bishop may make and also any move open to a rook. This is expressed by

(1.11.6) $Q \equiv B + R$.

Q is the *set theoretic sum* or *set sum* of B and R. It includes all the elements of B together with all the elements of R that are not also elements of B. This is expressed generally by

$Q = [q; q \ \varepsilon \ B$ *or* $q \ \varepsilon \ R]$.

There are no elements of R that are also elements of B, and of course this implies that there are none of B that are also elements of R. A concise way of stating this is

$B \cdot R = \Theta$.

B·R is the *set theoretic product* or *set product* of B and R, and it is defined as the set whose elements are elements of both B and R. In general, if A and B are sets,

(1.11.7) $C = A \cdot B \equiv [c; c \ \varepsilon \ A$ *and* $c \ \varepsilon \ B]$.

It is clear from definitions (1.11.2) to (1.11.7) that

$Kt \cdot B = Kt \cdot R = Kt \cdot Q = B \cdot R = \Theta$

but that $Q \cdot B = B$ and $Q \cdot R = R$.

1.12. The sets defined in (1.11.3) to (1.11.6) are all relations on $Z \times Z$, and they all have the property that for every $z_1 \ \varepsilon \ Z$ there are several $z_j \ \varepsilon \ Z$ such that $(z_1, z_j) \ \varepsilon$ B, or R, Kt or Q, as the case may be. That is to say, whatever the initial position of a piece may be there are, in general, several moves that it may make. Without this plurality there would be no game. We shall encounter several examples of this kind of relation in the course of our work.

But there is another type of relation that is of much greater importance in science. Let A and B be sets, and let F be a relation on $A \times B$. That is $F \subset A \times B$. If F has the property that for every $a \varepsilon$ domain of F there is one and only one $b \varepsilon B$ for which $(a,b) \varepsilon F$, then F is a *function.* It is sometimes called a single-valued function. It is important to note that the single-valued relationship does not necessarily operate in reverse. That is, if F is a function it does not follow that for every $b \varepsilon$ range of F there is one and only one $a \varepsilon A$ for which $(a,b) \varepsilon F$. There may be many elements of A that are paired with one and the same element of B, such that all these pairs are elements of F. This obviously must happen when the number of elements in A greatly exceeds the number in B. For example, if A is the set of children of age ten attending schools in a city, B is the set of values of the intelligence quotient as measured by a standard test, and F is the list of the names of the children together with their IQs, F is a function. Each child has one and only one IQ, but there are many children having one and the same IQ.

In this case the number of elements in F is identical with the number in A, and for every element of A there is a corresponding element of F. A briefer way of stating this is to say that F is *equivalent* to A, or $F \sim A$. It is obvious that $F \sim' B$, that is, F is not equivalent to B. The elements of A that are paired with one and the same $b \varepsilon B$ constitute an *equivalence class* of A, and A is said to be *partitioned* into equivalence classes by F. An equivalence class of A may be defined by

$$E(b) = [a \varepsilon A; \text{for every } a \varepsilon E(b), (a,b) \varepsilon F].$$

It should be noted that in this definition b refers not to *any* element of B but to a specific element. Thus if we put $b = 99$, we get

$$E(99) = [a \varepsilon A; \text{for every } a \varepsilon E(99), (a,99) \varepsilon F].$$

In mathematics an equivalence class of A is defined without any reference to other sets, but since in our work we shall be concerned only with equivalence classes that are determined by functional relations, the definition given here may be allowed to stand.

If A and B are sets and C is a relation on $A \times B$ such that for every $a \varepsilon$ domain of C there is one and only one $b \varepsilon B$ such that $(a,b) \varepsilon C$, and for every $b \varepsilon$ range of C there is one and only one $a \varepsilon A$ such that $(a,b) \varepsilon C$, then C is a one-to-one correspondence. Thus a table of squares of positive numbers is a one-to-one correspondence, but a table of square roots is not, unless we choose to neglect the negative roots.

1.13. Mathematical discourse is concerned primarily with the investigation of the logical implications of any abstract system the mathematician may construct; and one of his incidental tasks is to determine whether there can be an instance of such a system. If it generates mutually contradictory deductions there can be no concrete instance of it, and its further investigation is a waste of time.

A scientist also begins by setting up an abstract system, but his choice of a system is determined in the first instance by the observed properties of the natural phenomena he is seeking to understand. This, however, does not absolve him from the obligation to test the logical consistency of his system. If it does not survive this test it is a waste of time to continue work on it, no matter how close its superficial resemblance to the natural system may be. But whereas the mathematician's work is completed when he has exhausted the logical implications of his system, the scientist's work is completed only when he has demonstrated that the abstract system fits the concrete system in every detail. This means that in general he will be interested only in those implications of the abstract system that are capable of being tested by direct observation or by experiment, so that he may easily fail to detect logical inconsistencies that are fatal to his theory. If, however, he can incorporate in his theory a mathematical system that has survived all tests, he is to that extent relieved of the obligation to test for consistency: the job has been done already. A scientist is not bound to use the findings of mathematics, but if he does, his burden is made all the lighter.

For example, it will be assumed throughout this book that the spatial ordering of the terrestrial environment of any organism is adequately represented by the system of Euclidean geometry. Since the logical consistency of that system has been established, its theorems can be accepted without further proof.

In the same way a scientist is not bound to use mathematical symbols, since his business is with events in the real world. But neither is a mathematician obliged to use symbols. As Kershner and Wilcox point out, it would be quite possible to write mathematics without symbols, but in that case it would be so cumbersome as to be unreadable. Symbols are used not only because they permit brevity of utterance but because their neutrality, their availability for any purpose to which the writer may choose to put them, protects the reader from the misinterpretations that are all too common when everyday language is used. Even more important, it protects the writer himself against the unpardonable sin of equivocation. Consider, for example, the word *stimulus*, so frequently used in psychological literature. It has been used with a variety of meanings, but whatever meaning is assigned to it, it is nearly always represented by the letter S. As so used, however, the letter S is not a true symbol, with a specific meaning, but merely an abbreviation of the word *stimulus*, and therefore subject to all the ambiguity that attaches to that word.

From this it can be seen that the brevity of utterance that is made possible by the use of symbols is a hollow advantage unless it is allied with the logical stringency that is an essential feature of mathematical discourse. Brevity in conjunction with ambiguity may produce a resplendent offspring of wit, but we do not expect wisdom to result from such a marriage.

CHAPTER 2

The Beginnings of Adaptation to the Environment

2.1. Consider a newborn infant lying on his back and starting out on the long process of acquiring hand-and-eye coordination. At first he can neither fixate an object held in front of him nor reach for it with his hand; six months later he will be able to do both. This at once suggests that we are dealing with a system that is initially unstable but achieves stability in the course of time. Our first problem then is to define an unstable system that has a sufficient number of variables to permit the adaptation that generates stability.

The system must obviously contain variables that are determined by the position in space of the object that is to be fixated and reached for, and by the energy of the light reflected by the object. This requirement is so simple that nothing further need be said about it at this stage. But since the reaction is to be initiated by rays of light reflected by the object into the eyes, the system must also include certain afferent functions, or stimulus variables, and it is not immediately obvious how many variables of this kind are required. As the system is unstable in any case, it would appear that it does not matter how many or how few we choose.

Actually there is a very simple criterion. If we can determine that such-and-such variables are necessary for a specific response in the *adapted* system, we can say that the unstable system cannot achieve stability if one or more of those variables is omitted. We proceed therefore to enumerate the afferent variables that are necessary and sufficient to produce the response of reaching for an object, but in doing so we must remember that the infant can move only his head, eyes, and arms, and impose similar restrictions on our mature subject. That is, we shall simply hold constant all variables that are dependent on movements of the trunk and of the body as a whole.

2.2. With these restrictions, the apparently simple task of carrying the hand from an initial position Y to a goal at X requires at least 11 afferent variables. These are functions of

1. The angle at which a ray of light from X enters the left eye.
2. The corresponding angle for the right eye.
3. The horizontal deviation of the left eye from the median plane of the head.
4. The corresponding deviation of the right eye.
5. The vertical deviation of the eyes from a horizontal plane through the head.
6. The rotation of the head about its vertical axis.
7. The backward or forward tilt of the head from the vertical axis of the body.
8. The sideways tilt of the head from the vertical axis of the body.

9, 10, 11. The initial position of the hand referred to a convenient coordinate system.

We shall presently define these functions with some precision, but in the meantime it is necessary to point out that if the first or second variable were omitted the response would be indeterminate with respect to its distance unless some other variable were substituted for the missing one. As it happens, this aspect of the response is generously overdetermined by the organic system, since there are several afferent variables that are functionally related to the distance of the object. Indeterminacy in the direction of the response would result if variables 3 to 5 were eliminated while the eyes could still move in their sockets, or if variables 6 to 8 were eliminated while the head retained its mobility. Finally, there could be no determinate response if the initial position of the hand were not registered in the system by variables 9 to 11.

These statements flow directly from the geometrical relations of the various parts of the physical system and are necessarily true irrespective of any theory we may hold regarding perception. Analogously, a surveyor cannot determine the exact position of a beacon on a hilltop unless he trains his telescope on it from both ends of his base-line and records the angle of the telescope with the base-line, its elevation, the distinguishing name of the observed object, and the observation post at which the measurements were made. If he is very confident, he can neglect the elevation at one observation post, but if he fails to record any of the other variables he can arrive at no determinate result. Similarly, the organic system cannot generate an accurate movement from Y to X with fewer than the 11 variables listed above, and all of them must therefore be included in the system as it exists at birth. Our next task is to define them.

2.3. Let V_j be the set of all values that can be taken by variable j ($j = 1$ to 11). We have already run ahead of our task by describing these sets as functions; that is, each of them is a relation on the Cartesian product of two other sets, satisfying the definition of a function given in 1.12. The definition of V_j will therefore require the definition of at least two other sets.

We may begin with V_8 to V_{11}, which are similar to one another and all quite simple in structure. It will suffice to examine one of them, say V_8.

Let A_8 represent the set of all horizontal angular deviations of the left eye from the median plane of the head, and let P_8 be the set of all afferent impulses that can arise from the lateral rectus muscles of the left eye.[1] Then V_8 can be defined provisionally by

(2.3.1) $V_8 \equiv [(a,p); a \varepsilon A_8, p \varepsilon P_8, t_a = t_p]$

where t_a is the time at which a occurs. If it can be shown that p is exactly determined by the a that occurs synchronously with it, then V_8 is a function. It is known, however, that when a stimulus is applied continuously to a receptor organ, the discharge of the afferent fibers rises rapidly to a maximum and then diminishes more slowly. Consequently the afferent discharge at any moment is a joint function of the energy of the stimulus and its duration, and therefore (2.3.1) is not a function. To meet this all we need to do is to define T as a set of temporal durations, choosing a unit of time suitable for the purpose, and to define $B_8 \subset A_8 \times T$ by

$B_8 \equiv [(a,t); t \text{ is the duration of } a]$.

1. The existence of these afferents was long disputed but is now established. A simple way of proving their existence is presented in 11.17.

We can then redefine V_3 by

$$(2.3.2)\quad V_3 \equiv [(b,p); t_b = t_p].$$

We shall assume without further argument that V_3, as defined in (2.3.2) is a function. V_4 to V_{11} are similarly defined.

The reason for this apparently fanatic concern to prove that these sets are functions will become clear as we proceed.

2.4. The first two variables are obviously more complex than the others. To define them we need first to specify the position of any piece of matter that may reflect light into the eyes. Since the infant is assumed to be lying in a fixed position we can do this by defining rectangular coordinates with the origin at, say, the center of rotation of the head, and with one axis parallel to the vertical axis of the body and another parallel to the shoulders. We can then define a set, Γ, whose elements are ordered 3-tuples such that each $\gamma \varepsilon \Gamma$ specifies the position of a piece of matter in the immediate environment of the infant.

The only pieces of matter that are relevant to our inquiry are those that reflect light into the infant's eyes, and as this light varies in energy according to the molecular structure of the matter it will be necessary to specify the energy. Reflected light varies in wave length as well, but as this is almost certainly irrelevant at the present stage of our inquiry it will be neglected now.

It is customary to measure the energy of reflected light in millilamberts, but its absolute energy is of far less importance than the ratio of the energy to that of light reflected by some standard substance such as a matte black paper. The light reflected by any object varies enormously with the general level of illumination, but the ratio of the lights reflected by two different substances is much less variable. We may therefore define Ψ as the set of all energies of reflected light measured as ratios of the light reflected by a standard substance. This enables us to neglect variations in the general level of illumination, as well as the degree of contraction or dilation of the pupils and the state of adaptation of the retina.

We can now define

$$(2.4.1)\quad \Delta \equiv [(\gamma, \psi); \gamma \varepsilon \Gamma, \psi \varepsilon \Psi, \psi \text{ is light reflected by matter at } \gamma].$$

This definition implies that Δ is a function. It describes certain relevant aspects of the infant's environment, viz., its spatial ordering and the light it reflects. In general an element of Δ specifies the light energy, ψ, reflected by a piece of matter located at a point, γ, in space, but it will be convenient to include as elements certain subsets of Δ as determined by distinctive objects. Since the infant cannot be credited with our knowledge of the thinghood of such objects, we must define these subsets as being determined by surfaces at whose boundaries there is a sharp change in the energy of the reflected light. The definition then implies that elements of Δ can be determined both by entire objects and by details within any object.

2.5. To define V_1, the retinal variable for the left eye, we need to consider not only the position of the point that reflects light into the eye but also the orientation of the eye relative to the frame of reference. Together these determine the direction in which a ray of light enters the eye relative to the optic axis and therefore the specific receptor that is stimulated. We must also take account of the fact that the afferent energy generated by the light is jointly determined by the energy of the light and by the distance of the receptor from the fovea. We shall build up our definition of V_1 in stages to include all these variables.

We have already, in 2.3, defined A_3 as the set of horizontal angular deviations of the left eye from the median plane of the head. We can similarly define A_4 to A_8 as sets of angles in terms of which the orientation of the eyes and head can be measured, where the subscripts refer to the variables listed in 2.2. We can then define

$$O \subset A_3 \times A_5 \times A_6 \times A_7 \times A_8$$

as the set of all physically possible orientations of the left eye and the head. There is, of course, a corresponding set, with A_4 in place of A_3, for the right eye.

The direction of a ray of light relative to the optic axis is jointly determined by the position of the object reflecting the light and the orientation of the eye. It will be convenient to represent this compound independent variable by a single symbol, and accordingly we define

$$K \subset \Delta \times O$$

as the set of all elements, (δ, o), that result in stimulation of the left retina. It is clear that K must be a subset of $\Delta \times O$, because for every $o \in O$ there are some environmental objects that are outside the retinal field.

2.6. We must next define a set of retinal stimuli, that is, what Koffka called the "proximal" stimuli. Here again two variables have to be considered, viz., the position of the stimulated receptor and the energy of the light applied to it. We have already decided to neglect for the moment the wave length of the light. If we assume rectangular coordinates to be permanently drawn on the retina, the sets A_1 and A_2 may be defined as the horizontal and vertical angular deviations from the optic axis of rays of light entering the eye. Then $H \subset A_1 \times A_2$ defines the positions of all retinal points. The energy of the light may be represented by the set Ψ defined in 2.4. The energy is of course reduced by the light being filtered through the refracting media of the eye and is further subject to variation from changes in the pupillary aperture, but since the elements of Ψ are defined as ratios, their values at the surface of the retina may be assumed to be the same as their values at the source. We can now define

$$R \equiv H \times \Psi$$

as the set of all proximal stimuli applied to the retina.

2.7. The importance of R in the system is that its elements give rise to afferent events in the optic tract and the optic radiation, ending in the striate area of the cortex. Although there is reason to believe that the afferent processes determined by any element of R are to some extent modified by events taking place in adjoining parts of the retina, this is not inconsistent with the assumption that there is a one-to-one correspondence between R and N, the set of neural processes initiated by R. This assumption may be expressed by saying that R and N are equivalent sets, or $R \sim N$.

The relation of equivalence does not imply a relation of equality, and there is one important difference between N and R to which we shall refer in the sequel. If a pencil of rays of constant energy is applied to the retina, the volume of afferent energy generated in the optic tract is a diminishing function of the angle between the pencil and the optic axis. This of course depends on the fact that the number of fibers of the optic nerve per unit area of the retina is a diminishing function of distance from the fovea.

2.8. We can now define a relation on $K \times N$ by

$$(2.8.1) \quad V_1 \equiv [(k,n); k \in K, n \in N, k \rightarrow r \rightarrow n]$$

where the notation $k \rightarrow r \rightarrow n$ means that k determines a proximal retinal stimulus, r, which in turn determines an afferent neural event, n. It will be seen that the geometrical and physiological relations together ensure that V_1 is a function. For an element of K specifies the position of a piece of matter in the environment and the position and orientation of the eye relative to the same reference frame, and therefore determines the position, $h \varepsilon H$, of the retinal receptor that is stimulated. The element of K also specifies the energy of the light applied to h, and therefore determines n. Consequently we can say that for every $k \varepsilon K$ there is one and only one $n \varepsilon N$ for which $(k,n) \varepsilon V_1$.

V_2 is similarly defined for the right eye, and if we wish to define a single function incorporating both V_1 and V_2, we can do so by

(2.8.2) $V_0 \equiv [(v_1, v_2); t_{v1} = t_{v2}]$.

An element of V_0 describes two simultaneous events, involving both eyes, but it does not specify that one and the same external object is involved in both of them. If we wished to specify such an identity we could do so by adding to the definition the restriction that $\delta(v_1) = \delta(v_2)$, where $\delta(v_1)$ is the δ incorporated in v_1. An element of V_0 would then describe a binocular event involving a single external object. It is tempting to define V_0 in this manner, but the temptation arises from the fact that the elements of V_0 as thus restricted are the only ones that are of any importance in mature perception. Since the explanation of perception is the goal of our inquiry, it would be manifestly improper to allow our knowledge of the properties of perception to influence us in our description of the unadapted system. The definition given in (2.8.2) must therefore remain. The justice of this decision will become apparent when we discuss the perception of depth, in 7.8.

It will be seen that (2.8.2) offers a definition of the visual stimulus that is at once more comprehensive and more precise than any that has hitherto been proposed. It is still not complete, since it says nothing about the wave length of the light. But the flexibility of the notation is such that we can easily take care of any additional variables that may be required, and without affecting the validity of the definition as so far presented.

2.9. Our next step is to define a subset, S, of $V_1 \times V_2 \times \ldots \times V_{11}$ by

(2.9.1) $S \equiv [(v_1, v_2, \ldots v_{11}); t_1 = t_2 = \ldots = t_{11}]$.

S is the set of all possible states of the system consisting of the 11 variables defined above, and it has a number of important properties which must be thoroughly understood before we can proceed with our investigation.

The first property arises from the fact that the retina is capable of being stimulated simultaneously by a substantial subset of Δ. This implies the possibility of the simultaneous existence [2] of the elements of a subset of S. Let such a subset be defined by

(2.9.2) $\Sigma \equiv [s \varepsilon S;$ *for every* $s_i, s_j \varepsilon \Sigma, t_{si} = t_{sj}]$.

Since the eyes and head can have only one orientation and the hand only one position at any moment of time, it will be seen that the defining condition of (2.9.2) implies that for every $s_i, s_j \varepsilon \Sigma$, $(v_3, v_4, \ldots v_{11})_i = (v_3, v_4, \ldots v_{11})_j$. Hence it might appear that Σ could be just as adequately defined by

(2.9.3) $\Sigma \equiv [v \varepsilon V_o;$ *for every* $v_i\ v_j \varepsilon V_o, t_{vi} = t_{vj}]$, where V_o has the meaning assigned to it in (2.8.2).

The difference between the two definitions is that in (2.9.3) Σ does not specify v_3 to v_{11}, although specific values of V_3 to V_8 are implied. That is, it includes none of the proprioceptive components that are necessary for determining a movement of the hand from its initial position Y to a goal at X, and therefore does not satisfy the criterion stated in 2.1. We shall therefore adopt the definition of (2.9.2).

A second and closely related property of S is that every change in the orientation of the eyes or head, or both, and every change in the position of the hand transforms all the simultaneously existing elements of S into other elements of S. That is, Σ is transformed to Σ_1, and with further movements to Σ_2, Σ_3, through an endless succession. However, there is nothing haphazard about those changes. Since each of the sets, V_1 to V_{11}, incorporated in S has been shown to be a function, involving one or more of the sets A_3 to A_{11} defined in 2.3, and since the change from Σ_1 to Σ_2 is effected by a movement that changes some or all of the elements a_3 to a_{11}, it follows that the transformation is determinate. If the hand is included in the movement this produces a change in some of the elements of Δ, thereby producing a determinate change in elements V_1 and

2. The word "existence" is used here in a different sense from that current in mathematics. If a mathematician says, *there exists an x such that* $x^2 = -1$, he is asserting that the existence of such an x is compatible with his axioms. If his axioms refer to the ordinary system of numbers the assertion is false, but if they refer to the system of complex numbers it is true. When existence is asserted in this work, it will mean that the element or set referred to exists materially, in a concrete system.

V_2. The system defined by S is thus a regular one. That is, in Ashby's terminology, if it starts from state A (say Σ_1) and a specific primary operation, such as a movement of the eyes, is applied to it, it changes to another specific state B (or Σ_2) and always to the same state.

2.10. Since changes in the state of the system are brought about by movements of eyes, head, and hand, a complete description of the system requires the specification of those movements. The obvious way to do this is to adopt the device already used for specifying the moves in the game of chess. Let

$$(2.10.1)\quad Z(E) \subset A_3 \times A_4 \times A_5$$

be defined as the set of all physically possible positions of the eyes. It is necessarily a subset of the Cartesian product for the reason already given in 1.9. Then

$$(2.10.2)\quad M(E) = Z(E) \times Z(E)$$

is the set of all movements of the eyes. We can similarly define

$$(2.10.3)\quad M(H) = Z(H) \times Z(H)$$

as the set of all movements of the head, and

$$(2.10.4)\quad M(A) = Z(A) \times Z(A)$$

as the set of all movements of the hand. If we write

$$(2.10.5)\quad M = M(E) + M(H) + M(A)$$

we can say that, assuming Δ to be invariant apart from changes brought about by movements of the hand, for every Σ_i, Σ_j there is an $m \in M$ that transforms the system from Σ_i to Σ_j.[3]

2.11. The movements referred to above are not imposed from without but are initiated by the organic system itself. They must therefore have a source, and this source must be incorporated in the abstract system we are building. We shall assume that each movement, at its first appearance, is an unconditioned response to some pattern of stimulation that is different for each movement but always includes what Hull called a drive stimulus (S_D). Many of the drives that have been discussed in the literature are irrelevant to our purpose. For example, the infant is incapable of relieving hunger, directly or indirectly, by any of the movements defined in (2.10.5). We must obviously exclude from our system all drives that can be diminished only by the intervention of the mother.

If we do so, it is pertinent to ask whether anything is left that can determine critical states leading to adaptation of the system

3. This is one of the properties of what Henri Poincaré (in *La Valeur de la science*, 1905) called the continuum or group of displacements.

through actions taken by the infant himself. The answer is that we are not obliged to define as critical only those states of the system that call for maternal intervention. Lower levels of drive can also be considered as determining critical states that are not yet sufficiently severe to give rise to signals of distress. Such *minor critical states*, as we may call them, may well give rise to elements of M, and if one of these results in the carrying of an object to the month, the critical state is temporarily abolished. There is, of course, no actual diminution of hunger, but since hunger is assuaged by taking the nipple in the mouth, stimulation of the mouth quickly becomes conditioned to the cessation of all restless activities. The system arrives at a steady state.

Another drive that operates in early infancy was brought to light by J. B. Watson in the famous experiments in which he tried to discover all the stimuli that evoke unconditionally the responses he called "fear" and "rage." He produced major critical states by dropping the infant and by restricting the movement of the head or the arms. It seems reasonable to postulate that minor critical states are produced by less extensive falling movements, as when the infant is being carried, or by minor interference with the mobility of head and hands, such as may be produced by bedclothes too tightly tucked in.

These considerations suggest the postulate that each drive is a continuous variable with three distinctive ranges of values. At all values within the lowest range the system is in a steady state, which in the case of the infant means sleep. At all values within the intermediate range the system is in a minor critical state. The infant is awake and active, but the actions appear to be random. If any action results in the grasping of an object that can be carried to the mouth or of a fixed object that provides support for the infant, there is a temporary restoration of the steady state. Values within the highest range of the scale of drive determine a major critical state of the system. Action becomes violent, convulsive, and noisy, and, unlike that of the intermediate range, restores stability not directly but only through the intervention of the mother or someone else. We may define D as the set of all values of the drive, without specifying the nature of the drive. In what follows we shall be concerned only with elements of D drawn from the intermediate range, but there is no need to indicate this in the notation.

2.12. In our system we shall give Ashby's step-functions the specific interpretation of the neural impulses that give rise to elements of M(E), M(H), and M(A), as defined in 2.10. It is assumed that the responses in question are fully determined by the state of the nervous system at the moment each one occurs, but that the order of their occurrence is unsystematic. In short, the elements of M are unconditioned reflexes, and as such are subject to conditioning. This implies that Ashby's concept of fixing the value of a step-function is to be interpreted as the establishing of a conditioned reflex arc whereby the motor impulses that originally arose unconditionally out of the internal state of the nervous system are now aroused by a specific pattern of afferent energy including exteroceptive components.

2.13. We can now complete our description of the system as it exists at the birth of the infant by incorporating the sets D and M. We first define

(2.13.1) $Q \equiv [(d,s); d \,\varepsilon\, D, s \,\varepsilon\, S, t_d = t_s]$

as the set of states of the system as determined jointly by D and S. Finally, we define

(2.13.2) $U \equiv [(q,m);\ q \,\varepsilon\, Q,\ m \,\varepsilon\, M,\ 0 < (t_m - t_q) \leqq 10$ sec.].

The final condition means that (q,m) ε U only if the movement, m, occurs after q but not more than 10 seconds after it. This implies that if m ε M(A), several elements of Q, determined by a succession of m ε (M(E) + M(H)), may occur within the interval of 10 seconds. On the assumption that the afferent processes determined by these elements of Q persist, through the mediation of reverberating circuits, for at least 10 seconds, we can say that the traces of these q ε Q are all in existence at the moment when m occurs. It follows that if m is reinforced, a number of what Pavlov called short-trace conditioned reflexes will be established. But before we go on to that we must consider the properties of the set U.

We have defined M as a set of unconditioned responses, and have assumed that the stimulus for each m ε M is an internal state of the nervous system. This state is in part determined by the afferent processes resulting from the concurrent and preceding q ε Q, and particularly by v_9, v_{10}, and v_{11}, as determined by the initial position of the hand; but there may be other contributory factors that are independent of the relevent q ε Q. Even if there were no additional factors, we must remember that it is not just a single $q \varepsilon Q$ that is in operation but a subset, which we may represent by $(d, \Sigma) \varepsilon Q$. With so many afferent impulses pouring into the brain, and each one presumably contributing to the determination of m, it is inevitable that the infant's behavior must create the impression of being completely random and chaotic. This does not mean, however, that we must postulate a "principle of indeterminacy." Each response is in fact determinate, but we can point to no single factor, identifiable in terms of the notation we have developed so far, that can be described as *the* determinant. All this can be summed up in the single statement that U is not a function, but a one-many relation on $Q \times M$. That is, for every $q \varepsilon Q$ there are many $m \varepsilon M$ such that $(q,m) \varepsilon U$.

It can be seen that an element of U is essentially the same as what Hull called an "unlearned reaction" (${}_SU_R$ in his notation) although both stimulus and response are more rigorously defined than in his system. A more important difference is that whereas ${}_SU_R$ refers to a response in an organism that has already achieved some measure of maturity, the set U describes the behavior of a completely immature organism. In Ashby's terminology, U defines an unstable system; for, if it enters a minor critical state, the responses $m \varepsilon M$ are more likely than not to leave it in that state, and the same responses will completely fail to carry it out of a major critical state.

It is not immediately obvious that U is an ultrastable system, since, although it is provided with the necessary step-functions, we have not yet considered in detail the question whether the postulated conditioning process is adequate to the task it is expected to perform. Indeed it is highly probable that the reader has already made a quick calculation and arrived at the conclusion that the number of conditionings to be completed is so fantastically enormous that a million lifetimes would not be enough for the job. We therefore must turn next to the problem of the mechanism of adaptation.

2.14. It commonly happens that an infant's normal environment contains a few rigid objects of suitable dimensions to evoke the grasping reflex if the palm of the hand comes into contact with them. Let $\gamma_1, \gamma_2, \ldots \gamma_j \varepsilon \Gamma$ specify the positions of those objects, and let each of them be within reach of the hand. Similarly, $\delta_1, \delta_2, \ldots \delta_j \varepsilon \Delta$ will describe the positions of the several objects together with the energy of the light they reflect. In the immediately following discussion we shall concern ourselves with only one of the objects, whose description will be represented by δ, without any subscript. That is, until further notice δ will be understood to refer to one and only one object.

This selected object determines an equivalence class of S, and consequently of Q, which we may define by

$$(2.14.1)\quad Q(\delta) \equiv [q \in Q; \textit{ for every } q_i, q_j \in Q(\delta), \delta(q_i) = \delta(q_j)],$$

where $\delta(q_i)$ is the δ that is incorporated in q_i. This definition means that we assemble into a single set all the elements of Q in which the selected δ is incorporated. It will be seen that the definition implies that for every q_i, $q_j \in Q(\delta)$, $t_{qi} \neq t_{qj}$. That is, no two elements of $Q(\delta)$ can occur simultaneously. The equivalence class $Q(\delta)$ will be described as a *formal equivalence class* as opposed to the *functional equivalence classes* to be described later. It is clear that the elements of $Q(\delta)$ all differ from one another with respect to the afferent neural processes involved in them; and it is this that gives rise to one of the central problems of perception. How do these widely differing elements of $Q(\delta)$ all give rise to the same perception? We shall arrive at the answer in due course.

2.15. From (2.13.2) and (2.14.1) we can deduce that the traces of several elements of $Q(\delta)$ can be operating in the nervous system at the moment when the response m occurs. If this response should carry the hand to the position γ occupied by the rigid object postulated in 2.14, the system moves into a steady state, and this has the effect of conditioning the response m not only to the $q \in Q(\delta)$ that was in operation at the moment when the movement began but also to the traces of any other $q \in Q(\delta)$ that may have occurred within the preceding 10 seconds, provided the hand has not been in motion during that time.

By Pavlov's principle of irradiation, these reflexes generalize to neighborhoods of elements of Q surrounding each of the $q \in Q(\delta)$ that occurred within the critical period; and if these differ widely from one another, generalization will embrace a substantial subset of $Q(\delta)$. Sooner or later the same situation will recur. That is, the fixed object is in the same position as before and the hand is in the same initial position. On this occasion, however, the selection of elements of $Q(\delta)$ is likely to be different, and generalization will therefore extend to other elements of $Q(\delta)$ that were not affected on the first occasion. Of course the successful response m is not the only one that occurs, but the principles of conditioning enable us to deduce that those other responses will be eliminated, partly through extinction and partly because the probability that the successful response will be evoked immediately, thereby excluding all others, increases with every reinforcement. The final result of this double process of conditioning and extinction is that, provided the hand is in the same initial position, any $q \varepsilon Q(\delta)$ will suffice to evoke the specific response, m.

The initial position of the hand varies from one occasion to another, and this suggests the subdivision of $Q(\delta)$ into a number of subclasses according to the position of the hand. Let $z_1, z_2, \ldots z_n \varepsilon Z(A)$ be the initial positions of the hand as defined in (2.10.4). A subclass is then defined by

$$(2.15.1) \quad Q(z) \equiv [q \varepsilon Q(\delta);\ \textit{for every}\ q_i, q_j \varepsilon Q(z),\ z(q_i) = z(q_j)],$$

where $z(q_i)$ is the z incorporated in q_i. Further, let $m_1, m_2, \ldots m_n \varepsilon M(A)$ be the movements that carry the hand from the positions $z_1, z_2, \ldots z_n$ to the fixed object at γ. It is clear that the conditioning process described above must operate on all the subclasses $Q(z)$, so that ultimately m_1 is conditioned to all the elements of $Q(z_1)$, m_2 to all the elements of $Q(z_2)$, and so on.

It might seem that this must be an extremely long process, and so it would be if the conditionings of the several responses were completely independent of one another. But they are not independent, for as soon as m_1 has been conditioned to $Q(z_1)$, the probability that the hand, starting from z_2, will reach the goal within a period of, say, one second is nearly doubled. If the probability that any of the available responses starting from z_2 will be evoked at once is 0.01, then the probability that the hand will be carried from z_2 to either γ or z_1 is 0.02. If it is carried to γ there is of course immediate reinforcement, but if it is carried to z_1, an element of $Q(z_1)$ is thereby brought into operation, and as all the elements of $Q(z_1)$ have, *ex hypothesi*, been conditioned to a response carrying the hand to γ, that response will at once be evoked, and the result is a reinforcement not only of the movement (z_1, γ) but also of the movement (z_2, z_1). In Hull's terminology the latter response is secondarily reinforced. It follows that when another element of $Q(z_2)$ occurs, the hand will move from z_2 to z_1 and thence to γ.

Another factor that serves to accelerate the process is the fact that pin-point accuracy in the response is not essential for success. Contact with any part of the palm is sufficient to evoke the grasping reflex unconditionally, so that the response that is conditioned to the elements of $Q(\delta)$ is not in general a single clearly defined element of $M(A)$ but rather a neighborhood of such elements, that is, a subset of $M(A)$ having the property that the terminal points of its elements are centered round a single point, δ, with a limited range of deviation from this point.

2.16. It is evident that the structure of the system is such that the rate of acquisition of conditioned responses must increase with positive acceleration until the number of responses still to be acquired falls short of those already acquired. It would seem, however, that the great majority of the responses must involve roundabout paths to the goal. Indirect paths do in fact appear very frequently, but they are gradually eliminated. This process too is readily explained in terms of conditioning. Let us assume that responses (z_1, γ) and (z_2, γ) have been conditioned to $Q(z_1)$ and $Q(z_2)$ respectively, and also that on separate occasions the responses (z_3, z_1) and (z_3, z_2) have been secondarily reinforced. It follows that $Q(z_3)$ will tend to evoke both (z_3, z_1) and (z_3, z_2). These cannot occur simultaneously, but it does not follow that the response must be either one or the other. What is much more likely to happen is that the motor impulses tending to carry the hand to z_1 and z_2 operate jointly to determine a movement toward a point, z_4, midway between z_1 and z_2. If z_4 is nearer to γ than either z_1 or z_2, as it must frequently be, and a response, (z_4, γ), happens to follow, then the response (z_3, z_4) is secondarily reinforced, and the path from z_3 to the goal is thereby shortened.

It will be profitable to consider some of the properties that must characterize a system generated in this manner. We have already deduced that at an intermediate stage in the development roundabout paths to the goal must frequently occur, and direct observation of infants confirms this deduction. But what we are concerned with now is the properties of the fully developed system.

Let r be the distance between γ, the position of the goal, and z, the initial position of the hand. It is obvious that if we assign a minimal value to r, the number of subclasses, Q(z), satisfying the condition that r has this minimal value is very small. Let this number be x. Then if we write $k = x/r^2_{min}$, where r_{min} is the minimal value of r, the number of subclasses Q(z) at any distance r is given by

(2.16.1) $n = k\,r^2$.

From this we can deduce that the probability that an unconditioned response, m, will move exactly in the direction of the goal varies inversely as the square of the distance. The probability that the *extent* of the movement will be exactly equal to r is less easy to estimate. There would seem to be no reason why a movement of one extent should be inherently more probable than a movement of any other extent, provided they are both within the range of physically possible movements. But if the direction of the movement is correct and its extent is greater than r, the impact with the rigid object at γ will arrest the hand, and the response will be reinforced. We can say therefore that the probability that the extent of the movement will be not less than r is inversely proportional to r. Hence the probability that any movement, m, will reach the goal is inversely proportional to r^3.

An obvious consequence of this rapid decrease of probability is that as r increases there will be an increasing tendency, in the fully developed system, for the movement to the goal to be completed in two stages. This is quite simply determined by considerations of economy. An example will make this clear. Suppose that with $r = a$, the probability of reaching the goal in one move in the unadapted system is 0.01, then, with $r = 2a$, the probability is $0.01/2^3 = 0.00125$, but the probability of reaching any point whose distance from the goal does not exceed a is of the order of 0.01. Roughly speaking, this means that the probability that the hand will reach a point for which $r \leqq a$ is 0.01. It follows that when $r = 2a$, eight times as many conditioning trials will be required to enable the subject to reach the goal as when $r = a$. But the number of trials required to get within the cubic space for which $r \leqq a$ is the same as the number required to reach the goal when $r = a$. Assuming the level of drive to be relatively low, it is clear that a two-stage movement from the greater distance is adequately reinforced, and further refinement of the response is thereby precluded.

If, however, at a later stage in life, situations should be encountered in which a two-stage movement is not reinforced, the process of differential conditioning will result in the development of single-stage responses. For example, when a child uses a hammer for the first time, there is no reinforcement of responses that miss the nail, and there is strong negative reinforcement if the hammer falls on the fingers. What the child does at first is to hold the hammer quite close to the head and to aim the blows from a very short distance. That is, the action approximates quite closely a response that has already been acquired. But as the effect of such movements on the nail is negligible, the length of the stroke is increased, and direct conditioning has the effect that only accurately directed strokes are reinforced. There are many other life situations that similarly increase the accuracy of actions directed from a distance.

2.17. In the foregoing discussion we have run ahead of the argument by assuming that responses are conditioned not only to the elements of $Q(\delta)$ as defined in (2.14.1) but also to other equivalence classes determined by objects occupying different positions in space. We must now investigate this aspect of the process.

Let the position of the fixed object be changed, either by manipulation of the object or by changing the position of the infant, and let $Q(\delta_1)$ represent the equivalence class of Q as determined by the new position. By generalization the already acquired responses to $Q(\delta)$ will tend to be evoked by elements of $Q(\delta_1)$, but as these responses are defined relative to a frame of reference inherent in the infant's own body, they will be misdirected and will therefore fail to be reinforced. Other unconditioned responses $m \varepsilon M(A)$ will then be evoked until one of them reaches the goal and is reinforced. Ultimately all the elements of $Q(\delta_1)$ will be conditioned to either single-stage or two-stage responses that reach the goal.

Now let the object be moved to some intermediate position, represented by δ_2. By generalization the elements of $Q(\delta_2)$ tend to evoke both the responses appropriate to $Q(\delta)$ and those appropriate to $Q(\delta_1)$. These responses cannot be evoked simultaneously, but we may appeal here to Hull's principle that effective reaction potential ($_S\bar{E}_R$) is a decreasing exponential function of the difference, in j.n.d. units, between the stimulus actually applied and the stimulus to which the response was originally conditioned. Measurements along the j.n.d. scale are commonly supposed to be proportional to the logarithms of the corresponding physical measurements of the stimulus, although an exponential function would probably give a better fit. Accordingly, if we substitute a physical scale for the j.n.d. scale, we shall probably not be far wrong if we say that reaction potential diminishes as a linear function of the stimulus difference. However, the exact form of the function is not important for the following argument.

If, for any initial position of the hand, m is the response conditioned to $Q(\delta)$ and m_1 is the response to $Q(\delta_1)$, and the distances separating δ_2 from δ and δ_1 respectively are in the proportion of a:b, and δ_2 is on a straight line joining δ and δ_1, then $Q(\delta_2)$ will tend to evoke m with a strength proportional to 1/a and m_1 with a strength proportional to 1/b. The result of this simultaneous pull in different directions is that the hand will be carried to δ_2 in one move or two according to its initial distance from the goal. If δ_2 is not collinear with δ and δ_1, the reaction potentials will be weaker, but at least the hand will be carried in the general direction of the goal, thereby increasing the probability that a further movement will be successful and ensuring the more rapid conditioning of appropriate responses to $Q(\delta_2)$.

It is clear then that if the principle of generalization is incorporated in the abstract system described by the set U, it generates an automatic interpolation device that hastens the process of adaptation. At first the interpolated responses are likely to be crude approximations to those that will finally be reinforced, just as, when using a mathematical table, we may get erroneous results if we employ a simple interpolation formula. But as a wider range of equivalence classes $Q(\delta)$ gets conditioned to appropriate responses, interpolation yields more accurate results, just as accuracy in using a table increases when we choose a more elaborate interpolation formula.

2.18. The reader has no doubt detected a serious error that has permeated the whole argument from 2.15 onward. This is an error of the same order as that which we so carefully avoided in 2.8 in defining a binocular stimulus. The essence of it is that having defined the equivalence class, $Q(\delta)$, I seem to have assumed that only this particular subset of Q gets conditioned to the response of reaching for the fixed object. In everyday experience the object toward which a movement is directed appears to be the stimulus that evokes the response, but as it is precisely this perceptual experience that we are seeking to explain, it is grossly improper to allow that experience to affect our scientific reasoning. Actually the error was introduced quite deliberately, pending the discussion of another adaptive process that has been taking place simultaneously with that discussed in the last three sections. Since it is impossible to discuss simultaneously developments that occur together and that interact with one another, it is necessary to choose an order of presentation. Whatever the choice may be, some distortion of the facts is inevitable until the remaining aspects of the problem have been discussed. I have tried to minimize the distortion by anticipating the results of the discussion that now follows.

It is accepted that any neutral stimulus that regularly precedes the application of an unconditioned stimulus becomes conditioned to the resulting response. Now there are a great many elements of Q, besides those that comprise the equivalence class $Q(\delta)$, that satisfy this requirement. A substantial part of the infant's environment is permanent, and it follows that elements of Q determined by objects other than that which is to be grasped can become conditioned to the reaching response. But there is one important respect in which the elements of $Q(\delta)$ differ from other $q \varepsilon Q$: when grasping takes place, the object is obscured by the hand. To us, looking at the matter from the superior standpoint of maturity, this may appear to be a trivial or commonplace fact, scarcely worth mentioning, but let us consider for a moment what it means. The simplest way to do this is to compare the elements of $Q(\delta)$ with those of any other equivalence class $Q(\delta')$ where δ' refers to some object not within reach of the infant's hand. There are a great many elements of $Q(\delta')$ and they all differ from one another, so that within the number of trials required to establish a conditioned response the probability of any one $q \varepsilon Q(\delta')$ occurring more than once is quite small. Exactly the same statement may be made about the elements of $Q(\delta)$, but a certain number of them have the common property that they disappear immediately prior to the unconditioned evocation of the grasping reflex. Of course many other elements of Q disappear as a result of movements of the hand, but those disappearances are not followed by the grasping reflex, and they do not persist. We can say therefore that the disappearance of $q \varepsilon Q(\delta)$ becomes a conditioned stimulus for the grasping reflex, and this in turn has the effect of conditioning the preceding $q \varepsilon Q(\delta)$ to the response that carries the hand to the goal.

2.19. The explanation is not as yet very convincing, but there is still another factor to be considered. It depends on the fact that the afferent energy generated in the optical system by any element of Δ is maximized when $h = (0,0)$, that is, when δ stimulates the fovea. It is known that both the rate of conditioning and the strength of the conditioned response are increasing functions of the energy generated by the conditioned stimulus.[4] We can deduce then that the disappearance of an element of $Q(\delta)$ involves a maximum change of afferent energy when $h = (0,0)$, and therefore that the most rapid conditioning, both of the grasping reflex itself and of the preceding response, $m \varepsilon M(A)$, occurs when the infant's eyes are directed toward the object that is to be grasped.

It follows from this that if any $q \varepsilon Q(\delta)$ for which $h \neq (0,0)$ is insufficient to evoke a response $m \varepsilon M(A)$, and if an unconditioned response $m \varepsilon M(E)$ changes the direction of the eyes so that $h = (0,0)$, and the new element q of $Q(\delta)$ thereby brought into action is enough to evoke the manual response, the effect is to reinforce the response $m \varepsilon M(E)$ and establish it as a conditioned response to q.

This is an extremely important result, and its implications are worth considering in some detail. Let the system be in a minor critical state. At any moment a subset as defined in (2.9.2) determines an equivalent subset, Q', of Q, which we shall assume to contain an element of $Q(\delta)$. The afferent energies in the optic tract determined by the several elements of Q' vary over a wide range, and one of them, determined, let us say, by an object that is beyond reach, is maximized, while the energy determined by $q \varepsilon Q(\delta)$ is at a relatively low level. Despite this, the state of the system represented by Q' gives rise to an ocular response, $m \varepsilon M(E)$, which changes the state to Q'', such that $q'' \varepsilon Q(\delta)$ now maximizes the afferent energy generated by δ.

If, instead of Q', we have another subset, Q''', determined by a different initial direction of the eyes such that the retinal image

4. Some of the evidence has been collected by Hull in support of his principle of *stimulus intensity dynamism*.

of δ occupies another peripheral position, the state Q''' gives rise to another ocular response. This changes the state of the system to the same Q'' that resulted from the response to Q'. In general, no matter what the initial state of the system may be, provided it contains an element of $Q(\delta)$, it changes to a state in which the retinal image of δ is at the fovea. But if a large number of subsets, Q', of Q, each containing a $q \varepsilon Q(\delta)$ all give rise to responses having the common effect that $h(\delta) = (0,0)$, we cannot escape the conclusion that the $q \varepsilon Q(\delta)$ contained in each Q' is the most important component of the stimulus conditioned to the relevant ocular response.

This does not imply that the other components, $q \varepsilon Q'$, such that $q \varepsilon' Q(\delta)$, are not involved in the conditioning process. They are vitally involved, and we may here anticipate the argument of the following chapters by pointing out that when they are eliminated, as in experiments on the autokinetic phenomenon, the regularity of the fully adapted system is disturbed. All that the present discussion entitles us to say is that the elements of $Q(\delta)$ are the primary determiners of the ocular responses. And this is all that we shall mean when we speak of $Q(\delta)$ as being conditioned to elements of the set of ocular responses, $M(E)$.

2.20. We can now answer the question that was left unanswered at the end of 2.13. By writing conditioning, with the associated process of generalization, into the system defined by the set U, we have made it an ultrastable system. But that is not all. We have seen that any equivalence class, $Q(\delta)$, can become conditioned, subject to the qualification noted above, to appropriate subsets of $M(A)$ and $M(E)$, and this means that a subsystem, $U(\delta)$, of U has achieved adaptation independently of other subsystems. Thus the set U conforms exactly to Ashby's definition of a multistable system in which the subsystems can adapt independently of one another and in any order. But it has another property not envisaged by Ashby. The subsystems are so interrelated, through generalization, that when a few of them have adapted, the process of adaptation in the remaining subsystems is accelerated.

The condition postulated by Ashby for the independent adaptation of a subsystem is that it must be separated from the rest of the system by "a wall of null-functions," or alternatively by a wall of *part-functions* that are temporarily inactive and therefore are, for the time being, equivalent to null-functions. In the system defined by U this condition is given the specific interpretation that when it starts from any state, $Q' \subset Q$, there is one and only one $m \in M(A)$, viz. that which carries the hand to the fixed object, that results in stability. Since the only element of Q' that gets conditioned to this $m \in M(A)$ is $q' \in Q(\delta)$, we may say that the remaining elements of Q' are relatively inactive. They are, of course, fully active in the system defined by Q, but in the system that is growing out of the adaptation of U their activity is relatively unimportant. In this new system, to be discussed in detail in the next chapter, they may be considered as part-functions.

At the same time it is important not to overemphasize the mutual independence of the subsystems. They are, in fact, both independent and interrelated; and their interrelation, paradoxically enough, is precisely the factor that makes for their greater independence in the new system that is emerging. This interrelation is defined in terms of the Pavlovian principle of generalization. But together with this goes the related principle of generalization of inhibition, which is responsible for differential conditioning, that is, for increasing mutual independence of two or more subsystems. Finally, as shown at the end of 2.17, the interrelatedness of two or more subsystems that are already adapted contributes to the more rapid adaptation of many other subsystems. Generalization then helps to make those new subsystems independent of one another and of those that contributed to their organization.

CHAPTER 3

The Beginnings of Space Perception

3.1. We must now try to describe the system that emerges out of the developments discussed in Chapter 2. We can begin, in a tentative way, by defining

$$(3.1.1)\quad F \equiv [(q,m); q \varepsilon Q, m \varepsilon M, q \rightarrow m]$$

where the notation $q \rightarrow m$ means that m is a conditioned response to q. We have already, in (2.10.5) defined M as the set sum of M(E), M(H), and M(A), but for our present purpose it will be more convenient to redefine it by

$$(3.1.2)\quad M \equiv [(m(E), m(H), m(A)); t_{m(E)} = t_{m(H)} = t_{m(A)}].$$

Since zero movements are not excluded, M includes movements of the eyes alone or of the hand alone. It also includes all coordinated movements of head and eyes, and of hand and eyes, as well as independent movements of hand and eyes.

The movements with which we are chiefly concerned are reaching movements of the hand and joint movements of the head and eyes resulting in the fixation of an object in the environment. Since there are many different pairs, (m(E), m(H)), that can result in fixation of any fixed point, these can be considered as an equivalence class of M, which we may represent by $M(\gamma)$, where $\gamma \varepsilon \Gamma$, as defined in 2.4.

Since for any $q \varepsilon Q(\delta)$ there is one and only one reaching response that can be reinforced, and similarly there is only one equivalence class $M(\gamma)$ that is reinforced, we can conclude that for every $q \varepsilon Q$ there is one and only one $m \varepsilon M$ such that $(q,m) \varepsilon F$. Consequently F is a function. Its most important property is that it establishes a one-to-one correspondence, I, between Γ and the terminal positions of M. That is to say, to each element of Γ there corresponds a response that is invariant with respect to its terminus, although it may start from any one of a large number of initial positions and follow any one of a large number of different routes. Thus the set I has the effect of partitioning F into a number of equivalence classes, which we may call *functional equivalence classes.*

This result is obviously of the utmost importance for theoretical psychology. It has often been urged that one of the strongest arguments against conditioning as an explanatory principle in learning is that the response varies from one trial to the next although the stimulus remains constant. Actually the stimulus remains constant only if one defines it in relation to a physical reference frame. But this takes no account of the specific afferent processes as determined jointly by the objective stimulus and the orientation of the receptors. When S is defined as in (2.9.1) it becomes apparent that the variation in the response is exactly paralleled by variation in the stimulus, and the objection to conditioning as a principle of learning falls away.

It should be noted that F is *not* a complete description of the behavior of the system. It is simply a list of the stimulus-response pairs that have been linked by conditioning, and in particular it does not imply the impossibility of the subsequent occurrence of elements of U that are not included in F.

3.2. Although on the face of it F is a subset of U, this is true only in a superficial way. The elements of F have in fact a property that distinguishes them from the corresponding elements of U. Whereas the $m \varepsilon M$ in any $u \varepsilon U$ is an unconditioned response to an unspecified stimulus that includes d but may or may not include all the afferent processes defined by s, and almost certainly includes other components not incorporated in s, the m in any $f \varepsilon F$ is completely determined by q, apart from random sources of variation that do not affect the goal of m. In short, in u the conjunction of m with q is fortuitous; in f it is determinate. Again it must be said that when the conjunction is described as fortuitous all that is meant is that the system U is not regular; we have not included a sufficient number of variables to make it so. The reason for the omission is that the inclusion of the additional variables is unnecessary for our purpose, since the system U is an ultrastable one and develops a regular system through adaptation.

But if the conjunction of q and m is determinate, this implies a neural link or *engram* connecting the cortical termini of the afferent processes with the relevant motor centers. It is true that Lashley has given the weight of his authority to the opinion that there are no engrams and that the cortex as a whole is implicated in each and every action. But the conception of the engram that emerges from our discussion is completely consistent with the results obtained by his technique of extirpating portions of the cortex. For, in the first place, an engram is not a single chain of neurons connecting a single projection area to a specific portion of the motor cortex, but a complex network involving several projection areas and very likely one or more of the so-called "silent" areas, or association areas. And second, if we define an action by its terminus alone and not, as we have done, by both its initial and terminal points, there is not just a single engram mediating this response but thousands of them. It follows that extirpation of a comparatively small area of the cortex is likely to destroy some of those engrams but to leave a substantial proportion of them intact. Thus destruction of a portion of the striate area receiving afferent impulses from a specific part of the retina will make it impossible to perform a response $m \varepsilon M(A)$ if the light from the goal object falls on the affected part. But a simple movement of the eyes results in the activation of an intact engram mediating another response having exactly the same terminus.

The common practice of defining a response by its terminus is another example of the fallacy of deriving theoretical constructs from mature experience. It is quite true that in everyday life the specification of the goal is usually sufficient to determine the performance of an appropriate action, but in designing a machine an engineer is not content to define only the point at which each operation is to be concluded. In the same way we cannot construct a theoretical model of an organic machine if we insist that all we need to know about its actions are their end-results.

3.3. The set F, as defined in (3.1.1), is merely a list of the ordered pairs (q,m) satisfying the condition that m is a conditioned response to q. In order to investigate the implications of our hypothesis it will be necessary to incorporate in the system the engrams that mediate the conditioned responses. This problem has two aspects, structural and dynamic. From the structural point of view the engram is a network of neural connections such that if energy is fed into it, a specific response, m, will be evoked. Let E′ be defined as the set of those structures. Also let E″ be the set of energies that can be fed into the engrams. Then

(3.3.1) $E = E' \times E''$

is a set each of whose elements represents a specific engram operating as a specific level of energy.

If we substitute E for M in the definition of F we obtain

(3.3.2) $\Phi \equiv [(q,e); q \rightarrow e]$.

By (2.13.1) $Q \subset D \times S$. It is the component s in q that determines the engram, $e' \varepsilon E'$, that is to be activated, and d and s together determine e″, the amount of energy that is fed into e′. From this it follows that Φ is a function.

It is at once evident that there is an important difference between F and Φ. Since m is an actual movement, only one element of F can exist at any moment of time; but this limitation does not apply to Φ. There is no doubt a great deal of sharing of neurons between the several structures included in E′, but each $e' \varepsilon E'$ must nevertheless be unique, and it is therefore possible for many elements of E′ to be activated simultaneously. In particular, it is possible for each of the elements, s, of the simultaneously existing subset, Σ, of S to determine an element of E; and this leads at once to the definition of a set

(3.3.3) $\Pi \equiv [\phi \, \varepsilon \, \Phi;$ *for every* $\phi_1, \phi_j \, \varepsilon \, \Pi, \; t_{e1} = t_{ej}]$.

That is, Π is a complete description of a momentary state of the system that has emerged from the adaptation of the multistable system, U. It is a very remarkable set, and its properties are worth investigating in some detail.

3.4. As a preliminary to this investigation it will be useful to gather together in one place the chief links in the chain of definitions leading up to Π.

(3.4.1) $\Delta \subset \Gamma \times \Psi$

defines the positions of all objects in the immediate environment of the infant together with the relative energies of the light they reflect.

(3.4.2) A_3, A_4, A_5, A_6, A_7, and A_8 are the sets of angles in terms of which the position of the eyes in their sockets and the position of the head relative to the trunk can be described.

(3.4.3) $O \equiv [(a_3, a_5, a_6, a_7, a_8); t_{a3} = t_{a5} = t_{a6} = t_{a7} = t_{a8}]$ describes all physically possible orientations of the left eye and the head. There is a corresponding set for the right eye.

(3.4.4) $K \subset \Delta \times O$ describes all pairs, (δ, o), that result in retinal stimulation.

(3.4.5) A_1 is the set of all horizontal angular deviations of rays of light from the optic axis. A_2 is the set of vertical deviations.

(3.4.6) $H \subset A_1 \times A_2$ defines the positions of all retinal points.

(3.4.7) $R \equiv H \times \Psi$ is the set of all proximal stimuli applied to the retina.

(3.4.8) $N \sim R$ is the set of afferent neural processes induced by R.

(3.4.9) $V_1 \equiv [(k,n); k \varepsilon K, n \varepsilon N, k \rightarrow r \rightarrow n]$ defines the afferent process in the left optic nerve as a joint function of the positions of objects in the environment, the energy of the light they reflect, and the orientation of eye and head. V_2 is similarly defined for the right eye.

(3.4.10) V_3 to V_8 are the sets of afferent impulses generated in the lateral rectus muscles of the left eye (V_3), and of the right eye (V_4), in the superior and inferior rectus muscles of both eyes (V_5), in the muscles that rotate the head about its vertical axis (V_6), backward and forward (V_7) and sideways (V_8). These are all joint functions of the angles, A_3 to A_8, and the time during which the position has been held.

(3.4.11) V_9, V_{10}, and V_{11} are proprioceptive functions of the position of the hand.

(3.4.12) $S \equiv [(v_1, v_2, \ldots v_{11}); t_{v1} = t_{v2} = \ldots = t_{v11}]$ is the set of all possible states of the afferent system, V_1 to V_{11}, as determined jointly by the environment, the orientation of eyes and head, and the position of the hand.

(3.4.13) $\Sigma \equiv [s \varepsilon S;$ for every $s_i, s_j \varepsilon \Sigma, t_{si} = t_{sj}]$ defines the complete state of the system as determined by the subset of Δ that is operating on the retinas at any moment of time.

(3.4.14) $Z(E) \subset A_3 \times A_4 \times A_5$ is the set of all physically possible positions of the eyes.

(3.4.15) $M(E) = Z(E) \times Z(E)$
is the set of all movements of the eyes.

(3.4.16) $M(H) = Z(H) \times Z(H)$
is the set of all movements of the head.

(3.4.17) $M(A) = Z(A) \times Z(A)$
is the set of all movements of the hand.

(3.4.18) $M \equiv [(m(E), m(H), m(A); t_{m(E)} = t_{m(H)} = t_{m(A)}]$
is the set of all simultaneous movements of eyes, head, and hand.

(3.4.19) D is the set of all drive stimuli.

(3.4.20) $Q \equiv [(s,d); s \,\varepsilon\, S, d \,\varepsilon\, D, t_s = t_d]$
is the set of all states of the system as determined jointly by S and D.

(3.4.21) $Q(\delta) \equiv [q \,\varepsilon\, Q$; for every $q_i, q_j \,\varepsilon\, Q(\delta), \delta(q_i) = \delta(q_j)]$
is an equivalence class of Q as determined by a specific $\delta \,\varepsilon\, \Delta$. No two elements of $Q(\delta)$ can occur simultaneously.

(3.4.22) $Q(z) \equiv [q \,\varepsilon\, Q(\delta)$; *for every* $q_i, q_j \,\varepsilon\, Q(z), z(q_i) = z(q_j)]$
is an equivalence class of $Q(\delta)$ as determined by the initial position, $z(A)$ of the hand.

(3.4.23) $U \equiv [(q,m); q \,\varepsilon\, Q, m \,\varepsilon\, M, 0 < (t_m - t_q) \leq 10$ sec.]
is the set of all conjunctions of states $q \,\varepsilon\, Q$ with movements $m \,\varepsilon\, M$. U is not a function. It describes an irregular and unstable system.

(3.4.24) $F \equiv [(q,m); q \,\varepsilon\, Q, m \,\varepsilon\, M, q \rightarrow m]$
is the set of all conjunctions of states $q \,\varepsilon\, Q$ with conditioned responses $m \,\varepsilon\, M$.

(3.4.25) $E' \sim F$
is the set of neural structures or engrams mediating the conditioned responses, $q \rightarrow m$, of F.

(3.4.26) E″ is the set of energies applied to the elements of E′.

(3.4.27) $E = E' \times E''$
is the set of engrams in action.

(3.4.28) $\Phi \equiv [(q,e); q \,\varepsilon\, Q, e \,\varepsilon\, E, q \rightarrow e]$
is the set of states of the system including active engrams but not movements.

(3.4.29) $\Pi \equiv [\phi \,\varepsilon\, \Phi$; *for every* $\phi_i, \phi_j \,\varepsilon\, \Pi, t_{ei} = t_{ej}]$.

3.5 We may begin by observing that an element of Φ defines not a stimulus and a response, but a stimulus and a *state of readiness* for the execution of the response. The engram mediating the response is active, but whether the response actually occurs is dependent on the availability of the effector organs. It follows that Π describes a state of multiple readiness for all the responses that have been conditioned to elements of Σ. If there are any elements of Σ to which no responses have been conditioned, there are no corresponding elements of Π. This applies also to elements of Σ that do not, in conjunction with d, generate sufficient energy to activate the relative e′. We shall discuss the implications of this point at some length in the sequel.

Since the responses, M (3.4.15), are all directed to the positions of objects in space, we can see that Π describes a complex relationship between the organism and the spatial ordering of that sector of the environment that happens at the moment to be within the retinal field, and also, by virtue of the definition of U (3.4.23), those sectors that were within the retinal field at various moments during the preceding 10 seconds. But this is precisely the kind of relation that exists in perception, and accordingly I propose to identify Π with perception. If this is a valid hypothesis, the properties of perception should be directly deducible from the properties of Π.

3.6. Perception normally occurs *before* any action is taken, and this is commonly interpreted as meaning that it is a necessary link in the causal chain between stimulation and response. Thus Michotte writes:

> It is a commonplace that . . . the biological function of perception is to initiate and direct human and animal reactions. It not only enables us to contemplate our environment, but prompts us to action and enables us to adapt our behaviour to the properties of that environment [Michotte, 1954, p. 1].

The assumption here seems to be that the temporal priority of perception over action in the mature subject is so universal that its logical priority cannot be questioned.

It is at once evident that the temporal priority of perception in the mature subject is directly deducible from the definition of Π. At any moment of time only one $\phi \varepsilon \Pi$ can give rise to a response, $m \varepsilon M$, but by (3.4.29) there are many other simultaneously existing elements of Π, and some of these involve elements of Δ that will be the goals of subsequent actions. Those actions are therefore necessarily preceded by perception. But this has not always been true. The definition of U (3.4.23) shows that at birth $\Pi = \Theta$, but that responses m ε M can occur quite freely. During the process of conditioning that results in F (3.4.24), these responses are evoked as unconditioned reflexes, and it is their *consequences* that determine whether or not they become conditioned reflexes, and not their antecedents.

At the same time it must be clearly understood that there is nothing in the definition of Π to preclude the simultaneous existence of an element of U. The set Φ, (3.4.28), describes the system insofar as it has achieved adaptation, but does not imply that the entire system is adapted. There is still room for unlearned responses, and this will continue to be true, because new adaptations are constantly being demanded by situations for which the already existing conditioned responses are inadequate.

3.7. Since a new set Π is brought into being with every m ε M, an obvious way of investigating the properties of Π is to compare the sets Π_1 and Π_2 on occasions 1 and 2. It will be convenient to assume that the transformation has been effected by a movement of head and eyes, and that the hand is in the same position on both occasions. In general this means that different subsets of Δ are in the retinal field on the two occasions. We shall assume that these subsets have a substantial number of elements in common.

Let Δ_1 and Δ_2 be the subsets of Δ that are in the retinal field on occasions 1 and 2. Then

$$\Delta_0 = \Delta_1 \cdot \Delta_2$$

is the subset of Δ that is common to the two occasions. Let Π'_1 and Π'_2 be the subsets of Π_1 and Π_2 respectively that are determined by Δ_0 on the two occasions. At first sight Π'_1 and Π'_2 might appear to be equivalent sets, but this is not necessarily so. Some $\delta \varepsilon \Delta_0$ will stimulate the central area of the retina on one occasion and the periphery on the other occasion, and in the latter case it may be that the energy they generate is insufficient to activate the relative engrams, or even that no engrams exist. It follows that in general $\Pi'_1 \sim' \Delta_0$ and $\Pi'_2 \sim' \Delta_0$ (for $\sim'$ read: is not equivalent to), and therefore $\Pi'_1 \sim' \Pi'_2$. Let Δ'_1 be the subset of Δ_0 that is equivalent to Π'_1. That is, for every $\delta \varepsilon \Delta'_1$ there is a $\phi \varepsilon \Pi'_1$. Similarly, let

$\Delta'_2 \subset \Delta_0$ be selected so that $\Delta'_2 \sim \Pi'_2$. Then $\Delta'_0 = \Delta'_1 \cdot \Delta'_2$ is the subset of Δ_0 that is common to Π'_1 and Π'_2. Finally, let $\Pi'_1 \supset \Pi''_1 \sim \Delta'_0$, and $\Pi'_2 \supset \Pi''_2 \sim \Delta'_0$. It follows that $\Pi''_1 \sim \Pi''_2$—that is, for every $\phi_1 \varepsilon \Pi''_1$ there is a corresponding $\phi_2 \varepsilon \Pi''_2$, such that $\delta(\phi_1) = \delta(\phi_2)$.

To discover in what respects $\phi_1 \varepsilon \Pi''_1$ and $\phi_2 \varepsilon \Pi''_2$ resemble each other and differ from each other, we can follow them from their common origin in δ through the chain of definitions presented in 3.4, using the subscripts 1 and 2 to represent, at each stage, the elements that are operative on the two occasions.

By definition, $\delta_1 = \delta_2$. That is, ϕ_1 and ϕ_2 are equivalent with respect to δ. We have postulated that the orientation of head and eyes is different on the two occasions; that is, there are different elements of some or all of A_3 to A_8 as defined in (3.4.2). Hence, by (3.4.3), $o_1 \neq o_2$, and by (3.4.4), $k_1 \neq k_2$. By (3.4.9), $v_{1_1} \neq v_{1_2}$ and $v_{2_1} \neq v_{2_2}$. So far the difference between the two occasions has been expressed in purely geometrical terms, but with V_1 and V_2 we encounter differences in afferent neural processes. Since $\delta_1 = \delta_2$, and $o_1 \neq o_2$, it follows that $h_1 \neq h_2$ (3.4.6) and therefore that $r_1 \neq r_2$ (3.4.7). Hence, by (3.4.8), $n_1 \neq n_2$. In ordinary language, the retinal image of δ occupies different positions on the two occasions, determining two distinctive afferent processes.

Since $o_1 \neq o_2$ it follows from (3.4.10) that the elements of some or all of V_3 to V_8 are different on the two occasions. We have stipulated that the hand is in the same position on the two occasions, and hence, by (3.4.11), $v_{9_1} = v_{9_2}$, $v_{10_1} = v_{10_2}$ and $v_{11_1} = v_{11_2}$. Then, by (3.4.12), $s_1 \neq s_2$. It will be seen that the difference between the two occasions has expanded by the addition of up to six proprioceptive afferents. If we stipulate that the level of drive is the same on the two occasions, then, by (3.4.20), the difference between q_1 and q_2 is the same as the difference between s_1 and s_2.

Up to this point the difference between the two occasions has been steadily expanding, but when we come to F, defined in (3.4.24) there is a sudden convergence, which we can express by saying $m(f_1) = m(f_2)$. That is, the movement defined by f_1 is identical with that defined by f_2. Apart from that, f_1 and f_2 carry the same difference that characterizes q_1 and q_2. Then, by (3.4.27) and (3.4.28), $\phi_1 \neq \phi_2$, but $e(\phi_1) = e(\phi_2)$. But $\phi_1 \varepsilon \Pi''_1$ and $\phi_2 \varepsilon \Pi''_2$, and we can therefore generalize and say that Π''_1 and Π''_2 describe two different multiple states of readiness for one and the same subset of responses.

Generalizing to all occasions, and making use of (3.4.21) and (3.4.22), we can say that for every $\phi_1 \varepsilon \Pi_1$ and $\phi_j \varepsilon \Pi_j$ such that $q_1, q_j \varepsilon Q(z)$, where z is the initial position of the hand, and a common δ is understood, $e(\phi_1) = e(\phi_j)$.

If we now remove the restriction that the hand is to occupy the same position on each occasion, our generalization takes the form:

(3.7.1) For every $\phi_1 \varepsilon \Pi_1$, $\phi_j \varepsilon \Pi_j$, such that $q_1, q_j \varepsilon Q(\delta)$, $e(\phi_1)$ and $e(\phi_j)$ are equivalent with respect to the terminal points of m_1 and m_j.

In ordinary language, (3.7.1) states that no matter what the state of the system may be, as determined by the orientation of head and eyes and the position of the hand, the organism is always in a state of readiness to respond to a fixed object in the environment by a movement that will result in the hand making contact with that object.

Thus the system has, through the process of adaptation by conditioning, generated an invariant with respect to each $\delta \varepsilon \Delta$ that is within reach of the hand. If we are justified in identifying Π with perception, there must be an invariant of perception corresponding to that which we have just disclosed. There is. The positions of objects in the environment are perceptually invariant.

3.8. In our discussion of Π we have so far neglected an important concept that is incorporated in the definition of U, (3.4.23). There we decided to include among the elements of Q not only those that are in existence at a given moment of time but also those that were in existence within a preceding period of 10 seconds, and are represented by persisting reverberations in the nervous system. The neurological basis of those "traces" is no doubt the reverberating circuits that have been revealed by neurophysiology, but more important for our present investigation is the fact, demonstrated by Pavlov, that these traces can become conditioned stimuli. We have already, in 2.15, assumed that they operate in this way, and have seen how this speeds up the process of adaptation.

But if elements of Q can become conditioned stimuli even when they exist only as traces in the nervous system, it follows that an engram that has been activated by any $q \varepsilon Q$ can be kept active by the trace of that q. This has not been explicitly written into the definition of Π, since the dimension of time is not essential to that definition. On the other hand it has been made explicit in the definition of Φ, since the condition of simultaneity is stated as applying not to the elements of Q that are incorporated in the elements of Φ but to the elements of E. This means that Π includes not only pairs, (q,e), for which the activity of the engram, e, is concurrent with the actual stimulation of the receptor organs as defined by q, but also pairs for which the stimulus energies defined by q ceased to operate on the receptors a few seconds earlier, but the associated engram is still active. Thus, although a relation of simultaneity is posited in the definition of Π, the events that are occurring simultaneously may have been initiated at different moments of time.

The discussion in 3.7 was confined to those elements of Π for which the activity of the engrams is concurrent with that of the receptors. This was completely adequate for the immediate purpose of that discussion, which was to deduce one specific property of Π that has a counterpart in perception; and the validity of the conclusion is entirely unaffected by the exclusion of the elements to which attention is now directed. The recognition of those elements, however, enables us to deduce certain other properties of perception that would never be suspected otherwise.

Following the plan adopted in 3.7, we consider two occasions, at times t_1 and t_2, but we stipulate that $(t_2 - t_1) < 10$ seconds. Again we define Δ_1 and Δ_2 as the subsets of Δ that are within the retinal field at t_1 and t_2, but this time our interest is not in the elements that are common to the two occasions but in those that are active at t_1 but not at t_2, that is, in $\Delta_0 = \Delta_1 - \Delta_2$. We shall assume that $\Delta_0 \neq \Theta$. That is, the movement that transforms the state of the system from Π_1 to Π_2 includes a movement of the eyes. We shall also assume that $\Delta_0 \subset \Delta_1$. That is, the movement is not so extensive that nothing that was in the retinal field at t_1 remains in the retinal field at t_2.

The hypothesis that the elements of Φ remain active in the system for a few seconds after withdrawal of the stimulus implies that those elements of Π_1 that are determined by elements of Δ_0 are still active at t_2 and are therefore also elements of Π_2. It is obvious that this property of Π corresponds exactly to the property of perception that Gibson (1950) described by saying that the visual world is unbounded. Although Δ_0 is no longer in the retinal field at t_2, the state of readiness for responses directed to elements of Δ_0 persists, and this implies that Δ_0 is still perceived as being there although it is no longer stimulating the retina.

Another interesting deduction can be drawn if we specify three moments of time, t_1, t_2, and t_3, such that $(t_2 - t_1) < 1$ sec., and $(t_3 - t_2) > 10$ sec., and stipulate that a movement of the eyes occurs between t_1 and t_2, but no further movement occurs between t_2 and t_3. This means that $\Delta 1 \neq \Delta_2$, but $\Delta_2 = \Delta 3$. The argument of the previous paragraph shows that Π_2 contains elements of Π_1 derived from the elements of $\Delta_0 = \Delta_1 - \Delta_2$; but on the assumption that the traces left by the elements of Δ_0 have all faded within a period of 10 seconds, it follows that Π_3 contains no elements derived from Δ_0. That is Π_3 refers exclusively to that part of the environment that is within the retinal field, and may therefore be described as bounded.

It will be apparent that Π_3 describes precisely what Gibson has called the "visual field," whereas Π_2, which contains elements derived from subsets of Δ that were active at previous moments of time, describes the unbounded "visual world." Gibson recommends prolonged fixation as a means of studying the "visual field," and he seems to assume that what is revealed by this technique is, so to speak, the raw material of perception. Our analysis, on the contrary, indicates that the "visual field" is just as much a manufactured product as the "visual world," and that the only essential difference between them is that the latter contains elements derived from previous fixations while the former does not. We shall consider the differences between them in greater detail in 3.11.

3.9. We arrive at even more striking deductions if we consider not $\Delta_1 - \Delta_2$ but $\Delta_1 \cdot \Delta_2$. As before, we choose a single $\delta \varepsilon \Delta_1 \cdot \Delta_2$ and consider what happens to it on the two occasions. Let $\phi_1 \varepsilon \Pi_1$ and $\phi_2 \varepsilon \Pi_2$ be the elements of Φ generated by δ at t_1 and t_2 respectively. We have seen, in 3.7, that the neural processes defined by ϕ_1 and ϕ_2 differ in every respect except that $e_1 = e_2$ if the hand has remained in one position, and if it has changed its position, e_1 and e_2 are engrams mediating responses that have a common terminus.

So far there is nothing new, but now we must note that ϕ_1 is still in existence at t_2 and is therefore an element of Π_2 as well as of Π_1. And generalizing, we can say that Π normally contains two or more elements of $\Phi(\delta)$ where

$$(3.9.1)\quad \Phi(\delta) \equiv [\phi \in \Phi; \textit{ for every } \phi_i, \phi_j \in \Phi(\delta), \delta(\phi_i) = \delta(\phi_j)].$$

It will be remembered that it was said of the analogous equivalence class, $Q(\delta)$, defined in (3.4.21), that no two of its elements could exist simultaneously; but this does not apply to $\Phi(\delta)$, since, although the relevant $q \in Q(\delta)$ have ceased to exist, their effects persist in the corresponding engrams.

Consider now two or more simultaneously existing $\phi \in \Phi(\delta)$. They differ from each other with respect to the proprioceptive functions, V_3 to V_8, but more important than that, they differ with respect to H, (3.4.6), the position of the retinal images of δ, and therefore with respect to N, (3.4.8), the afferent processes aroused by δ in the optic apparatus. These differences have been a source of considerable bewilderment to psychologists. Why does the perceptual field not consist of a confused jumble of superimposed impressions, like a photographic film on which several exposures have been made? Actually the bewilderment arises from the assumption that perception is a direct function of stimulation. But if we assume that it is a function of learned behavior there is no more bewilderment, since the simultaneously existing elements of $\Phi(\delta)$ all mediate the same response, or at least responses that have the same terminus. It follows at once that the several simultaneously existing $\phi \in \Phi(\delta)$ mediate not several different perceptions but one and the same perception. And since, in the case we are considering, the perception in question refers to the position of δ in space, it follows that this position remains constant under all possible movements of the eyes. $\Phi(\delta)$ is a *functional equivalence class.*

3.10. We know that for any neural process to occur the stimulus must equal or exceed a threshold value. This may be measured in terms of the intensity of the stimulus or, in the case of a stimulus of constant energy, in terms of its duration. Thus a stimulus of a given intensity may produce a response if its duration is not less than 0.01 seconds, but if its duration is 0.001 seconds it will fail to produce any response. One of the things that have puzzled psychologists is that during the saccadic movements of the eyes that change the system from Π_1 to Π_2 there is no blurring of the visual field. An obvious explanation of this fact is that during a saccadic movement the energy generated by the retinal receptors does not persist long enough to arouse any engram to activity. There is adequate stimulation before the beginning of the movement and after its termination, but not while it is in progress. And even if the energy were sufficient it is obvious that the pattern of stimulation would be passing through a succession of elements of $\Phi(\delta)$, so that the external field would in any case be perceived as stationary.

3.11. The implications of the persistence of $\phi_1 \varepsilon \Pi_1$ into Π_2 are still far from being exhausted. As a preliminary to the further investigation of these implications it will be necessary to consider in more detail the properties of Π under prolonged fixation. We have assumed that the energy, e″, fed into any engram is a joint function of s and d. Consequently, if d is held constant the amount of energy can be deduced from s. If we also hold δ constant, it is evident that the chief source of variation in the energy generated by s is to be found in h, the position of the retinal image of δ. The cortical representation of a unit area of the retina diminishes from the fovea toward the boundary of the retina. If we now hold h constant and allow δ to vary, it is clear that there are two sources of variation in the resulting afferent energy. One is the difference between the light reflected by the chosen δ and that reflected by surrounding elements of Δ, and the other is the area of the retinal image of δ. If the former source is held constant, we can say that the energy generated by a retinal image centered at a given $h \varepsilon H$ is an increasing function of the area of the image.

From this we deduce at once that under prolonged fixation the probability that an element of S will be represented in Π is jointly determined by h and by the area of the retinal image of δ. Applying this deduction to perception, we can see that in what Gibson calls the visual field, small details are perceived in the center, but as the distance from the fovea increases there is an increase in the minimum size of objects that can be perceived.

All this time we have been holding d constant, and equal for all elements of Q. If we now allow d to increase for certain elements of Q that involve stimulation of the periphery of the retina, it follows that some of the objects that were previously imperceptible are now perceived. This is precisely what happens when we apply Gibson's technique for examining the visual field. His instruction is to fixate a prominent point but to attend to the whole field, a task that may require some practice, as he says. The effect of acting on his instruction is to increase d in the manner we require, and the set Π, which has, as a result of prolonged fixation, become sadly attenuated through the fading of the perseverative traces of previous fixations, now acquires a few more elements.

It will be seen that the properties of the visual field correspond exactly to the properties that Π must have under the stipulated conditions, and for this reason I consider that there is no justification for Gibson's distinction between the visual field and the visual world, and there is certainly no justification for considering the visual field as being somehow more primitive or basic than the visual world, or as being the raw material out of which the visual world is constructed. The visual field is merely the form that perception takes when specific values are assigned to some of the relevant variables, whereas the visual world is the form taken when the restrictions on the values of those variables is removed. One cannot even say that the visual field is the limiting form of visual perception when fixation is protracted, because the instruction to attend to the periphery alters the values of d for peripheral elements.

3.12. Returning now to more normal conditions, let us consider the effect of the numerous fixations that may occur within a period of 10 seconds. Let us suppose that there have been 20 fixations in that time, ranging over the whole of Δ. Our problem is to describe the state of the system at the 20th fixation, and we can do this by selecting a single δ and then generalizing to the whole of Δ. At the 20th fixation the image of the chosen δ may be anywhere on the retina, but it is most likely to be peripheral. Let its position be such that under prolonged fixation there would be no corresponding $\phi \in \Pi$. But in the preceding 10 seconds it has been at 19 other positions, and some of these have been at or near the fovea. Each of the twenty positions has determined an element of $\Phi(\delta)$ and therefore has contributed to the activation of an engram mediating a response terminating at δ even if the response is not actually evoked.

It is quite likely that during the 10 seconds the hand has been in two or more successive positions, so that the 20 elements of $\Phi(\delta)$ fall into two or more subclasses, $\Phi(z)$. It might seem that this must throw the system into a state of intolerable confusion, but in fact what is much more likely to happen is that the mutually incompatible features of the several engrams neutralize each other while the common features reinforce each other. The incompatible features are determined by the several initial positions of the hand, while the common features are determined by the common terminus of the responses for which the 20 engrams prepare the organism.

Translating into terms of perception, this means that the common goal represented by δ, of these prepared-for movements is clearly perceived in spite of the fact that its image is peripheral and it would not be perceived at all under conditions of prolonged fixation. Generalizing to Δ, we reach the apparently startling conclusion that when the eyes are flitting to and fro, $\Pi_1 \sim \Pi_2 \sim \ldots$ despite the contrary finding in 3.7. This means that the whole of the environment is perceived with equal clarity, and there is no focus and fringe of attention. In the words of Samuel Alexander, quoted at the beginning of this book, "The complexity as it were gathers itself together and is expressed in a new simplicity." The set Π is almost terrifying in its complexity; the spatial ordering of the environment as we perceive it is quite majestic in its simplicity.

To test the validity of the theory the reader may carry out what is surely the simplest scientific experiment ever proposed. On a sheet of blank paper make a dot of about 5 mm. diameter. Then, the paper remaining stationary, let the eyes wander far and wide over the immediate environment, and observe whether or not the dot remains in the perceptual field. Then choose a point of fixation some 35° or 40° removed from the dot and fixate it continuously for 10 seconds or more, again observing whether the dot remains perceptible. The experiment may then be repeated with the dot enlarged to double its diameter or more.

Despite its simplicity this is really a crucial experiment, and according to its results the reader may decide whether or not to go on reading this book. The theory leads to the deduction that the dot will remain in the perceptual field during the flitting movements of the eyes and that it will fade and vanish during the prolonged fixation. When the size is increased the fading will continue to be observed, but the dot will not necessarily vanish.

A further experiment is suggested by what we know about the afferent energy generated by a continuing stimulus. On application of the stimulus the afferent energy rises quickly to a maximum and then diminishes to an asymptote as an exponential function of time. This suggests that if, after the dot has faded during the prolonged fixation, it is covered for a few seconds by another sheet of paper and is then suddenly exposed, perception will be momentarily restored. This may also happen as a result of the involuntary movements that are constantly being made by the eyes during prolonged fixation, especially when the size of the dot is increased.

If these predictions are not confirmed, the theory is necessarily false and must be either abandoned or radically revised. If they are confirmed, this does not establish the theory beyond question. There are many other implications to be investigated, and these must also be confirmed by observation. But before we can do this it will be necessary to consider what changes take place in the system when the severe restrictions incidental to the helplessness of infancy are removed. Moreover, other developments have been taking place simultaneously with the adaptation of the subsystem to which we have so far confined our attention, and these are by no means irrelevant to our problem. They too must be incorporated in the system before we can subject the theory to a really searching test. Until that has been done we may conveniently neglect other implications of the restricted system described above.

CHAPTER 4

Further Development of Space Perception

4.1. Throughout the last two chapters we have assumed that the only movements available to the infant were movements of the eyes, head, and hands. This of course is a fiction, but it was deliberately adopted because it has enabled us to study the adaptation of a strictly limited subsystem without the complications introduced by movements of the trunk. As everybody who has watched the growth of an infant knows, the mobility of the trunk increases progressively, and this means that functions we have hitherto been assuming to be inactive are already active and gradually increasing the range of their activity long before the adaptations discussed in the preceding chapters have reached finality. In other words, the wall of inactive part-functions separating the system we have already described from the rest of the system is not broken down suddenly like the walls of Jericho, but rather suffers a gradual erosion. Nevertheless, we shall probably not go far wrong if we assume the expansion of the range of activity of the part-functions to be sudden rather than gradual, since the form of the adaptation is dictated not by chance or caprice but by the inherent properties of the system and must therefore yield the same results in either case. Moreover, we shall, in the next chapter, discuss other consequences of the process of acquiring control over bodily movements, and that will supply the required corrective to any error resulting from the procedure we are now going to adopt.

4.2. We assume that at the age of six months the process described in the last two chapters is well advanced and also that the infant is now able to sit without support, to twist his body about its vertical axis, and to lean backward, forward, and sideways. This means that the frame of reference defined in 2.4, which is implicit in the whole argument of Chapters 2 and 3, has now become mobile relative to Δ, or that Δ has become mobile relative to it. Clearly the further pursuit of our inquiry demands that a new frame of reference be defined, and apparently, there is an infinite number of ways in which this can be done. But since the infant, when he grows up, will continue to be the center of his own environment, the frame of reference that will be most useful for our purpose will be one that is centered in the infant's own body.

We shall choose rectangular coordinates with the origin at the point of contact of the base of the spine with the surface on which the infant is sitting. One axis runs along this surface parallel to the buttocks and another is the gravitational axis through the origin. The choice of the vertical axis may appear to be dictated by obvious considerations, but in fact those considerations arise out of mature experience, and it would therefore seem that I am violating the principle stated in 1.4, by adopting a vertical axis that is real to us but does not necessarily have any reality for the infant. We have no right to assume without proof that an axis from which his body is constantly deviating can serve as a frame of reference around which his perceptual experience can be built. The necessary proof will in fact be presented in Chapter 5, and in anticipation of that we may provisionally adopt the frame of reference defined above.

Another choice now confronts us. Having selected a new frame of reference we may either redefine Δ in relation to the new coordinates or allow the original definition to stand. If we choose the former course, all the sets in which Δ is incorporated will have to be redefined. But a more serious difficulty is that the visual functions V_1 and V_2 will have to be redefined by inclusion of variables that specify the position of the original reference frame relative to the new one. The elements of the original sets, V_1 and V_2, will be completely unrecognizable and the sets F and Φ will no longer exist. It follows that if we adopt the plan of redefining everything in terms of the new frame of reference, we lose sight of the system that has already achieved stability and throw away the opportunity of investigating the implications of the fact that the larger system with which we are now confronted contains this already stabilized system as a subsystem. Since this is one of the important objectives of our inquiry, it is clear that we must adopt the alternative plan.

This plan on the other hand has the serious disadvantage that we lose sight of the permanence of the environment. If we continue to define Δ with reference to a coordinate system with its origin at the center of rotation of the head, it is obvious that Δ suffers a succession of transformations and translations as the posture of the body changes. To meet this difficulty we may define Ω as the positions of objects in the environment related to the new coordinates, together with the light reflected by them. That is, Ω describes the same objective situation as Δ but related to a different and, for the time being, stationary frame of reference. For convenience we shall call this frame of reference $R(\Omega)$, and, analogously, we shall call the frame of reference of Δ $R(\Delta)$. Next we define A_{12} as the set of angles through which the trunk can be twisted about its vertical axis, A_{13} as the set of angles through which the trunk can be tilted backward and forward, and A_{14} as the angles of sideways tilt. Then

$$(4.2.1) \quad Y \equiv [(a_{12}, a_{13}, a_{14}); t_{12} = t_{13} = t_{14}]$$

is the set of all positions that can be taken by the trunk, described in relation to the frame of reference $R(\Omega)$.

Now since $R(\Delta)$ has its origin at the center of rotation of the head and one of its axes is parallel to the shoulders, it is evident that any element of Y determines a specific position of $R(\Delta)$ relative to $R(\Omega)$. It is therefore possible to deduce from any element of Y a transformation that will enable us to convert Ω to Δ. That is, if we know the coordinates of any point in the environment relative to $R(\Omega)$, the transformation deduced from $y \varepsilon Y$ will enable us to write the coordinates of this same point relative to $R(\Delta)$. Hence, although Δ changes with every change in the posture of the trunk, the set Δ, taken in conjunction with the relevant $y \varepsilon Y$, is equivalent to Ω. That is, a system that includes both Δ and Y is regular. Hence, if the organic system includes afferent functions of Y, it is a regular system. If we write $\Delta(y)$ as the transformation of Ω when the trunk takes the posture y, then it is clear that $\Delta(y_1) \sim \Delta(y_2) \sim \ldots \sim \Delta(y_n)$.

4.3. The newly acquired mobility of the body implies that the system is now enlarged by the inclusion of afferent functions of the position of the trunk. These include not only afferents that are dependent on the state of contraction or extension of the muscles but others that are dependent on the distribution of gravitational pressures in the body. We shall discuss the significance of these latter in the following chapter, but in the meantime it is not necessary to separate them from the former. All that is needed for our present purpose is to define three functions, V_{12}, V_{13}, and V_{14}, incorporating the sets of angles, A_{12}, A_{13}, and A_{14} defined in 4.2, the definitions being analogous to that of V_3 shown in (2.3.2), but including the pressure variables as determined by gravity.

We must now incorporate these functions in a new definition of S. We could obviously do this by a simple enlargement of the definition given in (3.4.12), making an element of S a 14-tuple instead of an 11-tuple, while at the same time noting that the Δ incorporated in V_1 and V_2 is no longer constant but varies with y, the position of the trunk. But to do this would be both uneconomical and scientifically foolish, for it neglects the fact that the elements of S as defined in (3.4.12), or at any rate a substantial proportion of them, have been conditioned to elements of M and therefore give rise, in conjunction with d, to determinate processes in the neural structures E′. It was legitimate, in the original definition of S, to assume the neural events to be determinate only up to the projection areas of the cortex, but as determinacy now extends to the motor cortex, we must recognize this in our new definition of S.

There is, however, another factor to be taken into account. The neural events initiated by S are in part determined by drive, and we have recognized this in the definition of Q (3.4.20). We have assumed, in 2.11, that when drive is at a minimum the system is in a steady state, involving sleep. In this state no engrams are activated by elements of S, and this suggests that a more realistic procedure will be to redefine Q rather than S. This need not involve us in any confusion, since at the present stage of our inquiry drive may be assumed to be a quite general state of the organism and not specific to any of the subsystems with which we are now concerned. Proceeding on these assumptions, we define

$$(4.3.1)\quad {}_2Q \equiv [(\phi, v_{12}, v_{13}, v_{14}); t_\phi = t_{12} = t_{13} = t_{14}].$$

If we now define ${}_2Q(y)$ as a subset of ${}_2Q$ that exists when the trunk is in any posture, y, it becomes evident that

$$(4.3.2) \quad {}_2Q(y) = (\Pi, v_{12}, v_{13}, v_{14}).$$

That is to say, ${}_2Q(y)$ describes a state of a system that includes an already adapted subsystem characterized by the emergent property of perception.

4.4. It must be observed, however, that by being incorporated in this larger system, Π has lost the property of invariance expressed in (3.7.1). More precisely, this property is retained as long as the body remains in a fixed posture but is destroyed by movements of the body. For consider two postures, y_1 and y_2, where $y_1 \neq y_2$. We select a single element $\omega \varepsilon \Omega$. This determines two elements, $\delta_1 \varepsilon \Delta(y_1)$ and $\delta_2 \varepsilon \Delta(y_2)$ and it is evident that $\delta_1 \neq \delta_2$. The difference between the two is, however, confined to γ. That is $\gamma_1 \neq \gamma_2$ but $\psi_1 = \psi_2$. In other words, ω has changed its position relative to $R(\Delta)$, the reference frame in terms of which Π is defined. It follows that the movements, $m_1(A)$ and $m_2(A)$, directed to ω, are not identical, since these are defined in relation to $R(\Delta)$. Hence, $\phi_1 \neq \phi_2$, and generalizing, $\Pi(y_1) \sim' \Pi(y_2)$. The environment is perceived as changing its position relative to the body. At the same time the conclusion reached in 3.12, that $\Pi_1 \sim \Pi_2$, remains true as long as y is held constant.

It may be objected that there is no ground for the statement that the environment is *perceived as changing* its position. We have deduced that it is perceived as constant so long as its position relative to $R(\Delta)$ remains invariant, but what right have we to assume that when $\Delta(y_1)$ is replaced by $\Delta(y_2)$, the infant perceives not a succession of *different environments* but rather a succession of different positions of the *same environment?* We might answer, in the manner of Gibson (1950), that the pattern of ordinal stimulation remains essentially the same. But in fact this is not true. If Ω were two-dimensional, the ordering of its elements would be preserved in its retinal representation through all changes of posture; but since it is three-dimensional, the ordering of the retinal image of $\Delta(y_1)$ is different from that of $\Delta(y_2)$. It is true that in mature experience the ordering is perceived as unchanged, but since that is precisely what we are seeking to explain, we obviously cannot use this result to explain itself.

To solve our problem we need only consider the elements $\phi_1 \varepsilon \Pi(y_1)$ and $\phi_2 \varepsilon \Pi(y_2)$ defined in the first paragraph of this section. By the hypothesis that an element of Φ remains active for a few seconds after removal of the exteroceptive stimulus, ϕ_1 and ϕ_2 are simultaneously active in the system. The brain is, so to speak, recording the information that an object was there a moment ago and is now here. Since the continuing existence of the perceived environment, when y is invariant, is already guaranteed by the simultaneous activity of elements of $\Phi(\delta)$ having different times of origin, there seems to be no reason why the simultaneous activity of elements of $\Phi(\omega)$, drawn from $\Phi(\delta_1)$ and $\Phi(\delta_2)$, should not also generate perception of a continuously existing though moving environment.

4.5. For any position of the trunk the conditioned fixation responses acquired in the first stage of development remain completely adequate, and this is equally true of conditioned reaching responses directed to objects that are within reach of the hand. That is to say, no matter what changes Δ may undergo as a result of movements of the trunk, a piece of matter occupying a specific position, γ, relative to $R(\Delta)$ will continue to evoke elements of the same equivalence class of fixation responses, and a reaching response that arrives at the same terminus. Hence the process of adaptation of the larger subsystem now under consideration does not involve any transformation of the subsystem that was adapted during the first stage of life. The set F, defined in (3.4.24), retains its identity, although there is nothing to prevent it from acquiring new elements during the further process of adaptation to be described now.

Since the conditioned responses defined by F retain their adequacy, it is clear that the adaptation of the new subsystem must be effected by conditioning a new class of responses to the more complex patterns of stimulation that are now in operation, and it is equally clear that the only class of movements available for this purpose is movements of the trunk. Following the same plan as before, we define

$$(4.5.1) \quad M(T) \equiv Y \times Y$$

as the set of all movements of the trunk including, as before, zero movements; and

$$(4.5.2)\quad {}_2U \equiv [(q,m);\ q \,\varepsilon\, {}_2Q,\ m \,\varepsilon\, M(T),\ 0 < (t_m - t_q) \leq 10 \text{ sec.}]$$

as the set of all changes in the system brought about by movements $m \,\varepsilon\, M(T)$.

Superficially, (4.5.2) is identical with the definition of U in (3.4.23), apart from the fact that in (4.5.2) the movements are of the trunk, whereas in (3.4.23) they are movements of eyes, head, and hand. But there is a much more important difference than that. In (3.4.23) the elements of Q define states of the afferent system as determined jointly by environmental and organic variables, but in (4.5.2) the elements of ${}_2Q$ define states of readiness for appropriate responses in a subsystem of a larger system that is still unstable with respect to the new variables that have been incorporated in it. The pattern of stimulation that precedes the response is not merely a pattern of afferent processes whose history after they reach the projection areas of the cortex is entirely unknown to us. It has three components, v_{12}, v_{13}, and v_{14}, of which this is true, but the full history of the remaining components is known, and this history is embodied in ϕ. In other words, the stimulus is not merely a stimulus, but a *perceived* stimulus. It will be very surprising if this fact does not have an important bearing on the process of adaptation now to be considered.

4.6 It will be well to guard ourselves at the outset against a logical error that might easily lead us astray. The stimulus specified by $q \,\varepsilon\, {}_2Q$ has been described as a perceived stimulus, but that does not mean that it is perceived in the sense in which a mature subject perceives. It is, in fact, a stimulus that sets in motion an acquired mechanism that mediates a very restricted type of response, and in particular does not of itself initiate any response, $m \,\varepsilon\, M(T)$. The perception must therefore be understood as being similarly restricted. For this reason it is obvious that it would be completely misleading to assert that the new adaptive responses that are now to be acquired are initiated by perception. They could not possibly evoke those responses unerringly because the exact determination of a movement of the trunk requires the cooperation of the afferents, v_{12}, v_{13}, and v_{14}, which contribute nothing to the engram specified by ϕ. In short, although it is true to say that the infant perceives his environment, it is manifestly false to say that he perceives what he ought to do about the position of his body. He perceives his environment but not his own position in it.

We must conclude then that the movements M(T) are in the first instance unconditioned responses to stimuli containing components that are not specified in our system, having exactly the same status as the movements M at the beginning of life. Within the framework of the system we have defined their occurrence has the appearance of being fortuitous.

Although the elements of ${}_2Q$ are now apparently much more complex than those of the set Q defined in (3.4.20), since (a) three additional proprioceptive functions have been added, (b) movements of the trunk introduce fresh sources of variation in V_1 and V_2, and (c) the components Φ involve much more complex neural activities than the remaining components; nevertheless, ${}_2Q$ is in fact much simpler than its predecessor. We may say that whereas Q describes an 11-dimensional continuum, ${}_2Q$ is 6-dimensional, since ϕ determines a 3-dimensional movement. In Alexander's language, the complexity of the earlier Q is now expressed in a new simplicity which we represent by Φ. The task of adaptation is therefore comparatively easy, since it only involves a set of appropriate 3-dimensional movements in a 6-dimensional continuum.

We are now ready to consider the process of adaptation in concrete detail. The infant is, let us assume, in a sitting posture. Somewhere in his neighborhood, but beyond his reach, is an object to which he has previously learned to respond by movements $m \varepsilon M$. There is an equivalence class, $\Phi(\delta)$, relative to this object, but it specifies states of readiness for fixation responses only, and not for reaching responses, since the object is beyond reach; but by generalization the pattern of stimulation evokes a response appropriate to some δ that was encountered in the first stage of development. That is, the infant stretches out his hand in the direction of the object but of course fails to reach it. This movement shifts the center of gravity of the body and a falling movement begins. This, as we have argued in 2.11, increases drive and creates a minor critical state. The result is a succession of unconditioned responses, $m \varepsilon M(T)$ and $m \varepsilon M$. In connection with the latter it must be emphasized, as we have already done in 3.1, that the development of the set F, (3.4.24), does not imply that elements of M can now occur only as conditioned responses. Nonadaptive movements of the eyes and hands can and must occur when the system is in a critical state to which it has as yet no adequate answer.

In the light of this finding the earlier statement that the process of adaptation involves only the finding of appropriate 3-dimensional responses in a 6-dimensional continuum needs some qualification. This continuum is not yet in fact *fully* organized, and its basic complexity can, in moments of stress, reassert itself and temporarily abolish the emergent simplicity. Regression to more primitive and complex levels of organization is a common phenomenon even in a mature subject. A simple example is the confusion that attends the first efforts to ride a bicycle, and at higher levels innumerable examples have been reported by Freud and his followers, but with an altogether different interpretation.

The inclusion of elements of M among the unconditioned responses to the critical state does not fundamentally affect the issue, since it is only elements of M(T) that can alter the state of the system so as to bring the relevant $\omega \varepsilon \Omega$ within reach of the hand. A movement that does this has the effect that the system now includes a $\phi \varepsilon \Phi(\delta)$, and the appropriate reaching response can be evoked, thereby terminating the critical state. The response $m \varepsilon M(T)$ is thus reinforced, and the principle of generalization, to which we have already appealed in Chapter 2, then operates to build up a new set

(4.6.1) $_2F \equiv [(q,m); q \varepsilon {}_2Q, m \varepsilon M(T), q \rightarrow m]$.

4.7. But that is not all. The reinforcement of $m \varepsilon M(T)$ at the same time serves to reinforce the reaching response, $m \varepsilon M$, which we have assumed to precede the movement of the trunk. This response was initially unsuccessful, and we might therefore expect it to be extinguished. No doubt a certain amount of negative reinforcement does in fact occur, but when the reaching response is followed by a successful $m \varepsilon M(T)$ it thereby receives positive reinforcement. It is only when the distance of the goal is such that the most extreme movement of the trunk fails to bring it within reach that the negative reinforcement prevails, and in that case both $m \varepsilon M$ and $m \varepsilon M(T)$ are extinguished.

This leads to a deduction that is fully confirmed by observation of the everyday behavior of a mature subject. This is that when a person is approaching an object that is to be grasped, the reaching response begins when the object is still out of range, but not before it can be attained by a combined reaching response of the hand and leaning of the body. If the inhibitory effects of the first unsuccessful reaching responses were to prevail, then the normal course of events would be that the movement of the hand would not begin before the object was within arm's length of the body. Commonplace actions of this kind are not often noticed by psychologists, but that does not mean that they stand in no need of explanation. Nor does it mean that they are of no importance, as we shall find when we discuss the new properties that are added to perception by the adaptation we have been considering.

4.8. We have so far been assuming that the reaching movements that are reinforced when a movement of the trunk succeeds in bringing an object within reach are identical with those that were conditioned to elements of the set Q defined in (3.4.20). This would be true if the reaching movement did not begin before completion of the response $m \in M(T)$, but if, as we have assumed, the movement of the hand begins first, it is not true. For every non-zero $m \in M(T)$ changes the position of the goal relative to $R(\Delta)$, and another movement of the hand is then required to reach the goal. We may call this a compensatory movement. Since a single reinforcement applies to the initial movement of the hand, the movement of the trunk, and the compensatory movement, we can deduce that the three movements will ultimately be combined into a single smoothly flowing response that carries the hand to the goal with a minimum delay.

The same argument applies to fixation responses. If the goal is fixated before the movement of the trunk begins, its position relative to $R(\Delta)$ changes with this movement, and a compensatory movement of the eyes, or of the eyes and head together, is required to maintain fixation. Once again the conditioning process has the effect that these responses are integrated into the complex pattern of motor activity already described.

These considerations indicate that we need a new symbol to represent the compound movements that are characteristic of this stage of the adaptive process. We therefore define

$$(4.8.1) \quad {}_2M \equiv [(m(E), m(H), m(A), m(T))]$$

I have in this case refrained from adding the usual defining conditions, partly because any brief statement indicating for example simultaneity, would be misleading, and partly because any $m \varepsilon {}_2M$ is likely to change its detailed organization as a result of conditioning. What I wish to convey by (4.8.1) is that any $m \varepsilon {}_2M$ starts from one state, A, of the system containing eyes, head, hand, and trunk, and ends in another state, B, of the same system. The transition from A to B may at first involve two movements of the eyes, of the head, and of the hand, and later on these two movements may be combined into a single smooth response. Whether a movement from A to B is executed in one or two stages, it is, for the purpose of our definition, one and the same movement. We may regard an element of ${}_2M$ as an equivalence class of responses that all start from A and arrive at B, but by different routes.

Like its predecessor, defined in (3.4.18), ${}_2M$ may be considered as being initially a set of unconditioned responses. It is true that some of the components are already conditioned responses, but they have this property only if q is such that an $m \varepsilon {}_2M$ for which $m(T) = 0$ can succeed, that is, if the goal can be reached without a movement of the trunk. The components m(E), m(H), and m(A) are *not* conditioned responses to any elements of ${}_2Q$ for which δ is beyond reach of the hand without a movement of the trunk.

This implies that the definition of ${}_2F$, in (4.6.1), must be amended to read

(4.8.2) ${}_2F \equiv [(q,m); q \varepsilon {}_2Q, m \varepsilon {}_2M, q \rightarrow m]$.

The difference between the two definitions is that in (4.8.2) the conditioned response is not simply a movement of the trunk but a complex pattern of movements that serves to establish contact with the goal. As before, the conditioned responses in (4.8.2) imply the existence of engrams, several of which can be activated simultaneously, and this enables us to define

(4.8.3) ${}_2\Phi \equiv [(q,e); q \varepsilon {}_2Q, e \varepsilon {}_2E, q \rightarrow e]$ and

(4.8.4) ${}_2\Pi \equiv [\phi \varepsilon {}_2\Phi; \textit{for every } \phi_i, \phi_j \varepsilon {}_2\Pi, t_i = t_j]$.

These definitions are identical in form with those given in (3.4.28) and (3.4.29), but the components, q and e, have the new meanings assigned to them in the present chapter.

4.9. It is clear that the set ${}_2\Pi$, as defined in (4.8.4), possesses all the properties we have already found in the set defined in (3.4.29), since, by (4.3.2), the earlier Π is included in the later one, and nothing has happened to extinguish the conditioned responses underlying the earlier one. But certain new responses have now been acquired, and it may be expected that these will have added new properties. In particular, it will be interesting to find whether the perceptual field still has the instability that we deduced in 4.4.

To answer this question we may follow the same procedure that was adopted in 3.7. That is, we define two sets, ${}_2\Pi_1$ and ${}_2\Pi_2$, determined by two positions, y_1 and y_2, of the trunk. We need not, for the purpose of the present investigation, specify the orientation of the eyes and head, or the position of the hand, since the argument of 3.12 shows that the perceptual field remains essentially unchanged whatever values may be assigned to those variables as long as y remains unchanged. We then select an object, $\omega \in \Omega$, that is beyond the reach of the hand from both y_1 and y_2 but can be reached by an appropriate rotation or inclination of the trunk, and consider the elements, $\phi_1 \in {}_2\Pi_1$ and $\phi_2 \in {}_2\Pi_2$, such that $\omega(\phi_1) = \omega(\phi_2) =$ the selected ω. It follows from the definitions of $R(\Delta)$ and $R(\Omega)$, and from the fact that $y_1 \neq y_2$, that $\delta(\phi_1) \neq \delta(\phi_2)$. The difference between ϕ_1 and ϕ_2 is thus even greater than the corresponding difference found in 3.7. But here again there is a convergence at the end of the chain of definitions, in that m_1 and m_2 terminate in postures that are equivalent in the sense that they both result in contact with ω.

The equivalence rather than the identity of the terminal states indicates that we cannot in this case generalize to ${}_2\Pi$ and claim that ${}_2\Pi_1$ and ${}_2\Pi_2$ are states of readiness for one and the same set of responses. However, if we examine the situation more carefully, we find that the number of ways of reaching an object diminishes as the distance of the object increases. Objects quite close to the body can be reached from any one of a large number of positions of the trunk, and from each of those positions the reaching movement of the hand has one and only one terminus. But as the distance of the object increases, the number of elements in the equivalence class of responses suffers progressive diminution, until we reach a subset, Ω', of Ω such that for each $\omega \in \Omega'$ there is one and only one terminal position of trunk and hand that is reinforced. Beyond that there is a large subset, Ω'', such that for every $\omega \in \Omega''$ there is no reaching response, with or without movement of the trunk, that is reinforced.

If now we define ${}_2\Pi_1'$ as the subset of ${}_2\Pi_1$ corresponding to Ω'

and ${}_2\Pi_2'$ as the subset of ${}_2\Pi_2$ corresponding to Ω', we can say that ${}_2\Pi_1'$ and ${}_2\Pi_2'$ specify two different states of compound readiness for sets of responses that terminate identically. The argument of 3.7 then enables us to conclude that the positions of all objects included in Ω' are perceived as being constant relative to $R(\Omega)$.

But what of the rest of the field? The constancy in the perceived position of Ω' does not in itself guarantee that nearer and more distant objects are likewise perceived as having a constant position. Consider first the subset Ω'', including all objects that can be fixated but cannot be reached by the hand. The easiest way to investigate this problem is to choose three objects in front of the infant, $\omega_0 \in \Omega'$, and ω_1, $\omega_2 \in \Omega''$, such that the distance of ω_2 is greater than that of ω_1. Let the body now move sideways from position y_1 to y_2, determining ${}_2\Pi_1$ and ${}_2\Pi_2$, and let ϕ_0, ϕ_1, $\phi_2 \in {}_2\Pi_1$, and ϕ_0', ϕ_1', $\phi_2' \in {}_2\Pi_2$ be the elements of ${}_2\Pi_1$ and ${}_2\Pi_2$ corresponding to ω_0, ω_1, ω_2 on the two occasions. Also let δ_0, δ_1, $\delta_2 \in \Delta_1$ and δ_0', δ_1', $\delta_2' \in \Delta_2$ specify the positions of ω_0, ω_1, and ω_2 relative to $R(\Delta)$ on the two occasions.

Simple geometrical reasoning shows that the angular shift from δ_0 to δ_0' is greater than that from δ_1 to δ_1', which in turn is greater than that from δ_2 to δ_2'. Since at the beginning of the developmental process discussed in this chapter only fixation responses have been conditioned to the three objects, we can deduce that at that stage the shift from y_1 to y_2 must have resulted in the perception of ω_0 as moving through the greatest distance and ω_2 through the least distance. But the result is radically changed by the conditioning of invariant responses to Ω'. By virtue of the common terminus of the responses specified by ϕ_0 and ϕ_0', ω_0 is perceived as occupying a constant position in space, and this implies that the change in the positions of ω_1 and ω_2 are perceived as being relative to ω_0 and not to $R(\Delta)$. The system has thus generated a new frame of reference, which may be denoted by $R({}_2\Pi)$ and defined by

$$(4.10.1)\quad R({}_2\Pi) \equiv [\phi;\ \textit{for every}\ \phi \in R({}_2\Pi),\ \omega \in \Omega'].$$

This definition implies that $R({}_2\Pi)$ is not an objective frame of reference, like $R(\Delta)$ and $R(\Omega)$, but a *perceptual frame of reference.* Furthermore, it contains not just one origin but a number of simultaneously operating origins. That is, it enables us to refer the position of any object in space simultaneously to the positions of all objects in the space of Ω'.

Returning now to ω_0, ω_1, and ω_2, we note that ϕ_0 and ϕ_0' are elements of $R({}_2\Pi)$, so that the perceived positions of ω_1 and ω_2 are related to that of ω_0. Again simple geometrical reasoning shows that the movement from y_1 to y_2 causes a displacement of ω_1 and ω_2 in the same direction as the movement and not in the opposite direction as when they are related to $R(\Delta)$, and that the displacement of ω_2 is greater than that of ω_1. From this we can infer that the elements of Ω'' are perceived by the infant as sliding past the fixed points of Ω' at different speeds, in the same direction as the movement of the body. He has as yet developed no differential responses to the varying distances of objects beyond the range of Ω', and for that reason we must infer that their distances are all perceived as equal. The reader may object that he can converge his eyes on objects at different distances and that the disparity between the two retinal images enables him to perceive the varying distances. But in fact those variables have been incorporated in ${}_2\underset{\sim}{Q}$ only with respect to objects in the environment that are within the range of Ω'. We have no right to extrapolate to Ω'', although it is not impossible that generalization may carry the range of perceived space a little beyond the boundaries of Ω'. We may therefore conclude that to the infant the space of Ω'' is filled with a series of rather closely packed transparent envelopes with pictures painted on them and sliding round him at varying speeds, rather like the pre-Copernican conception of the starry universe. It needed scientific exploration to break down the Ptolemaic cosmology; the infant's erroneous perception of his environment will similarly be reformed when locomotion enables him to explore farther and farther reaches of that environment.

4.11. We must consider next the effect of $R({}_2\Pi)$ on the perception of $\Omega''' = \Omega - \Omega' - \Omega''$, that is, the part of the environment that is within reach of the infant's hands. For every $\omega \in \Omega'''$ there are two or more successful responses such that the terminal positions of the trunk are different, and of course there are corresponding differences in the position of the hand relative to $R(\Delta)$. Obviously we cannot by any stretch of imagination claim that the engrams mediating those different responses are in any sense equivalent. To claim equivalence we must be able to demonstrate that there is at least one point at which the engrams converge, but there is none. The terminal positions of the trunk are all different, and so too are the terminal positions of the hand and of the eyes.

It is evident that we cannot escape the inference that Ω''' continues to be perceived as being in motion when the position of the trunk is changed. But the development of the perceptual reference frame, $R({}_2\Pi)$, implies that the extent of the perceived motion of any $\omega \varepsilon \Omega'''$ is no longer determined by the two directions of ω relative to $R(\Delta)$. Instead, the reference point by which its change in position is perceived is some point in Ω', which itself changes position relative to $R(\Delta)$ but is perceived as occupying a constant position in space. Thus the positional constancy developed by the infant is relative rather than absolute, and the relativity will remain with him for the rest of his life, because the structure of the system is such that there is no possible basis for absolute constancy. We shall see presently that even this relative constancy is only one of several different relative constancies.

4.12. The foregoing discussion suggests another absurdly simple, but by no means trivial, experiment that can be performed without special apparatus.

The subject sits in front of an array of objects at varying distances, some within easy reach without the necessity for moving the trunk and others attainable only by locomotion. A dinner table will provide as good a setting as any. The subject is requested to sway his body from side to side and to observe the displacements of the various objects relative to one another. No object should be fixated continuously but the eyes should be allowed to wander freely over the scene. The subject is asked to indicate whether there is any object or any limited area that seems to be relatively immobile, that serves, so to speak, as a pivot about which the movement of the remaining objects is centered.

What can the theory predict as the outcome of this experiment? We have seen in this chapter that the properties of the perceptual field developed in the first stage of life are not lost but are incorporated in the more complex field that results from sitting up. Assuming that this remains true throughout the further stages of adaptation that are still to come, we can predict that the center of rotation of the moving field will be in an area that can be reached by the outstretched hand with the aid of a forward inclination of the body.

But we can go further than this and anticipate that when the child begins to walk, the perceptual frame of reference developed during the sitting stage will prove to be too narrow and an additional one will have to be constructed. This at once suggests that if the subject repeats his observations on the moving scene while standing, the center of rotation will not necessarily be the same. If he sways about the hips while the legs remain stationary, the movement is essentially the same as when sitting, and the center of rotation is likely to remain virtually unchanged. But if the weight of the body is shifted from one foot to the other so that the hips are in motion, the center of rotation will be found to have receded to a more distant point, and the former center will now appear to be in motion. It is evident that in this case there are many variables that we have not yet considered, and a specific prediction is therefore impossible.

This experiment has been tried on a number of subjects. There is some variation, as might be expected from the complex character of the system, in the distance of the center of rotation, but all subjects are agreed that there is a definite center, that it is beyond reach of the hand when the body is held erect, and that it is unaffected by changes in the point of fixation. Of course deliberate fixation will transform any point one chooses into a temporary center of rotation, but the center revealed by this experiment is not dependent on fixation, since it remains constant while the eyes roam far and wide over the scene. This can hardly be accidental.

4.13 It is now necessary to take into account a feature of the system that has hitherto been deliberately neglected in the interest of simplicity of exposition. We have defined $R(\Delta)$ as having its origin at the center of rotation of the head, but have neglected the fact that every movement of the head changes the position of the eyes and therefore changes the retinal representation of Δ with respect to the ordering of its elements. If we had taken account of this fact it would have been necessary to define $R(\Delta)$ as having its origin at a point midway between the eyes and also to define the environment in relation to a frame of reference having its origin at the center of rotation of the head. This would have added complications to a system that was already difficult enough to comprehend. It therefore seemed advisable to say nothing about those complications in the hope that an opportunity would arise later for their restoration with a minimum risk of confusion. That opportunity is presented by the foregoing discussion of the effects of mobility of the trunk.

The reader will have no difficulty in recognizing that the arguments used in connection with the movements of the trunk are, *mutatis mutandis,* directly applicable to movements of the head. The space of Δ is divided into three regions analogous to the three regions of Ω. Following the same notation, Δ' is the envelope of space at arm's length. For every $\delta \varepsilon \Delta'$ there is one and only one reaching movement that can succeed, for the arm must be straight and it must be thrust out in the right direction. The Ptolemaic space, Δ'', of undifferentiated distances lies closer to the body than the corresponding Ω'', and its movement is less marked. Finally, there is the narrow space, Δ''', between Δ' and the body. We have hitherto assumed that for any $\delta \varepsilon \Delta'''$ there is one and only one terminus for a successful reaching movement; we must now recognize that while the position of δ determines the final position of the hand and the amount of bending at the elbow, the elbow itself may occupy any one of several positions.

There is thus a close analogy between the subspaces of Δ and those of Ω, and we may therefore infer that the process of stabilizing the system in which Δ remains constant follows the same kind of course as in the system in which Ω is constant. In particular we can infer that when perception of the spatial ordering of the environment emerges out of the conditioning process, complete positional constancy will be characteristic only of Δ'.

This enables us to infer that if a mature subject tilts his head from side to side or backward and forward, the center of rotation of the visual field will be a point at arm's length. Observations are more difficult to make in this case, on account of the comparatively narrow range of movement that is available, but such reports as I have been able to get confirm the inference.

CHAPTER 5

Gravity

5.1. In the system we have built up in the preceding chapters there are several variables that are in part determined by gravity. These are all afferent functions, but so far we have not included any response variables that are directly related to gravity. We have simply taken it for granted that any responses the infant may make to objects in his environment are at the same time adequately adjusted to the distribution of gravitational pulls operating on him at the moment. We must not assume, however, that this adjustment to gravity is an inherent or innate property of the system. The experience of mature subjects in mastering skills such as riding a bicycle or walking a tightrope suggests that responses to gravitational stimuli have to be acquired in the same manner as other skills. The fact that such responses do not stand out prominently in our conscious experience does not imply that they are unimportant or that they have been there all the time.

It has often been assumed that sitting, crawling, standing, and walking are not in the ordinary sense of the term learned activities but are fully explainable in terms of maturation, and some very impressive evidence has been adduced in support of this notion. Nevertheless I propose to reject it. By this I do not mean to imply that there is no such thing as maturation. It is obvious, for example, that locomotion within a few minutes or hours after birth could not occur in such species as the barnyard fowl, the goat, and the horse unless the reflex arcs providing for the reciprocal innervation of antagonist groups of muscles and of contralateral muscular systems were already fully developed. Similarly it is evident that a bird cannot take to the air before it is fully fledged. But this admission is not equivalent to an assertion that maturation is both necessary *and sufficient* to account for the facts. It may be sufficient, or nearly sufficient, to explain the swimming of a relatively simple organism such as the salamander, but it is certainly not sufficient to account for the flight of a complex organism such as the albatross. Sir William Jameson (1959) records that the young albatross requires a month to master the art of flight. The first attempts are clumsy and brief, invariably ending in crash landings. The mechanism of flight is there, fully matured, but it lacks a precise control system that will keep it in continuous operation through the constantly changing conditions of air currents and velocities, and will also permit instant change in the direction of flight when a source of food is detected, as well as modifications of flying technique adjusted to the direction of the wind. Since the whole receptor system, visual and olfactory as well as tactile and proprioceptive, seems to be implicated in this control process, it is reasonable to suppose that it is established by learning.

In the human organism too there are structures that must come to maturity before locomotion can begin. The human infant is in fact born at a lower stage of maturity than other vertebrates, thereby demanding a longer period of postnatal maternal care, but at the same time providing much more extensive opportunity for developing the system through learning. The human organism inherits the same kind of reflex mechanisms for the control of locomotion as the quadrupeds, and some of these mechanisms are already mature at birth. If an infant is suspended by his arms so that his feet are in contact with the floor, and he is then carried forward slowly, his legs will execute the coordinated movements of walking. But these movements cannot be carried out if at the same time the whole weight of the body has to be sustained by the feet. The infant's lack of readiness for this kind of activity is not merely a result of immaturity, but also depends on the fact that he must first solve a problem that does not exist for the quadrupeds. In a quadruped, standing on all fours requires nothing more than simultaneous tonic contraction of the muscles of all the limbs, and in the human infant this becomes possible only some months after birth. But the further problem he has to solve arises from the fact that when he assumes an erect posture, a relatively small movement of the trunk or of the arms or even the head can shift the center of gravity out of the safe region and threaten a fall. This means that random motor responses of a kind that would be perfectly safe in a quadruped are dangerous in a biped, whose feet cover a narrow area relative to his stature. The control system that the human organism requires must therefore make provision for compensatory adjustments that will immediately counteract the tendency to fall when the center of gravity is shifted.

5.2. The argument of the present chapter rests on the assumption that this aspect of the control system depends on learning. Some evidence in support of this came to light in the course of the first of the three experiments described in Chapter 9, in which the subject wore spectacles that reverse right and left. At the beginning of the experiment he could not stand on one foot without falling. Similarly, if he stood on his toes and turned his head to look sideways, he fell. There are no dangers attendant on these exercises when no spectacles are worn, since random deviations from erect posture are immediately corrected. The effect of reversing spectacles is that such deviations cause the retinal images of the environment to be displaced in the opposite to the usual direction, with the result that the compensatory adjustment is misdirected and increases instead of diminishing the deviation from verticality. There is positive instead of negative feedback. If these adjustments were dependent on an automatic control system that comes into operation through maturation, it is evident that the difficulties induced by the spectacles would persist as long as they were worn. But in fact they do not persist. A relatively small amount of practice is sufficient to enable the subject to remain erect when standing on one foot, or on his toes when looking sideways. This establishes beyond question that the control system is developed by learning.

I shall assume further that the control system is part of a multistable system that achieves stability by successive stages. We may think of the maintenance of erect posture as dependent on a system containing four subsystems, controlling the legs, the trunk, the arms, and the head, respectively. It is evident that if these subsystems were all active from the beginning a vast amount of time would be required for attaining stability of the system as a whole; but if the system can develop by stages, progress can be much more rapid. In fact, the course of postnatal maturation is such that the subsystems involving the legs and the trunk are initially inactive, in the sense that those parts of the body are unable to make any contribution to the maintenance of balance. In the following pages we shall investigate the properties of a system that develops by stages, starting with the head.

It is not claimed that the outline that follows represents what must happen in every individual. On the contrary, a good deal of variation is to be expected, since the traditional methods of rearing infants vary widely from culture to culture, and even within the same culture there are wide differences. It is not immediately obvious that such differences may have an effect on the development of perception, and yet this has been clearly demonstrated by Witkin (1960). Children who produced the largest errors in the perception of the vertical in his tilted room apparatus had been more consistently overprotected by their mothers than those with the smallest errors. We shall discuss this evidence in some detail at the end of the chapter.

5.3. A striking feature of the infant's behavior during the first few days of life is his inability to control the movements of his head. If the mother changes his position, as when she transfers him from one arm to the other, his head responds to the changed distribution of gravitational pulls by rolling into a new position as if it were a dead weight. This does not last long, however. Within two or three days the infant may be able to hold his head in a fixed position for a period of a few seconds, and the frequency and duration of this response increases gradually until the rolling movements have completely disappeared.

There is no direct evidence to show that this development is a result of adaptation rather than maturation, but there is some indirect evidence. If it were due to maturation we should expect infants born before full term to achieve stability at a later age than infants born at the end of a normal pregnancy, and that postmature infants should be able to hold their heads in a fixed position almost at once. But this expectation does not appear to be supported by the facts. There is consequently a reasonable case for the assumption that adaptation is the relevant mechanism. Moreover, since the most important function of the cerebral cortex is the formation of temporary connections (to use a term now favored by

Russian psychologists), we may legitimately assume that the cortex begins to form such connections as soon as it is exposed to variable stimulation.

Our immediate task then is to define a system that is initially unstable but is capable of achieving stability through conditioning. We have already, in (3.4.2), defined A_6, A_7, and A_8 as the positions of the head relative to the axes of $R(\Delta)$, and it will be convenient to retain those definitions. The initial instability arises from changes of position imposed on the infant by the mother, that is, by changes in the position of $R(\Delta)$ relative to the gravitational axis. To define these changes we may first define a gravitational reference frame, $R(G)$, as the radius of the earth that passes through the origin of $R(\Delta)$, that is, the center of rotation of the head. We then define Λ_1, Λ_2, and Λ_3 as the sets of angles between $R(G)$ and the three axes of $R(\Delta)$ and

(5.3.1) $\Lambda \equiv [(\lambda_1, \lambda_2, \lambda_3); t_{\lambda_1} = t_{\lambda_2} = t_{\lambda_3}]$

is the set of all positions of $R(\Delta)$ relative to $R(G)$. Changes of position may then be defined by

(5.3.2) $M(G) \equiv \Lambda \times \Lambda.$

Now any $m \varepsilon M(G)$ has a fourfold effect. It stimulates the semicircular canals, it causes a rolling of the head into a new position, and this in turn produces further stimulation of the vestibule, and also, following an assumption made in 2.11, an autonomic discharge creating a minor critical state. (We should, strictly speaking, include linear as well as angular displacements of $R(\Delta)$, but as they are less likely to produce rolling movements of the head, no serious error will be introduced if we neglect them for the present.) The rolling movements of the head may be specified in terms of $M(H)$, defined in (3.4.16); but as our interest in these movements depends on the assumption that they are a source of drive, it will be sufficient to specify them in the notation by a symbol representing the resultant drive. Similarly it will not be necessary to specify the vestibular stimuli resulting from the rolling movements. Since these movements are destined to be eliminated, the stimuli that become conditioned to the responses that prevent them must be stimuli that occur before the rolling begins.

We do need, however, to specify the vestibular stimuli resulting directly from any $m \varepsilon M(G)$. We can do this by defining C_1, C_2, and C_3 as the sets of stimuli aroused in the semicircular canals by rotations A_6, A_7, and A_8, as defined in (3.4.2). Actually these were defined as rotations of the head relative to the trunk, whereas here we are concerned with rotations of the head that are incidental to rotations of the whole body. This need cause no confusion, however, if the rotations are understood to be specified in relation to the position of the reference frame $R(\Delta)$ *at the beginning of the movement*. In other words, if the whole body is rotated, carrying the head with it, the effect on the canals is the same as if the head alone were rotated through the same angles while the body remained stationary.

Let λ be the initial position of the body from which $m \varepsilon M(G)$ starts. That is, λ defines the initial position of $R(\Delta)$ relative to $R(G)$. Similarly, let λ' be the terminal position. That is, $(m \varepsilon M(G)) = (\lambda,\lambda')$. If $z(H) = (a_6, a_7, a_8)$ is the position of the head relative to $R(\Delta)$ at the beginning of the movement, and this position does not change until the movement is completed, then its final position relative to λ, the initial position of $R(\Delta)$ is

(5.3.3) $z'(H) = (a_6 + \lambda_1 - \lambda_1', a_7 + \lambda_2 - \lambda_2', a_8 + \lambda_3 - \lambda_3')$.

We shall use the symbol $M'(H)$ to represent the set of movements of the head effected in this manner, while retaining $M(H)$ as the set of movements relative to $R(\Delta)$. Of course a movement may contain both $m \varepsilon M(H)$ and $m \varepsilon M(G)$, in which case $m' \varepsilon M'(H)$ will be the resultant of both movements; but for the moment we shall confine our attention to elements of $M'(H)$ for which $(m \varepsilon M(H)) = 0$.

Since the effective stimulus for the semicircular canals is angular acceleration, it will be necessary to incorporate this in our definition of the movements of the head. Let T be the set of temporal durations. Then

(5.3.4) $J \equiv [(m',t); m' \varepsilon M'(H), t \varepsilon T,$ t *is the duration of* $m']$

specifies the forces acting on the canals, and

(5.3.5) $B \equiv [(j,c); j \varepsilon J, c \varepsilon C,$ c *follows* j]

is an afferent function.

5.4. It is at once evident that B is not sufficient for our purpose, for although a given j always results in the same afferent process c, it may start from any one of a large number of different initial positions, λ, and the resulting rolling movements of the head will vary accordingly. Consequently the vestibular stimuli specified by any $j \varepsilon J$ cannot alone become conditioned to a determinate response that will serve to check the rolling movement.

To get over this difficulty we may define P as the set of patterns of pressure stimuli in the head and neck determined jointly by gravity, by Λ, by Z(H), and by the supporting structure on which the infant is resting. P is obviously a very complex set, including cutaneous stimuli and stimuli arising in the cervical vertebrae, and I shall not attempt to analyze it. In the present inquiry we are chiefly interested in the changes in gravitational stimulation brought about by changes in the disposition of the body, and these can most conveniently be expressed by

(5.4.1) $K \equiv P \times P.$

Then

(5.4.2) $N \equiv [(m,k);\ m \varepsilon M(G),\ k \varepsilon K,\ t_m = t_k]$

is a function. It defines changes in the position of the body and the resulting changes in pressure stimuli. Finally,

(5.4.3) $G(H) \equiv [(b,n);\ b \varepsilon B,\ n \varepsilon N,\ t_b = t_n]$

defines the total pattern of vestibular and pressure stimulation as determined by the movements imposed on the infant's body. The relation of simultaneity, expressed by the condition that $t_b = t_n$, implies that the movement m′ specified by b is identical with the movement m specified by n. But m′ is defined in relation to λ and therefore, by (5.3.5), determines the value of the independent variable that is responsible for the vestibular stimuli, whereas m is defined in relation to R(G), and therefore, by (5.4.2), determines the independent variable that is responsible for the pressure stimuli. Hence any $g \varepsilon G(H)$ specifies a movement of the body together with the resulting afferent processes. G(H) is thus analogous to S as defined in (3.4.12).

If we now add the drive that we assume to result from a rolling movement of the head, we can define

(5.4.4) $Q(G) \equiv [(g,d);\ g \varepsilon G(H),\ d \varepsilon D,\ d\ \textit{follows}\ g].$

5.5 We must next ask what means are available to the infant for getting out of the critical state induced by the rolling of his head or, alternatively, for preventing such a state from developing. Apparently the only possible response is a contraction of the muscles of the neck that will hold the head in a fixed position.

These responses can be defined in terms of M(H), whose elements, it will be remembered, include zero movements. The situation we are now considering makes it clear that a zero movement is not necessarily the result of a state of inactivity. On the contrary, inactivity is a necessary condition for the rolling movement that follows an imposed change in the position of the body relative to R(G), and an active response is required to prevent the rolling.

Following our usual procedure we assume that the drive induced by the rolling of the head gives rise to unconditioned responses including elements of M(H). But in this case there is an important difference. The head cannot roll beyond a certain distance, and when it comes to rest, the drive must be assumed to diminish in strength rather quickly, so that we cannot expect a prolonged succession of unconditioned responses as in the other systems we have considered. For this reason no reference need be made to the perseverative traces of stimuli. This implies not that the stimuli defined by G(H) leave no traces but only that they appear to be irrelevant in the situation we are now investigating. These considerations lead to the definition

(5.5.1) $U(G) \equiv [(q,m); q \in Q(G), m \in M(H), m \textit{ follows } q]$.

Like the set U, defined in (3.4.23), U(G) describes a system that is both unstable and ultrastable. The property of ultrastability is implicit in the description of the responses M(H) as unconditioned. Since any unconditioned response can be conditioned, the system U(G) is capable of adaptation through conditioning, so that the rolling movements of the head and the resultant sudden increases of drive can be eliminated.

The system described by U(G) is simple by comparison with the system U defined in (3.4.23), since it does not include any of the enormously complex patterns of combined retinal and proprioceptive stimulation incorporated in U. It is, in fact, the simplest of all the ultrastable subsystems with which we shall be concerned, and if it can be shown that it is separated from the rest of the system by a wall of null-functions, we can deduce that its adaptation will be relatively rapid. The infant is of course continuously bombarded by stimuli from the environment, and the rest of his body is subjected to changes in pressure stimuli, but all these functions are in effect inactive in the subsystem under consideration, since they do not affect the values taken by the variables of that system. The requirement of isolation is therefore satisfied.

The rate of adaptation will naturally vary with the frequency of the opportunities provided. Many mothers are so alarmed by the rolling of the head that they take precautions to prevent it, thereby delaying the process, while others, particularly if the baby is not their first, make little or no effort to control. While there is no direct evidence in support of this assumption, it is at least compatible with data reported long ago by Watson (1924). When infants were supported in a prone position, the earliest age at which the head was held in a fixed position for one second or more was found to vary from two to fifteen days. Watson, it is interesting to note, included this behavior in his list of instincts, on the ground that no learning is required for it.

The effects of the conditioning process envisaged here may be represented by the set

$$(5.5.2)\quad F(G) \equiv [(q,m);\ q \varepsilon Q(G),\ m \varepsilon M(H),\ m = 0,\ q \rightarrow m].$$

It must be emphasized again that although $m = 0$, it is not a zero response but a specific motor innervation that serves exactly to counterbalance the change in the gravitational force operating on the head as a result of the change in the position of the body specified by $q \varepsilon Q(G)$. Since for any $q \varepsilon Q(G)$ there is one and only one $m \varepsilon M(H)$ such that $m = 0$, it follows that $F(G)$ is a function.

5.6. We have assumed the development of $F(G)$ to have been determined in the first instance by the consequences of movements imposed on the infant by his mother, but it is clear that additional elements must be subsequently acquired as a result of movements initiated by the infant himself. In particular, if he is held in an erect position, any spontaneous movement of the head is likely to shift its center of gravity and start a rolling movement. The responses, $m \varepsilon M(H)$, that serve to prevent such movements are conditioned to the combined vestibular and pressure stimuli resulting from the spontaneous movement, and the outcome of this process is that the infant is not merely able to keep his head in any fixed position, but is able to change to any other position and retain it as well.

The retention of any position for more than a few seconds means that the vestibular stimuli induced by the movement into that position may have completely disappeared before a new position is taken up; and this applies equally to the traces of the pressure stimuli that were in operation before the movement began. This implies that the stimuli for the continuing response are changing as the response continues and ultimately consist only of the pressure stimuli dependent on the position that is now being held. Since these are single-valued functions of the position of the head relative to the reference frames R(Δ) and R(G), it follows that the establishment of the conditioned responses, F(G), entails the conditioning of the same responses to the attenuated stimuli that remain after the vestibular and other stimuli have faded out. The definition of F(G) given in (5.5.2) must therefore be understood to be amended by extending the meaning of $q \epsilon Q(G)$ to include patterns of stimulation as attenuated by the lapse of time.

5.7. Following the precedent of (3.4.28) and (4.8.3), we now define

(5.7.1) $\Phi(G) \equiv [(q,e); q \epsilon Q(G), e \epsilon E(H), q \rightarrow e]$,

where E(H) is the set of engrams mediating the conditioned responses M(H). It may appear that there is little justification for this, since only one $q \epsilon Q(G)$ can exist at any moment of time, and there is therefore no question of the simultaneous existence of a number of elements of Φ(G). Nevertheless it will be useful to be able to refer to an activity that goes on in the brain without having to speak at the same time about the accompanying motor activity, particularly when we want to investigate the part played by gravity in the perception of space.

Although only one $\phi \epsilon \Phi(G)$ can be fully active at a time, there is nothing to prevent this ϕ from coexisting with a set Π and thereby contributing to perception. In fact it can hardly be otherwise, since the afferent functions involved in $\phi \epsilon \Phi(G)$ are also incorporated in all the elements of Π. If Π contains any trace elements derived from the previous position of the head, those elements will be associated with a previous $\phi \epsilon \Phi(G)$, in which the terminal gravitational stimuli are the initial stimuli of the presently operating $\phi \epsilon \Phi(G)$. This ensures continuity in the process.

5.8. We may at this point interrupt the analysis of the development of adaptation to gravity in order to investigate the effect of this process on the perception of the spatial ordering of the environment. An examination of the sets Q and $_2$Q as defined in (3.4.20) and (4.3.1) shows that the patterns of stimulation to which responses to the positions of objects in space are conditioned contain the gravitational stimuli that are incorporated in the elements of Φ(G). That is to say, the elements of Q contain the elements of Q(G), and are therefore simultaneously conditioned to responses adapted to the positions of objects in space and to other responses adapted to gravity. It is therefore reasonable to expect that the perception of space will in some way be affected by this.

Briefly, the effect is that the perceptual field acquires a horizontal-vertical frame of reference that is not provided for in the definition of Π. We confine our attention for the moment to the definition given in (3.4.29), that is, the perceptual field as it exists at the end of the first stage of development, before the infant has learned to sit without support. At this stage the positions of objects and the movements of the hand are defined in terms of the reference frame R(Δ), but as the position of this frame is variable in relation to R(G), the gravitational axis, it follows that any change in the position of R(Δ) entails a change in the orientation of the perceptual field. The field, as determined by Π alone, is unstable. But if we redefine Π so as to include the element of Φ(G) that is in operation at the same moment, then it may be described as a state of simultaneous readiness not only for responses directed to objects in space but also for responses to the direction of the gravitational axis.

This leads us to another consideration that we have hitherto neglected. The proprioceptive stimuli, V_9, V_{10}, and V_{11}, (3.4.11), determined by the position of the hand, also contain components that are functions of gravity, and these necessarily have an effect on the efferent processes controlling the manual responses to objects in the environment. What this means may be understood if we consider two situations in which the position of an object relative to R(Δ) is the same and the initial position of the hand is also the same, but the position of R(Δ) relative to R(G) is different. The disposition of the gravitational forces operating on the hand is different on the two occasions, and consequently, although the movement $m \in M(A)$ is objectively the same in both cases, the efferent processes required to produce this movement are not identical. Each movement is at once a response to the position of the object and a response to gravity.

The stimulus components incorporated in Π include elements of V_9, V_{10}, and V_{11}, so that here again Π must be interpreted as a state of compound readiness for responses that are simultaneously adapted to the positions of objects in space and to the direction of the gravitational axis. The significance of this is that the perceptual field specified by Π possesses one fundamental stability that could not be deduced from our earlier analysis in Chapters 3 and 4. It has a horizontal-vertical reference frame that is derived entirely from the conditioning of responses to the direction of the gravitational axis.

Here we arrive at our first illustration of what I propose to call the *principle of interpenetration*. The essence of this principle is that when two sets of responses are conditioned to two sets of compound stimuli such that some of the components of the first set of stimuli are also components of the second set, any properties of the perceptual field determined by one set are incorporated in the perceptual field determined by the other set. In terms of the notation, let

$$\Phi_1 \subset Q_1 \times E_1$$

and

$$\Phi_2 \subset Q_2 \times E_2$$

represent two functional relations acquired by conditioning, where $E_1 \neq E_2$, but some of the components of the elements of Q_1 and also components of the elements of Q_2, then the properties of Π_1 are included in Π_2 and vice versa. Since Π_1 and Π_2 are simultaneous events they appear in consciousness to be a single event, and the origins of their several properties are not distinguished. There is one unified perceptual field.

Philosophers in the past have often spoken of what they called the "unity of the mind" as if this were some inherent property that must be accepted as a primary datum. Descartes, for example, was so impressed with this singleness of the mind that he could not believe its interaction with the body could be effected through any organ that was duplicated in the cerebral hemispheres, and accordingly he chose the pineal body as the seat of the soul. Modern psychologists smile at this naive idea, but many of them continue to be impressed by the unity of the mind and to insist that because the whole is apparently greater than the sum of its parts, there must be some organizing principle over and above any principles that may be found sufficient to account for the parts. This organization appears to be precisely what is done by interpenetration.

In normal circumstances there is no opportunity for direct investigation of this process, but it does sometimes happen that the development of one sector of the perceptual field is delayed, and in such cases the normal interpenetration does not exist. Senden, in his monograph on the effects of operations for congenital cataract (1935), reports that a patient may perceive the dog that he sees as being different from the dog that he touches, although only one dog is present and his own hand touching it is in his visual field. This striking absence of the expected unity of the mind finds a ready explanation in terms of the principle of interpenetration.

To understand this we must recall that the set F, defined in (3.4.24), includes both conditioned fixation responses and conditioned reaching responses, and that the stimuli for the former are components of the stimuli for the latter. Now a patient suffering from a congenital cataract is not totally blind—if he were, no surgeon would operate on him. Some light reaches his retina, and the volume of afferent energy can be altered by movements of the eyes. Consequently a certain amount of conditioning of oculomotor responses may be assumed to have taken place even before the removal of the cataract, although of course it will lack the fine differentiation that is characteristic of a person with normal vision. We can therefore expect that after recovery from the operation there will be a fairly rapid expansion of the oculomotor subset of F. The stimuli for the remaining subset are of a higher degree of complexity, and moreover it is almost certain that this subset is void. That is, there are no reaching responses that have been conditioned to patterns of stimulation including retinal components. What this implies is that the visual field as yet possesses none of the properties conferred on it by the conditioning of reaching responses. The incompletely developed field of visual perception, Π_1, and the fully developed tactile field, Π_2, are in effect two separate and distinct perceptual worlds. They will not coalesce into a single field until the patient has acquired a large number of specific motor responses to compound patterns of stimulation including retinal components.

5.9. When the subsystem U(G), defined in (5.5.1), has achieved stability by the development of the function F(G), (5.5.2), the process of adaptation to gravity can be extended to the larger subsystem that becomes active when the infant begins to sit without support. In this position he is in a state of unstable equilibrium, in that any movement he may make, such as stretching out an arm or tilting the head to one side, shifts the center of gravity and thereby initiates a falling movement. This creates a minor critical state, and any resulting unconditioned response that serves to terminate this state or prevent it from developing will become conditioned to the stimuli determined by the initial movement.

The system obviously has many more variables than that in which the head alone is involved, and the number of possible responses to any given critical state is very large, since the muscles of the trunk, the shoulders, the arms, and the head are all involved. The number of combined responses of these muscles that will suffice to prevent a fall is relatively small, and the probability that the muscles will all operate simultaneously to produce the required result is rather low. However, the system contains a subsystem that is already adapted, and this accelerates the adaptation of the new system. For any movement of the trunk generates an element of Q(G), as defined in (5.4.4), and by F(G) this gives rise to a conditioned holding response of the head. In this way the head is immobilized, and in consequence a response that is confined to the trunk will suffice to correct a falling movement. The probability that such a response will occur is much greater than the probability that responses of the trunk, head, and arms will occur simultaneously in such a manner as to prevent a fall.

As soon as appropriate responses of the trunk have been conditioned to the patterns of stimulation arising from spontaneous movements in all possible directions, there is no longer any need for immobilizing the head, since any change in the position of the head, involving a shift of the center of gravity, immediately evokes the necessary compensatory response of the trunk. The infant is thereby set free to react to his environment and proceed with the development discussed in Chapter 4. All responses to the external environment will now at the same time be adequate responses to the distribution of gravitational stimuli, and, by the principle of interpenetration, the direction of the gravitational axis becomes a property of the visual perceptual field that emerges from the conditioning of appropriate responses to the environment.

To give expression to these results in terms of our notation all we need to do is to redefine the sets describing proprioceptive functions by adding the vestibular functions and the pressure functions as determined by gravity. There is no need to redefine the sets M, describing unconditioned motor responses, since they already include all the responses that are required to maintain balance. But the sets F, describing patterns of stimulation and the responses conditioned to them, must be expanded to include balancing responses. The sets Φ are similarly expanded. It follows that any set Π, whose elements are simultaneously existing elements of Φ, describes a state of compound readiness for responses that are adapted not only to the positions of objects relative to a frame of reference, $R(\Delta)$ or $R(\Omega)$, defined by the body, but also to their positions relative to the frame of reference $R(G)$.

5.10. One very important consequence of this interpenetration is that the vertical direction is perceived as being absolutely constant. We have already seen that there is a relative constancy in the perceived positions of objects, but in the present case the constancy admits of no exception. I have elsewhere, in collaboration with Papert (Taylor and Papert, 1956), discussed this phenomenon, using a different notation; but the argument can easily be stated in terms of the notation used in this work.

We consider a situation in which the subject is sitting in an environment that contains a vertical line within reach of his hands. Let the set Ω be defined as containing this vertical line and nothing else. That is, we shall neglect all other elements of the environment. Following (3.4.13) we define Σ as the compound pattern of stimulation determined at any moment by Ω, together with the proprioceptive and pressure components determined by the orientation of the head and eyes and the posture of the body. There is a different set Σ for each setting of eyes, head, and body, and since Ω is a fixed vertical line, Σ is exactly determined by this setting. For the setting determines the values taken by the proprioceptive and pressure functions, and it also determines the orientation of the eyes relative to Ω, and therefore the retinal components of Σ. It should be noted in particular that any sideways tilting of the head produces a change in the direction of the retinal images of Ω, and any backward or forward tilting has the effect of changing the angle between the two retinal images.

Now consider a response such as moving the hand from one point on the vertical line to another. If we describe this response in terms of the reference frame $R(\Delta)$ the description remains unchanged as long as the position of the trunk is held constant, and therefore all the sets Σ for which this constancy holds can be considered as constituting an equivalence class, since the identical response $m \in M(A)$ is conditioned to each of them. The position of the line relative to $R(\Delta)$ is therefore perceived as being constant. A new position of the trunk means that a different $m \in M(A)$ is required, and the line is therefore perceived as having a different position relative to $R(\Delta)$. On the other hand the responses starting from different positions of the trunk are all identical in the sense that in each case the effort of lifting the hand through a given distance is maximized, since it has to be moved directly against the gravitational pull. Consequently, although the direction of the line relative to the body changes with every change in posture, its direction relative to the gravitational axis is perceived as being constant. It is evident that this relationship must continue to hold good when the infant learns to stand and walk.

5.11. When the infant has learned to sit without support, he is free to proceed with the much more laborious task of adaptation to the spatial ordering of the environment as discussed in Chapter 4. When that is reasonably well advanced he is ready to undertake locomotion. This takes a variety of forms, of which the commonest is crawling. Here too the acquisition of responses to gravity is of primary importance. Although the structure of the relevant reflex arcs is such that reciprocal alternating movements of the limbs are easily produced, these movements have to be conditioned to the massive pressure stimuli that develop when the limbs have to support the weight of the body. The first stage in this process is the conditioning of simultaneous motor responses in the arms, enabling the infant to raise his body above the level of the floor. This is a comparatively simple matter, since the probability of the simultaneous occurrence of extending movements of both arms is relatively high. If this has the effect of lifting the body, the independent relaxing of one limb entails a fall, and this has the effect that the maintaining of the combined response quickly becomes conditioned to the pressure stimuli. Here again rigidity of the head is likely to accompany the first efforts, but that is relaxed when the control of the arms is well established.

A similar process occurs in the legs, usually at a later stage, since falling movements of the lower part of the body presumably do not produce such extensive autonomic responses. They obviously have less effect on the vestibule. The response of maintaining the muscles of all four limbs in a state of contraction that keeps the body off the floor is then quickly conditioned to the resulting compound pattern of pressure stimuli. If now the infant responds to an object in front of him by stretching out a hand, he is likely to fall unless the ipsilateral knee is well forward. Consequently the response of bringing the knee forward prior to a stretching movement of the hand becomes conditioned to the previously existing pressure stimuli. The basic component of the activity of crawling is thereby established. The completion of the process involves the conditioning of alternating movements of the limbs to the constantly changing pattern of pressure stimuli. This entails changes in the pattern of exteroceptive stimulation as well, but we must postpone discussion of this to the next chapter.

Exactly the same principles are applicable to the process of learning to stand and to walk. At every stage the adaptation of the previously active subsystem is a necessary prerequisite of advance. Thus standing with support of the hands is made possible by the fact that the infant has already learned to hold both legs rigid in response to pressure; and standing without support is possible because, among other things, the head can be held in a fixed position. It is obvious that any extensive movement of the head would upset the balance and lead to a fall, and it is significant that the head is always held very rigidly during the first efforts to stand alone. As conditioning to the new patterns of pressure stimuli progresses this rigidity disappears. This simply means that differential conditioning enables the child to adjust to an increasingly wide range of variation in the distribution of gravitational stimuli.

The first walking movements introduce new patterns of gravitational stimuli to which as yet no adequate responses have been conditioned, and once more the previously adapted subsystems contribute to the process by getting into a steady state. The head and arms are held in a rigid position until the basic responses have been acquired, and gradually achieve freedom of movement as differential conditioning of balancing responses proceeds. Exactly the same rigidity of the upper part of the body can be seen during the first stage of learning to ride a bicycle.

5.12. We may now expand the definition of F(G) to include all the conditioned responses to gravity discussed above. At once it becomes evident that as thus amended F(G) is not subject to the limitation that only one of its elements can exist at any moment of time. The system contains a number of subsystems, and although these are not independent of one another there is a wide variety of ways in which their elements can be combined. That is, there are a great many postures that the body may take up, and each of them involves a different set of conditioned responses to gravitational stimuli. We may use the symbol $\Pi(G)$ to represent the subset of $\Phi(G)$ that is in operation at any moment of time.

We have hitherto used the symbol Π to represent states of the system in which engrams are active, but the relevant responses are not necessarily evoked. In the case of $\Pi(G)$ it would seem that this qualification does not apply, since, in an individual who is awake and active, responses to gravity are taking place all the time, and therefore there are no elements of $\Pi(G)$ that involve activity of engrams without the corresponding motor responses. Nevertheless there are good grounds for using Π rather than any other symbol. It is clear that any response to an environmental object must at the same time be adapted to gravity. Hence the numerous engram activities included in the set ${}_2\Pi$, as defined in (4.8.4), prepare the organism not merely for responding to the positions of objects in space but for doing so in such a manner that the posture of the body during the execution of those responses will be suitably adapted to gravity.

The implication of this is that $\Pi(G)$ is incorporated in ${}_2\Pi$. But this does not mean that $\Pi(G)$ has no independent existence of its own. In total darkness ${}_2\Pi$, as previously defined, is void, but $\Pi(G)$ is fully operative, and in these circumstances it constitutes perception of the posture of the body and the positions of the limbs. The perception of the position of the body is therefore an integral part of the perception of the visual world. Thus, although $_2\Pi$ and $\Pi(G)$ involve different response systems, those systems are fully integrated with one another, and the result is that the two perceptual fields constitute a single comprehensive perception. The visual world and the gravitational world are inseparable components of a unified perceptual world.

The relative importance of these two components varies enormously from person to person, and within one person it varies with the type of activity in which he is engaged. Thus $\Pi(G)$ is much more important in actors and acrobats than it is in people whose everyday activities are directed primarily to the manipulation of objects in the environment. A large part of the training of such people is directed to the production of specific sequences of movements, and we can therefore expect that in them the perception of their own posture is more prominent than it is in others. Thus the actors of the Moscow Art Theatre are sometimes required to rehearse a play without uttering a word, concentrating entirely on the movements and postures. The perception of their own bodies is consequently more highly developed and more detailed than it is in actors who are not required to submit to such training. In general, whenever accurate control of bodily movements is essential for the successful completion of a task, the corresponding segment of $\Pi(G)$ will have a larger number of elements.

5.13. There are several facts that support the inference that the horizontal-vertical frame of reference of the visual world is derived from $\Pi(G)$. One of the most striking is the effect produced on a passenger in a small aircraft that is making a steep turn. If the maneuver is properly executed, the direction of the thrust of the passenger's body against the seat remains invariant relative to the axes of the airplane. There is therefore an artificial gravitational axis that is oblique to the direction of the earth's gravitational pull. If the passenger looks at the ground below him he perceives it as being no longer level; it is tilted at an angle which is the negative of the banking angle of the aircraft. The frame of reference is thus not an inherent property of the visual world itself but is directly dependent on gravity.

Two supplementary facts that support this interpretation may be mentioned. The first is that the tilting effect is not so readily seen in a large airplane unless one is sitting near the center of rotation. In other positions there is a slight lateral thrust that is sufficient to destroy the illusion that one is still sitting upright. The second fact is that the illusion of the tilted earth disappears in an experienced pilot. The reason for this is that the banking is controlled by the pilot himself. He manipulates rudder and ailerons in such a manner as to keep the nose of the machine on the horizon, so that he is in fact responding to the level of the ground in a way that is incompatible with the responses that would be induced by the oblique gravitational axis. Thus in the situation "piloting an aircraft" some of the previously acquired responses to gravity have to be inhibited, and the associated elements of ${}_2\Pi$ are consequently eliminated.

An even more striking proof of the close dependence of the horizontal-vertical frame of the visual world on $\Pi(G)$ is seen in one of the effects of alcoholic intoxication. The locomotor instability characteristic of this state is explainable in terms of the blocking of proprioceptive and pressure afferents. This implies that at least some of the elements of $\Pi(G)$ are missing, so that the system shows some of the characteristics of $U(G)$. Now the afferents in question are at the same time components of the elements of ${}_2Q$, as defined in (4.3.1) but expanded in meaning to include the proprioceptive functions that become active in walking. Consequently we can deduce that ${}_2\Pi$ becomes unstable to the extent that the proprioceptive and pressure functions are disturbed. This means specifically that the visual world no longer has a stable horizontal-vertical frame of reference. When a drunk man falls and reports that "the ground came up and hit me," he is not merely indulging in picturesque or poetic language but is giving an accurate report of his perceptual experience.

5.14. Experimental evidence in support of the foregoing hypothesis is to be found in the researches of Witkin and his associates. His numerous experiments in which subjects sat in a tilted chair in a tilted room (Witkin, 1949) show that there is a wide range of variation in the perception of the vertical in the experimental situation. When the chair was erect and the room tilted, many subjects perceived the room as erect and their own bodies as tilted in the opposite direction to the tilt of the room; and relatively few perceived their bodies as erect and the room as tilted. At first glance this seems to contradict the hypothesis, since the horizontal-vertical frame of reference seemed to be determined solely by retinal stimulation in those subjects who saw the tilted room as erect. Evidently the theory must fail unless it can account for these cases as well as for those who had accurate perception of the vertical.

The first point to be noted is that the experimental conditions involved the activity of a very restricted subset of $Q(G)$. The subject sat in a chair equipped with head rest and side rests, so that he was in no danger of falling when the chair was tilted, and no active response to the direction of the gravitational axis was required. This implies that proprioceptive stimuli of the kind that are produced when the subject is maintaining his posture by his own efforts are eliminated, and also that there are patterns of pressure stimuli of a kind that are not found when posture is self-maintained. If we represent by $\Sigma(G)$ the subset of $Q(G)$ that is in operation when posture is self-maintained and by $\bar{\Sigma}(G)$ the subset that is in operation when the same posture is maintained by external supporting surfaces, it is evident that $\Sigma(G)$ and $\bar{\Sigma}(G)$ have relatively few elements in common.

Now any change in the content of $\Sigma(G)$, brought about by a change of posture, demands an active adjustment to the direction of the gravitational axis. In general this response will tend to the restoration of erect posture, so that it may be argued that all sets $\Sigma(G)$ are organized into a functional equivalence class and therefore determine a perceptual constancy, which in this case can only be the direction of the vertical. On the other hand, a change in the content of $\bar{\Sigma}(G)$, effected by a change in the tilt of the chair, demands only small intra-organismic responses to the changed distribution of gravitational pulls, since the supporting surfaces do all the necessary work. In other words, the responses to the sets $\bar{\Sigma}(G)$ are all different from one another and therefore determine no functional equivalence class and no constancy.

Now Witkin's experimental situation involves the operation of sets of the form $\bar{\Sigma}(G)$ rather than $\Sigma(G)$, and we need not therefore be surprised to find that for the great majority of the subjects the normal constancy in the perception of the vertical is more or less seriously disrupted. Indeed, in a few subjects the disruption was so severe that the direction of the vertical of the body space was literally indeterminate, and attempts to locate it had to be abandoned. At the other extreme there were a few subjects who showed virtually no departure from normal constancy. Neither the tilting of the room, the chair, nor of both together prevented them from locating the true vertical. The majority of the subjects fell between those extremes and displaced the vertical to varying extents toward the "vertical" axis of the tilted room. In extreme cases the room was perceived as erect under all degrees of tilt, and this was true whether the subject's chair was erect, tilted in the same direction as the room, or in the opposite direction. These subjects thus departed from constancy in a systematic manner by generating a spurious constancy, and it is significant that in doing so they displayed a systematic inconstancy in the perception of the direction in which their own bodies were tilted. Their reports may be best explained by considering first what happens in a subject with completely undisturbed constancy. If he sits erect in a room tilted 30° to the left, he will perceive himself as erect and the room as tilted. If, from this position, room and chair are rotated together through 30° to the right, the room will now be vertical and the subject tilted to the right. Although there has been no change in the pattern of retinal stimulation, the subject correctly reports the room to be erect and his own body to be tilted to the right. This is exactly the report given by the other type of subject when the room is tilted to the left and his body is erect.

It is evident that in this case the pressure stimuli, $\bar{\Sigma}(G)$, are consistent with the body being erect and with no other direction. If, nevertheless, the subject reports himself to be tilted 30° to the right, we are justified in concluding that in the life of this subject the sets $\bar{\Sigma}(G)$ have never been conditioned to responses adapted to the direction of the gravitational axis, and therefore do not generate accurate perception of the direction in which the body is inclined. But if the direction of the body is indeterminate, then a given pattern of retinal stimulation, produced by room and body being inclined at, say, 30° to one another, is consistent with any one of a large number of orientations of room and chair, provided only that the angle between them is always 30°. Why, then, in this ambiguous situation does the subject always perceive the room as erect and his body tilted at an angle consistent with the direction of the retinal stimuli?

This question cannot be answered in terms of the theory as expounded up to this point; and this is hardly surprising, since the subjects of Witkin's experiments were not infants but mature people. In particular, they are people who have had ample opportunity to discover, in circumstances in which sets of the form $\Sigma(G)$ rather than $\bar{\Sigma}(G)$ were in operation, that structures of the kind known as walls are almost invariably built vertically, while floors are commonly horizontal. This virtually invariant property of the structural features of rooms has an interesting consequence. Let $Q(w)$ represent the formal equivalence class of Q in which the exteroceptive components of the stimuli are determined by a wall. The responses conditioned to the elements of $Q(w)$ may be assumed to include up and down movements along the surface of the wall, and as these responses are at the same time adjusted to the direction of the gravitational axis, the resulting functional equivalence class, $\Phi(w)$, mediates perception of the wall as being vertical. But in a mature subject the elements of $Q(w)$ are also conditioned to a verbal response which may be symbolized by (wall-vertical), or (w-v). The consequence of this linkage is that the sequence $(q(w) \rightarrow (w\text{-}v))$ also becomes a conditioned stimulus for those responses to the wall that are dependent on its verticality. This implies that if a structure is identified as a wall and therefore vertical, the very act of identification, or naming, is sufficient to activate engrams putting the organism in a state of readiness for responses that move along the direction of the gravitational axis. But if such engrams are activated, then the wall is perceived as vertical even when it is objectively oblique. All that is required is that the pattern of stimulation should activate the engram mediating the response (w-v), which in turn activates engrams mediating vertical responses. There is no opposition to this response if the gravitational stimuli in operation at the time are of the form $\bar{\Sigma}(G)$, and if the past history of the subject is such that these have not been conditioned to responses adjusted to gravity. In that case the perceived direction of the body is indeterminate and can therefore be chosen to conform to the pattern of retinal stimulation that has generated a false perception of verticality. If, on the other hand, $\bar{\Sigma}(G)$ has been conditioned to responses adjusted to gravity, the engrams activated by $\bar{\Sigma}(G)$ will conflict with those activated by $(q(w) \rightarrow (w\text{-}v))$, and according to the relative strength of these two sets of engrams the perceived vertical will vary all the way from the objective vertical to the perpendicular to the floor of the tilted room. This is the range of variation actually found by Witkin.

5.15. In a subsequent study (already referred to in 5.2), in which the subjects were boys and girls ranging in age from eight to twenty years, Witkin inquired into the early history of his subjects, and found that those whom he described as "field dependent," that is, those with the strongest tendency to perceive the tilted room as vertical, had been subjected to massive overprotection by their mothers. An equally important finding was that the tendency to equate the perceived vertical with the floor-ceiling axis of the tilted room diminished with age.

These observations do not afford a direct test of the main thesis of this chapter, which is that the perception of the vertical is dependent on the conditioning of stimuli of the form $\Sigma(G)$ to responses adapted to the gravitational axis, but they are completely consistent with the further hypothesis that the adapted system can be gradually expanded by the conditioning of stimuli of the form $\bar{\Sigma}(G)$ to those same responses.

To understand the slowness of this process we must note an important difference between the two cases. When the unsupported body assumes an oblique posture, so that the stimuli are of the form $\Sigma(G)$, the resulting displacement of the center of gravity threatens a fall, so that immediate action is obligatory, and rapid conditioning is unavoidable. It is a necessary consequence of the structure of the physical world including that of the bipedal organism. But when the body is supported in an oblique posture, so that the stimuli are of the form $\bar{\Sigma}(G)$, there is no threat to stability and no immediate action is demanded. On the contrary, the conditions are often such that the most appropriate action is no action at all.

How, then, can stimuli of the form $\bar{\Sigma}(G)$ ever be conditioned to responses that are adapted to the gravitational axis? The answer is that occasionally circumstances arise which demand a sudden transition from a recumbent to an erect posture. It is evident that when the utmost speed is required, the act of assuming an erect posture cannot be executed in a succession of easy stages but must involve a coordinated and rapid sequence of movements that always yield the same end result, no matter what the initial posture may have been. The rapidity of the action must then have the effect that the stimuli, $\overline{\Sigma}(G)$, incidental to the initial recumbent posture of the body, become conditioned to the sequence of movements as a whole, and not merely to a preparatory movement, as when the action is performed in a leisurely manner. Since the actual components of the response must vary according to the initial posture, it is evident that each distinctive pattern, $\overline{\Sigma}(G)$, must be conditioned to a different response, so that, according to our main hypothesis, each one yields a different perception. At the same time they are all conditioned to responses that terminate in the same way, so that they constitute a functional equivalence class and therefore generate a perceptual constancy. It is evident that the constancy in question is the invariant direction of the perceived vertical, and the variable component is the perceived direction of the body. A subject who has had ample opportunity for this kind of conditioning will have correct perception both of the vertical and of his own position in the tilted room; whereas a subject who has seldom been required to leap into action from a leaning posture is likely to have false perception of both the vertical and his own position.

Since in most people the occasions for leaping into action occur spasmodically, we may deduce that the development described in the last paragraph is likely to be very slow, covering a period of years rather than months or days. This is confirmed by Witkin's report that in boys and girls there is a slow improvement from year to year in responses to the tilted room.

We can also deduce that mothers who are overprotective toward their children, or overindulgent, or lax in discipline, not insisting on immediate execution of orders, are likely to effect a substantial reduction in the natural frequency with which the children are required to leap into action, thereby slowing the process still further. Again Witkin's report confirms this deduction, although his own explanation of the data differs markedly from that proposed here.

A more rigorous proof of the dependence of perception of the horizontal on responses adapted to the direction of the gravitational axis is provided by the second of the three experiments described in Chapter 9. Perception of the horizontal was distorted by wearing prismatic spectacles. In situations in which stimuli of the form $\Sigma(G)$ were active, true perception of the horizontal was restored; while in situations involving $\bar{\Sigma}(G)$ but not demanding responses adjusted to the gravitational axis, distorted perception of the horizontal persisted. These divergent results were obtained not in two different subjects but in one and the same subject. On the basis of this experiment I venture to predict that if subjects whose perception of the vertical is erroneous when they sit in the tilted room are asked to stand instead, their perception will be nearly veridical.

5.16. There is one further aspect of Witkin's work that is relevant to the problem of perception in general and not merely to the problem of the present chapter. Several subjects in the tilted room experiments gave reports that, judged by an objective standard, were mutually contradictory. For example, with the room tilted at one angle and the chair at another angle, the subject reported the room to be erect and was then requested to adjust the angle of the chair until his body was perceived as erect. One might expect that the body would be perceived as erect only when it was aligned with the room, but the results frequently belied this expectation. One subject, in three successive trials, reported both the room and her body to be erect when in fact they were separated by angles of 43°, 25°, and 43° in the three trials. Witkin was not a little puzzled by such results, since the discrepancy was so gross that in his opinion it should have been clearly perceptible.

Since the expectation is belied it is evident that it must be derived from a false theory, most probably from a theory whose axiomatic foundation is false in some respect. Let us assume that one of the axioms is that each of the different components of an element of the set Q generates perception in its own right. If this axiom were valid, then the obliquity of the retinal image of the room should generate perception of an angular separation between room and body, so that it should be impossible to perceive both of them as erect.

If we reject this axiom and substitute for it the axiom that a component of an element of Q can generate perception in its own right only when it activates an engram mediating a conditioned response, and when this response is independent of the remaining components of $q \in Q$, the result ceases to be puzzling.

There is, of course, no inherent reason why the angle between a retinal image of a line and the retinal Y axis should not become an independent conditioned stimulus for some response, but the argument of the last three chapters suggests that in the circumstances in which a human being is reared there is no occasion for such independent conditioning. Adaptation to the spatial ordering of the environment, which is a matter of primary importance, demands the conditioning of responses to compound patterns of stimulation, and no unique response is conditioned to any of the components taken separately. This implies that if the room and the body are both perceived as erect, the obliquity of the retinal image of the room generates no independent perception that will reveal the discrepancy.

5.17. Our discussion of Witkin's researches may be summed up by saying that they provide additional strong confirmation of the principle of interpenetration stated in 5.8. The principle, stated in notational form, is that if

$$\Phi_1 \subset Q_1 \times E_1$$

and

$$\Phi_2 \subset Q_2 \times E_2$$

where $E_1 \cdot E_2 = \Theta$, but the elements of Q_1 and Q_2 have components in common, then the properties of Π_1 are incorporated in Π_2 and vice versa, yielding a single unified perceptual field. Specifically, let E_1 be a set of engrams mediating responses directed to the positions of objects relative to $R(\Delta)$. Since $R(\Delta)$ has no fixed position relative to the gravitational axis, it follows that Π_1 does not in itself possess any permanent horizontal-vertical frame of reference. Also, let E_2 mediate balancing responses in relation to the gravitational axis. This implies that the elements of Q_2 that are incorporated in Φ_2 are of the kind which, in 5.14, we have designated $\Sigma(G)$. It follows that a permanent horizontal-vertical frame of reference is an essential property of Π_2. Finally we define

$$\Phi_3 \subset Q_3 \times E_3$$

by saying that the elements of Q_3 are of the type we have called $\overline{\Sigma}(G)$, and the responses mediated by E_3 do not include any balancing responses. That is, $E_2 \cdot E_3 = \Theta$. This does not imply that $E_1 \cdot E_3 = \Theta$, since the responses to Q_3 may include moving a limb to another part of the supporting surface.

We now define two subsets of Q_1, viz., $Q_{1(2)}$ and $Q_{1(3)}$, where the elements of $Q_{1(2)}$ include elements of Q_2 as components, and the elements of $Q_{1(3)}$ include elements of Q_3 as components. The corresponding subsets of Φ_1 are $\Phi_{1(2)}$ and $\Phi_{1(3)}$, yielding perceptual fields $\Pi_{1(2)}$ and $\Pi_{1(3)}$. The principle of interpenetration then enables us to deduce that $\Pi_{1(2)}$ has a stable horizontal-vertical frame of reference, but $\Pi_{1(3)}$ has not. This means not that $\Pi_{1(3)}$ has no vertical at all, but rather that it is free to be determined by some nonessential criterion. Further, Π_3 has no stable vertical, by definition; and there too the vertical is free to be determined by some arbitrary criterion, although not necessarily the same as that which fixes the vertical of $\Pi_{1(3)}$. Hence there is no obstacle to the verticals of $\Pi_{1(3)}$ and Π_3 differing from one another when measured objectively, and the number of variations on this theme is theoretically infinite. Witkin, in fact, found a bewildering variety of discrepancies.

However, there is nothing to prevent the expansion of E_3 by the addition of responses that are adapted to the gravitational axis (although this is likely to be a slow process), and in that case $\Pi_{1(3)}$ will acquire a stable vertical from Π_3. When that has happened, perception of the vertical will be veridical throughout the whole range of experimental situations. The proportion of subjects conforming to this pattern was small, but it is not the frequency with which they occur that is needed to confirm the deduction but the simple fact of their existence.

CHAPTER 6

Expanding the Visual Field

6.1. With the advent of locomotion it is evident that the system is enlarged by the addition of several functions that have hitherto been inactive. On the afferent side there are two main types of function to be considered. First, locomotion involves patterns of proprioceptive and pressure stimuli that recur, with minor variations, in each locomotor cycle; and as the duration of a cycle is of the order of one second, we may assume that the perseverative traces of the earlier components of the pattern are still active in the system at the end of the cycle. It is therefore reasonable to assume that the cyclical pattern can operate as a unit. And second, there are changes of a progressive and continuous form in certain features of retinal stimulation. On the motor side there are new responses directed to objects that are beyond reach of the hands.

These new functions add enormously to the complexity of a system that is already extremely complex, but there are two factors that make the process of adaptation easier than it might otherwise be. The first is that the subsystem described in the preceding chapters is already an adapted system. This means that the multitudinous patterns of stimulation that can arise when the child is sitting or standing are already organized into a relatively small number of functional equivalence classes, so that the level of complexity has been substantially reduced. Hence the new developments to which we must now turn our attention involve additions to a system in which the existing variables are of the form Φ rather than Q or S.

It also has the welcome effect that the mathematical exposition can be greatly simplified. Consider, for example, the fact that the size of the retinal image of an object varies with its distance. At each distance, j, the pattern of stimulation involving this object may be any one of a whole class, $Q(\delta_j)$, of patterns that differ from each other in many respects, but have this in common, that the visual angle subtended by the object is the same in all of them. Assuming that the system Φ is fully developed, we can say that each of the elements of $Q(\delta_j)$ is conditioned to an ocular response that will carry the eye from edge to edge of the object; and since the visual angle is constant for the given distance, so is this ocular response. Hence there is a functional equivalence class, $\Phi(\delta_j)$, for each distance; and as the equivalence is directly determined by the size of the retinal image, it is evident that we can treat this size as if it were a simple variable stimulus that can be conditioned to a new class of responses. It has, in fact, become a simple stimulus through a long and laborious process; but in the discussion that follows there is no reason why we should carry along with us the machinery by which this simplicity was achieved. It will be restored to its rightful place when we express the results of our investigations in symbolic form.

The second factor can be most easily explained in the language of information theory. It has been shown by Shannon (in Ashby, 1956) that when the transmission of information is interfered with by "noise," the resulting ambiguity in the received message may be reduced to as low a level as we choose by the addition of other channels of communication. This is precisely what happens in the organic system. There is not just one afferent variable that is functionally related to the distance of the source of the stimuli but several; and any ambiguity or indeterminacy that might result from the operation of a single variable is subject to correction by the simultaneous operation of some or all of the others. If the "information" transmitted by these several "channels" is organized under a function Φ, any failure that might result from inadequacy of one channel is likely to be prevented by the remaining channels.

6.2. In dealing with the problems that arise here it will be convenient to discuss each of the new exteroceptive variables in isolation. We may begin with the variable commonly called *linear perspective*. It is at once evident that the customary treatment of this topic is quite inadequate, since the mere size of a retinal image is not a single-valued function of the distance of an object. In the case of familiar objects that have a standard size, such as the articles of furniture in the child's home, the size of the retinal image may conceivably *become* a signal for distance, but it is clear that the child's everyday commerce with these objects is a necessary prerequisite for this development. Thus even here the size of the image is not sufficient to account for the facts.

Since the child is now mobile we are prompted to ask not how the size of the retinal image is related to the distance of the object but how it *changes* with distance. We can define the size of the image as the visual angle subtended by the object, and of course we can do this in terms of the size of the object and its distance from the eye. Consider an object of unit diameter. Let x be the distance between the eye and one end of the diameter, and let the line along which x is measured be at right angles to the diameter. The visual angle is then given by

$$y = \cot^{-1}x$$

and the rate at which y changes as x changes is

$$u = \frac{dy}{dx} = -\frac{1}{1 + x^2}.$$

Since x diminishes as the child moves toward the object we can deduce from this that the visual angle increases with positive acceleration.

There is of course no afferent function that can be identified with u, but there is another way in which we can proceed. As the child crawls toward the object y increases as a continuous function of x, but the curve of this function is, so to speak, punctuated by the recurring cycles of proprioceptive and pressure stimuli incidental to locomotion. This suggests that we should take as our exteroceptive variable not the function u itself but the definite integral of u corresponding to the diminution of x effected by a single locomotor cycle. What this means will be most readily understood if we take a numerical example. For convenience we shall take as the unit of our linear scale the distance traversed in one locomotor cycle, and as before we shall take the diameter of the object to be unity. The following table shows x, the distance of the object, y, the visual angle at the beginning of each cycle, and z, the increment in y produced by each cycle. If the object is smaller, with a diameter of 0.2, say, the visual angles are smaller, but the increase

TABLE 6.2.1

x	10	9	8	7	6	5	4	3	2	1
y	5°43′	6°20′	7°7′	8°8′	9°28′	11°19′	14°2′	18°26′	26°34′	45°
z		0°37′	0°47′	1°1′	1°20′	1°51′	2°43′	4°24′	8°8′	18°26′

per locomotor cycle expands in the same manner, as Table 6.2.2 shows.

TABLE 6.2.2

x	10	9	8	7	6	5	4	3	2	1
y	1°9′	1°16′	1°26′	1°38′	1°55′	2°17′	2°52′	3°49′	5°43′	11°19′
z		0°7′	0°10′	0°12′	0°17′	0°22′	0°35′	0°57′	1°54′	5°36′

Although the values of z presented in Table 6.2.2 are much smaller than those in 6.2.1, it can be seen that the ratios of z to the preceding values of y are not so different. These ratios are presented in Table 6.2.3. It will be seen that although the smaller object at

TABLE 6.2.3. Proportions z_{x-1}/y_x for objects of two sizes.

	x	9	8	7	6	5	4	3	2	1
Size of	1.0	.11	.12	.14	.16	.19	.24	.31	.44	.70
object	0.2	.10	.13	.15	.17	.19	.26	.33	.50	.98

a distance of two paces subtends the same visual angle as the larger object at ten paces, a single locomotor cycle multiplies this angle by 1.98 in the one case and by a mere 1.11 in the other. Since the duration of a cycle is well below the maximum duration of perseverative traces, we may evidently consider the expansion of the retinal image as an adequate stimulus, capable of being conditioned to some appropriate response.

6.3. In considering how stimuli of this kind are to be incorporated in the adapted system it will be necessary to repeat the procedure adopted in 4.3, where we defined ${}_2Q$ as a set of compound patterns of stimulation including elements of Φ as essential components. In the subsequent process of adaptation those elements of Φ retained their identity, and the conditioned responses incorporated in them continued to be reinforced as usual. Adaptation at the second stage consisted in the conditioning of a new set of responses to the elements of ${}_2Q$ containing elements of Φ and this conditioning was brought within the bounds of possibility just because the organization of Φ had converted an extraordinarily complex system into a comparatively simple system. Obviously the same principles must apply in the case now under consideration.

It is evident that Tables 6.2.1 and 6.2.2 may be regarded as a small section of a set of numbers specifying a set of equivalence classes of a type we have not previously encountered. Each equivalence class is specified by two visual angles, presented at the beginning and end, respectively, of a locomotor cycle, which changes the position of the immediate environment relative to the frame of reference, $R(\Omega)$, from Ω_1 to Ω_2. If the x axis of $R(\Omega)$ is measured horizontally along the direction in which the child is moving, and if ω specifies the object that is responsible for the retinal image, then $x(\omega_2) = x(\omega_1) - 1$, where $x(\omega_1)$ is the x coordinate of ω_1. The x coordinates are not directly represented in the pattern of stimulation, but the y and z coordinates are, and our problem is to determine how perception of the xs can be generated.

The y (or z) coordinate is represented by a pair of visual angles, at the beginning and end of the locomotor cycle. By virtue of the existing adaptation of the system each of those angles generates perception of the positions of the boundaries of the object and therefore of its size. Since the second angle is larger than the first we can deduce that the object is perceived as increasing in size. We need a symbol to represent the state of the system as determined by this sequence of events. Let $\Phi(\omega_1)$, with elements ϕ_1, represent the equivalence class of patterns of stimulation in which ω_1 is involved, and $\Phi(\omega_2)$ the corresponding class for ω_2. At the end of the locomotor cycle the state of the system may be described by saying that it contains a trace element ϕ_1, a more active element ϕ_2, and a complex of proprioceptive and pressure stimuli conditioned to the motor responses involved in locomotion, which we may designate $\phi(GL)$. We now define

$$(6.3.1) \quad {}_3Q = [(\phi_1, \phi_2, \phi(GL))]$$

with the usual qualification of simultaneity. It should be noted that any $q \epsilon {}_3Q$ includes a specification of an object ω whose distance has changed from x to $x - 1$; but it does not specify any response adapted to the distance of this object or to its size. Thus although all the components of $q \epsilon {}_3Q$ give rise to perception, this does not include perception of the distance or the real size of the object.

6.4. There are three types of movement that serve to establish contact with the object. The first is turning movements of the body, which serve to bring the object into the line of advance. We may assume that these are already established as conditioned responses, but as locomotion may not start in the right direction, or may follow a curved path, these responses are not necessarily confined to the beginning of the process, and they will sometimes occur as modifications of locomotion. These movements may be represented by the set M(T). Second, there is locomotion, represented by the set M(L). If the surface on which the child is moving is level the elements of M(L) differ from one another only with respect to the number of paces included. Finally, when the object is within reach of the hands, there are the movements of seizing the object, involving extending the fingers sufficiently to grasp it, or placing one hand at each side. These may be designated M(S). Elements of M(S) occur only when $x \leq 1$, and they are already conditioned to patterns of stimulation that arise when this condition is satisfied. They are not, however, conditioned to elements of ${}_3Q$ for which $x(\omega) > 1$. Following our usual procedure we can use the symbol ${}_3M$ to designate compound responses including elements of M(T), M(L), and M(S). We now define

$$(6.4.1)\quad {}_3U \equiv [(q,m);\ q \in {}_3Q,\ m \in {}_3M,\ m \textit{ follows } q].$$

This, like other sets of the same form, describes an unstable system, and our next problem is to consider how it achieves adaptation.

6.5. It is at once obvious that any locomotor progression involves a succession of elements of ${}_3U$ in which the retinal image of ω increases with positive acceleration if it happens to be in the line of advance. The rate of increase diminishes as the object is removed from the line of advance. Since in the latter case contact is not established, the relevant $q \in {}_3Q$ do not become conditioned stimuli for the associated $m \in {}_3M$. We may therefore confine our attention to cases in which the object is in the line of advance.

As soon as the distance of the object is reduced to one pace, the pattern of stimulation evokes a conditioned reaching response, as determined by the adaptation that took place at the earlier stages.

But because this response is immediately preceded by an element of ${}_3Q$ for which the retinal image has been expanded by a factor of anything from 1.7 to 2.0, it is clear that this $q \varepsilon {}_3Q$ also becomes conditioned to the reaching response, as well as to the response of terminating the forward movement. But that is not all. By Hull's principle of secondary reinforcement the preceding $q \varepsilon {}_3Q$ becomes conditioned to the response of taking one step in the direction of the object.

This is clearly a situation to which Hull's goal gradient hypothesis can be applied. If we represent by q_n the element of ${}_3Q$ that is active in the system when the distance of the object is n paces, we can say that q_1 is conditioned to (a) stopping the forward movement and (b) reaching for the object. Let us say that b results in primary reinforcement. Then by virtue of the conditioned properties thereby acquired by q_1, the response of taking one step forward on the appearance of q_2 is secondarily reinforced, since this response generates q_1. When, on a subsequent occasion, q_3 is followed by a forward step, this generates q_2, which, because it is conditioned to one further step followed by a grasping movement, serves to establish q_3 as a conditioned stimulus for a forward step. This process of backward conditioning can continue until the expansion of the retinal image specified by q_n is insufficient to constitute a stimulus.

An even more important result is that at each stage in this process it is not just one response that is conditioned to q_n but $n - 1$ locomotor responses plus a reaching response. The reason for this is that Hull's principle of the gradient of reinforcement is applicable in this situation as well as the goal gradient. Actually in Hull's system the gradient of reinforcement plays a vital part in the theory of the goal gradient, so that, strictly speaking, we do not need to make a specific appeal to it. It is invoked now chiefly because it helps to establish an extremely important principle in the theory of perception. The essence of the gradient of reinforcement is that, in the absence of secondary reinforcement, the increment in habit strength resulting from a primary reinforcement is a diminishing function of the interval of time between the beginning of the response and the beginning of reinforcement. Hull's principle was derived from experiments on rats, in which the maximum delay beyond which there was no conditioning was approximately 30 seconds. But when, as in the case we are now considering, the subject encounters a series of secondary reinforcing stimuli after the initial response, the gradient drops much more slowly and extends backward almost indefinitely.

Applying these principles to our present problem we can see that if the time required to execute $n - 1$ steps plus a reaching response is less than 30 seconds, or whatever the limiting delay may be in human subjects, there is primary reinforcement of this whole action and q_n thereby becomes a conditioned stimulus for this total response and not merely for a single forward step. The strength of this connection is greatly increased by the operation of the secondary reinforcers that are encountered on the way.

6.6. The importance of this deduction for the theory of perception is that q_n arouses activity in an engram mediating a response that is adjusted to the distance of the relevant object and thereby generates perception of distances that are well beyond the limited envelopes that marked the boundaries of perceived space in the first two stages of life. The horizon has expanded, but not just to the limiting value of n at which the physiological difference between q_n and q_{n+1} is not sufficient to permit differential conditioning. The advent of locomotion has produced a revolution in the size of the world and in fact has converted it into an expanding universe.

One reason for the expansion is obvious enough and need not detain us long. As the child grows in stature the length of his pace increases, and there is a corresponding increase in the increment of the retinal image. Consequently the range of distances within which there is accurate discrimination, even if it remains the same in terms of paces, increases when measured by an absolute scale.

Let us now recall the argument of 4.10, where we concluded that in the second stage of development the infant perceives the spatial environment beyond reach of his hands as being akin to the Ptolemaic universe of cycles and epicycles. What is going to happen to this perceptual structure when locomotion begins? Obviously the radius of the cycles has increased to at least the limiting number of paces beyond which differential conditioning is impossible, but a simple consideration shows that in fact it extends far beyond that range.

Let k be the limiting number of paces, and let the environment contain, in the line of advance, objects at distances k — 2, k + 2, k + 10, 10k, and 100k. A single step produces, with respect to the nearest object, the stimulus pattern q_{k-3}, and its distance is therefore accurately perceived; but according to the argument of 4.10 the other four objects are all perceived as being equally remote. However, another two paces bring the second object within the range of determinate distances, and a further advance of eight paces does the same for the third, while the other two objects remain in the indeterminate beyond. We can see at once that this simple result explodes the Ptolemaic world of the preambulatory stage. For if objects 2, 3, 4, and 5 are at first perceived as being all at the same indeterminate distance, but three paces suffice to bring the second one out of the indeterminate beyond, and eleven paces do the same for the third, then objects 4 and 5 must be perceived as receding interminably.

This at once suggests another mechanism by which the radius of the perceived world is enlarged. Since the conditioning process has resulted in the establishment of a link between the stimulus q_n and the response of moving forward n — 1 paces, and this is in effect a single response and not just a sequence of n — 1 discrete responses, there is no reason why the n proprioceptive cycles, including the initial one that gave rise to q_n, should not also serve to punctuate the curve of the increasing retinal image of an object whose initial distance is m, say. Clearly the length of the sequence of steps that will serve this purpose is limited by the duration of the perseverative traces of the stimuli that were in operation at the beginning of the movement. We may designate by q^m_{m-n} the pattern of stimulation at the end of the n paces, where the superscript represents the initial distance and the subscript the final distance of the object. Assuming that the expansion of the retinal image specified by q^m_{m-n} is of sufficient physiological magnitude, we can conclude that it is capable of being conditioned to a movement consisting of m/n — 1 sequences of n paces each.

6.7. This argument seems to imply that locomotion is essential for the perception of distance, and of course this is not true in the mature subject. We must now consider briefly how this transformation takes place.

Nearly all the permanent objects in the child's environment are invariant in size, and many of them have a distinctive shape. Let us suppose that the child has on several occasions established contact with one such object, say a ball, reaching it from a variety of initial distances. These several encounters have the effect not only that the stimulus q_n becomes conditioned to a forward movement of n — 1 paces, or q^m_{m-n} to a movement of the appropriate extent, but also that the retinal image of the ball, whatever its size may be, is conditioned to the directing of locomotion toward the ball in preference to other objects in the vicinity. In other words, the ball, despite the variation in the angle it subtends at the eye, is in every case perceived as being the same desired object. In fact, as we shall see in 6.19, it will soon be perceived as being invariant in size. And because it is in fact invariant in size, the size of the retinal image at any moment of time can, after specific locomotor responses have been conditioned to q_n and q^m_{m-n}, become an independent conditioned stimulus for the appropriate forward movement. The reader will have no difficulty in recognizing that this is not a simple conditioned stimulus, analogous to the beating of a metronome in one of Pavlov's experiments. It is already a conditioned stimulus, evoking a response directed toward the ball in preference to all other available objects, before it becomes conditioned to a movement consisting of a specific number of paces. Without this prior conditioning, and without the conditioning of the locomotor response to q_n or q^m_{m-n}, it would be virtually impossible for the momentary size of the retinal image to become conditioned to the appropriate locomotor response.

6.8. We may now return to the question of the expanding visual world. It is clear that the detailed application of the principles discussed above must vary according to the circumstances in which the child grows up, and particularly on the amount of space in which he is free to wander. We can assume, however, that in every case there is a limit to the length of the excursions the child may make by his own efforts. Translocation by any other means may be neglected, since it does not involve the rhythmical sequence of proprioceptive and pressure stimuli which we have assumed to be essential to the process.

Assuming then that there is a limiting distance of m paces beyond which the child is not allowed to go, the argument of the preceding sections enables us to conclude that there will be reasonably accurate discrimination of distances within an area having a radius of m paces. Further, since he is allowed to go to the boundary of this area, he can, by virtue of the process discussed in 6.7, discriminate distances over a further range of m paces, and some of this discrimination may be retained when he returns to headquarters. Thus we may deduce that the outermost limit of discrimination is a circle of radius 2m.

How then is he going to perceive distances beyond this radius? To answer this question we may return to a conclusion arrived at in 6.6, that when the child is walking toward a series of objects at different distances, the most distant ones are perceived as continuously receding. Although this is a deduction that cannot be tested by direct questioning of the child, the phenomenon in question can occasionally be found in mature subjects, as the following example shows.

If a motorist drives from Cape Town to Johannesburg, he reaches, at a distance of about 250 miles, a point from which he can see ahead of him a low range of hills. They are about 50 miles away, but because the air is very dry and completely free from industrial effluents, they appear to a motorist who lives in a region where atmospheric humidity is higher and there are numerous factories to be very much nearer, say 20 miles. Supposing the height of the hills to be 1,000 feet, they subtend, at a distance of 50 miles, a visual angle of $0°13'1''$. A hill 400 feet high would subtend the same angle at a distance of 20 miles, and 10 miles farther on the angle would expand to $0°26'3''$. But in fact the angle increases in that distance only to $0°16'17''$, which is the angle subtended by a hill 400 feet high at a distance of 18 miles. Thus while the motorist has driven 10 miles toward the hills, they appear to be only 2 miles nearer than when he first saw them. That is, he has the illusion that they are receding from him almost as fast as he is approaching them. It is significant that on the next occasion when the motorist makes the same journey there is no trace of this illusion. The reason for this change is an interesting problem in itself, but to discuss it now would involve reference to higher levels of adaptation for which we are not yet ready. The significance of the illusion is that even in a mature subject rates of change that are outside his normal experience, and to which he has not yet learned to make the appropriate responses, can disrupt the spatial stability of his perceived world. For the time being his space has not only ceased to be Euclidean; it is not even metric. We should not therefore be surprised when the logic of our argument leads to the conclusion that the child's space is nonmetric.[1] There are many other questions that arise out of the foregoing argument, but it will be convenient to postpone discussion of them until we have considered some of the other "channels of communication" that are available to the child.

6.9. We have hitherto considered only visual angles subtended by distances measured in a plane at right angles to the line of advance, but angles subtended by distances in planes that are oblique to the line of advance, or parallel to it, are also subject to changes induced by locomotion. Of these the most important are angles subtended by distances along the floor in the line of advance. The reason for this is that the plane in which the head moves is necessarily parallel to the plane of the floor and at a fixed distance from it, with the result that the visual angle subtended by a distance along the floor from the child to an object can be expressed as a simple function of that distance. The change in the visual angle subtended by a horizontal distance measured along a vertical plane such as a wall is a more complex function, since the independent variables include the initial distance of the head from the wall, and the angle between the line of advance and the wall. In the case of distances along the floor these two variables have constant values and may therefore be regarded as parameters of the system. It is evident that an ultrastable system including these parameters is likely to achieve adaptation sooner than one in which they are replaced by variables.

Let us begin with the simplest possible situation, in which there is a single small object on the floor at a distance of x paces from the child. The geometrical relations are shown in Figure 6.9.1. The line OA represents the floor. E is the position of the child's

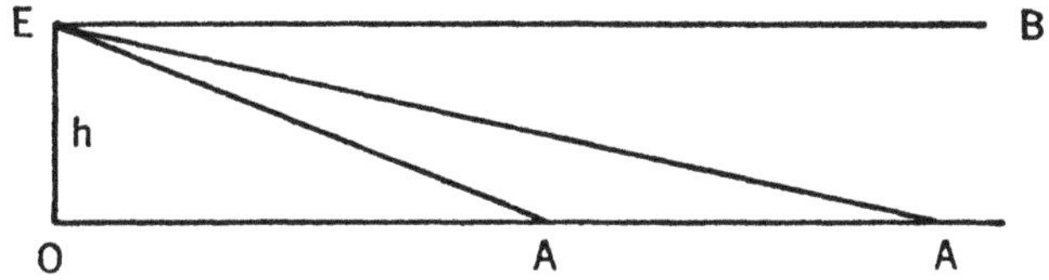

FIGURE 6.9.1.

1. One of the properties of a metric space, whether Euclidean or not, is that the distance between two points is completely determined by their coordinates. This condition is obviously not satisfied by the example given above.

eye and EB is the direction in which it moves. O is a point on the floor directly below the eyes, and h is the distance OE. A is the object at the initial distance $x = OA$. As the child crawls toward the object its position changes from A to A′, and this may be represented in the afferent system either by a decrease in the angle $OEA = \tan^{-1} x/h$, or by an increase in the angle $BEA = \cot^{-1} x/h$.

These geometric relations, simple as they are to us, would obviously present an enormously complex problem to the child were it not for the developments described in the last three chapters, since the position of the retinal image of the object changes not only with its distance but with every movement of the head and eyes. But by reason of the previous adaptations the position of the object in the child's visual field is constant for any fixed distance. The change in its perceived position may then be adequately represented by the angle AEA′. This, it must be remembered, is before the perception of distances beyond reach of the hands has been developed. The object is merely perceived as moving downward in the as yet indeterminate beyond. But there is nothing indeterminate about the angle itself, and we may therefore legitimately take this angle as sufficiently specifying a pattern of stimulation without once more describing the enormously complicated neural processes that are involved. It can operate as a simple stimulus precisely because it is perceived, and therefore has the acquired invariance implied by that statement.

It is at once evident that the downward displacement in the perceived position of the object as determined by a single forward pace and measured by the angle AEA′, increases with positive acceleration in exactly the same way as the visual angle subtended by a distance in a plane at right angles to the line of advance. In fact the two rates of increase can be made identical if we choose as the object a vertical rod of length h. The top of the rod is on a level with the child's eyes and of course remains there, so that its perceived position is constant. The increase in the visual angle subtended by the rod is thus brought about entirely by the downward displacement of its point of contact with the floor. This rate of displacement is independent of the size of the object, since it is completely determined by the length of the pace and the height, h, of the eyes above the floor, both of which may be considered as being invariant over the period during which the adaptation with which we are now concerned takes place. The importance of this invariance is that it provides a standard that enables the child to react differentially to the somewhat different rates of increase revealed in Table 6.2.3.

It is at once evident that the process of differential conditioning of locomotor responses described in 6.5 applies without alteration to the present situation, and the argument need not be repeated. The two processes will normally occur simultaneously.

6.10. We now complicate the situation slightly by having two objects, at distances x and x + c, in the line of advance, and assume that the second one is the goal toward which the child is moving. The visual angle subtended by the horizontal distance c increases with positive acceleration in much the same way as the other angles we have considered, and the increase resulting from a single locomotor cycle may therefore become a conditioned stimulus, but for what response? If the distance c is constant, while x is variable, we can deduce that the total pattern of stimulation becomes conditioned to a response that we can think of as being decomposable into two components, one of which is variable and the other constant. That is to say, the response consists of a variable component of x — 1 paces, bringing the nearer object within reach of the hands, followed by a constant component of c paces, bringing the goal within reach. When x > 1 the response to the angle subtended by c, or rather by increase in that angle produced by a single step, is of course a trace reflex, and its strength will naturally diminish as x increases, but this does not affect the invariant magnitude of the response.

If we now abstract from this total situation the variable stimuli due to the horizontal distance c and the constant terminal component of the locomotor response, it is evident that we have defined a functional equivalence class; and according to our hypothesis this should generate a perceptual constancy. Everyday experience shows that in fact such a constancy exists. If we walk along a level path paved with flagstones of uniform size, their widths, measured along the line of advance, are perceived as being identical despite the variation in the visual angles they subtend.

6.11. This leads naturally to a consideration of the gradients of texture which play such an important part in Gibson's theory of visual perception (Gibson, 1950). If we examine the illustrations depicting different kinds of texture, we shall find that each one of them is characterized by recurring patterns of light and shade or of coloration. The absolute magnitude of the individual units are subject to some variation, but they vary around a central tendency that remains reasonably constant from one sample of the same surface to another. Any surface of which this is true may be described as having a *uniform* texture, despite variations from point to point.

Consider now any plane surface having a uniform texture, and measure distances along a straight line in this plane starting from the foot of a perpendicular from the eye to the plane. The visual angle subtended by the distance between successive units of the texture diminishes with negative acceleration as the distance from the origin increases. It is easy to write an equation for this angle, and if we substitute for its general terms numerical values representing the length of the perpendicular from the eye to the plane, the average distance between units, and the number of units measured from the origin, we can write a series of angles that constitutes an objective description of the gradient of the texture. If the units are very small, such as the grains of sand on a beach, the angle quickly becomes too small to have any physiological effect, and the gradient may then be said to have reached an asymptote. But in such cases there are frequently larger units as well. Thus the beach may have ripples left by wind or by the receding tide, or even lines of footprints. All these provide supplementary gradients that stretch to much greater distances before reaching an asymptote.

Gibson argues that the existence of these gradients proves that the visual stimulus contains sufficient "information" to generate perception of the spatial ordering of the environment. But in fact this information, although necessary, is not sufficient. If we were to present to a mathematician the series of angles defining a gradient, but without indicating the units of measurement (to make the situation as similar as possible to that with which the brain has to cope), and ask him to say what physical system might produce this series, his answer would be that there is no unique solution. If, for example, there were some infinitely compressible substance, and slabs of it were piled on top of one another, the numbers might represent the thickness of the slabs, counting from the top downward. Even if we tell our mathematician that the numbers are angles subtended at a single point by a succession of uniform distances measured in one direction, he will tell us that the number of solutions is infinite. He can arrive at a unique solution only when we have told him the distance between the point at which the angles are subtended and the line along which the distances are measured.

Analogously, the child confronted with a gradient of texture has no means of converting this "information" into perception of the spatial ordering of the environment unless he has additional "information" representing his distance from the surface and the uniform size of the units of the texture. Neither of these is directly incorporated in the visual stimulus. The "information contained in light" appears to Gibson to be sufficient to account for visual perception only because he has failed to recognize that certain items of information that appear in our experience to be carried by light are in fact not carried by light. His error is of the same order as that which was corrected by Berkeley when he pointed out that a ray of light reaching the retina carries with it no information concerning the distance it has traveled. How then does the additional information get incorporated in the system?

At first sight it might seem that there is no possible solution to this problem, since values along a gradient of texture do not constitute objects toward which the child's behavior is directed. But we must remember that any neutral stimulus that is regularly associated in time with a stimulus for an unconditioned or even a conditioned response itself automatically becomes a conditioned stimulus, of the first or second order, for that response. Now the floor on which the child crawls or walks presents a gradient of texture that can be expressed as a simple function of distance from the child, since the distance of his head above the floor is constant. It follows then that the specific values of this gradient that are associated with objects to which the child has learned to respond by moving forward so many steps automatically become conditioned to those same responses. The result of numerous learnings of this kind is the incorporation into the system of the initially missing information that the diminishing angles subtended by successive units of the texture are derived from a succession of equal distances measured along a plane surface. The missing information about the distance of the eyes from the surface is at this stage irrelevant since it is not variable.

It is not necessary to assume that each value of the gradient must be separately conditioned to the appropriate response. As soon as a few responses of varying extent have been acquired, the automatic interpolation device postulated in 2.17 comes into operation, with the result that every value of the gradient tends to evoke its appropriate response, either by direct conditioning or by compound stimulus generalization. In this case, however, we may assume that it is not a simple linear interpolation that is involved. It is highly probable that, at least in the earlier stages of the process, the generalization gradients derived from the reinforcement of responses of several different magnitudes overlap to some extent. In that case a specific value of the gradient of texture is likely to generate supraliminal reaction potentials for more than two responses, so that the magnitude of the evoked response will be a weighted average of these, where the weights are supplied by the heights of the several generalization gradients at the given value of the stimulus.

The final outcome of this process may now be deduced. When the subject is confronted with a gradient of texture his retina is simultaneously stimulated by a discrete series of contiguous stimuli diminishing in magnitude, and in many cases another series with larger units will be superimposed on this. By the conditioning process we have postulated, this discrete series will activate a series of engrams mediating responses adapted to the distances of the several units of the texture. That is, the subject is put into a state of simultaneous readiness for all those responses, and therefore perceives the textured surface as stretching out in front of him.

It is important to note, however, that although the pattern of stimulation consists of a discrete series there are no discontinuities in the perceived space. The separate units are perceived, provided the angles subtended by them are above the threshold, but the space that carries the units is perceived as being continuous. This is directly deducible from the postulate of stimulus generalization. For there is no point on the whole surface that does not simultaneously activate a neighborhood of engrams. The weighted averages of such neighborhoods will obviously constitute something much nearer to a continuous series than the engrams themselves.

6.12. The gradients of texture presented by the floor are unique in the sense that the distance of the eyes from the floor is invariant during locomotion, so that the mathematical function describing the gradient has this distance as a parameter. In all other cases the distance from the surface has to be considered as a variable. However, as soon as the texture of the floor has been incorporated in the adapted system, the problem of adaptation to other gradients, generated by vertical and oblique surfaces, becomes comparatively easy. Suppose, for example, that the child is approaching a rising piece of ground. At the point where the rise begins there is a change in the gradient of texture, since the distance of his head from the plane of the rising ground is greater than the distance from the ground on which he is now walking. This does not necessarily produce the illusory perception of the slope being nearer than it is, since the rate of increase of the visual angles subtended by distances on the slope at right angles to the line of advance is inconsistent with that. What is more likely to happen is that the texture itself is perceived as having changed.

As the beginning of the slope comes nearer, the distance of the eyes from its plane diminishes until the child is actually on the slope, and if his body remains erect the distance of his eyes is slightly less than it was from the level ground. That is, the gradient of texture presented by the slope undergoes a progressive change of a determinate character, over and above the change that occurs in the texture of a limited piece of level ground as it is approached. The rate of this change depends, of course, on the angle of the slope. AB is the plane of the level ground and CD the plane of the rising ground. The angle between them is θ. If we take one pace as the unit of our linear scale it can be seen that each pace along

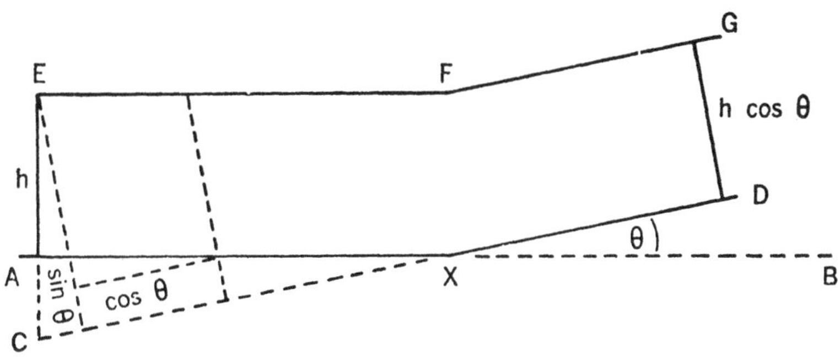

FIGURE 6.12.1.

the level ground decreases the distance of the eyes from the plane CD by an amount equal to sin θ, and the foot of the perpendicular from the eye to CD advances along CD by an amount equal to cos θ. Both these factors have the effect that the rate of expansion of the visual angle subtended by a unit of the texture on the sloping ground will be less than that of a unit at the same distance on level ground. Moreover, this angle is initially equal to that of a nearer unit on level ground, which of course expands not less but more rapidly. If the height of the eyes above the level ground is h, their distance from XD will remain constant at h cos θ after the point X has been passed. Hence the rate of expansion when climbing the slope is smaller than the corresponding rate of expansion on level ground.

When the subject reaches the slope a change in locomotor activity becomes necessary. The feet must be lifted to a higher level at each step, and more energy must be expended to lift the body through a distance of sin θ. The principles of conditioning then lead us to the conclusion that the initially larger angles presented by units of the texture on the surface XD, together with the diminished rate of expansion of those angles, become conditioned stimuli for a change in the pattern of locomotor activity as soon as the point X is reached. And if the texture is in fact uniform over the whole surface AXD, we can conclude that ultimately the stationary pattern of stimulation presented by this surface when the subject is standing will be sufficient to create a state of readiness for the appropriate locomotor behavior.

6.13. We can now deduce the nature of the perceptual experience that is generated by this state of readiness. Since our hypothesis is that perception is identical with the compound state of readiness, Π, it follows that new properties are added to perception whenever new elements are added to Π. What those new properties are is determined not by the stimuli themselves but by the responses that are conditioned to them. In the case we have been considering the response takes the form of altering the locomotor activity in such a way as to carry the body up the slope. Hence what is perceived is not the visual angles subtended by the units of the texture, or the altered rate at which they are changing, but the slope of the ground.

This, of course, is in complete agreement with everyday experience. If a subject who has no training in psychology or in art is confronted with a piece of sloping ground and is asked to say how he perceives it as sloping, he will probably be unable to give any answer. He will say that he just sees it as sloping and is likely to be completely unaware of the change in the gradient of texture. The texture itself is not the object to which his behavior is directed. On the other hand Professor Gibson would at once perceive the texture as well as the slope, not because his afferent processes are different but because, in the course of his professional activities, he has learned to make certain direct responses to the texture as such. Similarly, an artist who has learned to depict oblique surfaces by means of paint on canvas has acquired a set of direct responses to texture, and he too therefore perceives the gradient of texture as well as the slope. His responses are different in kind from those of the psychologist, but in a sense they have the same goal. His aim is to make other people see the slope in his picture, while that of the psychologist is to explain how ordinary people perceive the slope. Both ends are achieved by acquiring behavior, verbal-descriptive or manipulatory, that is directed to the gradient of texture itself. Both, however, continue to perceive the slope as before, since the originally acquired locomotor responses are not extinguished by the addition of these new responses.

6.14. When the child graduates from crawling to walking, the increased distance of his eyes from the floor implies a change in the gradient of texture presented by the floor. He has seen the floor from this height many times before starting to walk, but in the absence of actual conditioning it can only evoke indeterminate responses. The uncertainty of the first steps is due in part to the new proprioceptive and pressure stimuli that have become active in the system, but these are concerned with the management of the act of locomotion itself and not with the determination of the number of steps to be taken. A further measure of uncertainty arises from the altered gradient of texture, in that the visual angle subtended by a unit, measured along the line of advance, at a distance of x paces now arises from a unit at a distance of 2x or more, and therefore tends to evoke a locomotor response that is quantitatively insufficient. Consequently it frequently happens that a child who has already mastered the art of maintaining balance while walking, will start a journey to a relatively distant goal on his feet and complete it by crawling. The new gradient of texture evokes a response that terminates before the goal is reached, and the failure of reinforcement has the effect that other responses are tried. Obviously the most promising alternative is the well-established response of crawling, which has the advantage that it reinstates patterns of stimulation to which determinate locomotor responses have been conditioned. However, walking has such obvious advantages over crawling that the requisite differential conditioning of locomotor responses to the values of the new gradient of texture proceeds rapidly, with a concomitant decrease in the frequency of regression to crawling.

The transition from crawling to walking can be called a revolutionary event, since there is a sudden increase in the distance of the eyes from the floor and in the length of the pace, and adaptation of the new system thereby brought into action entails the expansion of discriminable space to more than double its previous limits. The essence of the matter is that the maximum distance at which physiologically differentiable stimuli can be generated has more than doubled; and when differential responses to such stimuli have actually been acquired, there must, according to our hypothesis, be a corresponding increase in the distance of the indeterminate beyond.

6.15. There is no direct means of testing this deduction, since the child who has just learned to walk has not as yet a sufficient command of language to enable him to report on his perceptual experience. But there is a further deduction that *can* be tested. As the child grows in stature and in the length of his pace there is a corresponding increase in the radius of discriminable space, with the result that distances that were originally in the indeterminate beyond become determinate. Now the child is not himself aware of his own growth, since no behavior is specifically directed to it. He does not measure his own stature. Hence the expanding radius of the perceived environment is likely to pass unnoticed, so that the outer limit of perceived space is likely to remain for him a constant.

Specifically, if the radius is n paces, this distance, measured by a standard scale, will go on increasing as the length of the pace increases, but in the perception of the child it will remain invariant. Thus the unit of the linear scale in terms of which perceived distances are measured is continuously increasing when measured in terms of a standard unit such as the yard or meter. On the other hand actual geographical distances remain constant as measured by a standard scale, with the result that the perceived dimensions of features of the child's immediate environment suffer a progressive shrinkage. But again this process is undetected, because the day-to-day adjustments in the extent of the locomotor response required to reach any goal are so minute that the distance appears to remain constant from day to day. We can deduce, however, that if the interval between two encounters with a given environment is made long enough to permit a substantial increase in stature and the length of the pace, the distances will, on the second encounter, be perceived as having shrunk.

This deduction depends on two assumptions. The first is that the general features of the environment, such as the positions of objects relative to one another, and their shapes, are capable of activating the engrams mediating the locomotor responses that were appropriate on the occasion of the earlier encounter. This presents no difficulty, since it is fully covered by the regular laws of conditioning. That is, the permanent features of the environment, just because they are permanent, automatically become conditioned to the responses that are initially conditioned to the patterns of stimulation described earlier in this chapter. The second assumption is that the engrams in question do not entirely fade out during the interval. While no direct evidence on this particular type of engram is available, there is plenty of evidence that engrams do in fact persist over long intervals of time during which they are not activated. We can then argue that by virtue of these persisting engrams the general features of the environment on the second encounter tend to evoke one set of locomotor responses, appropriate to the earlier occasion, whereas the specific patterns of stimulation now in operation activate engrams mediating responses involving a smaller number of paces. Since the latter set of engrams, depending on the present state of adaptation of the system, are well tried and tested, they must prevail, and the inevitable outcome is that the scene is perceived as having shrunk. The memory of the scene as it was perceived on the earlier occasion is, so to speak, embedded in the still persisting engrams mediating the locomotor responses that were appropriate at that time. The deduced phenomenon has been so frequently reported that there is no need to cite specific evidence.

6.16. While the floor on which he rests is the most important surface to which the child must adapt, locomotion soon brings him into contact with the vertical surfaces presented by walls. The first thing he must learn to do here is to arrest his forward movement in time to avoid a painful collision. To understand how this is done we must consider the changes in the gradient of texture presented by the wall as it is approached. For simplicity let us assume that the wall is decorated with a wallpaper that has a regularly recurring pattern. These patterns will be referred to as units of the texture. We begin by considering the gradient of texture when the child is in a fixed position facing the wall. If a perpendicular is drawn from a point midway between the eyes to the wall, and we imagine any radial line drawn on the wall from the foot of this perpendicular, the units it passes through present a diminishing series of visual angles. So far there is nothing to distinguish this gradient from that presented by the floor, except that the rate at which the angles diminish depends on the distance from the wall.

Let the child now advance toward the wall, along the perpendicular defined above. The gradient of texture changes, but in a manner altogether different from that of the floor. In a sense the gradient of the floor remains unchanged, since a forward step merely replaces one set of units by another, which stand in the same geometric relation to the eyes as the previous set. The nearest units are constantly increasing to a maximum and then vanishing. In the case of the wall the nearest units increase progressively but remain in the center of the field. All other units increase as well, and at the same time become progressively distorted in shape. But a more important change is that all units not at the center flow outward centrifugally. It will be seen that this involves an application of the argument of 6.2 to a situation in which there are many simultaneously presented distances, all measured from a common origin, viz. the foot of the perpendicular from the eye to the wall.

It will be instructive to draw up a table showing these changes as they apply to a small sample of units at different radial distances, r, from the foot of the perpendicular as the distance, x, of the subject from the wall decreases. Table 6.16.1 shows what happens to

TABLE 6.16.1.

	x	10	9	8	7	6	5	4	3	2	1
	a	5°43′	6°20′	7°8′	8°8′	9°28′	11°19′	14°2′	18°26′	26°34′	45°0′
r = 1	b	34′0″	37′41″	42′15″	48′2″	55′36″	65′51″	80′23″	102′5″	134′43″	163′35″
	c	.995	.993	.992	.989	.985	.979	.967	.944	.886	.690
	a	11°19′	12°32′	14°2′	15°57′	18°26′	21°48′	26°34′	33°41′	45°0′	63°26′
r = 2	b	32′59″	36′18″	40′20″	45′14″	51′18″	58′52″	68′4″	78′6″	83′50″	66′6″
	c	.980	.975	.969	.960	.946	.925	.890	.826	.699	.439
	a	16°42′	18°26′	20°33′	23°12′	26°34′	30°58′	36°52′	45°0′	56°19′	71°34′
r = 3	b	31′27″	34′16″	37′31″	41′16″	45′32″	50′6″	54′20″	56′19″	51′40″	33′23″
	c	.956	.947	.934	.916	.892	.853	.795	.701	.548	.312
	a	21°48′	23°58′	26°34′	29°45′	33°41′	38°40′	45°0′	53°8′	63°26′	75°58′
r = 4	b	29′32″	31′46″	34′12″	36′49″	39′24″	41′31″	42′26″	40′37″	33′42″	19′45″
	c	.927	.912	.892	.866	.829	.777	.703	.596	.443	.240
	a	26°34′	29°3′	32°0′	35°32′	39°48′	45°0′	51°20′	59°2′	68°12′	78°41′
r = 5	b	27′24″	29′6″	30′45″	32′18″	33′32″	34′5″	33′9″	29′54″	23′18″	12′59″
	c	.893	.869	.846	.811	.765	.705	.621	.511	.368	.194

five units of the texture as the distance, x, decreases from 10 paces to 1 pace. The units are assumed to be circular and to have a diameter equal to one-tenth of a pace. The radial distance, r, is the distance of the point on the edge that is nearest the foot of the perpendicular. That is, the radial distance of the center of the unit is $r + .05$. For each value of r, row a presents the visual angles subtended by r at the successive values of x. When $r > 0$, the projection of a unit at the eye is elliptical, the minor axis of the ellipse being collinear with r. Row b shows the minor axis of the ellipse, expressed as a visual angle. It was calculated by $b = \cot^{-1} x/(r + 0.1) - \cot^{-1} x/r$. Row c represents the ratio of the minor axis to the major axis. It was computed by calculating the distance of the center of the unit from the eye by $y = \sqrt{x^2 + (r + .05)^2}$. The visual angle subtended by the major axis is then given by $2 \tan^{-1} 0.05/y$. Continuous curves of function a for each of the five radial distances are presented in Figure 6.16.1, and of function b in Figure 6.16.2.

The first thing to be noted is that the system described by the table and the diagrams is absolute. That is, if we apply to it any primary operation such as changing the value of r or of x or both, the system moves to a determinate state. But in the organic system with which we are concerned only the functions a, b, and c are represented. The variables x and r are not initially represented, so that a primary operation such as reducing the unknown x to $x - 1$ can result in any one of a large number of states of the system. The change in proprioceptive and pressure stimuli resulting from a locomotor cycle is present in the organic system, but there is nothing representing the actual distance of the wall, or the fact that it is stationary, or the fact that its texture is uniform and invariant, or the fact that the line of advance is perpendicular to it.

All this information is available to us, of course, but we have no right to assume that it is automatically available to the child. To get some idea of the situation as it confronts the child we might take a large sheet of paper, cut a vertical slit in it, and place it over one of the diagrams so that a section of the curves is visible but the abscissal scale is concealed. We now decide on a lateral distance to represent one pace and move the paper to the right through that distance. The system changes to a new set of values as represented by the portions of the curves seen through the slit, but in the absence of the abscissal scale we have no means of interpreting this change. Besides, we have no means of knowing how much of the change is due to our own action and how much to the action of some unknown agency that may have been moving the diagram under the paper. Our problem is to discover how this missing information, so obvious to us that we are tempted to think it has been there all the time, comes to be incorporated in the organic system.

6.17. To answer this question we must make use of our knowledge that the wall is in fact stationary and its texture invariant. The table and diagrams of 6.16. were in fact constructed on that assumption. Let us look first at Figure 6.16.1. We can see

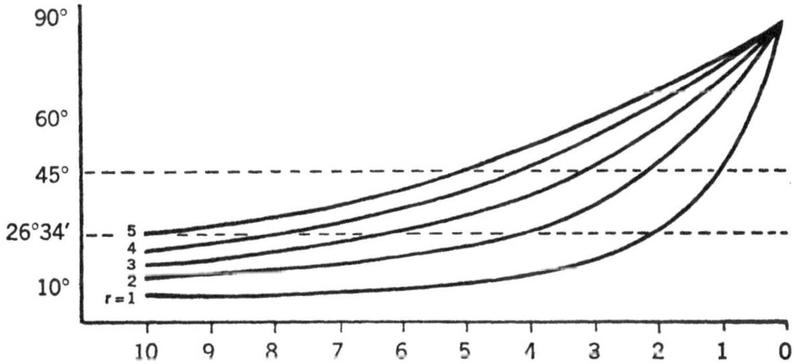

FIGURE 6.16.1. Centrifugal movements of units of texture.

at once that if, at x paces from the wall, a unit of the texture stands at 26°34′ from the line of advance, a forward movement of x/2 paces brings this unit to 45°, and another advance of the same extent brings the child into collision with the wall. To bring this out more clearly, broken lines have been drawn through the figure at 26°34′ and at 45°.

Now a collision constitutes a negative reinforcement and therefore tends to establish a conditioned inhibition of any response preceding it by a reasonably short period of time. The most recent response is the locomotor cycle that reduces the distance from x = 1 to x = 0, and it is this response that is primarily inhibited. Immediately prior to this response there is a state of stimulation which, following the notation of 6.5, we may designate $q_1 \epsilon {}_3Q$, where ${}_3Q$ is defined as in (6.3.1). That is, q_1 is the state of the system when the distance from the wall is one pace, and it includes, *inter alia*, the expansion of the visual angle subtended by $r = 1$ from 26°34′ to 45°, as well as the stimuli due to the locomotor cycle that effects this change. It should be noted that although q_1 is described as an element of ${}_3Q$, it is actually a subset of ${}_3Q$, since each unit of the texture determines a primary element, and they all operate simultaneously. Thus although we have selected for consideration only those elements of q_1 that are determined by units of the texture for which $r = 1$, the total stimulus is much more complex.

Figure 6.16.2 shows that q_1 also includes expansion of the visual angles subtended by the "minor axis" of all units of the texture for which $r \leqq 1$ and contraction for all units for which $r > 1$. Finally, rows c of Table 6.16.1 show a markedly increased distortion of the retinal images of all units not at the center in q_2 as com-

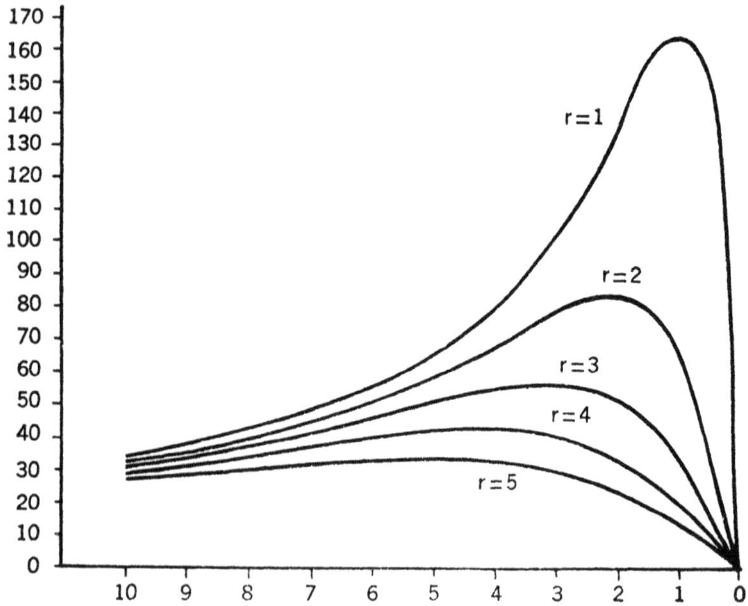

FIGURE 6.16.2. Visual angles, measured in minutes of arc, subtended by the diameter of a unit measured along the radius from the foot of the perpendicular from eye to wall.

pared with q_1. In short, q_1 describes a unique pattern of changing stimulation that can very easily become conditioned to the response of arresting the forward movement. But q_1 is preceded by q_2, in which the rates of change are smaller all round but, as shown by Figure 6.16.2, there is expansion of the minor axes of all units for which $r \leq 2$, and, as shown by Figure 6.16.1, the terminal value of $a \geq 45°$ for all units for which $r \leq 2$. Similarly, q_2 is preceded by q_3 and so on. Since the time required to execute the complete sequence of movements is well within the range of the gradient of reinforcement, we can conclude that $q_2, q_3 \ldots q_9$ all become conditioned to the termination of the movement at $x = 1$, but with progressively diminishing reaction potentials.

Since the primary negative reinforcement comes only at the end of the pace that reduces x from 1 to 0, we can deduce that the inhibitory potential acquired by q_2 will be insufficient to terminate the movement at $x = 2$, but will have the effect of diminishing the momentum, thereby making it easier to stop the movement at $x = 1$. The inhibitory potential acquired by q_3 will be smaller, resulting in a smaller braking force. We can see then that the negative conditioning resulting from a collision has the far-reaching effect that on subsequent occasions the wall is approached with diminishing speed and the final arrest is effected with a minimum of effort. It needs no argument to prove that this is exactly what happens in practice.

We can go further and deduce that if the system is changed by, say, riding a bicycle, the existing adaptation will initially prove to be inadequate. The main effect of riding a bicycle is that there is a sudden and substantial increase in the length of the "pace." There is also some change in the patterns of proprioceptive and pressure stimuli, but their cyclical character is retained, so that they still serve to punctuate the continuously changing pattern of retinal stimulation. As soon as the trick of balancing is mastered the appropriate motor responses soon become conditioned to the new stimuli of the form q_x; but these initially apply to stimuli presented by the ground. If the subject now suddenly finds himself riding toward an obstacle such as a wall, the appropriate responses are not immediately available and he is liable to apply his brakes too late or to turn aside too sharply. It does not require many experiences of this kind to establish adequate responses.

6.18. We are now ready to deduce the perceptual outcome of the conditioning process discussed above. Since q_x is conditioned to a deceleration of the forward movement, and the next step produces q_{x-1}, which is conditioned to a further deceleration, and so on until q_1 stops the movement entirely, the principle of secondary reinforcement leads to the deduction that ultimately q_x is conditioned to a progressive deceleration through $x - 1$ paces, culminating in complete inhibition of the movement. That is, q_x is conditioned to a response that is exactly adapted to the distance of the wall, and therefore, in accordance with our hypothesis, generates perception of that distance.

This, it must be understood, is a new perception, over and above that which is already implicit in the definition of q_x. The previously existing perception is dependent on the fixation responses that were established during the first stage of life, and of course this remains. If nothing new were added to the system, locomotion would give rise to perception of a constantly changing environment, like a motion picture taken by a camera that is itself in motion, but shown on a screen and viewed from a fixed seat in the theatre. This kind of perception in fact continues to exist, and it is easy enough to bring it into prominence by deliberately attending to it with the intention of describing it. The fact that this kind of perception appears to play such a relatively unimportant part in mature conscious experience does not mean that it is actually of little moment and has therefore fallen into the background. What has happened is that the elements of this perception have become conditioned to responses adapted to such relatively permanent features of the environment as walls, and the engrams mediating these responses have generated two new perceptual constancies, overshadowing the inconstancy of the primary perception.

The first constancy arises from the fact that every q_x is conditioned to a forward movement of $x - 1$ paces terminating in the invariant response of stopping, which always occurs at a position from which the wall can be reached by stretching out a hand. Since the variable component of this response is always reduced by exactly one pace when q_x is replaced by q_{x-1}, and since, by (6.3.1), q_x and q_{x-1} include perception of the movement of the body, it follows that the wall is perceived as occupying a fixed position in space.

The second constancy is determined by what happens after the wall is reached. To make this clear we may consider a specific instance. Assume that the child cannot walk but can stand without support. On the wall, above the level of his head, there are two objects, at distances $r = 1$ and $r = 2$. The patterns of stimulation determined by these objects will change in the manner shown in the table and diagrams. When the child reaches the wall, the movements required to establish contact with the two objects are determinate and invariant, if we neglect the details of execution. That is, he must stand up and stretch his hand out at two levels in succession. By the principle of the gradient of reinforcement, the stimulus patterns $q_1, q_2 \ldots$ are all conditioned to these invariant terminal responses, with the result that on subsequent occasions the heights of the two objects are, at all stages in the progress toward the wall, perceived as being constant.

Generalizing, we reach the conclusion that after some more experience the wall is perceived as being constant with respect not only to its position but also to the spatial relations between its parts. For example, it is perceived as being a plane surface because, once it has been reached, movements directed to its various parts must be executed by moving in a plane parallel to it.

6.19. This leads naturally to consideration of two other constancies that have been widely discussed by writers on perception, viz. the constancies of size and shape. It is clear now that there is a very simple explanation of these phenomena. No matter what distortions the retinal image of an object may suffer as a result of its position relative to the eyes, the final response of handling the object has certain components that remain invariant from one occasion to another. Thus, to take an example on which a vast amount of argument has been expended, a penny is perceived as being circular despite the fact that its retinal image is an ellipse that can vary all the way from a straight line to a circle. But if you expose a penny so that its retinal projection is elliptical, and ask a subject to place his finger and thumb at such a distance apart that what appears as the minor axis of the penny will fit into the space, an actual test will show that the distance selected is quite close to the diameter of the penny. As this response is the only invariant we can find in the whole system, we must conclude that it alone is responsible for the perceptual constancy. A similar argument, applied to variation in the size of the retinal image, enables us to deduce the constancy of size.

In all such cases, it must be understood, the stimuli are at the same time conditioned to the appropriate elements of variable responses, and the engrams mediating these responses determine properties of perception other than the size and shape of the object. The variable functions are the perceived directions and distances of objects relative to $R(\Omega)$.

6.20. We now have the full answer to the question asked at the end of 6.16. The missing information is built into the system by a process that is analogous to the solution of a mathematical problem by successive approximation. An example familiar to psychologists is that of determining the unknown communalities in a correlation matrix. A common procedure is to assign arbitrary values to the unknowns and factorize the matrix. This yields a set of calculated values which lead to an adjustment of the trial values. The process is continued until trial values and calculated values converge. Here the unique solution is inherent in the matrix of correlations, but trial and error is the only way of arriving at it. Similarly, if we think of the patterns of stimulation, $q_x, q_{x-1} \ldots$ as constituting a set of simultaneous equations in several unknowns, including x itself and the values of r of the several units of the texture, we can say that, on the assumption that the environment is stationary, a unique solution is inherent in those equations, but must be reached by trial and error.

The assignment of trial values to the unknowns consists in the evocation of elements of

$$(6.20.1)\quad {}_3U \equiv [(q_x, m);\ m\ \textit{follows}\ q_x].$$

As in other sets of this kind, m is an unconditioned response to a pattern of stimulation that may include q_x but is not identical with it. The positive or negative reinforcement of m is analogous to the mathematician's discovery that his trial values yield satisfactory or unsatisfactory results. If the results are bad he starts again; if they are good he retains the trial values as the solution of the problem. Analogously, if m is bad it is rejected; if it is good it is retained, and the result is the formation of an element of

$$(6.20.2)\quad {}_3F \equiv [(q_x, m);\ q_x \rightarrow m].$$

Then, by substituting activated engrams for m, we arrive at a compound state of readiness, ${}_3\Pi$, for a set of responses exactly adapted to all the unknowns in the original equations. Finally, by our hypothesis that Π can be identified with perception, the information that is *not* contained in the visual stimulus itself is now an integral part of perception.

6.21. Before we proceed further it will be useful to trace the genealogy of the set ${}_3\Pi$ we have just derived.

From (3.4.28) and (3.4.29) we have

(6.21.1) ${}_1\Pi \subset {}_1\Phi \equiv [(q,e);\ q \,\varepsilon\, Q,\ e \,\varepsilon\, E,\ q \rightarrow e].$

Here q represents a compound pattern of afferent activity in the nervous system as determined jointly by the external environment, the orientation of the head and eyes, the initial position of the hand, and drive. It carries with it no implication of consciousness. On the other hand the set ${}_1\Pi$ represents a limited perception of the positions of objects in the environment in relation to the reference frame $R(\Delta)$, defined by the main axes of the body. Hence any change in the position of the body implies a change in the perceived positions of objects.

At the next stage we have, from (4.3.1) and (6.21.1),

(6.21.2) ${}_2Q \equiv [(\phi, v_{12}, v_{13}, v_{14});\ \phi \,\varepsilon\, {}_1\Phi],$

and this, together with (4.8.3) and (4.8.4), leads to

(6.21.3) ${}_2\Pi \subset {}_2\Phi \equiv [(q,e);\ q \,\varepsilon\, {}_2Q,\ e \,\varepsilon\, {}_2E,\ q \rightarrow e].$

Here it is evident that ${}_2Q$ implies ${}_1\Pi$, so that we can write

(6.21.4) ${}_1\Pi \subset {}_2\Pi.$

That is to say, the new perception generated at this stage does not involve the abolition of ${}_1\Pi$. The newly acquired elements of ${}_2\Pi$, that is, ${}_2\Pi - {}_1\Pi$, are dependent on the engrams, ${}_2E - {}_1E$, mediating responses $M(T)$, as defined in (4.5.1). They represent perception of the spatial ordering of the environment relative to the reference frame $R(\Omega)$. However, this perception does not occur in the absence of ${}_1\Pi$. There is no separate and independent reality corresponding to the set difference, ${}_2\Pi - {}_1\Pi$.

Through this development certain important constancies of perception have been established. These we have represented by $R(\Pi)$, defined in (4.10.1) as a subset of Π such that all its elements arise from objects that can be reached by one and only one response. Following our new subscript notation, we can write

(6.21.5) $R({}_1\Pi) \subset {}_1\Pi,$

(6.21.6) $R({}_2\Pi) \subset {}_2\Pi,$

and, from (6.21.4),

(6.21.7) $R({}_1\Pi) \subset {}_2\Pi$.

It will be seen that although $R(\Delta)$ and $R(\Omega)$ are essential to the definitions of ${}_1Q$ and ${}_2Q$ respectively, they are not directly represented in Π. The frames of reference $R({}_1\Pi)$ and $R({}_2\Pi)$ are external to the body and consequently are not just perceptual representations of $R(\Delta)$ and $R(\Omega)$. They are true perceptual frames of reference in the sense that they are an integral part of the perceptual field, being generated by exactly the same kind of process as all the other elements of Π. In the same way a Cartesian frame of reference is part of the space it serves to define, and can therefore be defined in terms of itself. For example, in a 3-dimensional space the X axis may be defined by the set

$$X \equiv [(x,y,z);\ \textit{for every}\ (x,y,z) \in X,\ y = 0\ \textit{and}\ z = 0].$$

Similarly, $R({}_1\Pi)$ and $R({}_2\Pi)$ can be defined in terms of themselves. It must be clearly understood, however, that these definings take place within the field of consciousness. They are strictly private events, and it is no more possible for one person to make comparisons within another person's perceptual field than it is to describe the dimensions of personality in terms of centimeters, grams, and seconds.

Also incorporated in ${}_1\Pi$ and ${}_2\Pi$ are ${}_1\Pi(G)$ and ${}_2\Pi(G)$, involving still another perceptual frame of reference, viz. perception of the vertical-horizontal framework of the world. Again this is a strictly private frame of reference, as can be seen from the experience of the passenger in an aircraft making a steep turn, described in 5.13.

Turning to the developments discussed in this chapter we may first reword definition (6.3.1) by

$$(6.21.8)\quad {}_3Q \equiv [(\phi_1, \phi_2, \phi(GL));\ \phi_1, \phi_2 \in {}_2\Phi,\ t_{\phi_2} - t_{\phi_1} = 1 \text{ locomotor cycle}].$$

The definition of $\phi(GL)$ is given in 6.3. There are two important differences between ${}_3Q$ and ${}_2Q$. The first is that all the components of $q \in {}_3Q$ are elements of ${}_2\Phi$ and can therefore contribute to ${}_2\Pi$, whereas $q \in {}_2Q$ contains components that are not elements of ${}_1\Phi$. That is, all the elements of ${}_3Q$ are perceived stimuli already. This, however, makes no essential difference to the process whereby new perception is generated. The second difference is that whereas the elements of ${}_2Q$ imply a single position of the body relative to the environment, those of ${}_3Q$ imply a change in position effected by locomotion. Thus each element of ${}_3Q$ includes two elements of

${}_2\Phi$, and in all relevant cases these two elements belong to different equivalence classes of ${}_2\Phi$, thereby determining a change in those perceived properties of the object that are included in ${}_2\Pi$.

The new responses conditioned to the elements of ${}_3Q$ result in

$$(6.21.9) \quad {}_3\Pi \subset {}_3\Phi \equiv [(q,e);\ q \varepsilon {}_3Q,\ e \varepsilon {}_3E,\ q \rightarrow e].$$

It is now evident that

$$(6.21.10) \quad {}_1\Pi \subset {}_2\Pi \subset {}_3\Pi.$$

That is, the process of generating perception is essentially an additive process, in which the elements built up in the earlier stages suffer no transformation when they are incorporated in a more comprehensive subsystem of the multistable system. There may be changes in their relative importance or prominence, but that is another matter.

6.22. Perhaps the most striking feature of ${}_3\Pi$ is the wholesale manufacture of constancies that is made possible by locomotion. We have seen, in 4.11, that as long as the infant is anchored to one place he can develop a limited perceptual constancy, but this is strictly relative to his own body. The frames of reference that we have now called $R({}_1\Pi)$ and $R({}_2\Pi)$ imply that as long as the infant's position in the environment remains unchanged, objects that are just attainable by reaching are perceived as occupying a fixed position, but beyond that range positional inconstancy prevails. But this inconstancy is in fact completely lawful, in the sense that if we define a system in which the positions of objects are referred to arbitrary coordinates anchored to some fixed feature of the environment, and the child's own position relative to these coordinates is included among the variables of the system, then the changes produced in ${}_1\Pi$ or ${}_2\Pi$ by a primary operation such as changing the child's position can be exactly calculated.

During the first and second stages of life the child's own position provides the only possible arbitrary coordinates, but the positions of objects beyond his reach are not directly represented by variables in the ultrastable system whose adaptation has generated ${}_1\Pi$ and ${}_2\Pi$. That is, the systems ${}_1\Phi$ and ${}_2\Phi$ are not absolute in the sense in which Ashby uses that term. However, it is easy for us, as onlookers, to construct an absolute system, A, by adding to ${}_2\Phi$ three variables representing the position of the child relative to fixed coordinates. For we can now calculate exactly the elements of ${}_2\Phi$ that come into operation as a result of any change in the child's position. The changes in ${}_2\Pi$ that result from locomotion are not arbitrary but are exactly determined by the new values assigned to the variables defining the child's position, and it is precisely because they *are* determinate that it is possible for them to be conditioned to locomotor responses that are exactly adapted to the positions of objects in the environment. The system, ${}_3\Phi$, that is generated by this conditioning, contains in effect indirect representations of the three variables artificially added to ${}_2\Phi$ to form the system A. Although ${}_3\Phi$ is not identical with A, it is equivalent to it, for it is possible, in principle, to write transformations that will enable us to pass from one to the other.

Now an essential feature of the system A is that the positions of all objects, including the child, are defined in relation to a fixed frame of reference, and of course the coordinates of all permanent features of the environment are invariant as long as the frame of reference is retained. Any rotation of the axes or any shift of the origin changes the coordinates of all points in the environment but does not change the positions of the points relative to one another. These are invariants that are completely unaffected by the choice of the reference frame. It follows that if ${}_3\Phi$ is equivalent to A, ${}_3\Pi$ must show the same invariances that are found in A. Specifically, if we think of the subject himself as determining the frame of reference, so that his own coordinates are always (0,0,0), ${}_3\Pi$ should reflect the changing coordinates of objects in the environment as the frame of reference shifts and also the invariant relations of several objects to one another.

This in fact is precisely what happens. The conditioning of locomotor responses exactly adapted to the directions and distances (that is, the polar coordinates) of objects in the environment means that those coordinates are reflected in ${}_3\Pi$ and must change with every movement of the subject. But, as we have seen in 6.10 and again in 6.18 and 6.19, the elements of ${}_3Q$ are conditioned not only to responses that are adapted to the polar coordinates of objects in the vicinity and therefore vary when those coordinates are changed by locomotion, but also to further responses that can be initiated only when some intermediate goal has been reached. These further responses are adapted to the positions of other points relative to the intermediate goal, and, as the environment is assumed to be stationary, the responses in question are necessarily invariant. Thus the system $_3\Phi$ contains the invariants that are inherent in the system A, and those invariants are reflected in $_3\Pi$ as it changes from moment to moment.

We thus arrive at the momentous conclusion that a mobile organism, equipped with receptor and effector organs, and a brain capable of establishing temporary connections between afferent and efferent neurons, must generate a perceptual field reflecting the invariant relations between the several features of a stationary environment.

CHAPTER 7

Parallax

7.1. The general form of the set, ${}_3Q$, has been described, but some of the variables incorporated in it have been deliberately neglected for expository reasons. However, no harm has been done by this neglect, because the omitted variables are, so to speak, in parallel with those discussed in the last chapter and not in series with them. They, in fact, provide the basis for the additional "channels of communication," referred to in 6.1, that help to reduce the incidence of ambiguity in perception. The essence of the matter is that there are several variables, all elements of ${}_2\Phi$, that are functionally related to the distance of the stimulus-object that is responsible for the exteroceptive components of those elements. They are all asymptotic functions, but they reach their asymptotes at widely varying distances. Thus the function referred to in psychological textbooks as "accommodation" reaches its asymptote at between 1 and 2 meters, while the function known as "aerial perspective" reaches its asymptote at a distance that varies with atmospheric humidity and may be as great as 100 miles. Neither of these two functions is a component of ${}_3Q$, since the first one has its asymptotic value for all distances beyond reach of the hand, and the rate of change of the second one is so slow that no physiologically significant change is produced by a single pace.

Of the remaining functions that are components of ${}_3Q$ the most important is parallax, that is, the displacement of near and distant objects relative to one another under movements of the body in a plane at right angles to the direction of advance. The usual treatment of this subject in the textbooks takes no account of locomotion, but it is clear that parallactic displacements under movements of the head or trunk in the preambulatory stage cannot in themselves generate perception of distances beyond the reach of the hands. In the following pages I shall attempt to describe this function in some detail and show how it gets incorporated into the function ${}_3\Phi$.

There is another form of parallax that has been commonly treated by psychologists as the *primary* source of the perception of depth. This is binocular parallax, or retinal disparity. The remainder of the chapter will be devoted to discussion of this function.

7.2. The path of the head during locomotion is never a straight line. It undulates both up and down and from side to side. The vertical and lateral undulations are not separable from one another in actual locomotion, but for expository purposes it will be convenient to separate them and discuss the problem as if the lateral undulations alone existed. The results can then be generalized to the compound undulations. The lateral movement is often so small as to be negligible, but the argument that follows is equally applicable to vertical movement.

Let us assume, for convenience, that the lateral excursion of the head during one locomotor cycle is equal to one-tenth of a pace. We may then describe the situation by saying that the center of the head moves forward within a space bounded by two vertical planes parallel to the line of advance and separated from each other by a distance equal to 0.1. The head is, say, in the right-hand plane at the beginning and in the left-hand plane in the middle of each cycle. Now let a vertical rod be placed in the right-hand plane, at an initial distance of 10.5 paces. As we have not yet discussed binocular parallax, it will be convenient to neglect it for the moment and investigate the problem on the assumption that the subject has a Cyclopean eye in the middle of his forehead. This will simplify the geometry, and any errors that may result from this procedure will be corrected when binocular parallax is introduced.

The lateral movements of the head will result in a displacement of the perceived position of the rod relative to its background. These displacements are of course changes in ${}_2\Pi$ and not yet in ${}_3\Pi$. That is, they are initially perceived as lateral movements of rod and background relative to one another. We shall investigate two situations. In the first there is a background object in the right-hand plane at distance "infinity." That is, its distance is so great that its lateral displacement under movements of the head may be considered as virtually zero throughout. The displacement of the rod relative to this object is then given by $\tan^{-1} 0.1/x$, where x is the distance of the rod when the head is in the left-hand plane. As this is assumed to occur in the middle of each locomotor cycle, the successive values taken by x will be integers. The results are shown in column b of Table 7.2.1.

TABLE 7.2.1. Parallactic displacements of an object, a, relative to b, an object at infinite distance, and c, an object 10 paces beyond a.

x	b.	c.
10	0°34′23″	0°17′12″
9	0°38′12″	0°20′6″
8	0°42′58″	0°23′52″
7	0°49′6″	0°28′53″
6	0°57′17″	0°35′48″
5	1° 8′45″	0°45′50″
4	1°25′56″	1° 1′23″
3	1°54′33″	1°28′6″
2	2°51′45″	2°23′6″
1	5°42′38″	5°11′23″

In the second situation the background object is again in the right-hand plane, but it is only 10 paces beyond the vertical rod. The displacement of the two objects relative to one another is then given by $(\tan^{-1} 0.1/x - \tan^{-1} 0.1/x + 10)$. The resulting values are shown in the last column. Consider the first row of the table. The first half cycle brings the distance of the rod to 10 paces and brings the head into the left-hand plane. This displaces the rod through an angle of 34′23″ relative to an object at "infinity," as shown in column b. But at the same time it displaces an object at 20 paces through an angle of 17′11″ relative to the object at "infinity." Hence the displacement of the objects at 10 and 20 paces relative to one another is $34'23'' - 17'11'' = 17'12''$, and this is the value shown in column c.

7.3. It is at once evident that the angular displacement increases with positive acceleration as the distance decreases, and in much the same way as the functions discussed in 6.2 and 6.9.

Consequently exactly the same arguments that were applied to the latter functions can be applied to the present one. That is, the displacements can be considered as components of ${}_3Q$ and can therefore become conditioned stimuli for locomotor responses adapted to the distances of the relevant objects. This conditioning establishes another "channel of communication" carrying perception of distance; but it has one important property that distinguishes it from the other channels we have discussed. In the case of the other channels we have assumed that the "punctuation" of the curve of changing retinal stimulation depends on the recurrence of the patterns of proprioceptive and pressure stimuli incidental to locomotion. But in the present case there is a direct punctuation of the changing retinal stimulus in the sense that the position of a near object is perceived (in ${}_2\Pi$ of course) as undergoing a rhythmical change relative to that of a more distant object. That is, the particular stimulus we are considering here is by its very nature divided into clearly distinguishable slabs. It is essentially a discrete variable, whereas the others we have investigated are essentially continuous. Obviously this discontinuous variable can be considered as collaborating with the cyclical proprioceptive and pressure pattern (which is also discontinuous) in providing the necessary punctuation of the continuous variables. This illustrates once more the general proposition that the system is overdetermined.

7.4. Some subjects, when asked to observe parallactic displacement during locomotion, report that they can detect no such movement. In some cases this is attributable to an exceptionally steady gait; the oscillatory movements of the head are so narrow that the displacements are quite close to the threshold, and some training is required to detect them. Even when the oscillation is quite marked the subject may initially fail to detect the displacement; and this fact might be considered as an insuperable obstacle to the argument that perception of distance is generated by the conditioning of locomotor responses to these elements of ${}_2\Pi$. For if they are not perceived they are not elements of ${}_2\Pi$, at least initially.

There is an extremely simple answer to this argument. We have defined Π as a state of simultaneous readiness for conditioned responses to a wide range of environmental objects, and if we now identify Π with perception, it is clear that perception is determined not only by the stimulus but chiefly by the response that is conditioned to it. Now parallactic displacements, as elements of ${}_2\Pi$, have become conditioned to responses directed to objects beyond reach of the hands, that is, to locomotor responses more or less accurately adjusted to their distance. These conditionings determine elements of ${}_3\Pi$, and since the relevant responses are adapted to the distances of objects, it follows that what the subject perceives, within the field of ${}_3\Pi$, is primarily the distances. But that is not all. We have seen that the energy fed into an engram is a joint function of the stimulus energy and of drive. It then follows that if the drive in operation at any moment is more likely to be diminished by locomotion than by immediate manipulation, the activities aroused in the system by the stimulus-object will be elements of ${}_3\Pi$ rather than of ${}_2\Pi$.

We have hitherto thought of drives as being merely undifferentiated states of activity that are capable of supplying energy in any situation in which conditioned responses are to be established or evoked; but it seems clear that as the repertory of the organism's acquired responses increases in range and variety this ultrasimple conception becomes more difficult to maintain. We know from recent neurophysiological research that the Brain Stem Reticular Activating System (BSRAS) changes the mode of its activity as a result of conditioning. When some new stimulus is applied the BSRAS reacts with a widespread activity that apparently extends over the whole cortex; but when a determinate response has been conditioned to the new stimulus, the character of this activity changes markedly. The response of the reticular system is now confined to a restricted region, so that the resulting heightened cortical energy is confined to the areas that are relevant to the acquired response. This changed pattern is associated with the activity of inhibitory fibers that take their origin in the cortex. These fibers, it would seem, not only exercise an inhibitory effect on the BSRAS itself but also serve to diminish the responsiveness of the receptor organs to stimuli that are irrelevant to the ongoing behavior of the organism.[1]

The problem we are concerned with here is of a somewhat different character. Instead of two or more patterns of stimulation

1. For a detailed discussion of the reticular system see Berlyne (1960).

tending to evoke mutually incompatible responses, we have one compound pattern of stimulation arousing activity in two engrams mediating responses that are not in any sense mutually exclusive but are such that one of them is more directly relevant to the present needs of the organism than the other. Specifically, the stimulus is an element of ${}_3Q$, and it is conditioned to a locomotor response that establishes contact with some initially distant stimulus-object. But by definition this $q \varepsilon {}_3Q$ consists of two elements, q_1 and q_2, of ${}_2Q$, that have previously been conditioned to oculomotor responses serving to establish fixation. It follows that $q \varepsilon {}_3Q$ contributes to two successive sets, ${}_2\Pi$, as well as to ${}_3\Pi$. But since the organism is actually responding to $q \varepsilon {}_3Q$ with the appropriate $m \varepsilon {}_3M$, we may reasonably suppose that the inhibitory mechanism, operating through the BSRAS, tends to damp down the mainly irrelevant oculomotor responses conditioned to q_1, $q_2 \varepsilon {}_2Q$. Since this inhibition must necessarily diminish the energy fed to the relevant engrams, it follows that during locomotion toward a goal the perception of parallactic displacement is likely to be eliminated, or at least greatly diminished in strength.

7.5. This discussion has incidentally led us to a simple and satisfactory solution of the problem of the focus and fringe of attention. It is clear now that we do not need to think of attention as being some special kind of mental activity that acts as a sort of organizer or master of ceremonies to smooth the way for various other mental processes, such as perception and learning. Nor do we need to think of attention as a sort of torchlight which the subject can manipulate at his pleasure to illumine this or that sector of his mental field. All such conceptions are scientifically embarrassing, no matter how attractive they may be as poetic images, because they attribute causal functions to an agency that is defined only in terms of its own alleged effects. This is a classic example of the error referred to in 1.4.

The various "levels of attention" emerge as a necessary variable distinguishing the several elements of a set Π, and exactly determined by the amount of energy delivered to the several engrams. Assuming drive to be uniform for all elements of Π, the energy fed to the engrams varies solely with the afferent energy generated by the stimulus object. Thus if a movement of the eyes translates the retinal image of an object from the macula to the periphery, the volume of afferent energy is diminished and the engrams mediating the appropriate responses operate in consequence at a lower level of activity. The object recedes into the "fringe of attention." But, as we saw in 3.11 when discussing Gibson's "visual field," the energy applied to these engrams may be increased as a result of an instruction to report on the periphery, and the object moves to a higher level of attention. That is essentially what happens in real life situations where it becomes necessary to observe something without appearing to do so. The need to observe normally increases the energy by turning the eyes in the direction of the object, but when this response is inhibited some increase of energy is nevertheless available.

7.6. *Corresponding Points*

Ever since the publication of Johannes Müller's *Beiträge zur vergleichenden Physiologie des Gesichtsinnes* in 1826 the theory of binocular vision has been dominated by the doctrine of corresponding points. To define corresponding points, let x and y represent the horizontal and vertical angular deviations of a ray of light from the left optic axis, and x′ and y′ the corresponding deviations from the right optic axis. Then if rays of light enter the two eyes in such a manner that $x = x'$ and $y = y'$, the retinal points reached by the two rays are said to be corresponding points. We shall be mostly concerned with cases in which the two rays have a common origin in space. Since the eyes normally move up and down together, $y - y'$ may be considered as constant, although not necessarily zero, for each individual; consequently we need consider only the x coordinates. That is, if the rays have a common origin, corresponding points are sufficiently specified by the statement that $x = x'$.

The doctrine is in two main parts. First, if $x = x'$ the retinal images fuse to produce a unitary visual percept. But this also happens if $|x - x'|$ does not exceed a limiting value, say a. If $|x - x'| > a$, there is diplopia. Second, if $x = x' \neq 0$, the source of the rays is perceived as being at the same distance as the fixation point, for which, of course, $x = x' = 0$. But if $0 < |x - x'| \leq a$, the distance of the source is perceived as being different from that of the fixation point. The value of $(x - x')$ is known as the disparity of the two retinal images. Since there is no change in the perceived distance of an object when fixation changes to a nearer or more distant point, thus changing the degree of disparity, it is convenient to state the doctrine in a more general form.

Let d and d + Δd be the distances from a point O, midway between the eyes, of two objects A and B, where A appears to the left of B. If perception of distance is veridical, d and d + Δd are also the perceived distances, but to avoid confusion we shall represent the perceived distances by D and D + ΔD, retaining d for the objective distance. Also let α be the angle subtended at the left eye by the horizontal distance between A and B, and α' the angle subtended by the same distance at the right eye. Then the standard doctrine can be expressed by

$$\frac{\Delta D}{D} = f\,(\alpha - \alpha').$$

If perception is veridical we should be able to substitute d for D in this equation without loss of precision, but in that case we shall find that there is no function of $(\alpha - \alpha')$ that can satisfy the equation.

A substantial amount of research has been devoted to the measurement of the minimum value of $(\alpha - \alpha')$ to which a subject can respond by correctly reporting on the relative distances of A and B. The threshold is apparently of the order of 10 seconds of arc, the minimum on record being 2″. It must be understood, however, that such values are never obtained by direct measurement, but are calculated from linear measurements obtained with the aid of the Howard-Dolman apparatus or something similar. Such calculations are doubtless legitimate when the measurements are obtained under carefully controlled laboratory conditions, but they cease to have any meaning when those conditions are relaxed. Thus if the position of the head is such that its median plane does not pass between the two rods whose positions are to be compared, the actual value of $(\alpha - \alpha')$ will be significantly greater than the value derived from the setting of the rods, since the calculation is invariably based on the assumption that convergence is symmetrical.

It can be seen that the practice of converting the linear measurements into angular measurements exposes the investigator to a dangerous logical trap. It is all too easy to conclude that if a judgment that rod A is just perceptibly farther than rod B implies a specific value of $(\alpha - \alpha')$ when convergence is symmetrical, this angular difference is the necessary and sufficient condition for the judgment, and a similar judgment will be given whenever the same difference occurs. The standard doctrine of corresponding points gives direct expression to this fallacious conclusion. Occasionally one detects a certain uneasiness in discussions of this topic, but it never seems to rise to the critical level at which the doctrine is rejected outright. Thus Graham (1951, p. 885) writes: "We know that such a hypothetical construction is an approximation at best. Nevertheless it provides a basis for systematization not otherwise available." Actually a system based on this hypothetical construction alone lacks the necessary property of regularity, and is therefore scientifically worthless.

7.7. To demonstrate the irregularity of the system it will be sufficient to consider cases in which the distances of A and B are identical. In Figure 7.7.1, L and R are the nodes of the left and

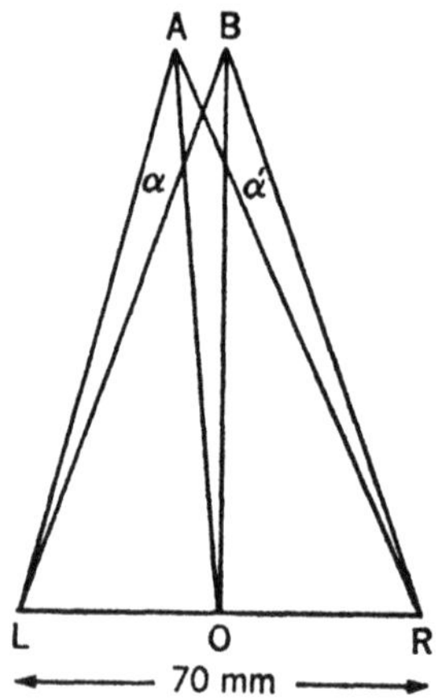

FIGURE 7.7.1

right eyes and O is a point midway between them. The interocular distance is taken to be 70 mm. Let OA = OB = 35 cm. We shall assume that in every case the eyes are converged on B. Three values will be assigned to the angle BOR, viz. 90°, 100°, and 110°. That is, convergence is symmetrical in the first case and asymmetrical in the others. For each value of the angle BOR we shall assign four values to the angle AOB, viz. 1°, 2°, 4°, and 10°. In each case we shall calculate the angles α and α', i.e. ALB and ARB, and record the values of $(\alpha - \alpha')$. The results are shown in Table 7.7.1. If the

TABLE 7.7.1. Values, in seconds of arc, of $(\alpha - \alpha')$.

BOR		90°	100°	110°
AOB	1°	6	127	246
	2°	24	266	503
	4°	98	581	1053
	10°	608	1811	3152

subject has a Howard-Dolman threshold of 10″, standard theory leads to the conclusion that on only one of the 12 occasions will he perceive the distances OA and OB as being identical. On every other occasion A must be perceived as being more distant. An actual test will show this deduction to be false. But that is not all. It is very easy to show that any one of the tabled values may be produced by many different settings in which the distances OA and OB are not equal, and they are readily perceived as being unequal. For example, if OA = 99.911 cm., OB = 100.552 cm., the angle AOB = 2°0′10″, the angle BOR = 100°2′56″, and the interocular distance is 70 mm. as before, $(\alpha - \alpha') = 6''$. In these circumstances A is quite easily perceived as being nearer than B; so that here we have the extraordinary phenomenon of a reputedly subliminal stimulus producing a result that would normally be expected only from a stimulus well above the threshold, while in other cases stimuli that are some hundreds of times the magnitude of the threshold produce no results at all.

7.8. As a preliminary to formulating a more satisfactory theory it will be useful to consider the problem as a mathematical one, and ask what is the minimum of information, in addition to the angles α and α', that is required to deduce the distances OA and OB, which we must assume to be initially unknown. First of all we must know that the angles α and α' are subtended by one and the same distance AB and not by two separate distances, as they could easily be. Second, we need to know the interocular distance; or, if this information is not available, we at least need to know that it is constant. The unknown distances may then be stated in terms of a linear scale in which the interocular distance is the unit. Last, we need to know the angles BLR and BRL. We now have one triangle in which one side is known, together with the adjacent angles. From this we can get the lengths BL and BR, and by a further trigonometrical operation we can deduce the distance OB. From the adjacent angles and the angles α and α' we get the angles ALR and ARL, and a similar set of operations yields the distance OA. For example, if $\alpha = 2°1'7''$, $\alpha' = 1°56'41''$, BLR $= 85°43'20''$, BRL $= 74°28'20''$ and the interocular distance is 70 mm., we find that OA $=$ OB $=$ 35 cm. and AOB $= 2°$. It will be seen that this is the case, in Table 7.7.1, where BOR $= 100°$, AOB $= 2°$, and $(\alpha - \alpha') = 266''$.

If all this information is necessary for the *calculation* of OA and OB, it is evident that the organic system cannot generate accurate *perception* of those distances unless it contains afferent analogues of the required information. As far as the angles α and α' are concerned there is no difficulty. The afferent analogue of α is a pair of elements of the function V_1 and the analogue of α' is a pair of elements of the function V_2. We may consider these four elements, two from V_1 and two from V_2, as constituting a single element of a formal equivalence class, V(A,B), which we may define by

$$(7.8.1)\quad V(A,B) = [(v_1(A), v_1(B), v_2(A), v_2(B))],$$

where $v_1(A)$ is an element of V_1 in which the component δ is represented by the object A, and the usual condition of simultaneity applies. It will be seen that this involves both an extension and a limitation of the set V_0 defined in (2.8.2). It is an extension in the sense that an element of V(A,B) has four components instead of two; it is a limitation in the sense that two elements of Δ are specified and that these remain the same throughout all the elements of V(A,B).

Now it is clear from the definitions of V_1 and V_2, as presented in (2.8.1), that the elements of V(A,B) all differ from one another with respect to the orientation of the eyes and head, and that these differences entail differences in the location of the retinal images of A and B, and hence in the resultant afferent impulses. They also entail differences in the functions V_3 to V_8, as defined in (2.3.2). Of these, V_3 and V_4 are functions of the horizontal deviations of the left and right eyes respectively from the median plane of the head, so that the organic system contains analogues of the angles BLR and BRL as determined by the convergence of the eyes. It should be noted that if convergence is not on A or B but on some other point C, the trigonometry becomes a little more complicated, but there is no loss of information in the organic system, since functions of the angles ALC, BLC, ARC, and BRC are represented in a new element of V(A,B), and functions of the angles CLR and CRL are represented in the new elements, $v_3 \varepsilon V_3$ and $v_4 \varepsilon V_4$. These functions are all one-to-one correspondences, so that each of the afferent events arises from one and only one angle. Hence the information contained in the afferent system is, in principle, sufficient to generate the required perception.

7.9. There is, however, one item of information for which we have not as yet found an analogue. This is the information that the angles α and α' are generated by one and the same pair of objective points, A and B. The standard doctrine of corresponding points postulated that the fibers from any such pair of points had a common terminus in the striate area, and the assumption seemed to be that if a pair of impulses arrived at a single cortical point the resulting perception was necessarily singular. Although Sherrington (1911) long ago demonstrated that the fibers from the two retinas have in fact different cortical termini, there are still writers who feel that the singularity of binocular vision cannot be otherwise explained. Thus Metzger (1953) postulates that the fibers approach each other diagonally in the thickness of the cortex and after meeting continue for a short distance on divergent paths. By this structure he claims to account both for the fusion of the retinal images and for the perception of depth.

Apart from Sherrington's demonstration, there is another type of evidence that completely disposes of the doctrine. If binocular fusion were dependent solely on the stimulation of corresponding points, a squinter could have singular vision only of objects within a few inches of his face, and for all objects beyond that distance he must have either diplopia or monocular vision. In the latter event there must be some mechanism for suppressing the response to stimuli applied to the squinting eye. The fact is, as every ophthalmologist knows, that many squinters develop true binocular vision. An image falling on the macula of the normal eye fuses with an image falling on a peripheral area of the squinting eye. This area is commonly referred to as a *pseudomacula*, and its central point as a *pseudofovea*. Clearly we need some other type of explanatory principle that will account for both normal and abnormal binocular fusion.

The experience of the squinter is valuable because it makes it quite clear that there is nothing trivial in the question how the information that the source of the two retinal images is singular gets incorporated in the system. Physiological congruence of the afferent impulses from the retinas does not provide the answer, since in the squinter noncongruent impulses seem to serve the same purpose. It is evident that there is no possible physiological correlate of the missing information. It must therefore get into the system in some other way.

7.10. The answer turns out to be extremely simple, and it satisfies the requirement that both normal and abnormal cases are explained. We begin by assuming that there is in fact no necessary physiological union between the two retinal impulses generated by a single object, just as we have previously assumed that there is no necessary union between exteroceptive and proprioceptive afferents. Now consider the formal equivalence class $Q(\delta)$ defined in (2.14.1), where δ refers to a specific fixed object. The elements of $Q(\delta)$ differ from one another with respect to the values of x and x′, as defined in 7.6, and $(x - x')$ is likewise subject to variation. But the only kind of response to any $q \varepsilon Q(\delta)$ that will be reinforced is a singular response that establishes contact with δ. Any double response to the double pattern of retinal stimulation, such as stretching out both hands in different directions, must be extinguished, because the source of reinforcement is in fact singular. It follows that when the function ${}_1\Phi$ has been established, all the objects within the field of ${}_1\Pi$ must be perceived as being singular. Thus the missing information is incorporated in the system not by any innate physiological disposition but by a process of conditioning.

Now let us suppose that, for some reason that we need not investigate, a subject fails to develop normal control over the internal and external rectus muscles, so that the mean value of $x - x'$ is not zero but some substantial value such as 20° or 30°. Like other subjects he learns to maximize the retinal stimulus due to any object toward which his activity is directed, by fixation responses. But instead of a single maximum involving both eyes, he has two maxima at his disposal. He can fixate with either eye, and in these circumstances two possible patterns of permanent behavior can arise. He may develop an alternating squint or a fixed squint. It is the latter in which we are at present interested.

In this case the patterns of stimulation arising from a specific fixed object may be represented by the equivalence class $Q'(\delta)$. The difference between an element of $Q'(\delta)$ and the corresponding element of $Q(\delta)$ in a normal subject is that the horizontal angles incorporated in v_1 and v_2 are x and $x' + k$ (assuming the squint to be in the right eye), instead of x and x′ as in the normal subject, where k is a constant, viz. the average angle of squint. There also appears to be a difference in the proprioceptive function V_4, but if we define the angles A_4 (horizontal deviations of the right eye) as being measured not from the median plane of the head but from k, then the components v_3, v_4, of $q \epsilon Q'(\delta)$ may be regarded as essentially the same as those of the corresponding $q \epsilon Q(\delta)$.

Now all the elements of $Q'(\delta)$ are conditioned to one and the same singular response, directed to δ, exactly as in the normal case. Therefore, despite the fact that the retinal images of δ always fall on widely disparate points or areas, our hypothesis leads to the conclusion that this type of retinal stimulation will generate perception of a single object.

We may arrive at the same conclusion in a slightly different way. If, in any $q \epsilon Q(\delta)$, we eliminate v_1 by covering the left eye, the remaining components of q are sufficient to prepare the organism for a reaching response that will be accurate with respect to its horizontal and vertical components, although it will suffer a certain indeterminacy with respect to the third dimension. Similarly, if v_2 is eliminated by covering the right eye, the attenuated q that results is again sufficient to determine the horizontal and vertical components of the response. Hence the two diminished patterns of stimulation mediate perception of the object as occupying approximately the same position in space. When the two patterns are combined by having both eyes open, there is no conflict between the two perceived positions, and the only possible result is the perception of a single object. This implies that physiological concurrence of the afferent impulses from the two retinas is quite unnecessary, and that the essential requisite is concurrence of the motor responses, as determined by conditioning. But there is nothing to prevent this condition from being satisfied when the retinal stimuli are located at x and $x' + k$ instead of x and x'. Our hypothesis then enables us to deduce that the permanent squinter can develop genuine binocular vision with a pseudomacula.

7.11. One of the very puzzling things about binocular vision is the fact that in ordinary life we are so seldom aware of diplopia. It is easy enough to demonstrate it by asking a subject to fixate a near object and report on the appearance of a distant object, or vice versa, but if the eyes are wandering over the scene, momentarily fixating objects at varying distances and in random order, the entire scene appears to be singular all the time. If the distance of the nearest object is 5 times the interocular distance, say 35 cm., the value of $x - x'$ for objects in the median plane of the head is likely to vary all the way from 0 to 11°, and the range is even greater for objects to the right and left of the median plane. Why is it then that the scene is not perpetually dividing itself into two at the near end when a distant object is fixated and at the distant end when a near object is fixated?

To answer this question we may appeal to the principles that were applied in the last five sections of Chapter 3. When any object, A, is fixated binocularly there is, as suggested in 7.10, concurrence of the engrams activated by the two retinal stimuli, and the object is therefore perceived as being singular. When fixation is transferred to another object, B, at a different distance, A now activates engrams mediating two mutually incompatible responses; but, following the argument of 3.11, we may assume that in normal circumstances the drive available for the activation of those engrams is relatively low, while, by the argument of 3.8, the activity of the engrams initially aroused by A continues at a high level for a few seconds. It follows that, despite the disparity of the retinal images of A when fixation is on B, A continues to be perceived as singular.

If, on the other hand, a subject is asked to report on the appearance of A while fixating B, this *Aufgabe* increases the energy fed to the new incompatible engrams aroused by A, and the subject has no difficulty in perceiving it as occupying two positions in space. In the circumstances of everyday life our activities are commonly directed to the objects in our environment, and very seldom to description of our perceptual experience. There is consequently little or no evidence of diplopia.

There is yet another factor that contributes to the unity of the binocular field. Let q_1, q_2 be two elements of $Q(\delta)$ that occur in quick temporal succession, such that in q_1, $(x - x')$ has a substantial value and in q_2, $x = x' = 0$. If now q_2 evokes a reaching response directed to δ, and this response is reinforced, it follows that q_1 becomes conditioned to this same response. Hence q_1, no less than q_2, mediates perception of a single object; and generalizing, we reach the conclusion that in all normal circumstances the binocular field is singular throughout. This is a truly remarkable result that could never have been deduced if we had based our calculations solely on the geometry of binocular vision.

7.12. It is now evident that the process by which the binocular field is welded into a unity serves at the same time to differentiate the field with respect to depth. In order to understand how this is accomplished, it will be instructive to examine some of the equivalence classes, $Q(\delta)$, for objects at varying distances from the subject. For convenience we shall assume initially that all these objects are in the median plane of the head when they are inspected. That is, convergence is to be symmetrical in every case. And again we shall take the interocular distance to be 70 mm. Our first step is to investigate the relation between the angle of convergence of the eyes and the distance of the point of intersection of the optic axes. Since convergence is to be symmetrical we need only record the angle between the optic axis of one eye and the median plane of the head. The angle for the other eye will be numerically identical but opposite in sign. Table 7.12.1 shows the distances in

TABLE 7.12.1

Angle of convergence	10°	9°	8°	7°	6°	5°	4°	3°	2°	1°	0°
Distance of point of intersection	19.8	22.1	24.9	28.5	33.3	40.0	50.1	66.8	100	200	∞

centimeters, of the point of intersection for angles ranging from 10° to 0.

Before we proceed it will be necessary to adopt a convention as to the positive and negative directions of the axes along which x and x′ are measured. Let us say that x, which refers to the left eye, is positive if it is on the temporal side of the retina, and x′, in the right eye, is positive if it is on the nasal side of the retina. Then, if any object, A, is at the point of intersection, $x = x' = 0$; if convergence changes to a nearer object, the images of A are on the nasal sides of the two retinas, so that x is negative, x′ is positive, and $(x - x')$ is negative; and finally, if convergence changes to a more distant object, $(x - x')$ is positive.

We can now construct a table showing the values of $(x - x')$ for objects at various distances according to the angle of convergence. A small portion of such a table is presented in Table 7.12.2. There are 66 entries in the body of this table, but there

TABLE 7.12.2

Angle of convergence	10°	9°	8°	7°	6°	5°	4°	3°	2°	1°	0°
Distance of object in centimeters 19.8	0°	2°	4°	6°	8°	10°	12°	14°	16°	18°	20°
24.9	−4°	−2°	0°	2°	4°	6°	8°	10°	12°	14°	16°
33.3	−8°	−6°	−4°	−2°	0°	2°	4°	6°	8°	10°	12°
50.1	−12°	−10°	−8°	−6°	−4°	−2°	0°	2°	4°	6°	8°
100.0	−16°	−14°	−12°	−10°	−8°	−6°	−4°	−2°	0°	2°	4°
∞	−20°	−18°	−16°	−14°	−12°	−10°	−8°	−6°	−4°	−2°	0°

are only 22 different numbers. That is to say, a given value of $(x - x')$ may be associated with any one of a variety of distances or with any one of a variety of angles of convergence. But if each entry is paired with the angle of convergence shown at the head of its column, we have 66 unique pairs. It follows that if afferent analogues of the components of such pairs can be shown to exist, each pair can be uniquely conditioned to a specific response. As we have seen, such analogues are available. They are incorporated in the first four components of the elements of the set S.

Since the pairs are all unique, it follows that each of the pairs represented by any one row of the table can be conditioned to responses accurately adapted to the distance of the object that is responsible for the retinal stimuli, provided, of course, that the distance is not too great. In the earliest stages of life the limiting distance is determined by the child's inability to make contact with any object beyond reach of his hands. With the advent of locomotion the range increases, but fine discrimination on the basis of locomotor responses alone cannot extend very far. The main reason for this is that as the child moves toward his goal the pattern of stimulation is constantly being replaced by new patterns, each of which is more likely than its predecessor to have been already conditioned to a locomotor response of a specific extent. It follows that the greater the initial distance of the goal the less likely it is that a response involving exactly the right number of paces will be directly conditioned to the initial pattern of stimulation.

However, action directed to distant objects is not confined to locomotion. We can throw stones, and we can increase the distance to which we can hurl a missile with the aid of slings, catapults, bows, and firearms. Now there is an important difference between these actions and walking or running. The action, considered as response, is completed as soon as the missile has left the hand or the weapon, and no further action that we can take has any effect on its flight. Consequently there is no reinforcement unless the initial impetus is accurately adjusted to the direction and distance of the target. Thus the acquisition of skill in throwing missiles, as well as in various ball games, has the effect that patterns of stimulation in which the exteroceptive components are due to objects at a distance put the organism into a state of readiness for actions accurately adjusted to the distances, and thereby generate perception of distance over a wider range than locomotion alone could account for.

7.13. It must now be admitted that the responses on which we propose to place the burden of explaining the perception of depth are extremely variable in execution and therefore appear to lack the required accuracy. If we aim a quick movement even at an object within arm's length, the range of variation in the extent of the movement is enormously greater than the perceptual threshold for distance. The direction of the movement is similarly subject to error. This means that if we investigate isolated elements of ${}_1F$, ${}_2F$, or ${}_3F$, it would appear that there is no justification for our assumption that those sets are functions, since the m that is evoked by any q is not in fact unique.

Before we conclude that this constitutes a fatal objection to the theory, however, it will be useful to consider what happens when the corresponding elements of Π are studied in isolation. We find that in these circumstances perception loses its precision. The best known example of this is the autokinetic phenomenon. A faint point of light in a dark room has no fixed position and appears to wander to and fro. The indeterminacy of its position is just as great as that of an isolated element of F, and would appear to be adequately explained by that.

The autokinetic phenomenon is commonly assumed to be explainable in terms of the absence of a frame of reference, but in fact this is no explanation at all. If there is no frame of reference of any kind, the position of a point is quite simply indeterminate. Such a point has no position. But the point of light seen in a dark room *has* a position, and this implies that there *is* a frame of reference. If there were none it could not possibly be perceived as changing its position. The only possible frame of reference would seem to be one provided by the subject's own body, that is, what we have called $R(\Omega)$.

The problem confronting us now is to explain why the operation of relating a point to $R(\Omega)$ should be subject to so much uncertainty when the point is isolated, but achieves such a high measure of precision when it is presented in a context. To answer this question let us consider a situation in which there are three objects, A, B, and C, at distances a, b, and c, where $a < b < c$. Let us suppose that the responses conditioned to a, b, and c are all subject to a measure of uncertainty, that the range of responses to b includes the distances a and c, and that the responses to a and c both include b. Thus if B were presented alone in an otherwise empty space, its perceived distance would be liable to vary within a range including a and c, but its most probable distance would be b. Let us try now to deduce what must happen when A and C are presented simultaneously with B.

To answer this question we must take account not only of the responses conditioned to the three distances but also of the circumstances in which these responses were acquired. The child is never called upon to react to an environment as drastically reduced as that which reveals the autokinetic phenomenon. It is an environment containing numerous objects, so that while he is acquiring appropriate responses to an object in one position he is simultaneously acquiring responses of another kind to *pairs of objects*. Assume, for example, that he is aiming at object B. When he succeeds, this implies that elements of the equivalence class Q(b) are conditioned to the appropriate response. But at the same time the total pattern of stimulation includes elements of the equivalence classes Q(a) and Q(c). To facilitate discussion it will be convenient to define another type of equivalence class, Q(a,b), as the set of patterns of stimulation in which the exteroceptive components are due to the pair of objects, A and B. Similarly, Q(b,c) is the set of patterns involving the pair B,C. Since $a < b < c$, it follows that a successful response to B carries the hand, or the body or the missile as the case may be, beyond A but not as far as C. The reinforcement of this response then implies that the elements of Q(a,b) are conditioned to a response that goes beyond A, and the elements of Q(b,c) to a response that does not go as far as C.

7.14. This incidental conditioning has quite momentous consequences. To understand this we may define

$$(7.14.1)\quad P \equiv \Omega \times \Omega$$

as the set of all pairs of objects or points in the environment. This set may be partitioned in three ways according to whether we consider the X, Y, or Z coordinates. We may express this by writing

$$(7.14.2)\quad P(X) = < + = + >$$

$$(7.14.3)\quad P(Y) = < + = + >$$

$$(7.14.4)\quad P(Z) = < + = + >.$$

In ordinary language, (7.14.2) means that the elements of P can be divided into three classes, viz. (1) that in which $x_1 < x_2$, (2) that in which $x_1 = x_2$, and (3) that in which $x_1 > x_2$, where x_1 and x_2 are the x coordinates of the objects forming a pair. A similar interpretation is given to (7.14.3) and (7.14.4). The class, =, in (7.14.4) includes all pairs of points in any plane parallel to the XY plane. The three partitionings simply give precise expression to the obvious fact that if we select any pair of objects we can always say that the first one is to the right of the second one or to the left or neither, that it is above or below the second one or on the same level, and that it is nearer or farther than the second one or at the same distance. Our problem is to discover how those relations get incorporated in perception.

The answer should now be clear. The responses incidentally conditioned to patterns of stimulation of the form Q(a,b), defined in 7.13, fall into three classes, <, =, and >, corresponding to the partitioning of P(X) or P(Y) or P(Z). Those responses are no doubt subject to errors that are proportionally just as great as those applying to the direct responses to single elements of Q, but there is an important difference that can be brought out by considering once more the three objects, A, B, and C.

We have assumed that the range of uncertainty in the direct response to B includes the distances a and c, so that if B were presented in isolation, without a background, its perceived distance would be subject to the same range of indeterminacy. But if A and C are also present, the engrams activated by elements of Q(a,b) and Q(b,c) have the effect that the direct response to B for which the organism is put into a state of readiness is greater than the response to A and less than the response to C. In other words B is perceived as occupying an intermediate position between A and C. Thus if the direct response to B should at any moment be in error to the extent that its perceived distance is less than a, or greater than c, the responses to $q \varepsilon Q(a,b)$ and $q \varepsilon Q(b,c)$, have the effect that A is still perceived as being nearer and C more distant than B.

We may now remove the restriction that there are only three objects in the field, and generalize to the normal situation in which the subject is confronted with an environment containing a multitude of objects and points stretching outward from his own body. The spatial ordering of this environment, as expressed by (7.14.2) to (7.14.4), has its counterpart in the system of engrams aroused to activity by patterns of stimulation of the form q(a,b). In short, the spatial ordering of the environment is *perceived*. And since this environment commonly contains objects that can be reached by stretching out the hand, the set Π will almost certainly contain elements of R(Π), as defined in (4.10.1). That is, there is a perceptual frame of reference, which, in conjunction with the responses to the elements of P, defined in (7.14.1), ensures a degree of stability in the perceived ordering that would appear to be impossible if each element of Π were subject to random and independent variation of the type revealed in the autokinetic experiment.

It must be observed, however, that although the ordering of the perceived environment reflects the objective ordering, it does not necessarily reflect exactly all the dimensions of the objective scene. All we can say is that the perceived environment is topologically equivalent to the objective environment. Thus if the objective space is Euclidean, it does not follow that the perceived space is also Euclidean. Our discussion throughout this work suggests that perceived space approximates Euclidean properties only within a very narrow range at first, and that this range expands as the subject's capacity for dealing with his environment increases, but never extends to the whole of the perceptual field. Piaget's observations on the child's perception of space are in full agreement with the statement about expansion, and there is a multitude of observations on adult perception to confirm the final deduction. The geometric illusions all represent deviations from Euclidean space.

7.15. We have seen, in this and the preceding chapter, that there are several components of ${}_3Q$ that vary as functions of the distance of an object, and we have assumed that all those components, or channels of communication, give rise to essentially the same perceptual experience because they are all conditioned to the same set of responses. More precisely, if $f_1(a)$, $f_2(a)$ . . . $f_n(a)$ are the values of n different functions of the distance a, they are all conditioned to a response adapted to that distance, and therefore all mediate perception of the same distance. We now consider the question what will happen if one of those functions, say f_i, is subjected to a transformation so that the afferent event $f_i(a)$ is produced by an object whose distance is greater than a or less than a, while the other functions remain unchanged. One of the commonest ways of doing this is to look through a binocular telescope at a distant landscape. This has the effect that the visual angles subtended by all objects within the field of the telescope are increased to values that normally are produced only by objects that are much nearer. But at the same time other functions of distance remain unchanged. For example, the binocular parallax function has the same values as when the scene is viewed with the naked eye.

It is well known that in these circumstances the distant scene is perceived as having less depth than it has in reality, but what is not so commonly realized is that the contraction is not as great as standard theory would lead us to expect. And no matter what transformation we apply, the distortion is never as great as we might expect. For example, suppose that we fit two prisms, of say

10°, into a spectacle frame, with the bases on the temporal sides. If we look through these prisms, converging the eyes sufficiently to fuse the two images, an object on the horizon will produce a pattern of proprioceptive stimulation similar to that produced by an object at a distance of about 40 cm. in normal circumstances. But we do not perceive the horizon as being only 40 cm. away. It is in fact perceived as being only slightly, if at all, nearer. The distances of nearer objects suffer a proportionally greater abbreviation, but nothing like so much as might be expected from the data shown in Table 7.12.2. And even this distortion gradually disappears if the spectacles are worn for an hour or more.

Does this mean then that the proprioceptive impulses from the ocular muscles do not in fact have the significance we have attributed to them? On the contrary, it merely confirms the conclusion that it is impossible to understand the perceptual system if we insist on examining its various components in isolation. The wearing of squint spectacles has the effect of altering one of the afferent functions on which the perception of distance depends, but it leaves other functions unchanged. If those other functions are eliminated by presenting a patch of luminous paint in a dark room and the subject is asked to estimate its distance by reaching for it, he will perceive it as being not more than 40 cm. away, even if its distance be several times that amount. The distances perceived in an ordinary environment when the spectacles are put on for the first time can be understood as representing a weighted average of the perceived distances mediated by the several afferent functions that are in operation at the time. In a dark room the weights carried by the remaining functions are reduced to zero, so that the transformed function alone determines the outcome. Its weight is unity.

When squint spectacles are worn in daylight, the initial error in the perceived distances of objects is corrected relatively quickly; this is readily explained by reference to the definition of the proprioceptive functions given in (2.3.2). The afferent impulse from any muscle is a joint function of the degree of contraction of the muscle and the time during which that state of contraction has been maintained. In normal circumstances the angle between the two optic axes varies from zero upward, and the relevant proprioceptive function is determined by the angle of convergence and the time during which that angle has been maintained. But when squint glasses are worn the angle of convergence varies from about 10° upward. That is, each eye is turned approximately 5° nearer the nose than it would be without the spectacles. The afferent impulses due to this basic 10° convergence soon drop to their asymptote, and any further convergence brought about by fixating an object nearer than the horizon produces a burst of afferent activity that is not essentially different from that which occurs when the same object is fixated in normal circumstances. There is therefore one aspect of the process of adaptation to the wearing of squint glasses that finds a ready explanation in terms of the physiological properties of the afferent system.

There are, however, other distortions that remain after the general error in the perception of distance has been corrected. For example, vertical straight lines are all perceived as being concave toward the subject. Those errors of perception diminish progressively if the spectacles are worn continuously, but the process is very much slower, and it can hardly be attributed to physiological adaptation. In the next chapter we shall consider a variety of experiments in which such adaptations have been studied, and shall find that they are all explainable in terms of the general hypothesis that has been presented in the foregoing chapters. But first we must consider another aspect of binocular vision.

7.16. The hypothesis that binocular fusion depends upon the conditioning of the disparate patterns of retinal stimulation arising from a single object to one and the same response affords a simple explanation of the well-known phenomenon of binocular rivalry. If the stimuli presented to the two eyes are such that they could not arise from one and the same natural object, the resulting elements of Φ are mutually incompatible in a special sense. In normal perception several elements of Φ can exist simultaneously despite the fact that the corresponding elements of F are mutually exclusive, but in the case we are considering there is a more fundamental incompatibility. Let a be a point on the contour presented to the left eye but not on that presented to the right eye, and b a point on the right but not the left contour. Then $\phi_l(a)$ specifies a state of readiness for a response that terminates in a, but $\phi_r(a)$ specifies no such state of readiness. Similarly, $\phi_r(b)$ embodies the knowledge that there is a solid object at point b, whereas $\phi_l(b)$ embodies the knowledge that there is empty space there. As a point in space cannot be simultaneously filled and empty, it must be either one or the other. Similarly, the organism cannot simultaneously be in a state of readiness for a response that will be arrested at a by a solid obstacle, and a response that will not be arrested at a, or for a response that will not be arrested at b and one that will be arrested at b.

Generalizing to Π, we may say that if Δ_r and Δ_l are the environments presented to the right and left eyes, and $\Delta_r \cdot \Delta_l = \Theta$, then Π_r and Π_l cannot exist simultaneously, and there are several possibilities. One is that either Π_r or Π_l is completely inhibited and the other one remains dominant. Another is that Π_r and Π_l alternate. This is the familiar rivalry phenomenon. Since Π_r and Π_l have many elements, it is evident that there are numerous ways in which the transition from one to the other may take place. It may happen suddenly, all the elements of one being simultaneously replaced by elements of the other; or the exchange may start at one point and sweep quickly or slowly over the whole field. Finally, if $\Delta_r \cdot \Delta_l \neq \Theta$, that is, if they have certain elements in common, there may be a stable perceptual field in which elements of Π_r dominate in one place and elements of Π_l in another place.

A beautiful example of the first type of result occurred many years ago when I was developing a batch of stereoscopic photographs. One negative turned out to be particularly good, and my enthusiasm to get it printed quickly prompted me to make the solution of "hypo-killer" too strong, with the result that a large blister developed in the emulsion in the middle of one half of the plate. I thought the picture was ruined, but out of curiosity I printed it. In the middle of the right side there was a meaningless jumble of shapes covering an area of about one square inch. To my great astonishment there was no sign of this blemish when I looked at the picture in the stereoscope. I had to shut my left eye to convince myself that it was actually there. Under prolonged inspection there was no trace of binocular rivalry. Evidently the meaningless subset of Π_r was completely suppressed by the corresponding meaningful subset of Π_l. Moreover, there was no evidence of discontinuity in the dimension of depth over the section of the picture covered by the blemish.

In this case the suppression may be accounted for by the paucity of the engrams activated by the blemish as compared to the wealth of engrams aroused by the corresponding area on the other side.

Within the blemish there were no familiar shapes. But suppression can also occur when there is a big disparity in the energy fed into the two subsets of engrams. As I write this I am facing an open doorway looking on to a sunlit garden. The door is flanked by two narrow windows, and if I squint I can bring the two windows together, so that I see one narrow window flanked by two open doorways. The brightly lit scene thus stimulates noncorresponding parts of the two retinas, while the corresponding areas are stimulated by objects inside the room, where the illumination is much weaker. While maintaining the squint I now scan the two doorways, and for the most part all I can see is the sunlit garden. The objects in the room are just as meaningful as those in the garden, but the engrams they arouse cannot compete with the more highly energized engrams aroused by the sunlit scene.

However, this is not the whole truth. I can myself increase the energy fed to a suppressed engram by selecting a particular indoor object, estimating where it should appear in the doorway, and deliberately looking for it. I have no difficulty in making it appear against the bright background, although it tends to waver and to disappear after a few seconds. Sometimes only part of the object is seen at first, particularly a part that is projected onto a uniform surface such as the sky. The rest of it, projected onto a more diversified background, comes more slowly or not at all. The importance of diversity is revealed by the following observation. I shut the door, which is almost entirely filled with rippled glass. The brightness of the scene is reduced, but the most important effect is that the details of the outdoor scene are obliterated by the uneven surface of the glass. Only vague areas of different color and brightness can be seen. I now repeat the squinting exercise, and the indoor objects are quite easily seen against the bright but poorly articulated background of the door.

If the squinting eyes are directed to objects in the room, showing little difference in brightness, the commonest initial effect is that each object is seen in part, as if each has had to sacrifice a part of its substance in order to occupy its share of the available space. If the inspection is continued for a minute or more, the conflict between the incompatible engrams is likely to be temporarily settled in favor of one object, which then stands out clearly, while the other has completely vanished. A very slow binocular rivalry then ensues. Only occasionally small parts of the two objects appear to occupy the same space, as in a photographic double exposure.

The binocular rivalry induced by presenting different colors to the two eyes is completely consistent with the theory. Alternation is rapid to begin with, but as the afferent energy is reduced by prolonged stimulation, the competition between the incompatible engrams becomes weaker, and the rate of alternation becomes progressively slower. The suppressed color then often makes its first appearance in a corner and slowly invades the field, sometimes being driven back before it conquers the whole area. The dependence of the rate of alternation on the energy fed into the afferent system was demonstrated in my very first piece of research, reported to the British Association for the Advancement of Science in 1921.

Instead of reflected light I used light transmitted through glass filters mounted in the focal plane of a stereoscopic camera. The source of light was a brightly illuminated sheet of milk glass in front of the camera, and the intensity of the light transmitted through the filters could be controlled by means of the iris diaphragms in the lenses. A stereoscope was mounted in a suitable position behind the camera. With the diaphragms wide open, the subject looked through the stereoscope for a specified period of time, recording the alternations by pressing a button. At the end of the prescribed period he immediately transferred his right eye to the left side of the stereoscope (or his left eye to the right side), and adjusted the diaphragm until the brightness of the color seen by the eye that was fresh to it was subjectively equal to that seen a moment ago by the eye that had been exposed to it. The diaphragm was left in this position, and after complete recovery from the initial stimulation the subject once more looked into the stereoscope. The rate of alternation at the beginning of the objectively reduced illumination was the same as it had been at the end of the preceding period of exposure to strong illumination. My conclusion then was that the rate of alternation was a function of the subjective intensity of the light, which in turn was a function of the objective intensity and a decreasing function of the duration of exposure to it. This may be summed up by saying that the rate of alternation is a function of the energy fed to the conflicting engrams.

One of the most interesting studies of the effect of presenting to the two eyes different stimuli that yet have something in common has been reported by Pettigrew, Allport, and Barnett (1958). Although their study refers to the perception of race, and therefore involves a higher level of behavioral organization than that with which we have been mainly concerned, nevertheless their results are readily explainable in terms of the behavioral theory.

Their stimuli were twenty pairs of passport photographs, each of which was viewed in a stereoscope for two seconds. The photographs represented European (white), colored (mixed race), Indian, and African faces, male and female. Each pair showed two male or two female faces. A male face of each race was paired with another male face of the same race and also with male faces of each of the other three races, and female faces were similarly paired. The subjects were resident in or near the city of Durban in South Africa, and included samples of all four races depicted in the photographs. They were required simply to judge the race of the "person" seen in the stereoscope.

We shall consider here only the judgments given when one of the faces was European and the other African. There are two obvious possibilities. Either one of the stimuli determines the response to the exclusion of the other, in which case either a white or a black face will be seen; or elements of both stimuli will contribute, and the face will be perceived as that of a person of mixed race. Since the shortness of the exposure time prevented binocular rivalry, it may be assumed that the readiness for response evoked by the ambiguous stimuli would be determined by the subjects' general behavior toward the several racial groups in the country. And since the structure of South African society has the effect that each group has its own characteristic patterns of behavior toward the races that make up the population, it was to be expected that group differences in response to the ambiguous stimuli would be revealed.

The major behavioral differences arise from the fact that the whites alone have political power, and exercise that power for their own economic advantage. But the picture is complicated by an important fact, not mentioned by the authors. Many of the whites, and particularly those whose families have been in the country for some generations, are in fact "colored," and have the appearance of being colored, although they are classified as Europeans. Similarly, many of the people who are classified as colored might, on their looks, easily be considered as European. Thus facial appearance alone is a very unsafe guide to a person's legal classification. Consequently the response of describing a person as colored on the basis of visual evidence alone tends to be inhibited. A white child who described as colored a person who is accepted as white would be reprimanded, and the repetition of this experience would have the effect of inhibiting the response.

The results reported by the authors show, in fact, that European subjects responded to the European-African pairs of stimuli more frequently by reporting either European or African than by reporting a mixture. In the other groups of subjects the distribution of the responses was reversed.

CHAPTER 8

Experimental Evidence

8.1. If Ashby's theory of the multistable system applies to an organism equipped with a brain, it follows that the properties acquired by the system are not fixed and immutable like the laws of the Medes and the Persians. The system continues to be adaptable, and in particular will adjust itself to any experimentally imposed transformation of one or more of its variables. One way of doing this is by surgical interference with the afferent or efferent system, but there are various objections to techniques of this kind. Drastic operations such as turning the eyeballs upside down can be performed only on dumb animals, which are incapable of reporting on their perceptual experience, or have a much simpler nervous system than man, so that they are incapable of achieving the adaptation that might be relatively easy for a man. Less drastic operations, such as Head's classical experiment in which he severed the radial nerve of his left arm and allowed it to regenerate, have the disadvantage that we cannot get an exact description of the transformation. When a nerve is severed we cannot guarantee that each fiber will follow the same channel as before the operation. There is even greater uncertainty when two nerves are crossed.

These difficulties are completely avoided by experiments in which an afferent function is temporarily transformed by some device that operates on stimulus energies from the environment before they reach the receptors, such as spectacles or pseudophones. Such devices can be applied to human subjects without causing any damage, although they may involve a good deal of temporary inconvenience, including motion sickness in some cases. But their most outstanding advantage is that we can have exact knowledge of the manner in which they transform the relevant afferent functions, so that we can calculate their effects on the sets Q, F, and Φ. (Since only mature subjects are used, it will be understood that all references to these sets are to their most highly developed forms. They will not therefore be distinguished by the subscripts previously used.) Hence we can calculate the errors of both behavior and perception that are induced when the device is applied for the first time to any subject.

8.2. The assumption that the system is multistable then enables us to calculate the changes in behavior that are induced by prolonged wearing of the device. In making this calculation we must be guided by our knowledge of the specific system of drives operating in each particular subject. Behavioral errors that are of primary importance in one subject may be of negligible significance in another, so that the details of behavioral adaptation are likely to vary from one subject to another. We have taken no account of individual differences in genetic equipment in our discussion of the development of perception in infancy and childhood, since our main purpose there was to discover the basic principles that are applicable to all multistable organic systems. But when it becomes necessary to test our theory by experimenting on mature subjects it is no longer permissible to neglect individual differences. For an experiment is performed not on a piece of raw material that may be expected to have essentially the same properties as any other sample of the same raw material. In each case the experimental subject is a highly complex multistable system that has long ago completed the adaptations discussed in the previous chapters, and has gone on from there to further stages of adaptation that tend to vary more and more extensively. Even if those new adaptations have no obvious bearing on the subsystems with which we choose to interfere experimentally, they may have important effects on the manner in which the subject adapts to the experimental conditions. To take an obvious example, a man who leads a sedentary life will be handicapped in a very different way from one who is constantly active, and the course of adaptation to one and the same transformation may therefore be expected to be different in the two cases.

The neglect of these considerations may lead to serious theoretical errors, as, for example when Hebb (1949) assumes that the development of visual perception in infancy follows much the same course as it does in congenitally blind subjects who have had their vision restored by removal of cataracts. In these subjects adaptation of the visual subsystem takes place after the rest of the system has achieved a satisfactory measure of stability. In particular, the subject is able to move about in his environment in response to a variety of stimuli, including unstructured retinal stimuli, so that after the operation the system that is to be adapted is a very much more complex one than in the helpless infant. Retinal stimuli are modified not only by movements of the eyes and head, but also by movements of the trunk, by standing and sitting, and by walking; and this implies that proprioceptive and pressure functions of all those movements must be included in the system that is to be adapted.

Analogously, we cannot assume that the process of adaptation to reversing or distorting spectacles will be entirely independent of the state of adaptation of the system as a whole, or that the only information we need to enable us to calculate the results is an exact statement of the transformation applied to the afferent function. That statement is necessary but not sufficient. In particular we must take account of the fact that the mature subject can understand and use language. After the early developments discussed in the previous chapters language plays an increasingly important part in the adaptation of the individual to his environment. It would be strange indeed if the readaptation of one of the simpler subsystems could take place quite independently of this.

8.3. This is even more important when we try to calculate the *perceptual* results of prolonged disruption of an afferent function. For the most obvious way we have of testing our deductions is by asking the subject to describe what he perceives. But the mere fact that we have to do this means that we are placing the subject in a situation that differs in several respects from the actual situations in which the readaptation takes place. For example, if he is wearing spectacles that invert the visual field, he makes numerous errors of movement in response to the transformed retinal stimuli, and his correction of those errors is effected by the extinction of the previously established responses and the reinforcement of a new set, and this process goes on independently of any verbal responses he may make at the same time. The subsystem that is in operation includes among its variables the physical effects of the subject's encounters with the material environment.

But when, in the laboratory, he is confronted with two objects, A and B, and asked to say whether he perceives A as being above or below B, a different subsystem is in action. The variables involving physical encounters are specifically excluded, and all the emphasis is placed on a behavioral system that plays a relatively minor part in the actual process of readaptation. If these laboratory tests constitute a regular part of the experimental routine, our calculations should be extended to include any possible effects they may have on perception. Clearly we cannot rule out in advance the possibility that such tests may modify the subject's behavior in some significant manner.

In short, the system on which we propose to experiment is vastly more complex than that which we have assumed to be active in infancy, so that while the results are in general calculable, we are likely to find some irregularity, because of course we shall not always know beforehand what hitherto unsuspected sources of perturbation are active in any specific subject. Consequently, if irregularities are found, that does not necessarily prove that the theory is false, since it may only mean that an essential variable has been neglected. On the other hand, if certain distinguishing characteristics of the subject are known, and we can deduce that these will affect the course of behavioral adaptation in a distinctive manner, the theory can be subjected to a searching test. For in that case we can calculate that the perceptual field must have distinctive properties corresponding to the behavioral peculiarities. If such deductions are not confirmed, the theory is condemned.

8.4. Apparently, the first man to propose an experiment with spectacles was Berkeley. In his *Commonplace Book* he wonders what would happen if an infant were fitted with "inverting perspectives" at birth. He does not venture to make any predictions, but if we may judge from the argument of *A New Theory of Vision*, it is reasonable to think he would have expected perception of the spatial ordering of the environment to be normal. It is interesting to note, however, that by stipulating that the spectacles be worn from birth he was, by implication, excluding the possibility that a subject could first learn to perceive the world as erect with normal retinal stimulation and could subsequently learn to see it erect with reversed stimulation.

It was not until nearly two centuries later that the first experiment with inverting spectacles was actually performed. Stratton (1897) constructed a monocular system of lenses that rotated the retinal stimulus through an angle of 180°, thus simultaneously inverting it and reversing right and left. He wore his spectacles for two periods, the second and longer one extending over eight days, and kept a diary recording his experiences, which is still well worth reading. The experiment was prompted not by any specific hypothesis regarding the genesis of space perception, but rather by the absence of any rational explanation of the fact that the world is perceived as erect despite the fact that the retinal image is inverted. Its purpose was nothing more than exploratory and Stratton himself apparently did not appreciate the full significance of what he found, for he did not follow it up.

Nevertheless Stratton's experiment deserves to be remembered as the most important experiment in the whole history of psychology, for it shattered once and for all the doctrine, widely held up to that time, that visual perception is a function of retinal stimulation alone. This implication has been strongly resisted by nativists, who have relied on certain ambiguities in Stratton's statements to prove that he never saw the world erect while wearing his spectacles. I shall not attempt to deny the ambiguity, for the simple reason that the doctrine is shattered by other statements in the report that are completely unequivocal.

Almost the first thing that Stratton observed when he put on his spectacles was that rotation of his head about its vertical axis caused the visual field to sweep past his eyes in the direction of the head movement but at twice the speed. This in itself constitutes a contradiction of nativist doctrine, for it implies that the direction in which the head rotates and the direction in which the images sweep across the retina are *both* involved in the perception of the world as stationary. But there is a more devastating result to come. As the experiment continued, the impression that the world was sweeping past his eyes became progressively less marked. On the sixth day there was only slight movement, and in the diary for the last two days there is no mention of it. There was, of course, no physical change; at the end of the experiment the images were sweeping across the retina in exactly the same way as at the beginning. Nevertheless this sequence of stimuli that originally gave rise to perception of a moving environment now evoked perception of a stationary world.

There is some ambiguity in Stratton's report that makes it difficult to be certain that he saw the world erect through his lenses; but there is no need to discuss the question, since other experiments, to be described below, have established beyond any doubt that the inverted perceptual field can be righted. On the other hand, the stabilizing of the initially unstable perceptual field is a fact that has been clearly stated and never questioned. That fact alone is enough to shatter the nativist doctrine. Stratton's experiment may not have established a new theory of perception, but it cleared the way for one by demolishing a false theory.

8.5. Stratton was acutely aware of the disruption of his overt behavior induced by the wearing of his lenses and of the progressive changes in this respect that took place in the course of the experiment, but it apparently did not occur to him that this had anything to do with the perceptual changes he reported. Fortunately, however, neither did he entertain the theory that simple exposure to reversed stimulation would be sufficient to induce a perceptual change, and consequently he made no effort to avoid normal encounters with his environment. He did not call on anyone to assist him or to protect him from the dangers to which he was exposed, except when he went for walks. He did not employ an amanuensis to record his observations but laboriously wrote them with his own hand. His everyday life therefore gave him ample opportunity for correcting at least some of the errors of behavior induced by the lenses. Thus there is nothing in Stratton's experiment to contradict the theory presented in this book.

An obvious test of the theory would be to perform a control experiment in which opportunities for behavioral adaptation are reduced to a minimum. If in this case no perceptual changes are reported, the results will be in agreement with the theory without adding much weight to it. If, on the contrary, both instability and inversion of the perceptual field are corrected, this will constitute a definite and final refutation of the theory.

It is, of course, extremely difficult to keep a subject entirely inactive, so that no adaptations of any kind are open to him. But an experiment in which the activity of the subjects was greatly curtailed was performed by Ewert (1930) some thirty years after Stratton's work. He was primarily interested in the effects of inverted stimulation on behavior and the process of correcting the behavioral errors induced by inverting spectacles. Accordingly he devised a series of tests and training procedures that occupied a substantial proportion of each day during which the subjects wore the spectacles. In most of the tests the subjects were seated, and were required to respond to stimuli verbally or by pointing with a finger, so that only a limited subsystem was active, and there was little opportunity for extensive interaction with the environment.

For example, in one test the subject was confronted with a screen divided into 16 squares. Two identical buzzers were placed on different squares, and one of them was sounded. The subject's head was held in a headrest, so that only ocular movements were available to him. He was required to name the square from which the sound was coming, and for this purpose what appeared to him to be the top row was to be named A, and what he saw as the left column was to be named 1. The spectacles were similar to Stratton's, but binocular, so that the field was rotated through 180°, and what the subject saw as the top left-hand square was actually the bottom right-hand square.

When the buzzers were placed symmetrically, that is, so that a rotation of the whole display through 180° in the plane of the screen would leave the visual pattern unchanged, the answers were nearly always correct, and there was no change in the proportion of correct answers throughout the experiment. The reason is quite simple. The subject saw the silent buzzer in the position from which the sound appeared to be coming, and named its square. As seen by the experimenter, this was the square occupied by the sounding buzzer, and the answer was recorded as being correct.

It will be seen that in this test the subject has literally no opportunity for correcting errors due to inverted vision. His head is immobilized, so that movements designed to fixate points involve the eyes alone, and these are just as invariably successful as if he were scanning an object that has been turned upside down. The only other behavior called for is a verbal response. Ewert does not say whether the subject was informed of his results. If he was not informed there could be no learning, and if he was informed he was in a sense misinformed, since the buzzer he *saw* as the source of the sound was actually the silent one.

The purpose of this test was to check a statement by Stratton that with prolonged practice audition swings into line with vision. Experiments subsequently performed by Erismann (reported in Kohler, 1951) and others have shown that it is vision that swings into line with audition; but for this to happen the whole system must be active. In Ewert's test many of the most important variables were held constant, so that the results can tell us virtually nothing about the state of adaptation of the system as a whole. For example, the headrest prevented the subject from turning his head so as to reduce the binaural differences to zero. If he had been able to do this, the sounding buzzer would have come into the center of his visual field, and in that case he would have given an answer that was true in the sense that he was correctly describing its position in his field; but the experimenter would have recorded it as false.

The test that seemed to involve the greatest amount of activity was a card-sorting test. The cards were numbered at both ends, so that the retinal stimulus they presented was the same as if no spectacles were worn, and no difficulty was experienced in reading the numbers. The time required for each sorting was recorded. At first, inversion interfered very markedly with the activity, but improvement was rapid, and for all subjects the learning curve showed the usual exponential form. When the spectacles were removed there was no aftereffect: on the contrary, the scores were better than on the last day of inversion.

Ewert thought this result contradicted Stratton's observation that motor habits were markedly disrupted after removal of the lenses, but this conclusion is unwarranted. What the subjects had learned to do was to react to the number on a card held in the left hand by moving the card with the right hand through one of nine trajectories, the path being predetermined by the number seen before the beginning of the movement and not by the position of the same number in the compartment at the end of the trajectory. On the restoration of normal vision, the conditioned stimuli for those nine motor habits were exactly the same as before, and the nine compartments still occupied the same positions at the ends of the nine trajectories.

But why should the performance have improved? The answer depends on the fact that the field of the spectacles was not wide enough to take in the whole of the sorting tray, so that movements of the head were frequently necessary to get a clear view of the goal. This means that it was not only a movement of the right hand that was conditioned to the seen number, but a movement of the head as well. Now this latter movement retained its objective validity on removal of the lenses from their tubes, so that the subject was already looking in the right direction when his hand was approaching the goal. But whereas, with the lenses in, the inversion still induced some hesitation in the final placing of the card, very little interference remained when the lenses were removed, because the subject had already spent two periods of an hour each without the lenses before taking the sorting test. It is true that he wore the lenses for two hours immediately before the test, but no serious work was done during that time, whereas the two hours without the lenses were devoted to testing. Thus the only possible source of postexperimental disruption of behavior had already been broken down to some extent.

Very little is said about the behavior of the subjects outside the laboratory, but we are told that an experimenter accompanied two of the subjects most of the time and one of them all the time, recording their observations and comments. This probably means that they were protected from many of the risks to which they would otherwise have been exposed, and thereby prevented from making full adaptation to the new patterns of stimulation. One form of behavior was specifically excluded: they were not permitted to write, on the rather strange ground that this would have involved the reinstatement of existing habits instead of building up new ones.

We can conclude then that the restrictions imposed on the subject's behavior, both outside the laboratory and more particularly in it, were so extensive that a complete reorganization of the perceptual field was virtually impossible. If, in spite of these restrictions, the subjects had reported that the world was perceived as erect, the behavioral theory would thereby be exposed to grave suspicion. In fact, nothing of the kind was reported. The final series of tests was designed to determine whether there was any reinversion of the field. The results were uniformly negative, although on two occasions one of the subjects gave a correct answer and immediately reversed it.

8.6. A few years before Ewert's work, Erismann began, in the

University of Innsbruck, a long series of experiments (reported in Kohler, 1951) on the prolonged wearing of spectacles of various kinds. He was subsequently joined by Kohler, and this brilliant and fruitful partnership has produced a wealth of knowledge that cannot fail to have the most far-reaching effects not only on the psychology of perception but on psychology in general. Erismann was the first investigator to follow up Stratton's lead, and the first to extend the field of investigation to other transformations of the retinal stimulus. He was in fact the first to recognize that Stratton's technique could be used not only to answer the rather restricted and even trivial question why the inverted retinal image yields perception of the world as erect, but as an instrument for the systematic investigation of perception.

The planning of his earliest experiments was apparently guided by the belief that the changes in perception reported by Stratton were closely bound up with the restoration of behavior adequately adapted to the environment, and although he has subsequently found evidence that has prompted him, mistakenly as I hope to show, to modify this belief, it was precisely this belief that was responsible for his work being so fruitful. For, in the first place, it led him to search for a less complex transformation than that produced by Stratton's lenses, which not only invert the field but reverse right and left as well, thus disrupting two dimensions of behavior. Accordingly he set about devising spectacles that would invert the field while leaving the right-left dimension unchanged. Later, spectacles that reverse right and left were constructed.

Second, having constructed a suitable instrument, he insisted that his subjects should not content themselves with gazing at the world through it but should go out and engage in the widest possible range of activities. Thus they were encouraged to walk along busy streets from the earliest possible moment. A companion was provided for the first walk, but thereafter the only protection was a walking stick and an armband such as is worn by the blind in Austria. Those protections were removed as soon as the subject could walk with confidence. He was then encouraged to undertake increasingly complex and even hazardous activities, such as riding a bicycle, mountain climbing, and skiing. For example, Kohler, while wearing spectacles that reverse right and left, designed a piece of electronic equipment, drew the circuit diagram, and built the apparatus, soldering all the joints, and without a guardian to protect him against making contact with the business end of the soldering iron.

Some of the subjects who volunteered for these extremely strenuous experiments found the discomfort unbearable and resigned after a day or two, but those who survived the initial difficulties ultimately reported changes of perception. In *every* case the positional instability of the perceptual field disappeared gradually, as it had done in Stratton's experiment, and in all but one case the world was ultimately seen the right way round. This latter change, however, had a different kind of gradualness. No change was observed for some days during which errors of overt behavior were gradually eliminated, and then the inverted world was suddenly seen as being erect, just as the appearance of an ambiguous figure such as the Schröder staircase suddenly changes. This impression lasted, as a rule, only for a moment, but as the experiment went on the duration of such experiences increased until finally perception of the world as erect was continuous. If our theory is correct these results should all be directly deducible from it, including the exceptional case in which the world was not perceived the right way round.

8.7. As a preliminary to this it will first be necessary to arrive at a clear understanding of the nature of the transformation applied to the afferent functions, V_1 and V_2. This depends on the kind of spectacles used, and it will therefore be convenient to treat each type separately. Let us assume then that the spectacles are in the form of total-reflecting prisms mounted in a suitable frame and placed in front of the eyes so that their bases are in a plane orthogonal to the vertical axis of the head. When the head is erect and the vertical deviation of the eyes is zero, a point at the same level as the eyes will stimulate a point on the retinal x-axis. Under these conditions the element of $\overline{V}_1$ involving the objective point in question is identical with the corresponding element of V_1 when no spectacles are worn. We shall use the symbol $\overline{V}_1$ to designate the set V_1 as transformed by the spectacles.

To determine the other elements of $\overline{V}_1$ we first assume that the head and eyes are held stationary. If θ is the angle between an approaching ray of light and the plane of the base of the prism, the angle at which it emerges from the prism to enter the eye is $-\theta$. There is no change in the angle it makes with the median plane of the head. Thus, with the orientation of head and eyes postulated in the last paragraph, the coordinates of the retinal image of any point in the environment will be (x, —y) instead of (x,y).

If, still without movement of the head, the eyes are now allowed to fixate any point whose objective position is (x,y), this movement will have to be through the angles (x, —y), instead of (x,y) as in normal circumstances. Hence any element of $\overline{V}_1$ involving a given δ, such that the image of this δ falls on the fovea, is equal to an element of V_1 involving a δ' whose y coordinate is equal to that of δ but opposite in sign.

Since the spectacles move with the head, any backward or forward tilt of the head through an angle ψ, say, means that the angle between an approaching ray of light and the base of the prism changes from y to $(y - \psi)$. The prism reflects this ray, and the angle at which it enters the eye is $-(y - \psi) = (-y + \psi)$. Without spectacles it enters at the angle $(y - \psi)$. To discover the objective position of the δ' that will give an element of V_1 identical with the element of $\overline{V}_1$ involving this δ, we note first that the initial position of δ must be (x, —y). If the object were stationary the rotation ψ would change this to $(x, -y - \psi)$, and in order to give $(x, -y + \psi)$, the object would have to move so that its y coordinate is changed by the addition of 2ψ. That is, only a moving object could produce the sequence of elements of V_1 identical with the elements of $\overline{V}_1$ that result from a tilt of the head in front of a stationary environment.

Finally, we must consider the effect of tilting the head toward a shoulder. A diagram will make clear what happens. Figure 8.7.1 shows the position on the retina of the image of a stationary cross when the head is erect (A) and when it is tilted 45° to the right (B). In each case the horizontal line (broken in B) represents the direction of the retinal X axis. It will be seen that rotating the head to the right has the effect that the retinal image of the cross rotates in the opposite direction. Figure 8.7.2 shows what happens when inverting spectacles are worn. Since the reflecting surface is always parallel to the retinal X axis, the images in Figure 8.7.2 can be derived from the corresponding images in Figure 8.7.1 by transferring each point from its position (x,y) in Figure 8.7.1 to the position (x, —y) in Figure 8.7.2. It is evident that in Figure 8.7.2 position B is arrived at by rotating the image in A in a *clockwise* direction through an angle of 45°, that is, in the same direction as the rotation of the head.

It is clear that the elements of $\overline{V}_1$ that occur in position A correspond exactly to elements of V_1 (that is, without spectacles) that would be produced by a cross in which the vertical line is inverted as in position A of Figure 8.7.2. But in order that this object should give rise to elements of V_1 identical with the elements of $\overline{V}_1$ arising in position B of Figure 8.7.2, it would have to be rotated in a clockwise direction through an angle of 90° while the head is tilting to the right through an angle of 45°. In general, if the head is tilted through an angle ϕ, while the spectacles are on, the resulting elements of $\overline{V}_1$ are identical with elements of V_1 that would be produced if, during the rotation of the head, the object itself were rotated through an angle of 2ϕ.

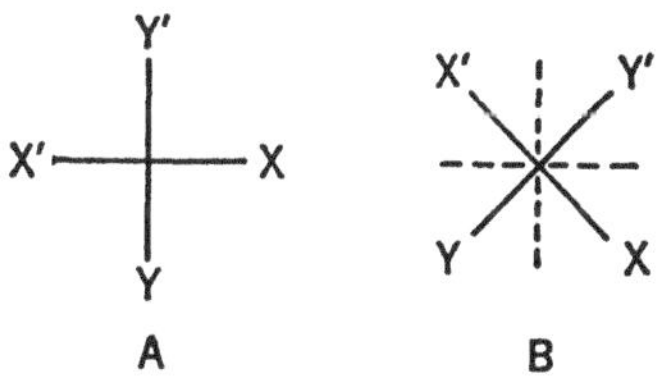

FIGURE 8.7.1.

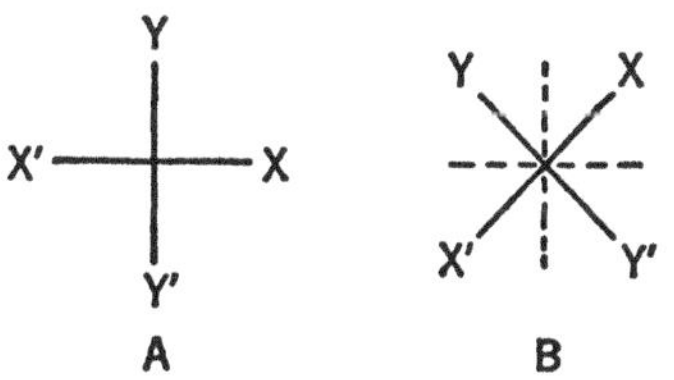

FIGURE 8.7.2.

The reader who is versed in mathematics will have found this description of $\overline{V}_1$ in terms of elements of V_1 intolerably prolix. He will find in the Mathematical Appendix a single expression that sums up all the results recorded in this section.

8.8 We are now able to deduce the immediate perceptual effects of wearing inverting spectacles. The reader may consider that such a deduction is quite superfluous, since the information can be obtained directly and more easily by simply putting on the spectacles. But the purpose of the deduction is not to obtain information but to test the validity of the theory.

The procedure is to substitute for the elements of $\overline{V}_1$ the elements of V_1 that have the identical afferent processes, and follow these elements through the sets of S, Q, F, Φ, and Π. Now an element of V_1 specifies an element $\delta \varepsilon \Delta$ as well as an afferent process in the optic tracts, and an element of Q containing this $v \varepsilon V_1$ is, by F, conditioned to responses that result in (a) fixation of δ, and (b) a movement of the hand that terminates at δ. By Φ, the engrams mediating these responses put the organism into a state of readiness for the responses in question, and by Π the organism perceives the positions of the several objects in the environment.

Since the δ specified by $v \in \overline{V}_1$ is not, except in rare cases, identical with the δ specified by the $v \in V_1$ having the identical afferent processes, it follows that the responses specified by the corresponding $f \in F$ will in general be misdirected, and consequently Π will not reflect the true positions of objects in the environment. The actual errors of perception can be deduced directly from the analysis of $\overline{V}_1$ in 8.7. The results may be summed up in five propositions.

(8.8.1) The field is perceived as inverted.

(8.8.2) Perceived positions are stable under rotation of the eyes provided the head is stationary.

(8.8.3) The field is stable under rotation of the head about its vertical axis.

(8.8.4) Backward and forward tilting of the head has the effect that the field is perceived as sweeping past the eyes in the direction of the head movement but at double the speed.

(8.8.5) Tilting the head toward a shoulder has the effect that the field is perceived as rotating about the axis of rotation of the head in the same direction as the head movement but twice as fast.

These statements are in complete agreement with observation.

8.9. The elements of Q incorporating elements of $\overline{V}_1$ give rise, by F, to conditioned reaching responses that are misdirected. The general direction of the error is indicated by statement 1 in 8.8, but statements 4 and 5 imply that the error with respect to any particular object varies quantitatively with rotations of the head in its median plane and with tilting of the head toward a shoulder. Statement 2 implies that the error is constant under rotation of the eyes while the head is stationary, and statement 3 that it is constant under rotation of the head about its vertical axis.

At the same time it is important to observe that fixation responses continue to be completely successful so long as they involve eye movements alone. But if an object appears to be near the upper or lower edge of the restricted visual field, and the subject makes a combined movement of head and eyes, the appropriate element of F shows that the movement of the head will be misdirected. The effect of this response is that the object moves right out of the visual field instead of coming into the center.

It follows that virtually all reaching responses evoked under F will be extinguished, and similarly the capital components of some fixation responses will be extinguished. Fixation responses involving ocular movements alone or including rotations of the head about its vertical axis will continue to be reinforced. (It is worth noting that if the prisms were incorporated in contact lenses, so that they moved with the eyes, the oculomotor components of fixation responses would be misdirected and would therefore be equally subject to extinction.)

Now this gives rise to a very interesting situation, in which certain elements are eliminated from F, while other elements, associated with the same elements of Q, are retained. To understand what this means, let us confine our attention for the moment to those elements of F in which fixation responses involve only oculomotor activity. Let F_0 be the subset of F for which this condition holds. Each $f \varepsilon F_0$ specifices a $q \varepsilon Q$ that is conditioned both to a reaching response and to a fixation response. Prior to the beginning of the experiment there was no conflict between these two sets of responses, and the engrams mediating them collaborated in determining perception of the environment. Now, however, they are at variance with one another. The perceived positions as determined by the fixation responses do not agree with the positions to which the hand must be directed in order to make contact with the objects. Nevertheless the fixation responses are always successful and therefore always reinforced. Consequently the perceptual field is for a long time dominated by the subsystem of F_0 that suffers no modification as a result of wearing the spectacles.

At the same time the subsystem of F_0 that involves reaching responses suffers rapid disintegration and is replaced by another subsystem in which the elements of Q are conditioned to different elements of M(A), i.e. reaching responses. This is necessarily a gradual process, both because a great many new responses have to be acquired, and because, according to Hullian theory, the strength of the new connections increases as a negatively accelerated exponential function of the number of reinforcements. Thus, although these new responses would, according to our theory, tend to establish a new, and veridical, perception of the spatial ordering of the environment, this cannot be done all at once, partly because of the initial relative weakness of the new connections and partly because the subsystem of Π that depends on the oculomotor subsystem of F_o remains intact. The new subsystem is not yet strong enough to interpenetrate with this intact subsystem and impose its frame of reference on it.

8.10. There are two other factors that must now be taken into consideration. The first depends on the fact that not all fixation responses can be carried out by ocular movements alone, and the narrow field of the spectacles greatly increases the number of occasions when a movement of the head is necessary. Let us therefore consider $F_c = F - F_o$, as the subset of F involving compound fixation responses. As we have seen already, the capital components of these responses carry the image of the object out of the visual field, and are therefore subject to extinction. New responses, carrying the head in the opposite direction, must therefore be reinforced. These new responses, although they are only part of the total fixation response, are nevertheless in agreement with the new reaching responses and therefore tend to favor the interpenetration that should impose on Π the frame of reference derived from the newly acquired behavior. This frame of reference, it must be remembered, ultimately depends on gravity.

The second factor is language. This obviously played no part in the building up of the system as described in the earlier chapters, but as the experimental subject is a mature human being we cannot assume that his linguistic habits are irrevelant to our problem. Before he started the experiment he acquired, in addition to reaching and fixation responses, certain verbal responses to elements of Q, including responses descriptive of the relative positions of objects in the environment. More particularly relevant to our present inquiry are responses describing A as being above B or below B, as the case may be. When the spectacles are put on those responses continue to give a true description of the direction in which the eyes must be moved to secure fixation, but they are false when considered as a description of the direction in which the hand must be moved to secure contact. They are thus reinforced by one set of results and extinguished by another set.

If we assume that there are no complicating factors, we can predict the outcome of this conflicting reinforcement. The words "up" and "down" describe not only the relative positions of objects in space but also the directions in which the hands move relative to the gravitational axis. Now an upward movement of the hand within the visual field generates a succession of elements of $\overline{V}_1$ and if there were no proprioception accompanying the movement, these elements of $\overline{V}_1$ would without question evoke the verbal description "downward." But in fact the response is not without question. There *are* proprioceptive impulses, and these give rise to elements of $\Pi(G)$, by which the movement is perceived as being upward. Thus the verbal responses "up" and "down" both tend to be extinguished, and a state of indeterminacy is likely to ensue. The subject may at times perceive himself as being inverted in an erect world. This has, in fact, been reported in some of the Innsbruck experiments. It is not, of course, entirely due to verbal responses. In the process of extinguishing the faulty reaching responses and establishing new ones, a stage must be reached in which new and old responses are about equally balanced in strength. If the opposing verbal responses are in a similar state of equilibrium, it is understandable that the subject does not know whether he is standing on his head or his feet.

As the new reaching responses became more firmly established, verbal responses to visual stimuli are more consistently negatived by responses descriptive of the direction in which the hand or the body has to move to reach a goal, with the result that in the end the visual stimuli become conditioned to verbal responses that are descriptive of the true positions of objects in space rather than the direction of eye movements. When this happens, all the responses conditioned to elements of $\underline{Q}$ are in harmony with one another and the result is that the world is perceived as erect. This is likely to occur, as Stratton found and the Innsbruck experiments have amply demonstrated, when the subject is actively engaged in adjusting himself to his environment. This activity supplies a drive that tends to activate the new engrams rather than the old ones. But as soon as the subject realizes what has happened, he is likely to stop the action in which he was engaged and ask himself whether it was really true. This tends to reinstate the old verbal responses to the visual stimuli, with the result that the world is once again perceived as inverted.

As the new verbal responses become more strongly conditioned to retinal stimuli, the periods of erect perception must increase in duration until finally the world is perceived as erect all the time. This is in complete agreement with the findings of Erismann and Kohler.

8.11. It may well happen, however, that special circumstances intervene to prevent the development described in 8.10, by reinforcing the original verbal responses to $\overline{V}_1$. One of the Innsbruck subjects who wore right-left reversing spectacles for 71 days, and subsequently inverting spectacles for a shorter period, achieved satisfactory behavioral adjustment in both cases but denied that he ever perceived the world the right way round through his spectacles. He described to me the technique he employed when, in the course of laboratory tests, he was asked to state the relative positions of objects as he perceived them. He defined the positions of the edges of his visual field as being next to his forehead, his nose, his right temple, and his left temple. Since those parts were not in his visual field, except when looking in a mirror, they constituted a frame of reference that remained invariant throughout the experiment. Since $\overline{V}_1$ is determined by the physical properties of the system and therefore remains invariant, it follows that any verbal response to an element of $\overline{V}_1$ that related this element to the frame of reference provided by the head also remained invariant throughout the experiment. Thus any tendency to the conditioning of veridical verbal responses to elements of $\overline{V}_1$ was counteracted by the use of a frame of reference that was irrelevant to all the other activities in which the subject engaged.

Erismann and Kohler were puzzled by the failure of this subject to report the righting of the perceptual field that had been found in all other subjects who survived the initial rigors of the experiment, and they devised a variety of ingenious tests in the hope of demonstrating that the field was in fact perceived the right way round. Apparently the only effect of this multiplication of tests was to reinforce still further the subject's laboratory behavior. Not one of them succeeded in evoking the expected response.

This experiment is particularly instructive, because the clear evidence that the subject's failure to perceive the world the right way round was associated with a specific mode of verbal behavior supports the hypothesis that the intermittent righting of the visual world is attributable to the gradual conditioning of verbal responses adapted to the true positions of objects in space. This particular subject's verbal responses were adapted not to the true positions of objects in space but to the positions of visual images relative to an artificial reference frame that was entirely irrelevant to his everyday commerce with the environment. The experiment was instructive in other respects as well, as we shall see in the next section.

8.12. We must next consider the perceptual instabilities described in statements (8.8.4) and (8.8.5). These instabilities arise, as we have seen, from the fact that the relevant rotations of the head cause the elements of $\overline{V}_1$ to change in the opposite direction to the corresponding elements of V_1 when no spectacles are worn. The result is that the reaching responses directed to objects in the environment are subject to variable errors. But as these errors are not random but systematic, they are relatively easy to correct. In fact they are automatically corrected simultaneously with the correction of the errors that arise from the inversion of the field.

To calculate the effect that this will have on perception we need only consider patterns of stimulation involving a single object occupying a fixed position in space. We may simplify the calculation by assuming that every time the subject reacts to this object its position relative to his body is the same, and also that his hand always starts from the same position. This will enable us to neglect those components of S that depend on the position of the trunk and the initial position of the hand. Since, by (8.8.2) and (8.8.3), stability is unaffected by movements of the eyes and by rotations of the head about its vertical axis, we may also neglect the proprioceptive functions, V_3, V_4, V_5, and V_6. Finally, it will be convenient to consider one source of instability at a time and to prohibit the subject from making movements of the head that give rise to the other type of instability. Thus we may allow him to move his head freely in its median plane but not to tilt his head toward either shoulder.

These restrictions enable us to write in a simplified form the elements of $\overline{S}$ that include elements of $\overline{V}_1$ arising from a single $\delta \epsilon \Delta$. We simply omit all reference to the variables that are irrelevant or that have been deliberately held constant. We must, however, specify with more precision than has hitherto been necessary the values of the elements of $\overline{V}_1$, and of V_7, the proprioceptive function of the position of the head in its median plane. The relevant components of $\overline{V}_2$ are the same as in $\overline{V}_1$, and $\overline{V}_2$ is therefore also omitted. In specifying the elements of $\overline{V}_1$ we can, for our present purpose, omit any reference to the x coordinate of the retinal image. The elements of $\overline{V}_1$ can thus be written simply as f(y), where y is the y coordinate of the retinal image of δ. The elements of V_7 can be written as $f(\psi)$, where ψ is the angle of tilt of the head from its vertical position, in its median plane.

If a ray of light enters the prism at an angle θ to the horizontal plane, it emerges at the angle $-\theta$. Hence if $\psi = 0$, the resulting element of $\overline{V}_1$ is $f(-\theta)$. If the head is tilted through the angle ψ_1, the ray enters the prism at the angle $(\theta - \psi_1)$ and the corresponding element of $\overline{V}_1$ is $f(-\theta + \psi_1)$. The element of $\overline{S}$ incorporating this $v \varepsilon \overline{V}_1$ may now be written as

$$(8.12.1) \quad \bar{s} = (f(-\theta + \psi_1), f(\psi_1)),$$

and the equivalence class of $\overline{S}$ determined by the chosen δ may be written as

$$(8.12.2) \quad \overline{S}(\delta) = [(f(-\theta + \psi_1), f(\psi_1)), (f(-\theta + \psi_2), f(\psi_2)), \ldots],$$

or, more simply, as

$$(8.12.3) \quad \overline{S}(\delta) = [(-\theta + \psi_1, \psi_1), (-\theta + \psi_2, \psi_2), \ldots].$$

To discover the effect that this will have on behavior when $\overline{S}(\delta)$ is written into F, it will be useful to write $S(\delta)$ in the same manner. Here the rays are not reflected before entering the eye, and hence

$$(8.12.4) \quad S(\delta) = [(\theta - \psi_1, \psi_1), (\theta - \psi_2, \psi_2), \ldots].$$

Now all the elements of $S(\delta)$ have been conditioned to the same reaching response, and we should therefore be able to discover what this invariant response is by manipulating the terms in any one of the bracketed expressions in (8.12.4). It is at once obvious that if we add the angle of the head implied by the proprioceptive function, $f(\psi)$, to the y coordinate of the retinal image implied by the retinal function, $f(\theta - \psi)$, we get the same answer, viz. θ, from every element of $S(\delta)$. And, of course, θ specifies the direction in which the hand must move to make contact with δ.

Applying this rule to (8.12.3) we get, as the direction in which the hand is conditioned to move,

$$(8.12.5) \quad (-\theta + \psi) + \psi = (-\theta + 2\psi).$$

If the spectacle field has a vertical range of 35°, this will represent the extent to which the hand may err, either upward or downward.

8.13. To predict how the subject will adapt to these unstable conditions, we must note that if $\psi = \theta$, that is, if the head is tilted so that the entering ray is parallel to the base of the prism, the resulting element of $\overline{S}(\delta)$ is identical with the corresponding element of $S(\delta)$. That is $\bar{s}(\delta) = s(\delta) = (0, \psi)$. By F, $\bar{s}(\delta)$ is conditioned to the same response as $s(\delta)$, and this response is therefore evoked and reinforced. Movements of the head from the position $\psi = \theta$ cause the response to err to a maximum extent of 35° in either direction, but it is obvious that these errors must be progressively eliminated. The largest errors will be subject to the strongest negative reinforcement and will be eliminated first. Accordingly we can deduce that the correction of errors proceeds by a gradual diminution of their range.

This implies that the elements of $\overline{S}(\delta)$ are being conditioned to responses that are approaching an invariant value, and we can deduce that if the experiment is continued long enough, this invariant response will ultimately be conditioned to all the elements of $\overline{S}(\delta)$. This means that F is replaced by a new function $\overline{F}$, determining a new $\overline{\Pi}$ that is characterized by stability, even if the field continues to be perceived as inverted. The re-inversion of the field depends, as we have seen, on the conditioning of a new set of verbal responses to $\overline{S}$, and this may or may not occur; but the stabilizing of the field must occur unless the subject is completely inactive throughout the experiment. Further, our discussion of the manner in which the errors are eliminated enables us to deduce that the stabilizing is a gradual process. This is confirmed by the reports of numerous experiments, from Stratton onward.

Additional confirmation of our hypothesis is provided by an experiment performed in Cape Town, to be described in more detail in Chapter 9. The subject wore right-left reversing spectacles, which initially produce the same kind of instability as inverting spectacles. As the experiment went on from day to day the subject reported that the instability described in (8.8.5) diminished. But he found a novel way of measuring this instability. If he tilted his head very slowly there was no apparent rotation of the perceptual field, but an increase in the speed of the movement gave rise to instability. The maximum rate of rotation below which the field remained stable increased from day to day. If the speed exceeded this maximum, the field appeared to be in motion during the movement of the head, but when the head came to rest the environment was perceived as occupying the same position as before the beginning of the movement. As the subject expressed it: "objects moved from their original position into their original position."

These phenomena are easily explained in terms of the growing strength of the new habits that were being acquired. We have already, in 3.10, appealed to the principle that if the duration of a stimulus is less than a certain threshold value it will fail to evoke the response that has been conditioned to it. We may now amplify this principle by saying that for a given intensity of stimulation the temporal threshold is a diminishing function of habit strength. That is, a longer exposure is required to evoke the response if habit strength is low. Now in the situation we are considering there are certain new habits that are growing in strength, and certain old and well-established habits, conditioned to exactly the same stimuli, that are being subjected to increasing inhibition. It is the old habits that are responsible for the instability and the new habits for the growing stability.

Let us postulate further that the inhibition of the old habits is a conditioned inhibition, and that its strength grows *pari passu* with the habit strength of the new responses. This would imply that if the duration of a stimulus is insufficient to activate the engram mediating the new response or to inhibit the engram of the old response, it may still be sufficient to energize the old engram and thereby give rise to perceptual instability. Consequently a relatively rapid movement of the head has the effect that the scene appears to be in motion, because the duration of the rapidly changing stimuli is enough to activate the old engrams but not the new ones. As soon as the head comes to rest, the stimuli can last long enough to arouse the new engrams, but because, for any δ, the $s_i \varepsilon \overline{S}$ now in operation and the $s_j \varepsilon \overline{S}$ that was in operation at the beginning of the movement are both elements of the new functional equivalence class, $\overline{S}(\delta)$, the environment is perceived as occupying the same position in space at the end of the movement as at the beginning, despite the apparent movement during the rotation of the head. Thus the paradox is resolved.

8.14. There is no need to discuss separately the disappearance of the instability that arises from tilting the head toward a shoulder. A somewhat different procedure is required for the specification of the stimuli, since both the x and y coordinates of the retinal image are changed by the rotation in question. But exactly the same principles are involved, and their application leads to the same kind of results. In the mathematical appendix a single expression is developed to specify the elements of $\bar{S}$ as determined by both types of rotation.

Similarly it is unnecessary to deal separately with spectacles that reverse right and left, or with Stratton's lenses. These are dealt with briefly in the appendix.

8.15. Finally we have to consider what must happen when the spectacles are removed after they have been worn continuously for a sufficiently long period to produce the perceptual changes discussed above. We can solve this problem by employing exactly the same procedure by which we deduced the characteristics of Π when the spectacles are first put on. That is, we must inspect the elements of $\bar{S}(\delta)$ and look for a mathematical operator that will enable us to deduce from any one of them the invariant response that has been conditioned to all of them. We then apply this operator to the elements of $S(\delta)$, which of course become operative again as soon as the spectacles are removed. As before, we shall confine our attention to the effects of movement of the head in its median plane.

For convenience I repeat here the specification of $\bar{S}(\delta)$:

$$\bar{S}(\delta) = [(-\theta + \psi_1, \psi_1), (-\theta + \psi_2, \psi_2), \ldots].$$

The invariant *reaching* response conditioned to the elements of $\bar{S}(\delta)$ moves in the direction θ, and we can easily see that this can be derived from any element by reversing the sign of the y coordinate of the retinal image and adding to it the angle of inclination of the head. Thus $-(-\theta + \psi) + \psi = \theta$. We have, however, two cases to consider with respect to the *verbal* responses conditioned to $\bar{S}(\delta)$. If the experiment terminates before new verbal responses have been firmly established, or if, as in the case discussed in 8.11, the acquisition of new verbal responses is effectively blocked, the perceived position of the object will be stable, but it will be $-\theta$ and not θ, since the verbal response describes it as being at $-\theta$. In this case therefore the appropriate operation is to *subtract* the angle of inclination of the head from the y coordinate of the retinal image. This gives $(-\theta + \psi) - \psi = -\theta$. In the event of the verbal responses being congruent with the reaching responses the operator, $-(-\theta + \psi) + \psi$, gives us the direction of the reaching response and the perceived position of the object as well.

We consider first the case in which the responses are congruent. On removing the spectacles we have

$$S(\delta) = [(\theta - \psi_1, \psi_1), (\theta - \psi_2, \psi_2), \ldots],$$

and applying to this the appropriate operator, we get

$$(8.15.1) \quad -(\theta - \psi) + \psi = -\theta + 2\psi,$$

which is exactly the same result as in (8.12.5). From this we can deduce that when the spectacles are removed the perceptual field is inverted and has exactly the same instability as when the spectacles were first put on. Strictly speaking we can deduce from (8.15.1) only the instability that arises from rotation of the head in its median plane, but in the appendix it is shown that the other instability is produced as well.

If the subject has continued throughout the experiment to perceive the world as inverted, we apply our second operator and get

$$(8.15.2) \quad (\theta - \psi) - \psi = \theta - 2\psi.$$

That is, the subject now perceives the world as erect, but it is unstable under rotation of the head in its median plane, and also, as shown in the appendix, under tilting toward a shoulder. In this case, however, the direction of the apparent movement is *opposed* to the direction of the head, as shown by the minus sign qualifying 2ψ.

The conditioned responses specified by $\overline{F}$ have not had nearly as much reinforcement as those of F, and when the spectacles are removed we may expect them to be extinguished rather quickly, thereby disinhibiting the F responses. The first to disappear will be the most recently acquired, that is, the verbal responses in subjects who perceived the world erect through the glasses. Consequently we may expect erect vision to be restored quite soon. The other responses will disappear more slowly, and evidence of their persistence will be apparent in misdirected movements. But what we are chiefly interested in is the question whether these behavioral relics of the experiment are likely to have any measurable effect on perception.

To answer this question we may consider the term 2ψ in (8.15.1) and (8.15.2). This represents not merely a perceptual error but an error in the direction of a reaching response. Such errors, we may expect, will not be corrected all at once, but will be reduced in extent as a negatively accelerated function of the number of negative reinforcements. If, therefore, we wish to describe the state of the system *after* the erroneous verbal responses have been corrected, we can do so by writing

$$(8.15.3) \quad (\theta - \psi) - f(\psi, t) = \theta - \xi$$

where ξ is a function of ψ that diminishes with t, the time elapsed since the removal of the spectacles. We can assume that ξ is a negatively accelerated exponential function of t, with zero asymptote, but its exact form is of little consequence. What is important is that if the subject is tested for the positional stability of his perceptual field after he has ceased to report inversion, (8.15.3) enables us to predict that he will perceive the field as moving in the *opposite* direction to the movement of the head, but that the extent of the movement will be substantially less than 2ψ.

Not one of the deductions listed here has been refuted, and some of them have been triumphantly confirmed. In the earlier Innsbruck experiments tests of the stability of the perceptual field were not carried out immediately after removal of the spectacles, since the experimenters were then understandably more interested in the phenomenon of inversion than in that of instability. When the field was no longer reported as being inverted, the experimenters turned their attention to the question of instability, and the answers they got were in agreement with (8.15.3).

The experiment discussed in 8.11 was carried out in 1954, and, on my suggestion, tests for stability were applied after removal of the spectacles. The results were in complete agreement with the deduction stated in (8.15.2). That is, the field was reported as moving in the *opposite* direction to the movement of the head and at twice the speed. As this is the deduction applicable to a case in which the verbal responses are not congruent with the overt motor responses, the agreement between theory and observation may be accepted as strong evidence in support of our hypothesis.

It may be of interest to report that in requesting the immediate test for stability I predicted that the result would be in accordance with (8.15.1). When, at the 13th International Congress of Psychology in Montreal, Kohler reported to me that the movement was twice as much as the head movement but in the *opposite* direction, it was he who pointed out that this was completely consistent with my prediction, because the subject had failed to perceive the world the right way round.

8.16. It would require several volumes to do justice to the immense wealth of experimental evidence accumulated by the Innsbruck School of Psychology. I shall limit myself here to one finding that illustrates in a striking manner the principle of multistability.[1] Two subjects who wore spectacles that reverse right and left ultimately reported that they perceived the world the right way round. But the reversal was not complete in every detail. A building on the right-hand side of a street was correctly perceived as being on the right, but an inscription on one of its walls was perceived as being mirrored. Even when correct perception of the spatial ordering of the environment had become continuous, printed matter continued to be perceived as mirrored. One of the experiments was terminated at this stage, but the other one was continued for several days longer, and in the end the subject reported that printed matter was no longer seen as mirrored.

The reader will find it an interesting exercise to postulate a system that will generate these results.

1. Personal communication.

Mathematical Appendix

BY SEYMOUR PAPERT[1]

In order to calculate the effects of wearing spectacles that reverse the retinal image along the vertical axis or the horizontal axis or both, it will be convenient to adopt certain simplifying fictions. We shall assume that the subject is monocular, and that all movements of his head can be executed in such a manner that the position of his eye relative to the environment remains constant. This enables us to choose the node of the eye as the common origin of three frames of reference, one for the external scene, one for the retina, and one for the head.

To define these frames of reference, let the head be erect and symmetrically placed. Then, if the optic axis is horizontal and parallel to the median plane of the head, the three frames of reference coincide. The optic axis defines one axis, and the others, through the node of the eye, are horizontal and vertical. The first frame of reference is stationary, the others can be rotated about the common origin. The rotations can be specified in terms of the sets A_3, A_5, A_6, A_7, and A_8, defined in 2.5. A_3 and A_5 refer to horizontal and vertical movements of the eye, respectively. A_6 refers to rotations of the head about its vertical axis, A_7 to rotations in its median plane, and A_8 to rotations that tilt the head toward a shoulder. Using complex numbers, we specify the position of the eye in the head by

(1) $\omega' = a_3 + ia_5$.

Similarly, the position of the head relative to the external frame of reference is represented by

(2) $\omega'' = a_6 + ia_7$, and

(3) $\phi = a_8$.

The direction of the optic axis relative to the external frame of reference is given by $(a_3 + a_6, a_5 + a_7)$. Hence we may express it as a complex number by

(4) $\omega = \omega' + \omega''$.

The position of the retinal reference frame relative to the external reference frame is then (ω, ϕ).

1. The mathematical argument employed here was developed by Dr. Papert before the book had taken its present form. I have accordingly adapted his argument to bring it into line with the notation used in the text.

Let x be the horizontal angular deviation of a ray of light entering the eye from any $\delta \varepsilon \Delta$ (defined in (2.4.1)), and y its vertical deviation, and let

(5) $z = x + iy$.

If $\omega = \phi = 0$, the position of the retinal point stimulated by this ray of light is

(6) $h(\delta) = z$,

where $h \varepsilon H$, as defined in 2.6.

If we put $\phi = 0$,

(7) $h(\delta) = z - \omega$.

If we put $\omega = 0$,

(8) $h(\delta) = ze^{-i\phi}$.

If we assume the rotation ϕ to be effected first, and then ω, we get, as a general expression for the position of the retinal point stimulated by the given ray of light,

(9) $h(\delta) = ze^{-i\phi} - \omega = \xi$, say.

Since the functions V_3, V_5, V_6, V_7, and V_8 may be considered as one-to-one correspondences we may represent (V_3, V_5) by ω', (V_6, V_7) by ω'' and V_8 by ϕ. Then, neglecting V_2, V_9, V_{10}, and V_{11}, we may write the set S, defined in (2.9.1), in the form

(10) $S = [(\xi, \omega, \phi)]$.

The elements of S are conditioned to responses directed to the positions of the objects responsible for the retinal components, thereby determining the perception of those positions. To deduce the perceived positions we need an invariant operator that can be applied to the elements of S. The required operator is

(11) $e^{i\phi}(\xi + \omega)$.

By (9) this yields

(12) $e^{i\phi}(\xi + \omega) = e^{i\phi}(ze^{-i\phi} - \omega + \omega) = z$.

Let the subject now wear spectacles in the form of total reflecting prisms with their bases parallel to a plane through the eyes and orthogonal to the vertical axis of the head. The spectacles are attached to the head and move with it. With $\omega = \phi = 0$,

(13) $h(\delta) = \bar{z} = x - iy$.

In calculating the effects of rotations ω and ϕ we must note that ω' does not affect the position of the spectacles but ω'' and ϕ do. Hence, putting $\omega'' = \phi = 0$, we get,

$h(\delta) = \bar{z} - \omega'$

and applying (11) we get

(14) $\bar{z} - \omega' + \omega' = \bar{z}$

as the perceived direction of the object, no matter what the direction of the eyes may be. This implies that we shall get exactly the same results from our further calculations no matter what value we assign to ω'.

For convenience let $\omega' = 0$. This means that the spectacles occupy an invariant position relative to the retinal frame of reference. Hence the position of the retinal image may be got at once by reversing the sign of the imaginary components in the expression for $h(\delta)$ in (9). That is,

(15) $h(\delta) = \bar{z}e^{i\phi} - \bar{\omega}''$.

The set S, as transformed by the spectacles, becomes

(16) $\bar{S} = [(\bar{z}e^{i\phi} - \omega' - \bar{\omega}'', \omega, \phi)]$,

and applying (11) to this, and recalling (2), we get

(17) $e^{i\phi}(\bar{z}e^{i\phi} - \bar{\omega}'' + \omega'') = e^{i\phi}(\bar{z}e^{i\phi} + 2ia_7)$

$= \bar{z}e^{2i\phi} + 2ia_7e^{i\phi}$

as the perceived position of the object. It will be seen that not only is the world perceived as inverted, but it is unstable under rotations ϕ and a_7. The term $\bar{z}e^{2i\phi}$ shows that when the head is tilted through an angle ϕ the world is perceived as rotating in the same direction as the head but twice as fast. Similarly, the term $2ia_7e^{i\phi}$ shows that with a rotation a_7 the world is perceived as rotating about the axis of rotation of the head, in the same direction and at twice the speed. There is no instability under rotations ω' and a_8.

Responses directed to the objects responsible for the retinal components of the elements of $\bar{S}$ are at first misdirected, as shown by (17). These responses are extinguished and new ones, accurately directed to the correct positions, z, are gradually established. Assuming all the elements of $\bar{S}$ to have been conditioned to appropriate responses, we can look for an operator that will enable us to calculate from any $\bar{s} \in \bar{S}$ the perceived position of the object.

There are two cases to be considered, depending on whether verbal responses, descriptive of the orientation of the perceived world, are at variance with the bodily responses or in agreement with them. In both cases positional stability is achieved, but in the former case the world is perceived as inverted and in the latter as erect. Every subject who persists with the experiment reaches the former stage, but not every one reaches the latter stage.

Writing ξ for the position of the retinal image, the required operator for the first stage is

(18) $e^{-i\phi}(\xi + \omega' + \bar{\omega}'')$.

Applying (18) to (16) we get

(19) $e^{-i\phi}(\bar{z}e^{i\phi} - \omega' - \bar{\omega}'' + \omega' + \bar{\omega}'') = \bar{z}$.

That is, the world is perceived as inverted, but it is no longer characterized by the positional instability revealed by (17). The operator for the final stage is

(20) apply (18) and reverse the sign of the imaginary component.

If the spectacles are worn continuously throughout the experiment, it is to be expected that the responses conditioned to $\bar{S}$ will continue for a short time to be evoked by S. We can therefore calculate the perceived positions of objects immediately after removal of the spectacles by applying (18) or (20) to the elements of S, according as the subject has reached the first or second stage. In the first case we get

(21) $e^{-i\phi}(ze^{-i\phi} - \omega' - \omega'' + \omega' + \bar{\omega}'') = e^{-i\phi}(ze^{-i\phi} - 2ia_7)$

$= ze^{-2i\phi} - 2ia_7e^{-i\phi}$.

Reversing the sign of the imaginary components we get, for the second case,

(22) $\bar{z}e^{2i\phi} + 2ia_7e^{i\phi}$,

which is exactly the same as (17). That is, if at the end of the experiment the subject has perceived the world as both stable and erect, removal of the spectacles will produce exactly the same effects as those that were experienced when they were first put on.

Inspection of (21) shows that when the subject who perceives the world as stable but inverted at the end of the experiment takes the glasses off, the world is seen as erect but positionally unstable. Rotations ϕ and a_7 have the effect that the world is perceived as rotating about the axis of rotation of the head but in the *opposite* direction and at twice the speed.

Spectacles that reverse right and left may be made by mounting the prism with its base parallel to the median plane of the head. This gives

(23) $-\bar{S} = [(-\bar{z}e^{i\phi} - \omega' + \bar{\omega}'', \omega, \phi)]$.

Applying (11) to this, we get

(24) $e^{i\phi}(-\bar{z}e^{i\phi} - \omega' + \bar{\omega}'' + \omega' + \omega'') = -\bar{z}e^{2i\phi} + 2a_6e^{i\phi}$.

A rotation ϕ produces the same instability as with the inverting spectacles, but the sweeping of the scene past the eyes occurs with rotation of the head about its vertical axis and not with rotation in its median plane. It can easily be seen that if a subject, wearing these spectacles, achieves positional stability but continues to see the world right-left reversed, the perceived positions of objects when the spectacles are removed are given by

(25) $ze^{-2i\phi} - 2a_6e^{-i\phi}$.

A subject in Innsbruck wore these spectacles for 71 days but failed to perceive the world as correctly oriented, although it was completely stable. On removal of the spectacles he was immediately tested for stability under rotations of the head. The results were in complete agreement with (25).

If the field is inverted by lenses, as in Stratton's experiment, we get

(26) $-S = [(-ze^{-i\phi} - \omega' + \omega'', \omega, \phi)]$,

and applying (11),

(27) $e^{i\phi}(-ze^{-i\phi} - \omega' + \omega'' + \omega' + \omega'') = -z + 2\omega''e^{i\phi}$.

There is no instability from rotations ϕ, but both components of ω'' produce instability.

As yet no experiments have been reported in which the spectacles have been incorporated in contact lenses. As this may yet be done it will be of interest to calculate the results.

Let us assume that the spectacles invert the field. With $\omega' = \omega'' = \phi = 0$, $h(\delta) = \bar{z}$. A rotation ϕ transforms $h(\delta)$ to $\bar{z}e^{i\phi}$. But as the prism moves with the eye it is evident that ω' produces the same kind of effect as ω'' when the spectacles move with the head. The final direction of the eye, and therefore of the prism, is given by $\omega = \omega' + \omega''$. Consequently the general expression for $h(\delta)$ is $\bar{z}e^{i\phi} - \bar{\omega}$. This leads to

(28) $\bar{S} = [(\bar{z}e^{i\phi} - \bar{\omega}, \omega, \phi)]$.

Applying (11) to this, we have

(29) $e^{i\phi}(\bar{z}e^{i\phi} - \bar{\omega} + \omega) = \bar{z}e^{2i\phi} + 2i\chi e^{i\phi}$,

where $\chi = a_5 + a_7$, that is, the vertical deviation of the optic axis as determined jointly by the direction of the eye in its socket and the forward or backward tilt of the head.

Comparison of (29) with (17) shows that whereas the field is stable under upward and downward movements of the eye when the spectacles are attached to the head, it swings in the same direction as the eye movement and at twice the speed when the prism is attached to the eye. On the other hand, movements of the head contribute to instability only to the extent that the eyes are carried with the head, whereas in (17) these movements are the sole source of instability.

It is clear from (29) that fixation responses must fail with respect to their vertical components, and this is true whether the response involves the eyes alone or both eyes and head. Hence new fixation responses must be conditioned to the elements of $\bar{S}$, and these will be objectively indistinguishable from responses to the same objects made by a subject who is not wearing spectacles. That is, the eye must always be turned so that the optic axis passes through the goal. This has the interesting consequence that an element of $\bar{S}$ involving a fixated point is identical with the corresponding element of S, and as this has already been conditioned to a reaching response, the manipulation of objects will be facilitated by first fixating them.

The operator required to calculate the perceived direction of an object when adaptation is complete is

$$(30)\quad e^{-i\phi}(\xi + \bar{\omega})$$

and reversal of the sign of the imaginary component. Applying this to (28) we get z as the perceived direction.

On removal of the spectacles (30) will still hold for a short time. We therefore apply it to the elements of S. This gives

$$\bar{z}e^{2i\phi} + 2i\chi e^{i\phi}$$

which is identical with (29). That is, the world is perceived as inverted and unstable. In particular, it moves up and down as the eyes move up and down, and at twice the speed.

CHAPTER 9

Three Experiments

9.1 The results of experiments hitherto reported can be accounted for in terms of the behavioral theory, and this adds to the probability that the theory is valid. But a more searching test is required. It is necessary to devise experiments in which some specific behavioral changes are to be induced and others excluded. We can then predict from the theory what perceptual results will flow from the induced changes. If the results agree with the predictions the theory is sustained. If the results do not agree, this disproves the theory, unless there is some variable that the experimenter has overlooked. In such a case the inclusion of the neglected variable will lead to new deductions that can now be tested. We aim at a test in which the predicted result cannot possibly fail to occur if the theory is true. If we can be sure that we have such a test, then failure of the results to confirm the prediction means that the theory is false. The most searching test then is one that exposes the theory to the risk of being disproved. Tests of this kind can be devised for the behavioral theory of perception. These tests differ in an important way from the usual type of psychological experiment, in which different groups of subjects are exposed to different sets of conditions, and the significance of any differences between them is tested by techniques such as analysis of variance. In each of the proposed experiments there is only *one* subject, and he is exposed to different treatments not at different times or in a succession of different experiments, but simultaneously or, when that is impossible, in alternating periods, within a *single* experiment. Since we assume man in his environment to be a multistable system, it should be possible to disrupt one of the larger subsystems by transforming an afferent variable, and then arranging the experimental conditions in such a way that the opportunities for readaptation vary over a wide range as between the smaller subsystems comprised in the larger one. Thus we can deliberately accelerate readaptation in one subsystem and retard it in another by the simple device of choosing a subject whose everyday habits of life are such as to provide strong motivation for the first adaptation and little or none for the second. The experiment then becomes, in part, a natural one, in the sense that the subject himself provides the differential treatment of the several subsystems, and without even knowing that he is doing so.

It will be still better if there are two subsystems, with different proprioceptive variables, say, and different behavioral variables, and adequate motivation for the readaptation of both, in addition to subsystems for which there is little drive. We then write the chosen transformation of V_1 and V_2 into the symbolic representations of the several subsystems, and in each case calculate the perceptual results of readaptation. Since the two motivated systems are *subsystems*, it is likely that the calculated results will refer to different properties of perception. By the principle of interpenetration those properties should fuse into a single general perception; but if the systems are so chosen that when either of them is active the other is necessarily inactive, there will be little opportunity for interpenetration, and two different perceptual results should be found. That is to say, the distortions imposed on visual perception should be corrected in different ways according to the system that is active at the moment.

9.2. There is another simple way of ensuring that some behavioral changes are to be induced and others excluded, and that is to wear distorting spectacles only for part of the day. Stratton, it may be remembered, took quite extraordinary precautions to avoid direct vision even for a moment during his experiment. Apparently he thought that even a brief exposure to normal retinal stimulation might suffice to obliterate any effects of wearing the spectacles, by reminding him of what the world really looked like. Other investigators have followed Stratton's lead by insisting on continuous wearing of the spectacles, usually without offering any theoretical justification for this procedure.

Now continuous wearing has the effect that new responses are conditioned not only to the patterns of stimulation as transformed by the spectacles, but also to the normal patterns that arise without the spectacles. Let us recall that an element of S, defined in (3.4.12), specifies the position of an external object and a compound pattern of afferent events including exteroceptive components due jointly to the object and the orientation of the eyes. Let $\bar{s}$ represent the corresponding system when distorting spectacles are worn. Now the afferent events specified by an element of $\bar{s}$ are not new; they are, in fact, events that could be produced, without spectacles, by an object occupying a different position in space. We can say, therefore, that for every $\bar{s} \varepsilon \bar{S}$ there is an $s \varepsilon S$, such that the afferent events specified by $\bar{s}$ and s are identical, but the exteroceptive components arise from objects occupying different positions. Since it is the afferent events that are immediately responsible for the arousal of an engram, it follows that the conditioning of new responses to $\bar{s}$ must have the effect that, when the spectacles are removed, the response evoked by any s will be that which has been conditioned to an $\bar{s}$ containing the same afferent events as s. But since the external object now occupies a different position, the response is misdirected.

This argument suggests that the aftereffects of wearing distorting spectacles are not an inevitable consequence of adaptation to the spectacles, but are due to the fact that continuous wearing denies to the subject the opportunity of correcting erroneous responses to S. We should therefore be able to eliminate them entirely by getting the subject to wear the spectacles for only a part of each day. Any erroneous responses to S induced by acquiring new responses to $\bar{S}$ will be avoided, and the standard responses to S will remain intact.

It may be objected that the proposed technique will not only correct erroneous responses to S but will also diminish the strength of the new responses to $\bar{S}$ acquired when the spectacles are on, so that the daily period without spectacles will obliterate the effects of the preceding period with spectacles, and the condition of the system at the end of the fiftieth day will be just the same as at the end of the first day. It may well be that some such argument was at the back of Stratton's mind when he decided to avoid even the briefest peep at the real world during his experiment.

My answer to this argument begins with a reiteration of one of the major assumptions of this book, viz. that the human organism has an almost unlimited capacity for differential conditioning to compound patterns of stimulation. It is true that for every $\bar{s} \in \bar{S}$ there is an $s \in S$ such that the afferent components of s and $\bar{s}$ are identical, so that the conditioning of those afferent events to one response in the morning and an entirely different response in the afternoon should, on the face of it, result in the continuing domination of the well-established standard responses. But in fact $\bar{s}$ is always accompanied by certain constant stimuli such as the pressure of the spectacles on the nose, narrowing of the visual field, and the like, while s always occurs in the absence of those stimuli. We may think of those stimuli as an afferent function having only two values, 1 and 0. Then the state of the system is more completely described by $(\bar{s}, 1)$ when the spectacles are on, and $(s, 0)$ when they are off. Although the afferent events specified by $\bar{s}$ and s are identical, those specified by $(\bar{s}, 1)$ and $(s, 0)$ are not. Consequently there is no obstacle to differential conditioning, and the subject can progressively increase the accuracy and strength of his response to $(\bar{S}, 1)$ despite the intervening periods without the spectacles.

In Ashby's terminology, the presence or absence of stimuli incidental to the wearing of the spectacles may be considered as a parameter to the reacting system. Complete adaptation would then imply that when this parameter changes from 1 to 0 or from 0 to 1, the system immediately moves from one behavioral field to another.

If experiment should prove that the system can in fact adapt to distorting spectacles worn intermittently, this will afford strong support for the theory of the multistable system; and at the same time it will create the conditions for another crucial test of the behavioral theory of perception. For if (a) the subject can pass from wearing the spectacles to not wearing them, or from not wearing to wearing, without showing any signs of behavioral disruption; and (b) perception is a function of behavior; then we can conclude (c) that there will be *no perceptual aftereffects* when the subject puts the spectacles on after a period without them, or takes them off after wearing them for a few hours; and (d) *the spatial ordering of the perceived environment will not be changed by putting on or removing the spectacles.* This does not imply that there will be no perceptual change of *any* kind. It is extremely unlikely that *all* the subsystems including $\overline{V}_1$ and $\overline{V}_2$ among their main variables will be completely adapted in the course of an experiment lasting a few weeks.

It is now evident that if the condition specified by (a) is satisfied, but (c) and (d) are not confirmed, then hypothesis (b) is proved to be false. Thus an experiment in which spectacles are worn intermittently exposes the behavioral theory of perception to the risk of being proved false. If it survives that risk, the probability of its being true is enormously increased.

Experiment I

9.3. In July 1953 S. Papert, the mathematician who is primarily responsible for the mathematical argument presented in the appendix to Chapter 8, volunteered to wear spectacles that reverse right and left. He was acquainted with the behavioral theory of perception, having read the first draft of this book, and consequently he participated fully in the planning of the experiment. One of our first decisions was that an effort should be made to accelerate the process of adaptation by giving the subject specific training in certain classes of response, and my colleague Mrs. A. Schermann undertook to devise appropriate training procedures and to act as trainer. There were thus three experimenters, including the subject himself.

The spectacles were a pair that had been presented to me by Kohler in the course of a visit to Innsbruck a few months earlier. One evening Papert put on the spectacles out of curiosity, and decided there and then to keep them on. The experiment thus began before it had been fully planned, and our initial intention was that it should follow the design of two experiments that had previously been performed in Innsbruck with similar spectacles. Any deviations from that design were adopted after the experiment had begun.

On the fifth day Papert deduced from the behavioral theory that he should be able to adapt to the spectacles even if he wore them for only half of each day, and that if this expectation proved to be justified, he should be able to perceive the world the right way round both with and without the spectacles. He therefore proposed that, beginning the following day, he should wear the spectacles each morning and remove them after lunch for the rest of the day. This plan was accepted by the other experimenters and put into operation forthwith.

9.4. The training procedures devised and applied by Schermann were based in part on the Hullian principle that the increment in habit strength resulting from a single reinforcement is a diminishing function of delay in reinforcement. Now if a subject wearing reversing spectacles stretches out his hand to grasp an object, the path of the hand starts in the wrong direction. This results in an increasing divergence between the perceived positions of the hand and the goal, and the subject responds to this by redirecting the movement. He reaches the goal by a roundabout path, and this total response, *including the initially misdirected movement,* is reinforced by the final grasping of the object. There is comparatively little negative reinforcement of the false beginning.

The trainer therefore got the subject to sit at a table on which there were a number of objects, which she named in random order as the goals toward which reaching responses were to be directed. He was instructed to move as quickly as possible, and if his hand started in the wrong direction she immediately gave it a sharp tap with a pencil. He was then required to withdraw his hand and aim at the next object to be nominated. This treatment quickly eliminated roundabout paths.

9.5. It was soon realized that the adaptation of one subsystem does not at all guarantee the adaptation of other subsystems, despite the fact that retinal stimulation is operative in all of them. This is well illustrated by the following observations. The subject held out both hands and a stick was held above them and midway between them. The experimenter moved the stick toward one hand and brought it back to the central position, and the subject was required to move the hand that had been indicated. The stick was moved quite slowly to begin with, and when correct responses were given every time, the speed of the movement was increased. This at first increased the proportion of false responses, but further training soon reduced this proportion to zero. Finally correct responses were evoked by the quickest movements the experimenter could produce. By a similar procedure the subject learned to move the foot that was indicated by the flicking of a stick toward it. We then tested the subject by asking him to move parts of the body not previously included in the training program, such as the knees, shoulders, and elbows, and in every case the first responses were wrong.

Experiments of this kind confirmed the theory of the multistable system. The subsystem including retinal variables and movements of the hands was evidently largely independent of the subsystem including the same retinal variables and movements of the knees, since adaptation of one of these did not automatically guarantee adaptation of the other. The same conclusion can be drawn from another test, carried out after adaptation of the subsystems referred to above. The subject was asked to stand with his hands behind his back, and a walking stick was aimed at the right or left side of his abdomen. He was required to avoid the threatened blow by swinging his body out of the path of the approaching stick, but at first he moved in the wrong direction. The force of the blow was sufficient to cause some discomfort, and the resulting negative reinforcement soon eliminated all errors.

Mrs. Schermann was prompted by this demonstration of the mutual independence of the several subsystems to devise more and more complex training procedures involving the simultaneous activity of two or more of the subsystems. For example, she would have the subject stand beside a small table on which two books were placed, with two chairs standing side by side in front of him. She then gave him a rapid succession of instructions such as: "Take the book on the right with your left hand and place it on the right-hand chair, at the same time putting your left foot on the left chair." To carry out this instruction the subject had to turn his head to the right to bring the books within his visual field, twist his body to the right in order to bring his left arm into a suitable position for grasping the book on the right, turn his body and head to the left so as to face the chairs, and then respond to one chair with his left leg and the other with his left hand. Such exercises could not fail to accelerate the interpenetration of the several subsystems.

9.6. The chief aim of this training was to ensure that compound responses should always begin in the correct direction and with the minimum possible latency. We argued from the theory that correct perception of the spatial ordering of the environment could not occur as long as the habit strength of the pre-experimental responses was higher than that of the new responses, since in that case the latency of the old responses was shorter, so that their engrams would be activated first and would therefore determine Π. Now Papert observed that in responding to the instructions he tended to repeat them subvocally. His actions were thus not direct responses to the instructions, but were mediated by his own verbal responses. He therefore proposed to eliminate the mediating responses by starting to count aloud as soon as he had heard the instructions and to keep on counting while carrying them out. The immediate effect of this procedure was to throw him into complete confusion. He was unable to take any action. The complexity of the instructions was then reduced, and with further practice he was able to carry them out while counting.

9.7. It would be tedious to give a complete catalogue of all the ways in which the various subsystems were combined, but mention must be made of some of the training procedures that were adopted by the subject himself. He found that if he stood on one leg he tended to lose balance and fall. Similarly, if he stood on his toes and turned his head to look over his shoulder he would fall. This of course is easily explained in terms of the interpenetration of the visual and gravitational systems. A swaying movement of the body, resulting from the withdrawal of the usual firm support, changes the pattern of visual stimulation in the opposite to the usual direction, and the resulting compensatory responses have the effect of shifting the center of gravity farther away from the safe region instead of into it. He therefore practiced standing on one leg, and on his toes with his head turned sideways, until he could make the appropriate compensatory movements. This did not prevent him from falling heavily when he attempted to ride a bicycle, since this brings a new and hitherto unadapted system into operation. But the earlier balancing practice undoubtedly helped him to overcome the difficulties of riding. It required only a few minutes before he was able to ride a few yards without support. An hour's practice was sufficient to enable him to steer a straight course.

Another of the training procedures he adopted was to walk round and round a chair or table, constantly touching it with his body, and frequently changing direction so as to bring both sides into action. It was during an exercise of this kind, on the eighth day of the experiment, that he had his first experience of perceiving an object in its true position. But it was a very strange experience, in that he perceived the chair as being both on the side where it was in contact with his body and on the opposite side. And by this he meant not just that he *knew* that the chair he saw on his left was actually on his right. He had that knowledge from the beginning of the experiment. The experience was more like the simultaneous perception of an object and its mirror image, although in this case the chair on the right was rather ghost-like.

9.8. The visual field of the spectacles is very narrow, and of course it cannot be extended by rotation of the eyes. Consequently when walking the subject tended to turn his head downward in order to get a direct view of his feet. As his competency increased, the trainer decided to correct this tendency. She would walk with him and encourage him to keep his head erect, tilting it into the vertical position herself when necessary.

The theoretical justification for this procedure is that in normal circumstances walking movements are initiated by stimuli that come into full operation some seconds before their source is reached, and then recede into the periphery. The appropriate responses to changes in the configuration of the ground are already determined when one is still a few paces away, and it is seldom necessary to look directly at the feet when the response is in process of execution. According to the argument of Chapter 6 it is predetermined responses of this kind that generate perception of distance. The spectacles do not destroy perception of distance, despite the reversal of binocular parallax, and therefore the motive for the training procedure had nothing to do with this. The motive was rather to ensure that correct responses involving right and left should be evoked by the traces of stimuli presented a few seconds earlier. It was considered that adaptation would be accelerated if responses could be conditioned to trace stimuli of somewhat longer duration than those in operation when the subject was able to look at the goal at the moment of action.

The theory leads to the expectation that correct perception of the right-left ordering of the world will be more likely to occur if correct responses are conditioned not only to objects that are within reach of the hands but also to objects beyond this range. The technique of keeping the head erect is one way of satisfying this condition, and riding a bicycle is another.

9.9. Another group of training procedures was directed specifically to the elimination of the perceptual instabilities incidental to the wearing of the spectacles. The subject would choose a vertical or horizontal line and trace it with a finger, not necessarily making contact with it. He would then tilt his head through various angles to right and left, all the time moving his finger to and fro along the line. At first any change in the angle of the head resulted in errors in the direction of the movement, but with practice these rapidly diminished, and finally the subject could change the angle of his head in the middle of a tracing movement without causing any significant change in its direction.

It was in the course of these exercises that the subject made the discovery, referred to in 8.13, that the maximum rate at which he could tilt his head without producing perceptual instability increased from day to day.

9.10. Some of our training procedures were directly inspired by the example of the Innsbruck school. Riding a bicycle is one of the exercises regularly adopted there. Another extremely valuable procedure that we adopted was to draw a curved line in chalk on the floor and get the subject to walk along this line, always keeping it between his feet. This is a very difficult task, not only because the direction of curvature is reversed but because the foot that is perceived as being the right foot is in reality the left. When the subject tries to move the foot that he perceives as being his right foot, he actually does move the right foot, but the foot that he sees moving appears to be his left foot. What he sees as his right foot remains stationary, and yet he feels his right foot to be in motion. The response is negatively reinforced, and this often has the effect that the subject is unable to move either foot for a time, as if he were rooted to the floor.

This exercise illustrates very neatly the principle of the relative independence of the several subsystems all involving retinal stimuli but different motor variables. If the subject finds that both feet are on the same side of the line, he wants to move the foot that is nearer the line to the other side of it, but the foot that actually moves is the more distant one, and it moves farther away instead of nearer. He responds to this failure by bringing the foot back to its starting point and moving the other one. But instead of moving this foot in the opposite direction of the previous movement, he often moves it in the same direction, crossing over the stationary foot.

Thus choosing the correct foot does not at all guarantee the choice of the correct direction. Similarly, if the subject first corrects the direction of the movement this does not guarantee that the appropriate foot will be moved. The task becomes very much easier if the subject is first trained with exercises of the type described in 9.5.

9.11. The results of the experiment fully confirmed the predictions made on the fifth day, which led to the change from continuous to intermittent wearing of the spectacles. As predicted, adaptation was not blocked by the daily periods of normal vision. On the contrary, it was more rapid than it had been in the two previous experiments in Innsbruck, and this can doubtless be attributed to the systematic training described above. Also there was no disruption of behavior when the spectacles were put on or taken off. And finally, the prediction that the right-left ordering of the perceptual field would remain unchanged when the spectacles were put on or removed was confirmed. This was strikingly illustrated when the subject rode a bicycle while wearing the spectacles, and took them off and replaced them without changing course or wobbling or showing any other signs of disruption. Objects that he perceived as being on his left while wearing the spectacles were still on his left when he took them off.

There is really nothing more extraordinary about this result than there is about the commonplace facts of perceptual constancy. We have explained these facts in terms of the partition of Q into functional equivalence classes, $Q(\delta)$, such that every element of any $Q(\delta)$ is conditioned to the same response. Whatever succession of elements of $Q(\delta)$ may come into action, the response for which the organism is thereby prepared is always the same, and therefore, by our hypothesis, the perceived position of the object specified by δ is always the same. What the training received in the experiment has done is to effect a partitioning of $\bar{Q}$ into functional equivalence classes $\bar{Q}(\delta)$, and by exactly the same kind of process as that whereby Q was originally partitioned. The elements of $\bar{Q}$ contain reversed retinal stimulation, but in addition they all contain the tactile and other stimuli incidental to the wearing of the spectacles, so that they can always be differentiated from elements of Q that are identical with them with respect to the other afferent functions.

We can say therefore that the effect of our experiment has been to enlarge the equivalence class $Q(\delta)$ by adding to it $\bar{Q}(\delta)$, since the response conditioned to $\bar{Q}(\delta)$ is necessarily the same as that conditioned to $Q(\delta)$. It follows that a transition from $q \varepsilon Q(\delta)$ to $\bar{q} \varepsilon \bar{Q}(\delta)$ has exactly the same effect as a transition from q_i to q_j or from $\bar{q}_i$ to $\bar{q}_j$. Hence the perceived position of the object remains unchanged when the spectacles are put on or taken off.

The subject's behavior, in riding a bicycle, for instance, proved that $\bar{Q}(\delta)$ was in fact conditioned to the same response as $Q(\delta)$. Hence, if he had reported that the perceived positions of objects did *not* remain invariant when the spectacles were put on or removed, the behavioral theory of perception would have been proved false, once and for all. It has survived the risk.

It should be noted that if $\bar{Q}(\delta)$ had been conditioned to the same motor responses as $Q(\delta)$ but to different verbal responses, as in the case of the subject discussed in 8.11, the theory leads to the deduction that putting on and removing the spectacles would result in an abrupt transition from one stable perceptual field to another with the opposite right-left ordering, and without aftereffects. While such a result would not be as spectacular as the one actually reported, failure to confirm it would be equally fatal to the theory. It should not be difficult to devise a training procedure that would have precisely this effect.

9.12. Apart from the confirmation of the theory afforded by its final result, this experiment is illuminating in other ways. In particular, it demonstrates in a striking manner the relevancy of Ashby's theory of the multistable system. Ashby has shown that a large ultrastable system cannot adapt easily if all the main variables are active, since the probability of adaptive responses occurring simultaneously in all the subsystems is very low. However, adaptation can take place very easily in any one subsystem if it is separated from the rest by part-functions that are for the time being inactive. The first point is vividly illustrated by the initial difficulty of walking along a curved line. The second point is illustrated by the fact that our subject very quickly mastered the simpler tasks in which he was trained, such as moving the hand or foot indicated by a visual stimulus, and subsequently found no difficulty with the more complex tasks.

It is significant that the first experience of perceiving an object in its true position occurred on the eighth day of the experiment, whereas the subjects of the two Innsbruck experiments did not report such experiences until they had been wearing the spectacles continuously for more than two weeks. But in their case the choice of the subsystem that was to be active at any moment was determined not by any specific theoretical considerations but by the general demand that the subject should be as active as possible. The attempt to meet this requirement almost certainly meant that the active subsystem would as a rule be too complex to permit rapid adaptation. The subjects were, so to speak, always biting off more than they could chew.

9.13. In the transitional stage of the experiment the subject reported some strange forms of perception, such as seeing two chairs, one on each side of the body, where only one existed. Many comparable experiences have been reported by other investigators. For example, in the film, *Die Umkehrbrille und das aufrechte Sehen*, made by Erismann and Kohler, the subject was confronted with two faces, one erect and the other inverted. At first the inverted face was seen erect and the erect one inverted; but when the owner of the erect face began to smoke a cigarette, the direction of the smoke was incompatible with the inversion, and it suddenly appeared to be erect. But again there was something odd about the perception. The subject explained it by saying that the face seemed to be both erect and inverted. The erect face appeared to have acquired a beard, as if the crown of the head had failed to jump with the rest and now occupied the same space as the chin. To common sense this is completely impossible, but it is not at all impossible if we assume that the new engrams, with the assistance of the direction of the smoke, were exactly equal in strength to the old ones that were in process of being inhibited. The two sets of engrams mediate mutually exclusive responses, but so do the several engrams specified by Π. This does not prevent them from being simultaneously active, and in the same way there seems to be no reason why engrams mediating perception of the face as erect should not be activated simultaneously with others mediating perception of the face as inverted. We can say then that Π has temporarily ceased to be a single-valued function and has become a two-valued function, in the sense that each element of Q activates two engrams instead of one within the same subsystem.

Anomalous experiences of this kind do not last long, since nonadaptive responses are constantly being inhibited and adaptive responses reinforced. The probability that the new engrams will be activated before the old ones therefore increases all the time. Moreover, this probability often receives a substantial increment by the addition of stimuli that strongly support the adaptive responses. For example, in the experiment depicted in the film referred to above, the subject suddenly saw a face erect if he held a plumb line in his hand and moved it up and down in front of the face. The gravitational stimuli evidently contributed a larger increment to the new engrams than the direction of the cigarette smoke had done, so that on this occasion the perception was not equivocal.

Other anomalous experiences, such as the perception of a building in its correct position while at the same time the inscription on it is seen as mirrored, belong to a different category. Here we cannot say that Π is a two-valued function, since the apparently conflicting perceptions do not belong to one and the same subsystem. Further strengthening of the responses on which the perception of the position of the building depends does not necessarily have any direct effect on reading behavior, and this implies that the anomalous experience can continue for a long time, in contrast to the double-image experience, which must of necessity be short-lived.

Experiment II

9.14. The next experiment to be described was performed in July 1954 at the University of Innsbruck, with the collaboration of Professor Kohler, and with myself as subject. The spectacles were in the form of 20° wedge prisms, mounted in an ordinary spectacle frame, with the bases to the left. The daily plan of the experiment was that I walked from my lodging to the laboratory, a distance of little more than 100 yards, at 8 A.M., without the spectacles. Kohler then applied a variety of tests for measuring the degree of perceptual adaptation to this kind of transformation of retinal stimulation. The spectacles were then put on and the tests were repeated. I then walked back to my lodging, wearing the spectacles, had breakfast, spent the rest of the morning mostly at my work table on a balcony overlooking the mountains to the south of the city. After lunch I walked back to the laboratory at 1:30 P.M., and the tests were repeated, first with the spectacles and then without them. I did not wear the spectacles again until the following morning.

Experiment I had demonstrated conclusively that the intermittent wearing of spectacles does not interfere with adaptation, and that there are no aftereffects when the spectacles are removed. This made it possible to predict that a direct comparison could be made between perception as it was at the end of the experiment and what it had been at the beginning. All that was necessary was to turn the spectacles round so that the bases of the prisms were to the right. The transformation applied to V_1 and V_2 may be described by saying that if (x,y) is the direction of a ray of light approaching the prism, the direction in which it emerges from the prism to enter the eye is $(x + \alpha, y + \beta)$, where α and β are two different joint functions of x and y. When the prisms are turned so that their bases are on the right, the direction of the ray entering the eye is $(x - \alpha, y - \beta)$. That is, the transformations with bases right and left are identical in form, but the coordinates of the retinal images are displaced in opposite directions. Now complete adaptation to prisms with bases left would entail that the subject would direct his movements not to an object in the direction $(x + \alpha, y + \beta)$ but in the direction (x,y). If the spectacles were worn continuously, the response when they were removed would be in the direction $(x - \alpha, y - \beta)$; and if the bases were turned to the right the direction would be $(x - 2\alpha, y - 2\beta)$. That is, the distortion would be doubled. Intermittent wearing means that without spectacles the response continues to be in the direction (x,y), and with bases right it will be in the direction $(x - \alpha, y - \beta)$. Thus, at the end of the experiment the distortion with bases right will be exactly the same in form as it was at the beginning with bases left. Hence any change in perception induced by the experiment can be detected at once and accurately described by the simple expedient of turning the spectacles around.

9.15. It is now necessary, in the interests of science, to disclose certain personal facts about myself, since it was my everyday habits of life that were to determine which of the various subsystems were to be readapted and what measure of interpenetration there should be between them. The most important fact is that an uncorrected infantile scoliosis left me with a legacy of a clubfoot. Excessive use of the motor car over many years has resulted in my leg muscles becoming weak and my joints stiff, so that I now have to exercise great care in walking, and to look at the ground in order to adjust to any irregularities there may be. Unexpected irregularities tend to upset my balance, since the corrective response is often insufficient to prevent stumbling. I carry a walking stick in my left hand. The deformity is in the right foot.

My walking movements are slow, and are usually initiated by stimuli coming from parts of the ground not more than two or three paces ahead. That does not mean that stimuli from more distant points do not put me in a state of readiness for the appropriate action, but in my case the appropriate action is to look down at the ground immediately in front of my feet and place them carefully so as to avoid a loss of balance. For example, if the distant stimulus-object is a curb at an intersection, the action for which I am prepared is a slowing down of my movement as I approach the curb, and the final action of stepping off the curb is a response not to the previously presented stimuli but to stimuli that come into operation immediately prior to the response. In negotiating stairs I look at each step before placing a foot on it.

Normally the only time I have to respond to stimuli from distant objects is when I am driving a car, but I had no car in Innsbruck and had no opportunity of driving while wearing the spectacles. Consequently the only occasions during the experiment when I had to take direct action relative to objects at distances beyond arm's length were when I was walking, and the most important of those objects were variations in the configuration of the ground.

Indoors I sat most of the time, either at the dining table or at my worktable, and my activities were thus largely confined to the manipulation of objects within reach of my hands. Apart from looking at other objects in my vicinity or at the view from my balcony, and observing and recording the distortions of their shapes produced by the spectacles, and particularly the instability of those shapes under rotation of my head, I had no occasion to take any direct action relative to those objects while sitting at the table. I did not throw balls or darts at any object, or take any other action that might be subject to reinforcement or extinction. The only actions that were open to correction by such means were movements of the hands relative to the table and the objects on it, and a few other objects that could be reached without leaving my chair.

It will be seen from this account that only two subsystems were regularly active during the experiment, and that, apart from retinal stimulation, the main variables of one subsystem were inactive when those of the other one were active. Thus gravitational stimuli were constantly varying during walking, and responses to those stimuli were constantly being evoked, and corrected for the errors induced by the transformed retinal stimuli. But when I sat at the table no errors in response to gravitational stimuli occurred, since I was supported by the chair and by my arms resting on the table. Here there was no risk that I might lose my balance, and therefore little or no drive to correct errors due to the distorted horizontal-vertical framework of the visual world. In any case the errors did not involve misplacements of my feet or faulty balancing movements of my body. Similarly the functions that were active while I sat at the table, mostly involving movements of the arms and hands, were inactive during walking.

Here then we have exactly the kind of situation envisaged in 9.1. Several subsystems are disrupted by the distorting spectacles, but in only two of these is there sufficient drive to ensure adaptation. We can therefore expect the behavioral changes induced in those systems to be reflected in perception. But the perceptual changes resulting from the two modes of adjustment will not necessarily be identical, and because the two subsystems are never active simultaneously, we may expect that the two perceptual fields will not interpenetrate to produce a single homogeneous field.

9.16. The perceptual distortions produced by wedge prisms have been fully described by Kohler (1951) and there is no need to repeat all the details here. It is sufficient to say that all horizontal surfaces below the level of the head appear to slope downward from right to left and with an increasing gradient. It is important to understand that this is due to a large extent to a disruption of normal binocular parallax. What happens is that the apparent width of an object varies with its position relative to the median plane of the head. If the head is turned so that the object is in the right of the visual field, and is then turned to the right so that the object moves to the left of the field, then the object appears to suffer a progressive contraction as the head turns. Now an object in the left of the field is more to the left for the right eye than it is for the left, and the right retinal image is therefore more contracted than the left. This is exactly what happens, without spectacles, when the left edge of the object is more distant than the right, and in that case the left edge is perceived as being more distant. It follows that if the subject looks at the ground under his feet it is perceived as receding with increasing rapidity from right to left. It is no longer perceived as level but as sloping down to the left. Exactly the same effect is produced by a table under the level of the eyes. The curvature is markedly diminished when the surface is viewed monocularly.

The radius of this curvature has its minimum value when the surface is immediately under the eyes, and increases with the distance of the part of the surface that is directly inspected. Thus if the subject holds his head erect and looks at a distant level surface it is perceived as level. The fact that the curvature of the ground is most pronounced underfoot is of obvious importance in view of my need to look at the ground in front of my feet when walking. The near edge of the worktable was also directly under my eyes when I sat at it, so that here too the portion of the environment that was included in the active subsystem was the portion that was subject to maximum distortion by the spectacles.

9.17. At the time when this experiment was performed I had not yet incorporated the theory of the multistable system into my theoretical structure, and consequently it did not occur to me that the subsystems active in walking and sitting at the table were largely independent of one another and might therefore produce different perceptual results. I feel it necessary to mention this in case the reader should suspect that the results were determined not by the adaptation of the transformed systems but by predictions derived from the theory. In fact my predictions were derived mainly from the results of previous experiments with similar spectacles in Innsbruck. In particular, I expected that there would be a progressive leveling of horizontal surfaces, and that this would apply to the table as well as to the floor. With this in mind I measured the apparent slope of the table twice daily, at approximately 9:30 A.M. and at noon.

The procedure was to place my walking stick on the table, always in the same position relative to my body, and to raise it at the left end until it appeared to be level. I then measured the height of the raised end above the table. Two different methods were adopted. In the first I kept my head in a fixed position and scanned the stick with ocular movements alone. In the second the scanning was done by rotating the head so that the two ends of the stick came into the center of the visual field in alternation. This double procedure was dictated by theoretical considerations. Since the displacement of a ray of light when it passes through the prism is a function of its angle of incidence, the displacements of the two ends of the stick should be identical if they were viewed in alternation in such a manner that the angle of incidence of the rays reflected by them was always the same. The apparent slope should in that case be much less, as in fact it was. The measurements were less than half those obtained when the head was held in a fixed position.

Despite this daily preoccupation with measuring the slope of the table, and the confident expectation that it would show a progressive diminution, the measurements on the last day of the experiment were not significantly less than those on the first day. On the other hand it had not occurred to me to make any measurements of the apparent curvature of the table, and I had not formulated any expectations about that. And yet it was precisely this distortion that was most completely eliminated. Again, I had expected that because the greatest proportion of my time was spent at the table, the responses acquired there would be the chief determiners of any perceptual changes that might occur; and I did not anticipate that the brief period spent in walking—not more than 15 minutes each day—would have any marked effect, or that that effect would be strikingly different from that produced by the behavior at the table. Yet that is just what happened. It is abundantly clear therefore that in experiments of this nature the theoretical expectations of the subject have no effect on the outcome if they are based on an inaccurate or incomplete analysis of the subsystem that is brought into action by the experimental conditions.

9.18. The experiment lasted for thirteen days. The daily tests applied by Kohler after removal of the spectacles at 1:30 P.M. had shown that the aftereffects had increased slowly for a few days and then diminished to zero. It was therefore possible to make a direct comparison of perception as it was at the end of the experiment with what it had been at the beginning, by simply putting the bases of the prisms on the right. This comparison showed that when I was walking, level ground was no longer perceived as sloping downward to the left with an increasing gradient. Instead, there was a level path, about a yard wide, stretching in front of me. To the right of this path the ground sloped up very gently, and to the left it sloped downward more steeply. The direction of this path was completely unaffected by changes in the direction of my eyes and even in the direction in which my head was facing. It was always bisected throughout its length by the median plane of my body. In fact, its direction was always the direction in which I was walking or might have intended to walk.

If I stood in an open doorway and looked down at the threshold it appeared to be level throughout its whole width. When I removed the spectacles it was displaced to the left, but I could detect not the slightest change in slope; it remained in exactly the same plane as before. But when the spectacles were put on again with bases right, the threshold was perceived as sloping downward to the right, and convex upward. This phenomenon was so striking that I unfortunately neglected to observe whether the displacements effected by the transitions from bases left to no spectacles and from no spectacles to bases right were equal in extent. I cannot assert that there was no difference, but it was certainly not enough to prompt me to make comparisons.

When I sat at the table I perceived it as sloping down to the left, at approximately the same angle as at the beginning of the experiment, but there was no trace of curvature over its whole width. It had become an oblique plane. Now the visual angle subtended by the width of the table when I was sitting at it was very much greater than that of the level path on the floor when I was standing or walking, but the table showed no signs of curvature at the right or left, and there was no level section in the middle. Another very striking change was that whereas at the beginning of the experiment the perceived width of the table was highly variable under rotation of my head about its vertical axis, at the end it was completely stable as long as the rotations were confined within the range that had been customary as I sat working at the table. There was a slight residual instability when the rotations went beyond that range.

If, while still sitting at the table, I observed other objects in my vicinity, such as a wardrobe about ten feet away from me, or the window frames, or the houses and mountains seen through the window, the instability in the shapes of those objects was just as great as it had been at the beginning of the experiment. I could detect no difference in this respect when I turned the bases of the prisms to the right. It was only the table and the objects on it that had ceased to be variable in shape.

9.19. It is at once evident that these results disprove once and for all the common-sense notion that visual perception is a function of retinal stimulation alone. But the question we must now consider is whether they afford support for the theory advanced in this book. To answer this we must consider the behavioral disturbances produced by the spectacles and the extent to which they were corrected. We can then deduce the perceptual changes that must, if the theory is valid, result from those corrections, and compare the deductions with the recorded results.

It will be convenient to represent by $|V_1$ and $|V_2$ the sets V_1 and V_2 as transformed by the spectacles with bases left. Similarly, $V_1|$ and $V_2|$ will represent the same sets as transformed by the spectacles with bases right. When the subject is seated at a table the active afferent system may be represented by $|_2Q$, and when he is walking by $|_3Q$. It will be appreciated that the drives operating in $|_2Q$ and $|_3Q$ are not identical. For example, the drive to maintain balance and avoid a fall is of primary importance in $|_3Q$ but plays no part in $|_2Q$. Again, $|_3Q$ includes among its active functions the gravitational and proprioceptive stimuli incidental to walking, but the proprioceptive functions incidental to the manipulation of objects with the hands are inactive, and in $|_2Q$ the position is reversed. This does not mean that the hands are inactive during walking, but simply that the relative functions play an insignificant part in the maintenance of balance. Similarly, the legs are not completely inactive when sitting at the table, but the relative functions play a negligible part in controlling movements of the hands. Thus, in Ashby's terminology, each subsystem is separated from the other by a wall of inactive part-functions.

My first action after putting on the spectacles each morning was to walk first through a corridor to the vestibule, then down a short flight of steps, unprotected by a rail, to street level, then along the street, across one intersection, to my lodging, and finally up a staircase, protected by a rail, to the first floor. There was one behavioral disruption that was common to all sections of this activity. For every $|q \varepsilon |{}_3Q$ such that the source of the retinal stimulus is a point on the ground a few inches to the left of my left foot and from 12 to 18 inches ahead of it, there is a $q \varepsilon {}_3Q$ such that the afferent events specified by q are identical with those specified by $|q$. By ${}_3F$ this q is conditioned to a movement of my left hand that carries the ferrule of my walking stick to a point that is an inch or two below the level of my left foot. Similarly, any $|q \varepsilon |{}_3Q$ for which the retinal stimuli arise from a point in front of my right foot is conditioned to a movement of the right foot aimed at a piece of ground about half an inch higher than that on which my left foot is resting. In short, I not only *perceive* the ground as sloping but walk as if I were actually on sloping ground. Since the ground is actually level, this means that my stick is arrested in its downward movement before it has reached the goal prescribed by the response conditioned to $|q$, so that my walking is characterized by a succession of furious bangs with my stick on the floor, with consequent shocks to my left hand and arm. Similarly the downward movement of my right foot stops before it has actually reached the ground, so that there is a slight, though not dangerous, disturbance of balance.

9.20. Both the shocks sustained by my left hand and arm and the disturbance of balance arising from the inaccurate placing of my right foot involve negative reinforcement of the responses previously conditioned to the relative elements of $|{}_3Q$, and consequently readaptation starts at once. Gradually the action of the left hand is modified until at the end of the experiment it is indistinguishable from the normal action. Similarly, the action of my right foot is restored to normal. But this means that the elements of $|{}_3Q$ are now conditioned to the same responses as are the elements of ${}_3Q$ that come into operation when I am walking on level ground without spectacles. That is, the elements of $|{}_3Q$ and of ${}_3Q$ determined by a point on the ground in a specific position relative to my body constitute a single equivalence class and therefore determine a perceptual constancy.

It is important to realize, however, that we cannot now generalize to the whole of $|{}_3Q$, since the new responses have been conditioned only to elements of $|{}_3Q$ for which the retinal stimuli arise from the narrow section of the ground to which my walking movements are confined. We can therefore generalize only to the subset of $|_3Q$ that satisfies this condition. This generalization leads to the deduction that that portion of the ground on which I am walking must be perceived as level, but that this will not extend to right and left of that portion, since I am not given to walking sideways. Then, by an application of the goal gradient hypothesis analogous to that of 6.5 and 6.17, we can deduce that the perceived level path will stretch on in front of me in the direction in which I am walking.

From the definition of a functional equivalence class of Q we can deduce that the location of the perceived level path is independent of the direction of my eyes in their sockets and of the direction in which my head is facing. For the invariant response that is conditioned to all the elements of an equivalence class of $|_3Q$ is a movement directed to a point that has a specific position relative to my body but constantly varies relative to my head and eyes.

9.21. In addition to distorting shapes the spectacles displace the visual field to the right, the average angle of displacement being 10°, that is, half the angle of the prisms. This has little effect on walking as long as the surface of the ground is unbroken, but it involves some risk if there are irregularities on the right-hand side. For example, if I walked along the street with the curb on my right, there was a risk that I might put my right foot on the edge of the curb and slip into the gutter. There was no such risk if the curb was on my left, since the pre-existing responses to elements of $|_3Q$ tended to make me move along a line well away from the curb. The danger here was rather that I should collide with the wall on my right; and in fact I did this a few times in the early days of the experiment.

Since walking close to a curb on the right exposed me to the danger of stepping off the curb without preparing for the necessary downward movement of my right foot and therefore falling, I adopted the expedient of always keeping close to the wall on the left. Similarly, when the curb was on the left I kept close to it and thereby avoided collisions with the wall. This cautious procedure, which violates the Innsbruck tradition that the subjects of such experiments should expose themselves freely to all reasonable risks, had the effect that I deprived myself of the opportunity of acquiring locomotor responses accurately adjusted to the lateral displacement of the retinal stimuli.

Climbing or descending steps presented no serious difficulty provided I approached them squarely, but if I approached them obliquely, the retinal displacement exposed me to danger. On one occasion early in the experiment I approached the steps leading to the laboratory obliquely. The steps were on my left as I approached, and I turned through an angle of 45° intending to climb them obliquely. Since the spectacles displaced the images to the right, I lifted my right foot and brought it down on a nonexistent step. The result of this experience was that for the duration of the experiment I always walked to a point opposite the center of the steps, turned left through an angle of 90°, and approached the steps squarely. Here again, therefore, I missed the opportunity to acquire accurate responses to the lateral displacement of the retinal images.

Science, as it happens, has benefited from my pusillanimity. For we can deduce from my failure to acquire adequate responses to the laterally displaced stimuli that, despite the leveling of the perceived ground underfoot, there is not likely to be any significant change in the lateral position of a perceived point on the floor as a result of prolonged wearing of the spectacles. This is fully borne out by the results. When I stood in a doorway, looking down at the threshold, and removed the spectacles, the threshold was perceived as being horizontal in both cases, but it appeared to jump to the left when the spectacles were taken off.

9.22. In considering the process of readaptation while sitting at the table we must take account of an important formal difference between the systems that are active here and in walking. At the table the hand that is about to execute a reaching movement is frequently in the visual field at the moment when the response is initiated, and it usually remains visible throughout the whole action. In walking, on the other hand, the foot that is about to be moved forward is invisible at the moment when the movement begins; and similarly the point of the walking stick is invisible when its forward movement begins. Since the course of such movements is already fully determined at the moment they begin, there is little opportunity for modifying them before their completion.

There is hardly any feedback to correct errors. In contrast to this, a misdirected movement of the hand is capable of being corrected before it has reached the goal predetermined by the initial impulse, since the hand and the goal are both determining elements of $|_2Q$ throughout the movement.

Since the retinal image of the hand is itself displaced, this means that the errors in reaching movements are very much less than the displacement effected by the spectacles would lead us to expect. Let the actual position of the goal be (x_1, y_1) and the initial position of the hand (x_2, y_2). The spectacles transform these positions to $(x_1 + \alpha_1, y_1 + \beta_1)$ and $(x_2 + \alpha_2, y_2 + \beta_2)$. If the hand were initially invisible and a rapid movement were made toward the goal, giving no opportunity for feedback, the error in its terminal position would be (α_1, β_1); but if the hand is initially visible the error is more likely to be $(\alpha_1 - \alpha_2, \beta_1 - \beta_2)$, which in general will be very much smaller than (α_1, β_1). Hence the corrections that have to be made through the process of readaptation are, in this situation, substantially less than we might expect.

This is particularly important in relation to the slope of the table. If the left hand is resting on the table, its perceived position is lower than its real position, so that when it is moved to pick up an object on another part of the table, the error is equal to the difference between the perceived levels of hand and goal, and not the difference between the real position of the hand and the perceived position of the goal.

From this we can deduce that whatever changes may occur in the perception of the table, these will not include a change in the slope unless there is some independent training process that will correct the errors in the perceived positions of the hands. I did not in fact think of this until long after the experiment had been completed and therefore no special training procedure was adopted. The only behavioral changes that were imposed on me were those arising out of the activities in which I was engaged. Since in those activities my hands were always moving in relation to the table and other stationary objects, the natural situation provided no opportunity for the necessary independent training.

It has been argued in 5.8 that the horizontal-vertical framework of the visual world is derived from the adaptation of the system to the direction of the pull of gravity. Obviously this force was fully operative when I was walking, and as any faulty response exposed me to the risk of a fall, there was a strong drive to correct such errors. There was no such drive in operation when I sat at the table, in the sense that balance was not imperiled by my manual responses to objects on the table. Thus the situation did not supply any motive for the kind of readaptation that would have corrected the errors in the perceived positions of my hands. It would be interesting, in some further experiment of this kind, to have the subject hold a tray with a ball on it, and to practice tilting the tray to make the ball roll in any desired direction or to stand still.

9.23. The errors that had to be corrected were of two main kinds, and both were subject to variation with rotation of my head. The first arose from the apparent curvature of the table. In moving objects from one part of the table to another, I acted at first as if the table were actually curved. In writing I tended to press the pen too hard against the paper at the beginning of each line and to decrease the pressure toward the end of the line. Daily practice eliminated those errors, and ultimately my actions were indistinguishable from ordinary manipulations of objects lying on a plane surface. This should, according to the theory, result in the table being perceived as plane.

The second type of error arose from the distortion of the shape of the table—contracted at the left and extended at the right. Reaching movements directed to objects on the left stopped before the goal was reached, while movements to the right carried the hand too far. Experiment I had already provided evidence in support of the notion that perceptual changes are likely to develop more quickly if the subject is encouraged to make the response start in the right direction and not to rely on feedback generated during the course of the movement. Accordingly, I devoted a portion of each morning to exercises in which I aimed rapid movements of the hands at objects in various positions, and with my head at various angles. Gradually the errors were eliminated until I could reach any object on the table with a single quick move and with the same measure of accuracy as in normal conditions. We can then deduce that at the end of the experiment the table should be perceived undistorted in shape and not subject to changes with rotation of the head. This is precisely what happened.

Finally, since the only responses directed to objects beyond the reach of my hands as I sat at the table were fixation responses, and these were invariably successful, we can deduce that such objects must have been perceived in the same way at the end of the experiment as at the beginning. In this particular subsystem there were no errors of behavior and therefore no need for readaptation.

This kind of result—complete or nearly complete perceptual stability with respect to an object within reach of the hands together with undiminished instability with respect to objects beyond that range—is completely impossible if one tries, as Erismann and Kohler do, to account for the perceptual changes resulting from the wearing of spectacles in the form of wedge prisms by an appeal to some automatic process of physiological adaptation in the visual system. For if this were the true explanation, it would be impossible for the perception of near objects to be transformed while that of distant objects remained unchanged, since the visual system is equally implicated in both cases.

9.24. We return now to the question that was raised in 9.1, whether any failure of the observed results to confirm the deductions would constitute a fatal objection to the theory. It is important here to understand clearly what is meant by failure. It means not just that the predicted perceptual result does not occur, but that it fails to occur despite the fact that the postulated behavioral transformation has been completed. Thus if the experiment had been terminated before the new behavioral patterns had been established, the nonappearance of the deduced perceptual results would have no significance. This would simply mean that the appropriate test had not in fact been applied.

If any of the predicted perceptual results had occurred while the relevant behavior was still disrupted, that would also constitute a failure, and it is obvious that this kind of failure would have fatal consequences for the theory, since it would imply that some mechanism other than behavioral adaptation was responsible for the result. It should be noted, however, that the mere occurrence of behavioral and perceptual changes does not constitute a real test of the theory. If we assume, as many psychologists have done, that the function of perception is to control behavior, then any change in perception would automatically bring about a change in behavior, so that the concurrence of behavioral and perceptual changes is consistent with both theories. Consequently a failure of concurrence is extremely unlikely to happen even if the behavioral theory is false, and the theory is therefore not exposed to a serious risk of being disproved. Failure, it should be noted, would be equally damaging to both theories.

We must be certain that the deduced result is the only one that can possibly be produced if the theory is true. It is conceivable, for example, that in our calculations we may have neglected some variable that is active in the system. The failure of such a deduction to be confirmed would not damage the theory. If we are satisfied that there has been no such error of omission, failure of the experimental results to confirm the deduction can mean only one thing—the theory is false. If it should survive this test the probability of its truth is greatly increased.

It seems to me that, assuming the behavioral theory to be true, there is one way in which the results could have deviated from the deductions. If the subsystems involved in walking and in sitting at the table had not been as completely separated from each other as I have assumed, so that there was a much larger measure of interpenetration than I have supposed, the theory would have led to the deduction that the two perceptual fields would have tended to coalesce into a single unified field. That is, the leveling of the path would have generalized to the table, and the flattening of the table would have generalized to the ground. This might well happen in a subject enjoying more freedom of movement than I have, but in that case he would not be under the same compulsion to correct errors in placing his feet in response to visual stimuli, and the deductions would therefore be different.

From this it is clear that we cannot test the theory by comparing the results reported by one subject with deductions drawn from the behavioral adaptations of another subject having a different set of properties. The question we have to ask therefore is whether the theory can generate a different set of results not in another subject but in the same subject. And by the same subject I mean not merely the same person, but the same person engaged in the same kind of activities. If, for example, I had spent part of my time standing at the worktable, the character of the experiment would have been changed, and it would have been necessary to draw another set of deductions. The question must therefore be formulated in the following way: given the actual subject who performed the experiment, and given the activities in which he actually engaged and the behavioral adjustments he actually achieved, is it possible for the theory to mediate any deductions other than those recorded above?

The answer is that in their specific case no other deductions are possible. We have, so to speak, assigned specific values to the general terms of the theory, just as we might assign specific values to the coefficients of the unknowns in a set of simultaneous equations. Just as there is one and only one set of values of the unknowns that can be derived by applying the rules for solving simultaneous equations, so there is one and only one set of results when the rules of the behavioral theory of perception are applied to any system that has been fully specified. It can therefore be stated with complete confidence that if the deduced results do not occur in the system so specified, the theory is necessarily false. The results are in fact in agreement with the deductions, and the theory therefore has survived another crucial test.

Experiment III

9.25. In the experiments described above the transformations of V_1 and V_2 were effected by prisms mounted in spectacle frames. One effect of this arrangement is that the image formed by the prism remains invariant as long as the head is held in a fixed position, and can be scanned by the eye without loss of precision. It follows that neither of these experiments affords an opportunity to test the hypothesis that fixation movements of the eyes are acquired by conditioning, and that the visual perception of space is in part determined by the activation of engrams mediating such responses. To test this hypothesis it is necessary to transform the functions V_1 and V_2 in such a manner that fixation responses involving the eyes alone will be in error. An obvious way to do this is to incorporate a distorting prism in a contact lens. Since the angle at which a ray of light emerges from the prism is a nonlinear function of its angle of incidence, and the prism moves with the eye, it follows that when fixation is transferred from point A to point B, the angle of deflection of the light from B is no longer the same at the end of the response as it was at the beginning. A diagram will serve to clarify the geometric relations.

Figure 9.25.1 shows the normal geometric relations. A and B are fixed points and O is the node of the eye. If fixation is initially on A, it is evident that the eye must be rotated through the angle AOB in order to transfer fixation to B. (Actually a correction is required in view of the fact that O is not the center of rotation of the eye, but as this correction is systematic it can be neglected for the purpose of the present argument.) Figure 9.25.2 illustrates the transformation effected by a prism mounted in a spectacle frame. It will be seen that as long as the position of the prism is unchanged, that is, the head is held stationary, the directions in which the rays from A and B enter the eye are independent of the direction in which the eye is pointing. Consequently, if fixation is transferred from A to B, the eye must be rotated through the angle A′OB′, which in general is not equal to the angle AOB. In Figure 9.25.3 the prism is in contact with the eye, and fixation is assumed to be on A. With the prism in this position the deflection of the rays from A and B is essentially the same as in Figure 9.25.2, although by reason of the curvature of the prism the angle A′OB′ is likely to deviate from AOB less than in Figure 9.25.2. Now if the eye is rotated to the right is order to fixate B, the prism is carried with it, with the result that when the light from B falls on the fovea its angle of deflection is identical with that of the light from A in Figure 9.25.3. Hence, if the eye be rotated from direction A′ to direction B′ as shown in Figure 9.25.3, it will be carried to the right of the direction B′ as shown in 9.25.4. That is, this particular fixation response will go beyond its goal, with the result that the point B will be perceived as having changed its position. It is clear that in order to reach the goal the eye must be rotated from the direction A′ in Figure 9.25.3 to the direction B′ in Figure 9.25.4, that is, through an angle equal to the angle AOB in Figure 9.25.1.

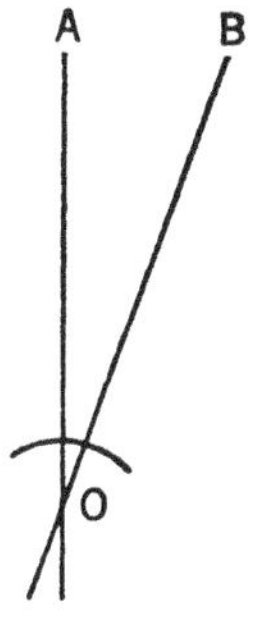

FIG 9.25.1.

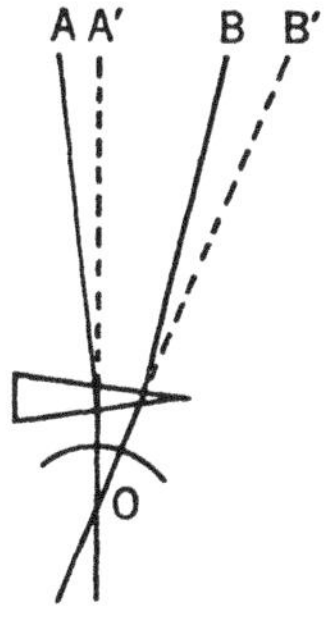

FIG 9.25.2.

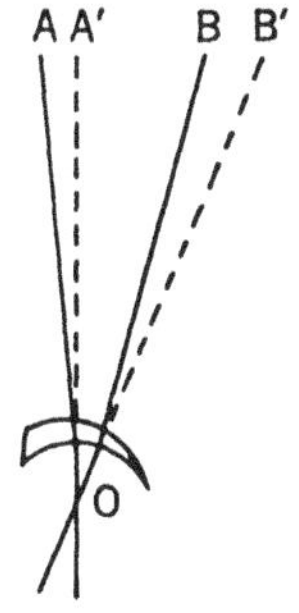

FIG 9.25.3.

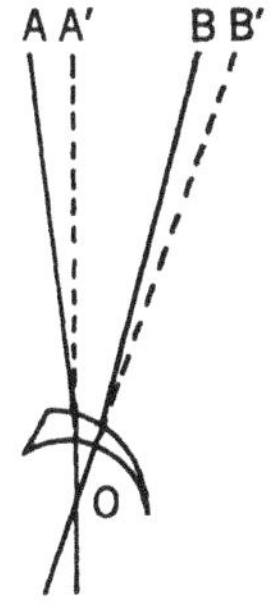

FIG 9.25.4.

Generalizing, we may say that no matter what actual distortions of the retinal image the prism may produce, the fixation movements required to scan any object must of necessity be identical with those that are required under normal conditions. It follows that if fixation movements are, as I have assumed, conditioned responses to compound stimuli including peripheral retinal components and proprioceptive components from the ocular muscles, the initial effect of wearing a prismatic contact lens will be that those responses will be subject to error. Readaptation will begin at once, and ultimately the transformed patterns of stimulation will evoke exactly the same responses as the corresponding normal patterns. Then, by the hypothesis that Π is identical with perception, we can deduce that the perceptual distortions produced by the prism will disappear, *and without the intervention of the manipulations that were necessary in the first two experiments*. That is, if the subject merely looks at his environment, scanning objects, and particularly outlines, but without attempting to establish any other kind of contact besides fixation, normal perception should be restored. If this prediction is not confirmed, the hypothesis that the proprioceptive functions V_3, V_4, and V_5 are essential components of the set Q will be proved false. But this will imply that the entire behavioral theory of perception is false, since without those functions it is logically impossible for conditioning to establish a one-to-one correspondence between Γ and the terminal positions of M, as shown in 3.1. An experiment with a contact lens thus exposes the theory to yet another critical test.

9.26. An opportunity of performing such an experiment was afforded me during a visit to Johannesburg in July 1959, when the Obrig Contact Lens Laboratories generously undertook the unusual task of building into a contact lens a curved prism of at least 10°. A mold of my left eye was made, and as the position of the base of the prism was of no consequence, it was agreed that the makers should choose a direction for the base that would enable them to maximize the angle of the prism. The position chosen was midway between the nasal and lower sides of the eye, and the angle was approximately 11°45′. The lens also incorporated corrections for the refractive errors of my eye.

The folding of the prism over the cornea has the effect of reducing the range of variation in the angle of incidence on the outer face of the prism of rays of light that reach the retina, with the result that the distortion over the whole field is much less marked than that produced by a prism with plane surfaces worn in a spectacle frame. Nevertheless my prism produced a sufficient measure of distortion to permit the hypothesis to be tested. Straight vertical lines appeared to be curved, with the convexity to the right, and horizontal surfaces below the level of the eyes appeared to dip down in the middle, being higher at the left than at the right. There was very little of the instability of shapes that is such a characteristic feature of perception when prisms are worn in a spectacle frame. The main evidence of this instability was that if attention was transferred from one point to another by means of a combined movement of head and eye, the second point appeared to have suffered a slight change of position. No noticeable changes of position were produced by fixation movements involving the eye alone, but careful observation showed that when two points were fixated in succession, the distance separating them was not identical in the two cases.

9.27. The lens was worn for several periods of approximately one hour each, the right eye being blindfolded. The first session was held in the office of the Johannesburg *Sunday Times* in the presence of a number of people who were interested in the outcome of the experiment, and there was consequently little opportunity for making careful observations, although even in these circumstances it was evident that some adaptation was taking place. In particular, the curvature of vertical straight lines appeared to diminish, and at the end of the hour I could not detect any positional instability under fixation movements, even when the head was involved. The clearest evidence of adaptation came about half an hour after removal of the lens. Sitting in a stationary car I got the impression that the vertical lines of a tall building in front of me were not quite straight. I then inspected the lines monocularly, and found that with the right eye they were straight but with the left eye they were curved, the convexity being to the left, that is, the opposite of what I had seen through the lens.

This result was all the more striking because the aftereffects observed on removal of lens and blindfold appeared to fade rather rapidly, presumably because perception was now dominated by the unaffected subsystem involving the right eye. No doubt if I had continued to wear the blindfold over my right eye after removal of the lens, the distortion would have disappeared quite soon. The significance of this finding is that it establishes the relative independence of the subsystems, (V_1, V_3, V_5) and (V_2, V_4, V_5), thus substantiating once more the correctness of Ashby's theory of the multistable system. These two subsystems normally operate in such close collaboration that psychologists have seldom had occasion to suspect that they are in fact independent. Yet it is precisely this independence that makes it possible for them to collaborate to generate binocular perception of space. If they were indissolubly linked with one another, as, for example, through the fibers of the two optic nerves having common terminal stations in the striate area, the range of their collaboration would be strictly limited, and it would be virtually impossible to account for the singularity of the binocular field discussed in 7.11. This singularity was there deduced from a hypothesis that included the assumption of the mutual independence of the two ocular subsystems, but at the time when the deduction was made no direct evidence of independence was available. The observation reported above supplies the missing evidence.

9.28. The argument of Chapters 2 and 3 rests on an axiomatic basis that includes the assumption that the set Q is divisible into a large number of subsects, $Q(\delta)$, each of which is capable of being conditioned separately to a response directed to the object specified by δ. If we assign fixed values to the functions V_6, V_7, and V_8, and neglect V_9, V_{10}, and V_{11}, the elements of $Q(\delta)$ are all the patterns of stimulation, (v_1, v_3, v_5), arising from a single object occupying a fixed position relative to $R(\Delta)$, through all possible directions of the eye. The theory assumed that the perception of this object as occupying a fixed position is determined in part by the conditioning of all the elements of $Q(\delta)$ to oculomotor responses that result in the fixation of the object. Since the contact prism has the effect that these responses are misdirected, the theory leads to the following deductions.

First, the correction of the errors induced by the prism must have the effect that the perceived positions of points will be stabilized. This does not mean that these positions will be *correctly* perceived; that can be effected only by the correction of errors in manual and other bodily responses. A corollary of this deduction is that when the subject has stabilized the perceived positions of a group of points forming a straight line that is initially seen as curved, the line will be perceived as straight. Second, the assumption of the mutual independence of the several subsystems, $Q(\delta)$, implies that the correction of a distortion in one part of the field has little or no effect on perceived distortions in other parts. Thus the straightening of one particular line does not mean that all other straight lines will automatically be perceived as straight. In short, the distortion has to be ironed out bit by bit.

These deductions were confirmed on the second day of the experiment. On that day the lens was worn for an hour in the morning and again for an hour in the afternoon. The morning session yielded disappointing results, but it subsequently became clear that this failure was completely consistent with the theory. Since the distortion was less than I had hoped for, I rather naïvely assumed that the best way to get results would be to make long sweeping movements of the eye from the middle of an apparently curved line to its extremities. I had for the moment forgotten the argument, presented in 2.16, that responses to a near goal are more likely to succeed and therefore to be reinforced than responses to a more distant goal. Accordingly in the afternoon session I decided to scan lines by means of very short movements of the eye, and in a remarkably short time such a line was perceived as being quite straight. At a later session I got a friend to time the process. A typical result was that a vertical line subtending a visual angle of approximately 35° was seen as completely straight after scanning it for twenty seconds. On the other hand a line parallel to the edge of a carpet was not seen as straight throughout its length even after two minutes. Subsequent inspection with the unencumbered right eye revealed that it was in fact curved at the section where I had failed to straighten it. This was confirmed by a witness with normal eyesight who inspected the line from the chair I had occupied.

On the basis of their experiments with wedge prisms mounted in a spectacle frame, Erismann and Kohler have concluded that there is some kind of physiological adaptation tending to straighten curved lines that are subjected to prolonged inspection. But the straightening is never complete. It is evident therefore that we cannot appeal to such a process here, since the straightening was complete, and more particularly because it failed when the line was objectively curved.

9.29. The second deduction, from the assumption of the mutual independence of the subsystems, was strikingly confirmed during the afternoon session. I sat on a chair near a bookcase with three shelves. One of the uprights of this case was about 60° to the left of the median plane of my body. I inspected it with my head turned to the left, and my eyes also turned to the left. Keeping my head in a fixed position I scanned the two lower sections of the upright, and presently these sections appeared to be completely straight. Then, still without moving my head, I turned my eyes up to inspect the top section. *It was still curved,* and a further process of scanning was necessary to straighten the whole line. It is clear that if the straightening were due to field forces in the visual cortex, no further exposure should have been necessary to straighten the top portion. (It must be remembered that there was no binocular parallax to complicate the stimulus.) The result is, however, completely consistent with the assumption that the conditioning of adaptive responses to $Q(\delta_1)$ (the lower part of the upright) does not guarantee the conditioning of responses to $Q(\delta_2)$ (the upper part), even if v_1 is essentially the same in both cases. It will be seen that in the circumstances of this part of the experiment the only important difference between the active elements of $Q(\delta_1)$ and $Q(\delta_2)$ is in the values taken by v_5, the proprioceptive afferents from the superior and inferior rectus muscles. If my head was not erect during the scanning, $Q(\delta_1)$ and $Q(\delta_2)$ also included different elements of V_3, the proprioceptive function of the internal and external rectus muscles of the left eye; but this involves no new principle.

Immediately after making the observations reported above I changed my position and inspected a vertical line in the median plane of my body, and also of my head. This line was just as markedly curved as the upright of the bookcase had been a few minutes earlier, and a further process of detailed scanning was necessary to straighten it. The difference between this situation and that presented by the bookcase is confined to V_3, the function of the lateral deviation of the left eye from its zero position, and V_6, the function of the deviation, about the vertical axis of the head, of the median plane of the head from the median plane of the body.

We thus have direct evidence not only that the proprioceptive afferents from the ocular muscles are implicated in the perception of space, but also that each of the compound patterns of retinal and proprioceptive stimuli must be separately conditioned to the appropriate oculomotor response.

9.30. Experiments II and III together help to explain the changes that take place in the visual perception of patients who undergo successful bilateral removal of cataracts. When correcting spectacles are fitted to such a patient there is a substantial increase in the size of the retinal image and it is characterized by spherical aberration. Since the latter phenomenon is a joint product of the condition of aphakia (absence of the crystalline lenses) and the properties of the correcting lenses, it can be readily understood that the distorted visual field is unstable under movements of the eyes, of the head, and of the body. According to a physician who himself was operated on (*Am. J. Ophthalmology*, 1952), the most disturbing instability arises from movements of the eyes. The difficulty caused by spherical aberration "is augumented when he discovers that the movements of his eyes, which were part of his former existence, suddenly cause the curved outside world to squirm like writhing snakes."

A well-motivated patient reacts to this instability by minimizing the movements of his eyes and learns to scan objects by slow movements of his head, looking all the time through the optical centers of his glasses. "When this simple trick is mastered," says the writer of the article, "the spherical aberration disappears, and, once gone, can only be elicited and reproduced with difficulty."

Although this statement must be accepted at its face value, it is not very easy to interpret. The difficulty is that it is almost certainly impossible to immobilize the eyes during scanning movements; but if the patient succeeded in doing so, it would be very easy to restore instability, and therefore spherical aberration, by deliberate movements of the eyes, since the patterns of stimulation when the eyes deviate from the central position have not been incorporated in the readapted system. I venture to think that what actually happens is something similar to what happened during the third session of Experiment III. The attempt to immobilize the eyes while the head is moving slowly must have the effect that the movements of the eyes are restricted to a very narrow range, so that the optimum conditions are established for the acquisition of correct fixation movements. Needless to say, correct movements of both head and eyes are acquired. When this results in the straightening of straight lines, it is reasonable to expect that the rate of movement will be increased, and that this will entail an increase in the range of ocular movements. If this is a true interpretation of what happens, then it is easy to understand the patient's difficulty in restoring spherical aberration. It is hard to restore precisely because most of the elements of $\bar{Q}$, the patterns of stimulation as transformed by aphakia and the correcting lenses, have become conditioned to effective fixation responses involving movements of both head and eyes. Here $\bar{Q}$ is assumed to include the drives that prompt the patient to go about his normal everyday activities. If he attempts to restore the spherical aberration he is temporarily substituting another and weaker drive, viz. curiosity regarding what he saw at the beginning of his aphakic career. This drive would tend to activate the pre-operational engrams, but because of its insignificant strength in comparison with the prevailing drives, it is to be expected that it will be more and more frequently overruled by the latter. Obviously some detailed investigation of the process of adaptation in aphakic patients is required.

Finally, it is important to note that the restoration of Euclidean space by this procedure does not guarantee that manual activities can now be carried out with ease. On the contrary, a long and arduous process of re-education is required. As the author of the article says, "Nothing can restore his confidence except constant practice. Self-assurance and the cajolery of his friends and admirers are unavailing. There is nothing to do except patiently repeat some manual task until confidence is again regained." Obviously it must be so if the theory of the multistable system is true. The elements of $\bar{Q}$ have become conditioned to appropriate fixation movements, but they still have to be conditioned to adequate manual responses. Clearly this presents a more formidable problem than the former, because the proprioceptive impulses determined by the initial positions of the hands are now relevant components of $\bar{Q}$, whereas the variables V_9, V_{10}, and V_{11} must be considered as inactive part-functions in the subsystem controlling fixation movements.

The author says nothing about perceptual instabilities experienced during this stage of the rehabilitation, but it is highly probable that there must be some shifting of the perceptual field when the hand fails to reach its goal. This, of course, would not be nearly such a disturbing experience as the initial instability arising from movements of the eyes, and the author may not have considered it worth mentioning. What is reasonably certain is that the regaining of manual dexterity must involve interpenetration of the subsystems generating Π and Π(G), thereby producing once more a unified perceptual field.

The same kind of argument applies to the enlargement of the retinal images. The author does not specifically state that the magnified objects are gradually scaled down to their true dimensions, but it is evident that this is precisely what must happen as a result of the acquisition of manual dexterity. The only permanent linear scale that is at the disposal of the patient is supplied by the dimensions of his own body, and the enlarged scale of visual perception must in the end be trimmed to fit this. What the author does say is that the difficulties of orientation arising from magnification are readily overcome. That can only mean that the visual scale is adjusted to fit the scale of Π(G).

CHAPTER 10

The Perception of Color

10.1. Ever since men began to speculate on the phenomena of conscious experience it has been customary to distinguish between sensation and perception, and this distinction has persisted to the present day. Sensation, it is usually held, is the raw material out of which perception is built. Today most psychologists would be willing to admit that learning plays an important part in building up perception, but they would claim that the sensory raw material belongs to a different category. It is "immediate experience," in the sense that it is not mediated by any independent variables that we can specify. It just happens, and we must accept it as being ultimately unexplainable. We can, of course, investigate the physiological process on which sensation depends, but the ultimate reason why those processes should generate specific sensory experiences remains a mystery. We can, for example, investigate the substances found in the rods and cones of the retina, and discover that they have the interesting property that they are levorotatory when stimulated by certain wave lengths of light and dextrorotatory when stimulated by other wave lengths. But this still leaves unanswered the question why light of one wave composition should generate the sensation we call red and lights of other compositions generate orange, yellow, green, blue, and violet sensations.

Now this last sentence, innocent as it may seem, contains a gross error. The assumption that the colors we perceive are completely determined by the wave composition of the light is false, and we should have realized this long ago. Hering's famous experiments on simultaneous color contrast demonstrated quite clearly that there is not just one stimulus that gives rise to any given color. When he illuminated a vertical screen of milk glass with two lights, white and red, and placed a vertical rod between the lamps and the screen, two shadows appeared, one lit by the red light only and the other by the white light. The red shadow was seen as red, and this seems to present no problem; but the shadow illuminated by the white light was seen to be green. If we use a green light instead of a red one, the white shadow appears to be red, and in fact we can give it almost any color we like by varying the color of the illuminant. Thus white light can produce a "sensation" of white or of any one of a wide range of other colors. Hering's explanation of these and similar phenomena was that there must be some kind of irradiation from the surrounding part of the retina, illuminated by both red and white light, to the area illuminated by white light alone. But this hypothesis was conclusively disproved by numerous experiments cited by Koffka (1936). For example, if sheets of red and green paper are placed side by side and a gray ring is laid on them symmetrically, the ring appears to be gray. But if a narrow strip of paper is laid over the whole, coinciding with the red-green intersection, the two portions of the ring now take on contrasting colors. Clearly some central process must be postulated to account for such facts.

Recently the assumption that color is a function of wave length has been subjected to a much more serious attack by the remarkable experiments reported by Land (1959). He made two photographs of a scene containing a wide range of colors, one through a red filter and the other through a green filter, using ordinary black and white film. Positive transparencies were made from the negatives. The picture made with the red filter he called the long wave record, or simply the long record, and the other one he called the short record. The long and short records were then put in a double projector so constructed that the two images could be exactly superimposed on one another on the screen. If the long record was illuminated by red light and the short record by white light, the picture on the screen reproduced the colors of the original scene with almost complete fidelity. When the short record was illuminated by the red light and the long record by the white light, each color was replaced by its complementary. In other experiments Land used pairs of bands from the spectrum as his sources of illumination. If the two wave lengths were quite close to one another no colors were seen. Thus no color was produced by wave lengths of 5990A and 5900A. (An Ångström unit, A, $= 10^{-10}$ meter.) But if 5990A was used for the long record and 5790A for the short record, colors of a relatively low saturation were seen. These are both within the yellow range of the spectrum.

The important thing about Land's experiments is that, with certain limitations that need not be discussed here, the longer and shorter waves used to illuminate the long and short records can be chosen from anywhere in the spectrum without materially altering the distribution of colors on the screen. That is, just as Hering demonstrated long ago that one and the same light stimulus can produce a wide variety of color perceptions, so Land has shown that one and the same color perception can be produced by a wide variety of different light stimuli.

10.2. In seeking to interpret these results we must keep in mind that in both sets of experiments the result produced by any given stimulus is not independent of the stimuli from the surrounding field. Land points out that if two spectral lights are mixed in the ratio determined by any point in one of his dual photographs, the result is what can be predicted by classical theory, and concludes that in order to produce the true color it must be surrounded by a random distribution of intensity ratios of the same waves. Be that as it may, the fact that the surroundings play an important part in the experiments of both Hering and Land prompts us to consider the circumstances in which colors are perceived in ordinary natural settings.

If we look at a red apple in a variety of situations we see it as red in every case, and the most obvious common-sense explanation of this uniformity is that it is reflecting light of exactly the same composition on each occasion. But a moment's consideration shows that this cannot be so. If it is placed on a sheet of white paper and illuminated only by the light from the blue sky, the apple reflects light of one composition; if the sky is overcast the reflected light is changed by the elimination of some of the blue rays; if it hangs on the trees the apple is illuminated by green light reflected by the leaves and transmitted through them, so that once again the reflected light has a different wave composition. In short, the composition of the light reflected by any object is not constant but undergoes an endless succession of transformations according to the contributions made to the incident light by colored objects in the environment.

Why are we not aware of this in everyday experience? I believe the answer is that we are misled by perception itself. If we look at the colored objects in our environment we see the colors as being located in the objects, but we do not see that those objects are radiating light in all directions and therefore changing the composition of the light reflected by neighboring objects. If this were not so the colors would not be visible to us, nor could they affect the emulsion of a color-sensitive photographic film. The fact that they do reach our eyes and penetrate the camera means that they *must* affect the wave composition of the light reflected by neighboring objects. The fact that we are aware of nothing of all this in our daily lives but obstinately see the apple as having the same red color in all circumstances constitutes a challenge to science. Our first problem in dealing with the perception of color must therefore be to discover the source of this remarkable constancy.

10.3. We begin by defining

(10.3.1) $\Lambda \equiv [\lambda;$ *λ is the wave length of a ray of reflected light*$]$.

It will be remembered that a set is defined as a collection of elements, and that the elements may include subsets of two or more primitive elements, extending even to the whole set. This mathematical convention is particularly useful for our present purpose, since the light reflected by natural objects can never be represented by a single primitive element, λ. It is only a high grade spectroscope that can isolate the primitive elements from one another. In everyday life the elements of Λ are always subsets.

Since colors are always seen as being located in objects (if we exclude film colors), the obvious way to incorporate Λ in our notational system is to redefine Δ so as to specify the wave length of the light reflected by an object. But here we encounter a difficulty. The wave composition of the reflected light changes, as we have seen, according to the character of the incident light. But the composition of this incident light is not available as a stimulus, even if the eye be placed in the position of the object receiving the light, in which case, of course, it cannot at the same time respond to the reflected light. It would seem, therefore, that there is no possibility of constructing a completely regular system including Λ. Nevertheless we can construct a system that achieves a reasonably close approximation to regularity by specifying the composition of the light reflected by objects surrounding any element of Δ. Since the contribution of any colored area to the composition of the incident light varies inversely as the square of its distance from the object, it is clear that the reflected light is most powerfully affected by the immediate environment of the object. If this environment is exposed to the same general illumination as the object itself, it follows that a system in which the variables include λ, the wave length of the light actually reflected by an object, and $\lambda(i)$, the wave length of that portion of the incident light contributed by the immediate environment, will be reasonably regular. Thus if $\lambda(i)$ be changed by moving the object into other surroundings, λ will change to a new value that will be determinate within certain limits of error. One possible source of error is that a surface, differently colored from the rest of the environment, may contribute to the incident light but be invisible. That is, it may affect λ without contributing to $\lambda(i)$.

We can now redefine Δ by

(10.3.2) $\Delta \equiv [(\gamma, \lambda, \psi, \lambda(i))$; γ, λ, ψ *refer to one piece of matter*].

Here, as in the earlier definition, (2.4.1), γ specifies the coordinates of a piece of matter referred to the reference frame, $R(\Delta)$, located in the child's body, λ is the wave length of the light reflected by that piece of matter, and ψ is the intensity of the reflected light.

It is evident that the situation has once more become exceedingly complex, in the sense that the wave composition of the light reflected by a substance whose molecular structure changes only very slowly, if at all, is subject to a wide range of variation according to the environment in which it is placed. We shall see presently that the process of adaptation generates a new simplicity out of this complexity, and in doing so creates a variety of side effects that have long fascinated and puzzled psychologists.

10.4. It might appear that the next step should logically be to incorporate the new definition of Δ into the definition of V_1 and V_2, since these are the only afferent variables directly affected by wave length. This would be a reasonable procedure if it could be shown that the perception of color is entirely independent of the perception of space. But it is obvious that this is impossible. Since the composition of the light reflected by an object is in part determined by its surroundings, the conditioning of appropriate responses to Δ, as defined in (10.3.2), cannot be begun until adequate responses to the spatial ordering of the environment have been established. It is clear that we cannot maintain the view that colors are subjective experiences fully determined by retinal processes, and that perception is the resultant of a process whereby those subjective experiences are externalized and given "a local habitation and a name"; for it is difficult to see how a local habitation can be assigned to a subjective experience that is liable to vary from moment to moment. It seems more reasonable to assume that the habitation is constructed first and the paint is put on afterward. Our problem will then be to disclose, if possible, the technique of the painter.

These considerations suggest that the most satisfactory way to deal with λ and $\lambda(i)$ is to add them to the elements of the already adapted system ${}_3\Phi$. The reason for the choice of ${}_3\Phi$ rather than ${}_2\Phi$ or ${}_1\Phi$ will become clear when we discuss the form of behavior that is available for the organization of color perception. We can then define

$$(10.4.1) \quad {}_4Q \equiv [(\phi, \lambda, \lambda(i)); \phi \varepsilon\, {}_3\Phi, \delta(\phi) = \delta(\lambda)]$$

where the last conditional statement means that λ describes the light reflected by the object whose specifications is implicit in ϕ. The term $\lambda(i)$ refers to the light reflected by the immediate environment of this object, which means that several elements of ${}_3\Phi$ are operating simultaneously. This suggests that a more appropriate definition would be

$$(10.4.2) \quad {}_4Q \equiv [(\phi, \lambda, \lambda(i)); \phi \varepsilon\, {}_3\Pi, \delta(\phi) = \delta(\lambda)].$$

That is, the perception of color can be developed only within a system that has already adapted in such a manner as to generate perception of the spatial ordering of the environment, with all the constancies that this implies.

10.5. In the earlier chapters we have seen that it was a simple matter to partition the sets ${}_1Q$ and ${}_2Q$ into formal equivalence classes such that all the elements of any one class could be conditioned to one and the same response. The criterion for the formation of such a class is that all its elements specify the same δ or ω. We must now seek an objective basis for the partitioning of ${}_4Q$.

An ideal solution would be to classify on the basis of the molecular structure of natural substances, since it is this structure that determines which rays are to be absorbed and which reflected. Hence λ is exactly determined by the molecular structure of the substance and the wave composition of the incident light. But this basis of classification cannot be adopted because the molecular structure cannot, at this stage of development, be an objective toward which behavior is directed, except in a very crude manner. It is not until one becomes a student of physics or chemistry that behavior is specifically directed to this aspect of matter. This is not to say that the structure of a substance is irrelevant: it is, on the contrary, highly relevant to our problem, but not in such a systematic way as the position occupied by an object is relevant to the acquisition of space perception.

Our basis of classification must satisfy two conditions. First, it must be objective, in the sense that the equivalence class to which any element of ${}_4Q$ belongs can be established by some standard physical operation; and second, it must be defined in terms of variables that can be included in the multistable system. It will be seen that molecular structure satisfies the first condition but not the second. We can solve our problem by defining

$$(10.5.1)\quad W \equiv [\lambda; \textit{for every } \lambda_j, \lambda_k \,\varepsilon\, W, \lambda_j(i) = \lambda_k(i)].$$

That is to say, W is the subset of Λ obtained by placing all natural substances in turn in a standard environment, such as a dark room with gray walls, and exposing them to a standard illumination. The formal equivalence class to which any element of ${}_4Q$ belongs can be determined by placing the object specified by it in the standard environment and illumination. This ensures that the first condition is satisfied. Since Λ is already included in our system, the second condition is satisfied as well.

We can now define a formal equivalence class of ${}_4Q$ by

$$(10.5.2)\quad {}_4Q(w) \equiv [q \,\varepsilon\, {}_4Q; \textit{for every } q_i, q_j \,\varepsilon\, {}_4Q(w), w_i = w_j].$$

It is important to remember that any element of ${}_4Q$ specifies both λ and $\lambda(i)$. Now consider two substances, a and b, such that $w_a \neq w_b$. It is conceivable that under different incident lights a and b may reflect lights of exactly the same wave composition, that is, $\lambda_a = \lambda_b$. But in that case $\lambda_a(i) \neq \lambda_b(i)$. Again, if $\lambda_a(i) = \lambda_b(i)$, then, since $w_a \neq w_b$, it follows that $\lambda_a \neq \lambda_b$. Hence, for every w_a, w_b, such that $w_a \neq w_b$,

$$(10.5.3) \quad {}_4Q(w_a) \cdot {}_4Q(w_b) = \Theta.$$

This has the important consequence that all the elements of ${}_4Q(w_a)$ are available for conditioning to one response, and all the elements of ${}_4Q(w_b)$ to another response, thereby making possible the construction of functional equivalence classes, ${}_4\Phi(w_a)$ and ${}_4\Phi(w_b)$, and laying the foundation for constancy in the perception of color.

10.6. We must next turn our attention to the question of the behavior that is to be conditioned to the elements of ${}_4Q$, and at once it is evident that there is an important formal difference between the responses evoked by the wave composition of the light and those that are conditioned to the position of the object reflecting the light. We may sum up the distinction by saying that whereas the latter set of responses vary as a continuous function of the variable in terms of which the equivalence class is specified, there is no evidence of any such continuous function in the case of responses to the wave composition of light. The reader will appreciate that I am not here speaking about sensory or perceptual responses, but about overt responses that can be measured and recorded by objective means. More precisely, if an approaching response is evoked by an element of an equivalence class, ${}_3Q(\delta)$, the position of the object is specified in terms of Cartesian coordinates referred to the initial position of $R(\Delta)$, and, assuming that there are no intervening obstacles, the response may be predicted by transforming to polar coordinates. This yields a vector that defines the path of the response. If one or more of the coordinates specified by δ should be altered, there is a corresponding quantitative adjustment of the response.

We look in vain for any corresponding quantitative relation between W, the set of terms that specify the equivalence classes of ${}_4Q$, and the responses that are evoked by the elements of ${}_4Q$. But if the responses to ${}_4Q$ cannot be ordered along a quantitative scale, it is clear that they must differ from one another in kind; and as far as verbal responses descriptive of color are concerned this is obviously true. The terms red, yellow, green, blue, purple, brown, black, white cannot, as responses, be arranged along any natural scale, but are all qualitatively different from one another. However, this represents a relatively advanced kind of behavior that almost certainly does not come into operation before some crude form of color perception has been generated by other means. And it is certainly not available to those infrahuman species that are known to be able to discriminate on the basis of color. This does not mean that verbal responses play no part in the development of color perception. We shall later consider experimental evidence that shows how powerful they can be. It just means that the foundations of color vision must be laid through the mediation of nonverbal behavior.

Perhaps the simplest way to discover the characteristics of this nonverbal behavior is to list some of the actions of mature persons in response to color. If we are picking apples or tomatoes, we choose the red ones and leave the green ones. When a motorist is approaching an intersection controlled by traffic lights he applies his brakes if the light is red but keeps going if it is green. When the bank submits a statement of your account you add to the balance at the top the amounts shown in black and subtract the amounts shown in red. If the balance at the top is in black it is treated as a positive number, if in red as a negative number. In a family one member always dries himself with the yellow towel and does not touch the others, while another member always chooses the blue towel. A woman chooses from among a number of available pairs of gloves one that harmonizes with the costume she is wearing, rejecting all the others. A group of children engaged in a rough-and-tumble will choose a springy green lawn as the theater of their activities rather than a gritty red, yellow, or brown gravel, or a gray unyielding concrete surface. An artist selects one pigment for a particular area of his canvas and rejects all others. A photographer using color film selects a scene in which there is a red object in the foreground.

It is evident that the one thing common to all these examples is that each of them involves a choice between two responses, which we may describe as acceptance or rejection, taking or leaving. In the simplest examples it involves reaching with the hand or refraining from reaching. Now by ${}_3F$ this reaching response is already conditioned to the elements of ${}_4Q$ that are brought into operation by the objective situation, so that the act of reaching or refraining from reaching must be interpreted as meaning that a strengthening or weakening of the reaching response has been conditioned to the additional components contained in $q \varepsilon {}_4Q$, that is, the wave composition of the reflected light. But conditioning does not occur by chance. There must be something in the natural situation that can serve as a reinforcing agency, positive or negative.

10.7. There is, in fact, no lack of reinforcing agencies. One of the most obvious is the varied effects of eating different substances. The effect of an ingested substance depends on its molecular structure. It may combine with the digestive enzymes to provide nutrition for all the body cells, or for certain selected tissues. It may supply some needs of the cells but not others. It may not react with the enzymes at all and pass through the body unchanged. It may form substances that cannot be absorbed by the tissues and are ejected by vomiting. Or it may form substances that destroy some of the tissues or interfere with their functioning, endangering the life of the organism.

Here we have reinforcing agencies in plenty, but it is not immediately obvious how they can operate to strengthen or inhibit reaching responses according to the wave composition of the light reflected by the substance, since, although positive reinforcement comes fairly quickly through the elimination of hunger pangs, negative reinforcement in many cases is delayed so long that its effect is negligible. However, there are physiological mechanisms that serve to speed up the process. The swallowing reflex is evoked by a wide range of substances taken into the mouth, and in the human child it seems that the chemical receptors do not evoke an unconditional inhibition of the swallowing reflex when the substance happens to be a noxious one. The child has to learn to accept substances that are beneficial and to reject those that are harmful; and this means that chemical stimuli that come into operation when the substance is in the mouth have acquired conditioned properties, and can therefore serve as secondary reinforcers for any response that precedes the stimulation of the chemical receptors, such as putting the substance in the mouth.

In order that this may happen it is necessary that beneficial and harmful substances should stimulate some other receptor differentially before they are put into the mouth. This requirement is satisfied by the olfactory receptors, which come into action both when the substance is in the mouth and before it reaches the mouth. Thus the odor of a substance becomes a conditioned stimulus for the response of putting it in the mouth or for the inhibition of that response. It is necessary to observe, however, that the responses conditioned to olfactory and gustatory stimuli do not operate in an absolutely uniform manner, but vary according to the nutritional state of the body. The response to a given odorous substance may vary all the way from voracious eating to complete rejection, and not only because of variation in the level of hunger. The response varies with the extent to which the tissues are depleted of the ingredients supplied by the food in question. This presumably means that interoceptive stimuli collaborate with the chemical stimuli in determining the response.

10.8. Now the molecular structure of a substance, which is the source of the primary reinforcement, is also responsible for the chemical stimuli and is therefore the secondary reinforcing agency as well. In addition, this structure determines which rays of the incident light are to be absorbed and which reflected. That is, it determines the equivalence class, ${}_4Q(w)$, of the patterns of stimulation in which the substance is involved. There is, of course, no one-to-one correspondence between the retinal response to the composition of the reflected light and the effects that the substance produces when it reaches the stomach, or even when it reaches the mouth, but that is of no consequence, since the responses to be conditioned to wave length involve nothing more than the strengthening or inhibition of responses already conditioned to the corresponding elements of ${}_3Q$. The important thing is that the natural situation sets the stage for a classical conditioning experiment in that it provides both the conditioned stimuli, in the form of elements of ${}_4Q(w)$, and the unconditioned stimuli, in the form of chemical stimuli, that in conjunction with interoceptive stimuli have already been conditioned to the response of swallowing or rejection.

Now let us assume that there are several substances, determining elements of ${}_4Q(w_1)$, ${}_4Q(w_2)$, . . . ${}_4Q(w_n)$, such as boiled potatoes, fried egg, lettuce, tomato, in fact all the substances that appear in the child's normal diet. These foods are presented in a variety of combinations, so that the colors surrounding any one food will vary from one occasion to the next. If plates of different color are used on different occasions, that too will result in variation in the light reflected by any one substance. In addition to this there is a wide range of variation in the composition of the light entering the room, which is not detected by ordinary mature subjects because they have already developed color constancy. For example, if the sun is shining on grass and green trees outside the window, the light entering the room will be predominantly green. If the sun is low in the sky the proportion of long waves is greater than it is at noon, and of course clouds have a direct effect on the amount of blue light reflected by the sky.

The stimulus situation appears to be hopelessly confused, but by (10.5.3) the patterns of stimulation from two foods that are presented simultaneously can never be identical. Consequently, if the child has a favorite food that he likes to eat first, or last, the relevant (λ, $\lambda(i)$) automatically becomes a conditioned stimulus for this act of choice. The conditioned properties already acquired by the chemical stimuli delivered by the preferred food are sufficient to guarantee immediate reinforcement. It will be apparent that this process necessarily involves differential conditioning to the lights reflected by the several foods that are on the plate, since the choice of one implies the momentary rejection of all the others.

10.9. The necessary outcome of a multitude of such conditionings is that some of the formal equivalence classes, ${}_4Q(w)$, are transformed into functional equivalence classes, ${}_4\Phi(w)$; but it may be expected that initially the w specifying any such class will not represent a single standard color but will include rather a wide range of elements of W. In the earlier stages there will be a certain amount of overlapping between the classes. One obvious reason for this is that the standard light, w, reflected by a particular type of food, varies from one sample to another. Even if several samples are initially identical, the culinary treatment to which they are subjected may change them all to different elements of W. All this implies that the functional equivalence classes are initially few in number, wide in range and not sharply demarcated from one another. The laboratory of life will, however, provide many situations that demand more refined differentiation, so that the number of equivalence classes should increase, with a corresponding narrowing of their range. But before we consider this process of subdivision it will be useful to investigate some of the implications of the conditioning described above.

The most obvious implication is that some new property has been added to perception; and since this new property is superimposed on ${}_3\Pi$ without altering it in any way, it must have the same local habitation as the elements of ${}_3\Pi$. In our mature experience the only property that seems to satisfy this condition is color. We may therefore formulate the hypothesis that color is a perceptual property involving the activity of engrams mediating responses of which the essential feature is choice from among a number of alternatives, the stimulus being the wave composition of the light reflected by the several objects between which the choice can be made. We may use the symbol ${}_4\Phi$ to represent the states of readiness including these new engrams, and ${}_4\Pi$ to represent a simultaneously active subset of ${}_4\Phi$. It must be understood, of course, that ${}_3\Pi$ is included in ${}_4\Pi$. That is, the perception of color is inseparable from the perception of the positions of the objects that carry it.

A second implication flows from the character of the behavior that is conditioned to the wave composition of the light. Unlike the behavior that generates ${}_3\Pi$ this is not quantitatively graduated to adapt to quantities measured along some continuous physical scale. It is true that wave length is measured by such a scale, but the behavior in question does not vary continuously with wave length. On the contrary, the same response may be evoked by any one of a collection of lights that would be matched with lights taken from a substantial range of the spectrum. Moreover, the same response may, under different conditions of organic need, be evoked by any one of an entirely different range of lights. The response, although it is evoked by the wave composition of the light, is not in any sense related to wave length; it is related to the relevance of the substance reflecting the light to the organic needs of the body. It is that relevance that is the source of the primary reinforcements on which the whole system is built. The essence of the behavior is selection, but what we select is not a wave length but a substance that is good to eat. Since, then, the behavior is not related to any variable that can be expressed in simple quantitative terms, we can deduce that the perceived colors do not fall into any obvious quantitative sequence, but are distinguished from one another qualitatively.

Since reflected light may include any combination of wave lengths, there is nothing to prevent the emergence of color qualities that cannot be matched by any color produced by a single wave length. The purples and browns, which are not to be found in the spectrum, confirm this deduction.

We can also deduce that when a child who is in the process of developing color perception is tested by being asked to name colors presented in isolation, and not in any of the contexts in which his discrimination is being sharpened, he will be likely to make mistakes, or to give different responses on different occasions. Thus if he is shown a red object at noon, in a room flooded with green light reflected by grass and trees outside the window, he might easily report it to be yellow, whereas the same object, seen in a room illuminated by late afternoon sunlight, might be correctly reported as red. I have observed confusion of this kind in several children between the ages of two and three.

Now acccording to all the well-known theories of color vision, color is a sensory experience that is primarily determined by the biochemical and physiological events induced in the retina by the wave length of the stimulus light. But if this were true it would seem that an intelligent child of two could hardly be confronted with a simpler task than naming the colors red, yellow, green, and blue. To people with normal color vision they are so sharply differentiated from one another that a child would seem very dull if he failed to attach the right names to them. Yet the confusion is found in bright children who are capable of what seem to us to be far more difficult differentiations, such as attaching their correct names to people they have met only once. The mystery disappears at once if the stabilization of color vision depends on the organizing of functional equivalence classes each of which may contain many hundreds of elements. If the chosen test stimulus, which it must be remembered includes $\lambda(i)$ as well as λ, has not yet been incorporated in an equivalence class, the response must necessarily be indeterminate.

10.10. There are many other natural situations that provide occasions for the conditioning of selective responses to the wave composition of the light, but there is no need to describe, or even enumerate, them. If the mechanism that operates in the case of food has been correctly described, then the same mechanism must operate in all the other situations. But there is one important source of refinement of color discrimination that is available to man and to no other species. This is language. It is unlikely that language is ever the medium through which color is created for the first time, since the child normally acquires selective responses to food and to other objects and substances in his environment while his command of language is still quite primitive; but language is unexampled as a means of subdividing the relatively small number of wide ranging equivalence classes that are established through interaction with the natural environment.

The manner in which language operates may be gathered from a beautiful experiment reported by Howells in 1944. The procedure was to present a color and a tone simultaneously and to require the subject to name the color. Two colors were used, a red with a tinge of blue, and its complementary. After the first 5,000 trials saturated and unsaturated colors were presented in alternation. We may call the saturated colors R and G, and the unsaturated colors r and g. Two tones were used, differing only in pitch. We shall call the lower one 1 and the higher one 2.

In each group of 20 trials the stimulus combination (1,R) was presented nine times, (1,G) once, (2,G) nine times and (2,R) once, the order being randomized. After the first 5,000 trials the same procedure was followed, except that if R or G was presented in one trial, r or g was presented in the next trial, and again R or G in the next. The subjects were paid for their services and warned that they would be dismissed if they made too many mistakes.

It is evident that in this situation the response of naming red became conditioned to the low note, and that of naming green to the high note, so that when (1,g), or even (1,G), was presented there was a tendency to call the color red, and similarly to name green when (2,r) or (2,R) was presented. But the subjects actually saw red as green or green as red, and this was conclusively proved by a supplementary experiment in which the subjects were asked to adjust the filters so as to make the color change from its initial R or G to white. If the adjustment was made to the accompaniment of the low note, the light which the subject declared to be white was actually an unsaturated green. If the high note was sounded during the adjustment, the color that to the subject looked white was an unsaturated red.

10.11. There are two important conclusions that can be drawn from this experiment. The first is that it is not only $\lambda(i)$ that can collaborate with λ in determining the equivalence class to which a pattern of stimulation belongs. In this case presumably both λ and $\lambda(i)$ were constant, but in addition there was one tonal stimulus that nearly always accompanied the red light, and this became a powerful conditioned stimulus for one of the responses —saying the word "red"—that had previously been conditioned to the elements of the "red" equivalence class. So powerful was this that when a green light was presented with the low note the total pattern of stimulation was still an element of the "red" equivalence class, and the color was accordingly seen as red. We may be reasonably sure that if odors were used instead of tones the results would be the same, although fewer trials would probably suffice.

The second conclusion is that what determines the perceptual outcome is not the stimulus but the activity of the engram mediating the response conditioned to it. This is particularly clearly brought out by the supplementary experiment, in which the responses of pronouncing the words "red" and "green" were not evoked at all. The subject was asked to adjust the filters to make the light white. When it was white by normal standards it was seen as red if the low note was sounding, and green was added to neutralize the red. If the subject responded to this green light by calling it white, this can only mean that an engram was operating to push the perception in the direction of red. We may perhaps describe the action of this engram by saying that it delivers to the motor system an instruction of the form: Act as if red has been added to the light. The engram is still active when the adjustment has been made, but there is no evidence of the overt response in the subject's verbal behavior.

It will be seen that in this respect the perception of color has the same formal properties as the perception of space. That is, the building up of a stable behavioral field is a necessary condition for the emergence of perception, but it is the activity of the engrams that constitutes perception, and not the actual performance of the responses. If this were not so it would be impossible to perceive a variety of colors simultaneously.

10.12. It is now possible to understand how language contributes to the refinement of color perception. The essence of the matter is that when a language contains a rich vocabulary of color names, the number of available responses from which a selection can be made is enormously increased, and the equivalence class defined by each name has a very much narrower range. In the natural situations discussed above positive reinforcement is obtained if the response is evoked by any one of a number of substances covering a wide range of elements of W; but in social situations a verbal response is likely to be extinguished if it does not agree with the response that would be given by another person who hears it, and to be reinforced if it agrees. It is of no consequence that such responses have no direct relevance to physiological needs: they are relevant to social needs, and that is enough to ensure their reinforcement, whether positive or negative.

Similarly it is of no consequence that the response is an arbitrary phonetic sequence having no relation whatsoever to the composition of the light to which it refers. The important point is that this response is conditioned to all the elements of some narrowly limited equivalence class, ${}_4Q(w)$, and the state of readiness for this response that is induced by the action of any one of those elements is sufficient to generate perception of the relative color. There is no need to analyze the process in detail: it is essentially the same as that already described.

We can deduce from this that the rate at which color discrimination develops will depend in part on the size of the color vocabulary that is in common use in a community. This in turn depends on the variety of colors in which common household goods are supplied. There has been an enormous increase in this variety during the first half of the twentieth century, and we can therefore deduce that children today develop color perception at an earlier age than they did at the beginning of the century. This seems to be confirmed by the fact that the test of naming the colors red, yellow, green, and blue was assigned to a mental age of seven in the 1911 revision of the Binet-Simon scale for the measurement of intelligence. In Burt's version of the scale, published in 1921, the test was assigned to the age of five; and in the modern Terman-Merril scale it is placed at the age of three.

10.13. We must now test the validity of the theory by investigating its logical implications and comparing those with the observed facts about color perception.

The conditions under which children are brought up vary enormously, and as we have assumed that color discrimination cannot begin until a child is able to do quite a number of things for himself, we can assume that there is considerable variation in the child's freedom to make choices. For example, freedom of choice is reduced by uniformity of diet, or if food is cooked in such a manner that all the ingredients take on approximately the same color. From this we can deduce that there is likely to be a much wider range of variation in color vision than there is in the perception of space. Where there is adequate freedom of choice, which probably applies to the majority of the population, there is likely to be a large measure of agreement with respect to the number of primary color qualities that are distinguished. But if the area of choice is severely restricted during the period when color perception normally develops, one or more of the primary qualities may fail to come to maturity. If the child then learns to make his choices on the basis of stimuli other than the wave composition of the light, the opportunity for developing normal color vision may be lost forever, since the alternative stimuli will generally suffice to mediate the appropriate choice, and there will not again be sufficient drive to allow responses to be conditioned to the composition of the light. There is a great variety of ways in which freedom of choice on the basis of wave length may be restricted, and it follows therefore that there will be a corresponding variety in the forms of color blindness.

This deduction is confirmed by the facts of color blindness, but of course color blindness may also result from deficiencies or abnormalities in the retinal apparatus, and the confirmation therefore carries less weight. However, no physiological theory of color vision has yet been able to account satisfactorily for the great variety of color deficiency, whereas it is precisely this variety that is accounted for by the behavioral theory.

10.14. Turning now to normal color vision, and neglecting individual differences, let us consider the implications of the hypothesis that color constancy is determined by the conditioning of all the elements of an equivalence class, ${}_4Q(w)$, to one and the same response. It will be remembered that the significant components of any $q \varepsilon {}_4Q$ are λ, the light reflected by the object, and $\lambda(i)$, the light reflected by the immediate surroundings, and that

$\lambda(i)$ is assumed to make an important contribution to the incident light by which the object is seen. Since $(\lambda, \lambda(i))$ is assumed to produce a determinate response appropriate to w, the standard light reflected by the object, it will be useful if we can find an invariant operator that will enable us to calculate w from λ and $\lambda(i)$.

For this purpose it will be convenient to assume that the standard light used for the determination of w is pure white containing all the wave lengths, that is, Λ. Then $\lambda(i)$ can differ from Λ only by not containing certain elements of Λ. Let the missing elements be represented by $\lambda'(i)$. Then $\lambda(i) + \lambda'(i) = \Lambda$. In other words, $\lambda'(i)$ is the complementary of $\lambda(i)$, since the mixture of the two gives white light. Now if the object absorbs none of the rays of $\lambda'(i)$, we can calculate w at once by

$$(10.14.1) \quad w = \lambda + \lambda'(i).$$

But if the object absorbs some of the rays of $\lambda'(i)$, say $\lambda''(i)$, then w is given by

$$(10.14.2) \quad w = \lambda + \lambda'(i) - \lambda''(i).$$

It must be understood that the invariant operator we are looking for has nothing in common with the physical operation by which w is determined objectively. It is an operator that utilizes nothing but the afferent processes generated by the objective situation. For this reason it is clear that (10.14.2) is in general unsuitable for our purpose, since, although the information expressed by $\lambda'(i)$ is implicit in $\lambda(i)$, the actual light reflected by the surroundings, there is no direct representation of $\lambda''(i)$ in the afferent system. Of course it may be represented indirectly, but we shall defer consideration of this point till later. Assuming that there is no indirect representation, the only possible operator is that expressed in (10.14.1).

Naturally we do not know the exact nature of the physiological counterpart of this operator, but we must assume that it has such a counterpart, since in the living system the varying lights reflected by a red apple, say, all give rise to the same color perception. But we can express this physiological operation in symbolic form, and use it to deduce what will happen in specific situations. The symbolic expression can, of course, be translated into another symbolic form, using words. Thus it might be translated: add to the color reflected by the object the complementary of the color reflected by the surroundings, and that will reveal the real, permanent, inherent color of the object. This is more cumbersome than (10.14.1), but it says the same thing.

Now let us apply (10.14.1) to Hering's window. The surfaces illuminated by the red light only, by the white light only, and by both lights are all in the same plane. Hence, in contrast to most natural situations, in which the reflecting substances in the environment are 3-dimensional, the light reflected by the surface surrounding the "white" shadow has no effect on the light reflected by the shadowed part of the glass. Nevertheless (10.14.1) comes into operation and transmits to the effector part of the cortex the instructions: add to the light reflected by that shadow the complementary of the surrounding light. Since the shadow is actually a white light of low intensity, the result is that it is perceived as being tinged with green.

Now consider what will happen in an ordinary 3-dimensional situation in which an object that is actually green is set in a pink environment. The red light reflected by the surrounding objects will neutralize the green light reflected by the object, so that the light it reflects into the eye is white light. In these circumstances (10.14.1) operates in the same way. It dictates the addition of the complementary of the surrounding red to the white light reflected by the object, and the result is that it is perceived in its true color—green.

It will be evident now that there is no need to invent a concept of retinal irradiation to account for the phenomena of simultaneous color contrast. This is not to say that there is no such thing as irradiation, but just that the facts of color perception would be the same whether it were involved or not. But actually there are two facts that stand against the hypothesis of irradiation. The first is the indeterminacy that is characteristic of the early stage in the development of color perception. This would hardly be possible if the change in λ induced by $\lambda(i)$ were automatically corrected by irradiation from the area stimulated by $\lambda(i)$. The second fact brings us to the case, mentioned earlier in this section, in which the operator defined in (10.14.1) does not suffice to give the required correction. It must frequently happen that the molecular structure of a substance is such that it will absorb a large proportion of the rays included in the complementary of the incident light. In that case the reflected light will be not

$$\lambda_1 = w - \lambda'(i)$$

but $$\lambda_2 = w - \lambda'(i) + \lambda''(i),$$

where the operations of subtraction and addition are to be understood as set theoretic operations. Thus λ_1 is the set of all the wave lengths included in w except those that are also elements of $\lambda'(i)$. But if we accept the irradiation hypothesis and also the hypothesis that the perceived color is entirely determined by retinal events, then the perceived color must be given by

$$\lambda_2 + \lambda'(i) = w + \lambda''(i).$$

But this means that it is impossible to explain color constancy if we rely entirely on events taking place in the retina.

10.15. This argument makes it clear that the operator (10.14.1), although it may suffice to explain the facts of simultaneous color contrast, is incapable of explaining color constancy in general. There is nothing surprising in this, since, according to our hypothesis, a functional equivalence class is formed by conditioning the elements of ${}_4Q(w)$ to one and the same response. But as $\lambda''(i)$ varies from one element of ${}_4Q(w)$ to another, it is evident that some other piece of information is needed in addition to λ and $\lambda(i)$. In many cases this information is available in the form of knowledge of the relative permanency of the substance reflecting the light. That is, if the subject can identify the substance by properties other than those that determine the reflected light, there is no obstacle to the conditioning of all the elements of ${}_4Q(w)$ to a single response.

There are, however, many cases where this identification is impossible. For example, the majority of people are not sufficiently acquainted with the chemistry of dyes to enable them to identify the substance that is responsible for the color added to a fabric. The result is that two dyes that appear to be identical in one light may be seen to differ when they are exposed to another light.

From this we can deduce that the degree of completeness of color constancy is likely to show a considerable range of variation within those members of a population whose color vision is normal as measured by standard tests. It is highly improbable that any person will ever be found in whom constancy is complete. The multiplicity of new substances that are constantly being produced by the chemical industry is such that nobody could possibly become acquainted with the reactions of all of them to all possible forms of illumination.

10.16. We turn next to the phenomena of successive color contrast. These are usually demonstrated by asking the subject to fixate for 30 seconds a point in the middle of a colored square on a neutral gray ground. The colored square is then suddenly removed, so that the subject is now looking at a uniform gray ground. Alternatively he may be asked to shut his eyes at the end of the 30 seconds fixation. In either case he reports seeing a square whose color is the complementary of the stimulus color. This persists for some time but begins to fade almost at once.

The fact that negative after-images occur whether the eyes be open or shut indicates clearly that they depend on some physiological aftereffect of photic stimulation. Hence they are of physiological rather than psychological interest. It is evident that their duration, their gradual fading, and the fluctuations to which they are subject during the fading may provide useful information to the physiologist who is trying to discover how the retina responds to different wave lengths. On the other hand no information concerning the *perception* of color can be gathered from these facts. The colors of the after-images are determined not by the intrinsic character of the physiological processes in the retina, but by the responses that have been conditioned to those processes when, in the course of normal interaction between the organism and the environment, they have been aroused by reflected light.

However, the persistence of the physiological processes raises a new question. It frequently happens that fixation of a brightly colored object gives rise to retinal events that are quite sufficient to generate negative after-images, but in the circumstances of everyday perception we are seldom aware of them. What happens to them? Are they suppressed, and if so, by what means? They can in fact be detected whenever we choose to look for them, by directing the gaze to a suitable blank surface. This means that if there is a mechanism of suppression it does not operate directly on the retina.

Actually there is no need to postulate any such mechanism, since the concept of equivalence classes is sufficient to account for the facts. Indeed, if it were not for this it is difficult to understand how our perception of color could be anything but chaotic. On the occasions when fixation is sufficiently prolonged to give rise to a physiological aftereffect the retinal response to a new object of regard is modified, but since the first object is still perceived as occupying the same position in space, the system contains enough information to serve as a conditioned stimulus for the invariant response that specifies the equivalence class to which the color of the second object belongs. Searching for the after-images involves a change of drive, with the result that the pattern of stimulation now belongs to a different equivalence class and a different color is perceived.

10.16. It is now possible to offer an interpretation of Land's results, briefly referred to in 10.1. Let us begin by making the assumption that for any substance there is a range of incident lights —a subset of Λ—such that for each element of this subset the longer and shorter waves are reflected by the substance in an invariant proportion. Thus if the longer waves are orange and the shorter are yellow, and the substance reflects 0.6 of the orange and 0.2 of the yellow; then, with the longer waves yellow and the shorter blue-green, these waves will also be reflected in the proportion of 3 to 1. This assumption is put forward not as a serious physical hypothesis but as a hypothesis designed to apply to the limited physical system set up by Land.

Now let us assume that the spectral lights used to illuminate the long and short records satisfy the above condition with respect to two or more of the substances represented in the dual photograph, and also that the condition is satisfied by a mixture of the lights transmitted by the red and green filters used in making the photographs. Then it follows that each of the substances is represented on the screen by a mixture of long and short waves in the correct intensity ratio, since that ratio is incorporated in the dual photograph. This mixture is, in fact, one of the mixtures that can be reflected by the substance itself, provided the appropriate incident light falls on it. However, this reflected light cannot in itself determine correct perception of the color of the substance unless, according to our hypothesis, the incident light is also represented in the afferent system. That is, we need both λ and $\lambda(i)$. But by the conditions of the experiment, the light that illuminates any one object, determining λ in conjunction with the intensity ratio supplied by the photographs, also illuminates the immediate environment of the object, thereby providing $\lambda(i)$. Hence the total pattern of stimulation, $(\lambda, \lambda(i))$, is an element of the equivalence class, ${}_4Q(w)$, conditioned to the invariant response that determines the perceived color of the object. Generalizing to the whole picture, we can deduce that all those substances for which the stated conditions are satisfied both by the lights used in making the photographs and those used for illuminating them will be perceived in their normal colors. Other substances for which the conditions are not fully satisfied will be perceived as having undergone some color transformation. This is precisely what Land found.

10.17. In our discussion of the perception of the spatial ordering of the environment we have relied for confirmation of the behavioral theory on experiments in which the exteroceptive afferent functions are subjected to systematic distortion. The theory of color perception demands a similar test. If the composition of the light reaching the retina is transformed in a systematic manner, the behavioral theory enables us to deduce that the colors of objects will be perceived in a different way. But by the theory of the multistable system readaptation should begin at once, and, by the behavioral theory of perception, when the process of adaptation is complete, the colors of objects in the environment should be perceived in exactly the same way as they were before the transformation was applied. These deductions are exactly confirmed by two experiments reported by Kohler (1951), in which changes in color perception were brought about by prolonged and continuous wearing of spectacles.

10.18. In one experiment the right half of each lens was yellow and the left half blue. Since the spectacles were attached to the nose in the usual way, the dividing line between the two colors was always in the median plane of the head. Consequently the color superimposed on any object was jointly determined by the position of the object relative to the median plane of the body and the angle between the median plane of the head and the median plane of the body. It was unaffected by movements of the eyes.

The effect of the filters was to prevent certain rays from getting through, and we may therefore represent the stimulus presented by any object by $(\lambda - \beta, \lambda(i) - \beta)$, where $\beta \varepsilon \Lambda$, and takes either of two values, β_1 and β_2, according as the light enters the eye through the blue or the yellow filter. Since this depends jointly on the position of the object and the orientation of the head we can specify the conditions determining which of its two values β will take. To simplify the argument we shall confine our attention to occasions when the head is erect on the shoulders, and the only rotations that occur are about its vertical axis. We then define x as the angular deviation from the median plane of the body of a ray of light reflected into the eye by an external object, and ξ as the angular deviation of the median plane of the head from the median plane of the body.

We shall adopt the symbol ${}_4\bar{Q}$ to represent the set of states of the afferent system as modified by the spectacles. Omitting irrelevant components, we define it by

$$(10.18.1)\quad {}_4\bar{Q} \equiv [(x, \xi, \lambda - \beta, \lambda(i) - \beta); \text{ if } (x - \xi) > 0, \beta = \beta_1, \text{ if } (x - \xi) < 0, \beta = \beta_2].$$

Since $\lambda(i)$ refers to the surroundings of the object to which λ refers, β will take one value for some of its components and the other value for the remainder.

If we now select some object whose relevant properties are specified by $\delta \epsilon \Delta$, as defined in (10.3.2), and write an equivalence class, ${}_4\bar{Q}(\delta)$, including all the elements of ${}_4\bar{Q}$ incorporating the selected δ, we shall have to divide it into two subclasses, ${}_4\bar{Q}_1(\delta)$ and ${}_4\bar{Q}_2(\delta)$, according as the third component of the element is $\lambda - \beta_1$ or $\lambda - \beta_2$.

Now the afferent processes specified by the elements of ${}_4\bar{Q}(\delta)$ have already, by ${}_4F$, been conditioned to specific responses, thereby determining elements of ${}_4\Pi$; and since it is evident that ${}_4\bar{Q}(\delta) \cdot {}_4Q(\delta) = \Theta$, it follows that the object will not be perceived as having its standard color. Further, since ${}_4\bar{Q}_1(\delta) \cdot {}_4\bar{Q}_2(\delta) = \Theta$, there will be one color when $(x - \xi)$ is positive and another color when it is negative. However, the colors may be expected to show some instability owing to the varying effect of the subtraction of β from $\lambda(i)$. Thus if the object is in the middle of the yellow field, the pattern of stimulation will approximate more closely to an element of ${}_4Q(\delta)$ such as might arise when the whole scene is illuminated by artificial light; but the nearer it gets to the boundary between the yellow and blue fields, the more it will be influenced by the neighboring blue, so that it will appear to be rather more strongly tinted with yellow. This, of course, is a Hering's window effect. Successive color contrast effects will be observed as well, when an object is transferred from the blue to the yellow field, or vice versa.

10.19. We consider next what changes are likely to occur as a result of prolonged wearing of the spectacles. It is a well-known fact that when ordinary tinted spectacles are put on, all colors are at first perceived as having changed, but within a few minutes they are restored to normal. We cannot expect the same thing to happen when the two-tone spectacles are put on, not because a different set of principles is applicable here but precisely because the same principles operate in both cases. The effect of putting on the tinted spectacles is essentially the same as that produced by a sudden change in the composition of the general illuminant. In both cases traces left by the $\lambda(i)$ that were in operation prior to the change persist for some time, with the result that the colors of all objects appear to have undergone a sudden change. But the new patterns of stimulation are in fact elements of the same equivalence classes as those they have replaced, and the result is that when the traces of the previous stimulation have faded, all objects are once more perceived as having their standard colors.

There can be nothing like this rapid adjustment when two-tone spectacles are put on, because the new patterns of stimulation are not elements of the same equivalence classes as those they have replaced. That is, ${}_4\overline{Q}(\delta)\cdot{}_4Q(\delta) = \Theta$. This is not because the components we have called λ have been changed—they are changed by tinted spectacles as well—but because the associated change in $\lambda(i)$ is one that does not occur in nature. There are two reasons for this. The first is that the transformation imposed on $\lambda(i)$ does not entail any change in the light reflected on an object by its surroundings. If a part of the environment were actually yellow and another part blue, as for example, two adjacent beds of flowers, then both yellow and blue rays would contribute to the light falling on an object of another color, and this color would be correctly perceived. But the composition of the light reflected by an object is not affected at all by the colors that seem to be imposed on the surroundings, because in fact no colors are so imposed. The change is effected by subtraction only when the light reaches the spectacles. This is equally true of single-toned spectacles, but whereas in this case the transformation is equivalent to that produced by a change in the general illuminant, there is no natural source of light that separates its long and short waves and distributes them on opposite sides of a dividing line. One could, of course, have two sources of light with directed beams, and this brings us to the second reason. These two sources could not produce the effect of the spectacles unless they were attached to the forehead, so that the dividing line between the beams changed its position with movements of the head. Even this would not produce the same stimuli as the spectacles, because the light reflected by an object in the yellow part of the field would be modified by the light reflected onto the object by the blue part. If anyone were to fix such a projector to his forehead the light actually reflected by an object would change its composition with every change in the direction of the beams; but this is not so when the transformation is effected by two-toned spectacles.

Despite the fact that the elements of ${}_4\overline{Q}$ do not occur in nature, they are derived from ${}_4Q$ by a systematic transformation, and provided it can be shown that the terms of this transformation are represented by analogues in the afferent system, there is no reason why the elements of any ${}_4\overline{Q}(\delta)$ should not be conditioned to the same invariant response that, before the experiment, was evoked by the corresponding ${}_4Q(\delta)$. By (10.18.1) the character of the transformation depends on whether $(x - \xi)$ is positive or negative; hence if it can be shown that the system contains an analogue of this quantity, we can predict that stable color perception can be restored. The required analogue in fact exists. By ${}_3\Pi$ the position of an object relative to $R(\Delta)$ is perceived despite changes in the direction of the head and eyes; and ξ is represented by an element of V_6, the afferent function of ξ.

There is no need to investigate the process of readaptation in detail. It is sufficient to say that the afferent system has the regularity required for adaptation, and, provided there is adequate motivation, for every δ the elements of ${}_4\overline{Q}_1(\delta)$ and of ${}_4\overline{Q}_2(\delta)$ can be organized into a single functional equivalence class, ${}_4\overline{\Phi}(\delta)$. And generalizing, we reach the conclusion that when the spectacles have been worn long enough, ${}_4\overline{\Pi}$ will be identical with the pre-experimental ${}_4\Pi$. This conclusion is confirmed by Kohler's report. The blue and yellow colors imposed on the scene faded out, and the colors of objects no longer suffered a change when the head was rotated.

10.20. When the spectacles are removed at the end of the experiment normal color stimulation is restored, but the responses conditioned to the elements of $_4\overline{Q}$ are not immediately extinguished; and we can therefore deduce that normal color perception will not be re-established at once. To calculate the properties of the postexperimental perception all we need to do is to write a symbolical representation of the behavioral modifications involved in organizing $_4\overline{Q}_1(\delta)$ and $_4\overline{Q}_2(\delta)$ into a functional equivalence class and apply this to $_4Q$.

The required behavioral rule may be stated as follows:

(10.20.1) If $(x - \xi) > 0$, act as if β_1 were added to the light reaching the retina. If $(x - \xi) < 0$, act as if β_2 were added.

Since $\lambda - \beta + \beta = \lambda$, the application of this rule when the spectacles are on means that whether an object be seen through the blue or the yellow filter, the response will always be appropriate to the same pattern of stimulation, $(\lambda, \lambda(i))$. When the spectacles are removed, the pattern of stimulation is $(\lambda, \lambda(i))$ whether $(x - \xi)$ be positive or negative; but application of (10.20.1) has the effect that when $(x - \xi) > 0$ the subject acts as if the pattern of stimulation were $(\lambda + \beta_1, \lambda(i) + \beta)$, and when $(x - \xi) < 0$ he acts as if the patterns were $(\lambda + \beta_2, \lambda(i) + \beta)$. Now β_1 specifies the wave lengths that are stopped by the yellow filter and β_2 those that are stopped by the blue filter. Thus β_1 contains mainly short waves and β_2 long waves. Hence the application of (10.20.1) means that when an object is to the right of the median plane of the head the subject acts as if it were reflecting more blue light than in fact it does, and if it is to the left of the median plane he acts as if it were reflecting more yellow light. By $_4\Pi$ this means that he perceives everything to the right of the median plane as tinted blue, and everything to the left as tinted yellow. It is easy to see that the dividing line between the two colors moves with the head and is unaffected by movements of the eyes. This calculated result is confirmed in every detail by the report of the experiment.

10.21. The second experiment involved the wearing of 20° wedge prisms with bases to the left, exactly as in the second experiment described in Chapter 9. The spectacles were worn continuously over a period of four months. One of the effects of wearing these prisms is that there are bands of color at all vertical edges where there is a sharp transition from bright to dark. The effect may be explained with the help of a diagram. In Figure 10.21.1

			3	4	5	6	7	8		
	A	B							C	D
3	r	y	g	b	v					
4		r	y	g	b	v				
5			r	y	g	b	v			
6				r	y	g	b	v		
7					r	y	g	b	v	
8						r	y	g	b	v
retinal points	1	2	3	4	5	6	7	8	9	10
color	r	o	y	y	w	w	b	b	v	v

FIGURE 10.21.1.

ABCD represents a horizontal line through a white object, BC, lying on a black ground, AD. Six numbered points have been marked along section BC, and we are to consider what happens to the rays of light reflected by those points after they have passed through the prism and entered the eye. The prism splits the light from each point into a spectrum, and these spectra are all projected on the same retinal line, but in order to make things clearer the several spectra are shown in separate rows, carrying the same numbers as the points of origin of the light. Wave lengths are represented by the initial letters of the colors red, yellow, green, blue, and violet. To determine the composition of the light reaching any retinal point, we add together all the wave lengths appearing in the column representing that point. The result is shown in the final row of the table.

This shows that beyond the left edge of the white object there is a band of red. Moving to the right the red changes through orange to yellow, which becomes paler and merges into white. As we approach the right-hand side the white light changes to a pale blue, which becomes deeper and then changes to violet. It should be noted that the retinal area covered by the light from BC is more extended than it would be in the absence of the prism. The significance of this fact will appear in due course.

10.22. These colors introduce erroneous components into perception, but the question whether the errors will be eliminated must depend on whether they also induce errors of behavior that need to be corrected. Clearly no such errors occur if the subject is simply contemplating a scene, and there is thus no motivation for the elimination of the colors. On the contrary, they add variety and brilliance to a scene such as a snow-covered landscape, and in this case motivation would favor their retention. But there are other circumstances in which the colors are something of a nuisance. If the subject is reading or writing, for example, they fill up the spaces between letters and tend to blur outlines, with the result that the action cannot be carried out at its normal speed. The colors are particularly troublesome in writing, because they are more vivid when the ink is still wet. As an academic man Kohler had adequate motivation for the elimination of errors arising in these situations, but little or none for the correction of errors that might have been induced when he was out-of-doors.

In order to read accurately it is essential that the stimuli presented by the letters be unambiguous. This means not only that each letter must be physically unique in shape, but also that each unique shape should evoke a unique response in the subject. If the letters are subjected to a systematic distortion without destroying their unique identity, some learning may be required before the distorted shapes will invariably evoke the standard responses. When that happens each shape is perceived as falling within the permitted range of variation of the standard shape. The distorted shape is, in fact, incorporated into a functional equivalence class to which it did not previously belong. This is essentially what happens when we learn to read a difficult handwriting.

The distortion applied to printed characters by the wedge prisms is systematic, in that every left edge is decorated with bands of blue and violet, and every right edge with bands of red and yellow. This decreases the speed of reading for a time, partly because the colors themselves tend to evoke verbal responses that compete with responses that should be evoked by the printed words, and partly because some of the letters seem to be lost in a mass of color. A thin vertical black line, for example, is overlaid by violet rays derived from the white area to its left and also by red rays from the white area to its right, with the result that no black is seen at all. The direct verbal responses to the colors are irrelevant to the purpose served by the reading and are therefore subject to rapid extinction. But how is the subject to meet the difficulty that some of the characters are blurred beyond recognition?

The answer turns out to be very simple. Just because the color is applied to right and left edges in a systematic way, it follows that each character, despite the distortion applied to it, continues to present a pattern of stimulation that is unique, that is, a pattern that is distinct from the patterns presented by all the other characters. Hence there is no obstacle to the conditioning of each pattern to the response previously conditioned to the undistorted character.

The process is greatly assisted and accelerated by the fact that most of the letters show enough black to be recognizable. We know from tachistoscopic experiments, and from the frequency with which typographical errors escape the attention of an inexpert proofreader, that words may be perceived as having their correct form in spite of distortions. That is, a limited part of the word is a sufficient conditioned stimulus to evoke the response that initially required the collaboration of all the characters; and provided that response is evoked, the word is perceived as being correctly spelled. (This, it should be noted, is another powerful piece of evidence in support of the hypothesis that it is the response rather than the stimulus that determines what is perceived.) The conditioned properties of the attenuated stimulus then make it possible for the subject to respond to an apparently chaotic pattern of color by naming a letter of the alphabet.

But if a pattern of color becomes a conditioned stimulus for the response of naming a letter of the alphabet, it follows that this pattern becomes an element of a functional equivalence class of stimuli that are all conditioned to the same response. It is therefore perceived as having the same essential shape as all the other patterns included in this equivalence class. That, of course, does not prevent it from being perceived at the same time as having an unnecessary and irrelevant decoration of colors. But the color no longer interferes with reading, and the stage is therefore set for the extinction of the direct responses to color.

The extinction of the color responses occurs exactly in the manner postulated by Hull. That is, reactive inhibition comes into operation first, and in a remarkably short time. After half an hour's reading the subject is scarcely aware of the colors; but when, after an interval when he has been otherwise employed, he resumes reading, the colors are once more prominent. In Hull's terminology, the reactive inhibitory potential has almost completely dissipated. However, some conditioning of inhibition has taken place during the first session, and in subsequent sessions there is a progressive diminution in the initial strength of the responses, until finally no colors are seen at all.

10.23. Needless to say, there are many other activities in which responses to the edge colors are irrelevant, and in these the inhibitory process will proceed in the same manner. The only activities to which they are not irrelevant are simple contemplation of a scene and direct observation of the colors for the purpose of reporting on them. In both these cases the drives operative in reading and other behaviors to which the colors are irrelevant are out of action. We may think of drive as being a many-valued parameter to the multistable system, with each value determining a different behavioral field. Inhibition of responses to the edge colors is characteristic of most of those fields, but not of the field determined by the drive that motivates description of the colors. Hence if the subject stops in the midst of his reading to ask whether the colors have really disappeared, he has no difficulty in seeing them. Or if he goes out-of-doors, where the level of general illumination is much higher, and boards a tram from which he can view the passing scene without having to take any action relative to it, the colors can once again assume their initial prominence.

However, there are so many activities to which the colors are irrelevant that we may expect the inhibition to generalize to other situations as well. Thus there is likely to be a gradual diminution in the brightness of the colors seen out-of-doors, and by interior lighting they should ultimately cease to be visible even when attention is deliberately directed to them.

These deductions are confirmed by Kohler. On the twelfth day of the experiment he says of the colors: "Most of the time they are not noticed, but they can be seen very clearly any time I wish. . . . When I compare this with the impressions of the first day I find it hard to detect any falling off." In the report of the fiftieth day of the experiment we read: "With the spectacles I no longer see any dispersion bands in an artificially illuminated room, unless it be in the immediate neighborhood of the source of light." At the same time there is evidence of a reduction in the saturation of the colors seen when looking at a bright sunlit landscape.

10.24. It is now necessary to consider in more detail the nature of the behavioral adaptation by which the colors are eliminated. We have so far discussed it as if it involved nothing more than the simple extinction of conditioned responses; but a moment's thought will show that it must be more complex than that. For if a letter l appears as nothing more than an area of color, the extinction of the color responses would have the effect that nothing would be seen in its place. But that is not what happens. This patch of color, as we have seen, becomes conditioned to the response of naming the letter l and therefore mediates perception of that letter. So if the letter is perceived and the color is not perceived, this means that the two conditioning processes must combine to generate perception of a black figure on a white ground.

In order to effect this transformation by physical means it would be necessary to filter out the red and violet rays that are superimposed on the black surface, and add their complementaries to the yellow and blue rays that occupy the adjacent white areas. Evidently if the system could develop behavioral analogues of these physical processes, printed letters would be perceived as black spaces on a white ground. Howells' experiment has revealed that a tone can become a conditioned stimulus for a response that has the same perceptual effect as the addition of light of a specific wave composition. Evidently this could also happen under the conditions of Kohler's experiment provided there is some invariant stimulus, other than the wave length of the light, that can serve as a conditioned stimulus for the postulated response. There is. The edge itself provides a stimulus, in the form of an element of $_3\Pi$, that is entirely independent of wave length.

Referring to Figure 10.21.1, let us define a left edge as one in which the black area is to the left, and a right edge as one in which the black is to the right. This ordering is, of course, represented in $_3\Pi$, so that different responses can be conditioned to right and left edges. Each response, however, has two components. In the case of a left edge one component takes the form of a statement that the area to the left of the edge is black, and the other that the area to the right is white. In the case of a right edge the responses take the form of statements that the area to the left of the edge is white and the area to the right is black. Since these areas are in fact illuminated by red and yellow rays in the case of the left edge, and by blue and violet rays in a right edge, the effect of the responses is exactly the same as if they took the form "subtract the red rays from the left part of the area and add blue to the right part," in the case of a left edge, or "add yellow on the left and subtract violet on the right," in the case of a right edge. It is not necessary to assume that the responses ever take this form explicitly: it is enough to know that they are implicit in the simpler responses that employ only the terms black and white.

Activities such as reading provide ample opportunity for the reinforcement of the simple black-white responses, and they are all the more easily established because the irrelevance of the colors to the purposes served by reading helps to extinguish verbal responses to the colors.

10.25. If we are right in assuming that the responses of subtracting and adding colors are implicit in the black-white responses to edges, we should be able to deduce what must happen when the spectacles are removed. The stimuli are now actually black and white areas, but the edges still determine elements of $_3\Pi$, and as such they still evoke the responses acquired during the continuous wearing of the spectacles. To determine the perceptual aftereffects it is clearly not sufficient to consider the explicit form of the black-white responses: we must take account of the implicit processes whereby red and violet areas are converted to black, and yellow and blue areas to white, that is, the responses of subtracting and adding.

Now the black areas have a low reflectance, so that the amount of red and violet light to be subtracted is negligible. Hence the response is likely to have no noticeable effect on the perceived color of the black surfaces. On the other hand the addition of the complementaries of yellow and blue can hardly fail to produce a perceptual effect. Hence we can deduce that all left edges will appear to be decorated with bands of blue and all right edges with yellow. Since the subtractive response produces no result when applied to a black surface, it follows that the aftereffect colors are narrower than those initially seen with the spectacles.

Our assumption that adaptation was motivated by activities such as reading by interior illumination leads to the deduction that the implicitly added colors are bright enough to neutralize the yellows and blues seen at the edges of printed characters under such illumination, and that the response is not graded in strength according to the intensity of the light. This implies that the aftereffect colors will be relatively faint in bright daylight and will become brighter with decreasing luminance.

Another obvious deduction is that since the conditioned stimulus is an element of ${}_3\Pi$, the response is independent of the composition of the light by which an edge is viewed. Thus if the scene is viewed by sodium light all right edges (as defined in 10.24) will be decorated with bands of more saturated yellow, and all left edges with bands of blue, despite the fact that there are no "blue" rays in the sodium light. Since sodium light is monochromatic, this result will be obtained whether the spectacles are on or off.

10.26. These deductions are confirmed by Kohler's findings, as shown by the following passages, translated from his report. The aftereffect colors were first detected on the twelfth day of the experiment. In the report of the thirteenth day we read:

> It is true that these color bands were much less distinct and much narrower than those seen through the glasses in the same circumstances, but they were quite clearly above the color threshold. . . .
>
> 16th and 17th days. Quite slowly and gradually the color bands seen without the spectacles became more distinct. At the same time I observed that the most favorable conditions for the seeing of those colors were not the same without the spectacles as with them. While brilliant daylight produces extraordinarily clear color bands, it is exactly the reverse with the aftereffect, which becomes clearer and more brightly colored the darker the room is. There is a limit however: in the colorless twilight my color aftereffect also vanishes. The optimum is a somewhat subdued electric light. . . .
>
> 50th day. The aftereffect colors have developed to such a degree of clarity that there is no longer any doubt about them. In fact, by artificial light in the evening they approach the brightness and color of a solar spectrum. That is, they have become as clear as those I used to see through the spectacles when looking at a bright sunlit landscape. With the spectacles

> I no longer see any dispersion bands in an artificially illuminated room unless it be in the immediate neighborhood of the source of light. In weaker light, as in a corner of the room, color bands become clearly visible, but they are the opposite of the normal dispersion colors . . . This is none other than my aftereffect [pp. 50 f.]

It will be seen that this last observation finds a ready explanation in terms of our hypothesis. Since the strength of the conditioned responses is assumed to be adapted to the level of illumination normally employed for reading, it is more than sufficient to eliminate the dispersion colors at an edge seen by light of a substantially lower intensity. There is, in fact, overcompensation of the weak color bands, with the result that the aftereffect colors appear. It should be noted that this could not happen unless the edge were sufficiently illuminated to determine a conditioned stimulus in the form of an element of ${}_3\Pi$. Since this condition is not satisfied in the colorless twilight, no aftereffect colors are seen then. It is impossible to read by such light because the edges of the characters do not exist as stimuli.

The sodium light test was applied (although not as a test of the hypothesis presented here) a few days after the first appearance of the aftereffect colors, and the result was in complete agreement with the inference recorded above. The same result was obtained on subsequent repetitions of the test.

Finally, it must be recorded that no trace of red or violet ever appeared in the aftereffect colors, but only blue at left edges and yellow at right edges. Throughout the experiment the aftereffect colors remained narrower than the dispersion bands.

The experiment was subsequently repeated by Papert, who used 45° prisms in order to maximize the width of the colors. His results agreed with Kohler's in every detail.

10.27. The explanation of the aftereffects offered here is the outcome of a long process of trial and error in which other hypotheses were tried and rejected. Although it is not customary for an author to present an account of his own erroneous solutions to a problem, I feel that in the present instance it is worthwhile doing so, since the "solution" in question could have been rejected on purely logical grounds even before it was tested experimentally.

It is well known that if a prismatic solar spectrum is passed through another prism the dispersed rays are reassembled to produce white light. Consequently, if we can find some behavioral analogue of this physical process, it is conceivable that this could cause the disappearance of the edge colors and restore perception of the black and white surfaces. Now in the preceding chapters we have seen that there is ample evidence to support the hypothesis that the perceived position of a point in space is determined by the conditioning of elements of Q to responses accurately directed to that position. Therefore, referring once more to Figure 10.21.1, there seems to be no inherent reason why the dispersed rays from external point 3 should not be jointly conditioned to a response directed to that point, and similarly for the rays from all the other points. But if all the rays of one spectrum are perceived as coming from a single point in space they should be perceived as mixing to form white light.

This would imply that all red rays are displaced two units to the right, yellow rays one unit to the right, blue rays one unit to the left, and violet rays two units to the left. (The scale is not linear, of course, but as the theory is false in any case, accuracy in this respect is supererogatory.) When the spectacles are removed these displacements continue to be effective, but as the rays from any one point in space now fall on a single retinal point, the perceptual result must be identical with that produced by prisms with their bases to the right when worn by a fresh subject. That is, the aftereffect colors should include red and violet, and they should increase in brightness with increased illumination. Most important of all, no edge colors should be seen at all when sodium light is used, since it contains only yellow rays. The hypothesis thus generates at least three deductions that are at variance with the experimental results.

It was only after these discrepancies had enforced the rejection of the hypothesis that it became evident that it implies the very axiom that I have been explicitly rejecting throughout this book, that is, the axiom that a sensory or perceptual experience is sufficiently determined by afferent processes alone. It assumes that perceived colors are fully determined by the wave length of the light, and that the way to change a perceived color is to redistribute the rays so as to produce a different mixture. Moreover, it postulates a kind of behavior that operates in the subsystem that generates $_{1}\Pi$, that is, behavior that results in the perception of locality. It therefore offers no explanation of the color experiences themselves, and in particular it does not account for the supposed combining of the relocated rays to generate white light. Thus the results which the hypothesis seeks to explain are surreptitiously included among the unstated axioms. In short, this is a blatant example of the logical fallacy of *petitio principii.*

Despite the efforts of logicians to train us in the construction of scientific hypotheses by illustrating the numerous ways in which we can fall into fallacious arguments, the sad fact remains that errors of this kind do not proclaim themselves for all to see, but as a rule become evident only when discrepancies between theory and observation compel us to examine anew the logical basis of our theories. I offer the reader this example of my own logical errors in the hope that he may scrutinize other arguments in this book and detect other fallacies that I may have overlooked.

CHAPTER 11

The Modalities

11.1. From the remote beginnings of psychology to the present day the receptor organs have been thought of as organs of sense, each one giving rise to its own specific form of sensory experience. Since destruction of the eyes puts an end to vision and destruction of the ears to hearing, it seemed eminently reasonable to assume that vision and hearing were directly determined by the functioning of those organs. But when physiologists began to ask how they contrived to produce such remarkably different results, serious difficulties were encountered. They found that every receptor organ transmits afferent impulses to the brain, and that destruction of the afferent fibers was just as effective a means of abolishing sensation as destruction of the receptor organ itself. When it was demonstrated that exactly the same result was produced by destruction of the cortical terminus of the afferent fibers but not by destruction of any other part of the brain, it appeared reasonable to conclude that each cortical projection area had some specific property or mode of action that was responsible for sensory experience. But physiologists have searched in vain for evidence that would support this view. Nervous impulses are essentially the same wherever they occur. Neurons vary in their maximum frequency of firing, fibers vary in their rate of transmission of impulses, and of course there is an infinite variety in both the spatial and temporal patterning of groups of impulses; but nothing has been found that will explain unequivocally why the several projection areas should generate sensory experiences of such widely different types.

The search continues, but in view of what has been said in the preceding chapters it is safe to predict that neurophysiological methods, however necessary they may be, will not in themselves suffice to solve the problem. It was the outstanding achievement of Pavlov that he recognized that the most effective way to investigate the cortex is to observe the manner in which it determines the behavior of the organism in a carefully controlled situation. The techniques he developed led him to the important conclusion that the main function of the cortex is the establishing of temporary connections. These connections he recognized to be specific to the individual organism in which they occurred, and conditional upon the maintenance of the relations between organism and environment under which they were first formed.

I submit that by following Pavlovian lines of thinking we are much more likely to solve the problem of the modalities than by peering at the cortex with the electronic microscope or the oscillograph, by seeking for minute chemical differences between the projection areas, or by studying the gross electrical activities of the several areas with the aid of the electroencephalograph or the toposcope. All those procedures may be expected to yield valuable information, but it is hard to see how any of them could reveal the multitudinous connections that enable us to perceive a fixed object as occupying a constant position in space; and if they cannot do that it is unlikely that they will reveal the secret of the modalities.

11.2. Perhaps the greatest obstacle to a scientific approach to the problem of the modalities is that our own sensory experiences appear to us to be immediate, that is, not mediated by anything else that we can discover. We do not see them growing, in ourselves or anyone else, as we can see growth in the ability to speak a foreign language or play the violin. They give the impression that they have existed in their present form all our lives and that nothing in human experience could be more permanent. We are ready enough to admit that the ability of a master chess player to estimate the offensive and defensive possibilities by merely glancing at the disposition of the pieces is the product of extensive practice at the game, but we find it hard to believe that our ability to perceive the difference between a red and a green apple can have a similar foundation, or that learning has anything to do with the difference between taste and smell.

We may find it possible to accept that learning can give rise to changes in quality within one and the same modality—the evidence presented in Chapter 10 makes it very difficult to reject this—but the idea that the modalities themselves are explainable in a similar manner appears absurd and even repugnant to some people. Let us suppose that it were possible by surgery to direct the impulses from the retina to the auditory projection area and from the cochlea to the visual cortex. The doctrine of specific energy implies that the victim of such an experiment would hear with his eyes and see with his ears, although in both cases there would be nothing but a meaningless jumble of impressions, and that this sad state of affairs would continue for the rest of his life. It would be considered monstrous to suggest that the auditory cortex might ultimately mediate visual experience and the visual cortex auditory experience. And yet there is one authentic case where it has been established that a single sense organ mediates experiences that belong to two different modalities.

It is now well known that the so-called "sixth sense" of the blind is mediated by auditory stimulation, but in consciousness takes the form of a sensation of very gentle pressure against the skin of the face. If this phenomenon can be explained in terms of the behavioral theory, the general problem of the modalities will cease to be a mystery.

11.3. Some blind people, but by no means all of them, have developed a rudimentary perception of the positions of relatively large objects in their immediate environment, and can move about without fear of collision. They can walk confidently along a street without having to maintain constant contact with the wall, but can remain at a uniform distance from it. They at once know when they reach an intersection, and having crossed it they are never in any danger of colliding with the wall at the other side or of wandering too far into the street. In short, they behave as if they had some kind of dim vision of their immediate surroundings. When questioned as to how they do it, they reply that as they approach a large obstacle such as a wall, they begin to feel a very light pressure against the skin of their faces, and that this pressure increases as they get nearer the wall.

We know now that the stimuli for these sensations are not pressure on the skin or any other kind of cutaneous stimuli but auditory stimuli in the form of the echoes of the subject's own footsteps, or the tapping of his stick on the pavement, reflected back to him by the obstacle. The question naturally arises: how does this auditory stimulus fail to be perceived as auditory and come to be perceived as cutaneous?

Assuming the subject to have been blind from an early age, we can try to reconstruct the process. When he begins to walk he will inevitably suffer a few collisions with objects in his environment, and particularly with walls. In these encounters his face is likely to suffer more damage than any other part of his body, and he will automatically react to such damage by putting his hands to his face. If his parents, recognizing that he is blind, seek to protect him from danger by having him under constant supervision or otherwise restricting his movements, he will never develop any protective skills of his own. But if he is left to his own devices, the echo of his own voice and footsteps will soon become conditioned to the protective responses of putting his hands to his face and arresting his forward movement.[1]

There is no need to expound the matter in detail, since the principles are exactly the same as those we have employed, in 6.17, to account for the visual perception of the distance of a wall. Here the conditioned stimuli are auditory and, as in the other case, the rate of change increases as the distance diminishes. The amplitude of a sound wave varies inversely as the square of its distance from the source, and as the pattern of auditory stimulation includes both the sound waves that reach the ear directly from the feet or the mouth and the waves reflected back from the wall, this total pattern is eminently well fitted to become conditioned to a graded series of responses of a protective character.

Once the basic responses are established various refinements become possible. For example, since a sound wave can be intercepted only if the diameter of the obstacle is not less than half the wave length, it follows that an object such as the trunk of a tree

1. In a carefully designed study of echolocation in rats, Riley and Rosenzweig (1957) have shown that blinded rats can learn to avoid a barrier when the only possible cue is echoes of sounds produced by themselves and reflected by the barrier. These authors make the important suggestion that auditory cues were operative in the experiment reported by Lashley and Russell (1934) in which rats reared in darkness were able to jump from one platform to another immediately after exposure to light. This is supported by their own finding that several blinded rats could jump gaps of 15 to 20 cm., but became erratic in their performance when longer distances were used.

will reflect waves above a limiting frequency, so that the composition of the reflected waves will be different from that of the waves reflected by a wall. Since the human voice, like other musical instruments, produces compound sound waves with overtones, and in addition to that the tones contained in spoken words cover a wide range of fundamental frequencies, it follows that the blind subject has at his disposal an instrument that can enable him to respond, within limits, both to the distances and sizes of the objects in his environment.

Finally, if a sound wave comes from a source that is not in the median plane of the head, it stimulates the two ears in different ways, and if appropriate responses are conditioned to this binaural difference, the direction from which the sound is coming is perceived. This occurs in people with normal vision, but in the blind the differentiation is more refined. However, the important thing here is that this differentiation applies to reflected sounds as well as to direct sounds. Consequently the echoes of his own voice are capable of providing a blind man with information concerning the distance, direction, and size of the objects in his immediate environment. In an unfamiliar setting he only has to talk for a few moments to get a reasonably adequate knowledge of his environment.

11.4. Now one of the interesting things about this is that many blind people are completely unaware of the fact that their knowledge is derived from auditory stimuli. Just as people with normal vision would say that their knowledge of the environment is mediated by retinal stimuli alone, so blind people say their knowledge is mediated by faint pressures exerted on their skin. At the same time this has apparently no effect on their responses to auditory stimuli other than the echoes of sounds which they themselves originate. Auditory stimulation, in fact, gives rise to conscious experiences falling within two totally different modalities. Clearly neurophysiologists would have a hard task if they were to try to disentangle the events in the superior temporal gyrus that are responsible for those two forms of "sensation."

The solution to the puzzle must be sought not in the primary projection area but in the engrams that are aroused to activity by the impulses arriving in that area. Again we cannot investigate these by neurophysiological techniques, but fortunately it is an easy matter to observe the behavior of a subject who is in process of acquiring the "sixth sense." With the object of training those victims of blindness who have failed to acquire the "sixth sense," Kohler has devised an instrument in the form of a miniature loudspeaker that can be carried on the chest.[2] When switched on it emits a succession of sharp clicks that produce a more satisfactory echo than either the footsteps or the voice. The volume can be increased for use in a noisy environment such as a busy street. Even a person with normal vision can, when blindfolded, learn to find his way about with the help of this instrument. Naturally the subject of such an experiment knows that his movements are to be guided by auditory stimuli, and at first he listens for and can easily detect the changes in the quality of the sound. But as he acquires skill and confidence he ceases to attend to the sound as such and becomes aware of exactly the same kind of pressure sensations reported by the blind, and becomes aware of the positions and sizes of the larger objects in his environment. Blind people who have hitherto relied on companions to guide them in dangerous areas quickly learn to move about without assistance when they carry the loudspeaker, and after some training they can discard the apparatus and rely on the sounds produced by themselves. They then experience the full range of pressure sensations.

There seems to be only one possible conclusion. The pressure sensations associated with the "sixth sense" of the blind are due not to some innate connections between the auditory and somesthetic projection areas but to the character of the behavior that has been conditioned to a specific subset of auditory stimuli. This behavior has two main aspects: it is adapted to the positions of the objects in the environment, and it serves to protect the subject from painful contacts with those objects. It is the protective aspect that is responsible for the sensations of pressure, while the other aspect mediates perception of the spatial ordering of the environment.

11.5. We are now in a position to formulate a general hypothesis regarding the genesis of the modalities. We start from the assumption that there are no specific energies, either in the afferent fibers or in the projection areas. This is justified not merely by the failure of physiology to find any evidence of specificity, but by the logical and philosophical difficulties that we encounter if we accept specific energies. We would still be faced with the

2. Personal communication.

insoluble problem of explaining how physiological events get themselves transformed into events of an entirely different order. The rejection of specific energies is of course a purely negative statement and therefore does not form an essential part of an hypothesis.

The receptor organs are so constructed that they can respond to various energies in their environment, such as light waves, sound waves, pressures, including pressures within the organism as determined by gravity, and others determined by acceleration, particles given off by volatile substances, temperature, and the like. Stimulation of the receptors generates afferent impulses that travel to the spinal cord or brain stem and thence are relayed to the cortex. On their way to the cortex they stimulate the brain stem reticular activating system (BSRAS) which raises the general level of cortical activity, so that although the afferent impulses reach determinate parts of the cortex, they can be relayed to virtually any other part, and it is largely a matter of chance what behavior will result from any given impulse. That is, at the beginning of life the impulses from the several receptors are differentiated with respect to their cortical termini but not with respect to their ultimate destinations.

The function of the cortex, as Pavlov has shown, is the formation of temporary connections, and we must assume that it starts its characteristic mode of activity as soon as birth exposes the organism to variable stimulation. That is, the cortex first of all produces an apparently random succession of movements involving the whole motor system—the so-called mass activity of infancy. This includes movements of the limbs and the head, of the eyes and eyelids, of the mouth and vocal apparatus. Most of the components of the mass response leave the general condition of the organism unchanged, but when a critical state arises certain specific components are effective as a means of terminating this state. If it can be shown that certain forms of stimulation invariably precede the action that serves to terminate a given type of critical state, we can assume that the stimuli in question become conditioned to the successful response. Then, if there are two or more types of critical state, if the successful responses are different in kind, and if the conditioned stimuli operate on different receptor organs, it follows that the perceptual experiences generated by activation of the engrams mediating the conditioned responses must be qualitatively different.

It will be seen that this is the same argument that has been used, in 10.9, to account for qualitative differences within the field of color vision. If the conditioning of different types of behavior to lights of different composition can generate qualitatively different perceptual experiences, then we may expect even more markedly different experiences to emerge from the conditioning of different types of behavior to stimuli operating on different receptors.

11.6. There is no need to make an exhaustive list of the critical states into which the system may move in the earliest stage of life, since the methods of dealing with them are extremely restricted. Thus we may include in one class all those that are due to localized irritation such as colic, inflammation of the skin by urine, pressure on a limited area of the skin, and the like. In all these cases relief can be obtained only through the intervention of the mother, who must therefore be included as an essential part of the system. The baby has only one response to all such sources of irritation, a vigorous but chaotic activity of the whole musculature, including that of the vocal apparatus. It seems probable that the violence of the reaction arises not from the intensity of the stimulation but from the fact that the postcentral gyrus, which is the cortical projection area in all these cases, is situated alongside the precentral gyrus or motor cortex. The projection areas of the exteroceptors are more remotely situated, so that impulses from them are likely to be considerably diluted before they reach the motor cortex, and will therefore arouse a much weaker response. The nearest are the auditory projection areas, in the superior temporal gyri, and it is probably for this reason that a sudden loud noise produces the same kind of reaction as colic or inflammation of the skin.

It is reasonable to suppose that the stimuli that evoke this vigorous response do not appear suddenly but rise by gradual stages to the critical level. Consequently, if the mother reacts promptly to the baby's crying and succeeds in eliminating the source of irritation, the violent response will become conditioned to the less intense stimuli that occur before the critical level is reached. And the more prompt the mother is the weaker will be the stimuli that suffice to evoke crying as a conditioned reflex.

According to our hypothesis this conditioning, if it can be shown to exist, should give rise to a specific variety of perceptual experience, and I suggest that the essence of that experience is pain. Evidence in support of this view is afforded by the remarkable experiments at McGill University (Melzack and Scott, 1957) in which dogs were reared in cages so small that there was no opportunity for them to accelerate their movements to such a velocity that contact with a solid body would be sufficient to evoke the chaotic response unconditionally. Apparently young dogs do not suffer from the colics that occur so frequently in human infancy, so that if they are protected from collisions, from contact with fire and other stimuli that might evoke the chaotic response, there is no chance of conditioning it or any of its components to stimuli that are below the critical level. Meanwhile the cortex goes on with its work of establishing temporary connections, and by the time the dog is grown its brain is already highly organized, and stimuli that would evoke a howl of pain in a normally reared dog evoke only conditioned reactions of other kinds, mediating other forms of perception. No doubt if we could get an accurate history of the infancy of those human subjects who display "pathological" insensitivity to pain, we would find that there had been a similar lack of opportunity for conditioning.

11.7. Apart from the heterogeneous collection of critical states that arise from local irritation there are two that depend on the general condition of the organism. For convenience we may call them hunger and fatigue, although both these terms carry meanings that are not intended in the present context. In particular we exclude the subjective experiences that are usually thought of as being included in the meanings. As we shall use the term here, the essence of hunger is that as the concentration of food particles in the blood stream diminishes, the cells throughout the body become more active. Each cell is of course limited in its activity by its own structure and the structure of the surrounding tissue, but one of the effects of the increased activity is the transmission of an increasing volume of afferent impulses to the somesthetic area of the cortex, which in turn brings about an increasing activity of the motor apparatus. Ultimately this mass response becomes as violent as that induced by local irritation, and it may therefore be assumed that a prompt reaction by the mother will have the effect of establishing crying as a conditioned response to the less intense stimuli that precede the critical stage, so that hunger should, according to our general hypothesis, come to have the same subjective quality as pain.

In mature experience there is of course some affinity between hunger and pain, and this is doubtless due to the common means by which the infant relieves both. But there is an important difference between the two cases. Crying secures the attention of the mother whether it be induced by hunger or by a local irritation, but the relief of hunger requires a further action by the infant; in other cases, however, relief is entirely dependent on the ministrations of the mother. Hence searching for the nipple becomes a conditioned response to hunger stimuli but not to painful stimuli. Hunger and pain, as subjective experiences, therefore have something in common because in both cases the stimuli are conditioned to crying; they are nevertheless differentiated because there is a further conditioned response in the case of hunger but not in the case of pain.

It may be objected that the foregoing argument is absurd because it postulates that a stimulus can become conditioned to its own unconditioned response. But in fact there is no absurdity at all. The essential law of conditioning is that if a neutral stimulus, no matter what its character, regularly precedes a stimulus that evokes an unconditioned reflex, then the neutral stimulus acquires the power of evoking the reflex. Pavlov used a wide variety of conditioned stimuli in his experiments, but for obvious reasons he could not use a lesser quantity of meat powder or acid as a conditioned stimulus, since that would itself evoke an unconditioned reflex, although doubtless the quantity of saliva secreted would have been less. Nevertheless it seems likely that if a minute quantity of meat powder is regularly followed by a more substantial quantity, the minute quantity would soon evoke a flow of saliva appropriate to the larger quantity. In that case the secretion of a large quantity of saliva in response to a mere crumb of meat would indicate the establishment of a conditioned reflex.

Exactly the same kind of result follows if we consider a case where the reflex is evoked only when the stimulus reaches a certain level of intensity, and this level is reached by a gradual process. For example, the knee jerk can be evoked by a rapid stretching of the patellar tendon, as by tapping the tendon with a suitable hammer. But when a child learns to walk the stretching of the tendons occurs more gradually, and the effective tension for the evocation of the reflex is preceded by lesser and ineffective degrees of tension. It seems reasonable to suppose that learning to walk smoothly implies the conditioning of the tendon reflexes to tensions that are originally inadequate. This notion is strongly supported by the fact that if the knee jerk is conditioned to, say, an auditory stimulus, the conditioned response resembles a "voluntary" movement rather than the unconditioned reflex. The so-called voluntary movements of walking may well be conditioned tendon reflexes. I submit therefore that there is nothing outrageous or absurd in suggesting that a weak stimulus can be conditioned to a response that is originally evoked only by a quantitatively greater stimulus of the same kind.

11.8. This hypothesis raises another question. According to the theory of conditioning any stimulus that regularly precedes an unconditioned stimulus acquires conditioned properties. Since we have assumed that initially all stimuli are alike except with respect to intensity, it would seem that the general cortical activity induced by exteroceptive and proprioceptive stimulation should become conditioned to the crying response, and that there is no justification for thinking that only the interoceptive impulses are so conditioned. There is a simple answer to this. It is precisely during the periods when activity is increasing as a result of the slow depletion of the stored food that the infant is acquiring the enormously complicated system of responses described in Chapters 2 and 3. This means that the level of activity is much higher than it would be if the interoceptors alone were active, since the cortex is constantly being bombarded by afferent impulses from the exteroceptors and proprioceptors. But those impulses are rapidly becoming more specific in their effects on the motor system and losing their initial character or undifferentiated stimulators of motor activity. That is to say, we cannot describe the events leading up to the cry of hunger by saying that there is a single form of massive stimulation that has been gradually building in intensity until it reaches the critical level and triggers the crying response. As the days go on, more and more of the stimuli that precede the hunger cry are becoming organized as elements of ${}_1\Phi$ and therefore increasing in diversity and specificity. Such stimuli are not available for conditioning since they do not occur regularly in temporal conjunction with the unconditioned stimuli for the crying response. The only invariant stimulus that can qualify for conditioning is the interoceptive impulses due to the gradual depletion of the store of food.

Now the conditioned responses specified by $_1\Phi$ differ in kind from those that are conditioned to interoceptive stimuli, and our hypothesis therefore enables us to deduce that the perceptual experiences aroused by the stimuli specified by $_1\Phi$ and by interoceptive stimuli are qualitatively different. Every reader has within himself the evidence that confirms this deduction.

11.9. We turn next to fatigue. Activity at a high level, if continued for a long time, endangers the life of the active cells, but long before the danger becomes acute the cortical cells generate inhibitory impulses which appear to have a threefold effect. First, there are inhibitory fibers that run from the projection area of the cortex to the receptor organ and diminish the responsiveness of the receptor cells to the stimuli to which they are exposed. That is, excessive activity of a receptor generates inhibition in its cortical projection area and thereby protects both the receptor cells and the cortical cells. Second, the localized cortical inhibition diminishes the strength of any responses that have been conditioned to the stimuli. This of course is facilitated by the reduction in the volume of afferent impulses. And third, the inhibition spreads to other parts of the cortex until all but vegetative activities cease. Pavlov gives an example of how inhibition spreads. A dog that has been subjected to a monotonous succession of conditioned stimuli gives the first sign of inhibition when its tongue hangs limply from its mouth as if paralyzed. It still eats when food is offered, but the speed of the response is decreased. A little later, although it still takes food, the movement of the jaws is seen to be sluggish, and still later the animal will not even turn its head toward the food. The inhibition then spreads to the limbs, until finally the dog hangs in its harness fast asleep (Pavlov, 1955, pp. 374 f).

The spreading of inhibition can be counteracted by stimulation of another receptor, and of course it is facilitated by reduction of stimulation. Pavlov refers to experiments in which a dog is simultaneously deprived of olfactory, visual, and auditory stimulation by severing the olfactory and optic nerves and destroying both cochleae. Such an animal sleeps for twenty-three hours per day, waking up only for eating and evacuation. Something essentially similar is done by the intact organism. One important form of stimulation can be reduced to a negligible level by simply shutting the eyes. Proprioceptive stimuli are similarly eliminated by the inhibition of the skeletal muscles, which at the same time reduces stimuli due to gravity. When the individual is inactive the gravitational stimuli are relatively constant, with the result that their cortical centers send inhibitory impulses to the receptors. The same rule applies to constant or frequently recurring auditory stimulation. It is only when unusual sounds occur that sleep is broken.

All this may appear to be very remote from the problem of the modalities, but it is in fact directly relevant. When the system gets into a critical state as a result of excessive activity, it is not a single response that carries it out of the critical state but a collection of discrete responses that immobilize the limbs, the trunk, the head, the mouth and vocal apparatus, and the eyes. And finally there is the active response of shutting the eyes. All these responses are subject to conditioning, the conditioned stimulus in each case being a stimulus that has already been conditioned to an active response but is now allied with reactive inhibition developing in some other part of the cortex. If the localized inhibition spreads in the normal way over the whole cortex, it follows that all engrams whose activity constitutes perception become inactive, and as a consequence there is no perception and therefore no consciousness. The disappearance of consciousness in sleep is thus a direct consequence of a generalized state of inhibition, and is directly deducible from the theory of perception presented in this book and from Pavlov's theory of inhibition.

Although the normal course of events, particularly in infancy, is that inhibition starts at one point and spreads over the whole cortex, it frequently happens that this is prevented for a time by excitatory processes in another part. In that case we may assume that many of the engrams mediating perception are only partly inhibited, or that certain stimuli arouse both positive and inhibitory engrams. But this implies the emergence of some new form of conscious experience, reflecting the increased difficulty of performing actions that at other times are easy. This is none other than the subjective feeling of fatigue. Since inhibition involves no change in the actual form of the inhibited responses, the feeling of fatigue must be located not in the external environment but in the body.

11.10. The fact that inhibition spreads over the cortex, taken in conjunction with the complex character of the stimuli specified by the elements of Φ, enables us to draw an important deduction regarding the perception of the spatial ordering of the environment at times when the subject is getting drowsy. Since the perception of the position of an object in space depends on retinal stimuli and also on proprioceptive stimuli from the muscles of the neck and eyes, it is quite possible for the proprioceptive impulses to be inhibited while retinal impulses are still coming through and the motor centers controlling the head and eyes are still active. The effect of this partial inhibition must be that the positional constancy of visual perception is temporarily lost. The visual field will be perceived as if it has become detached from its firm foundation and is moving in an erratic and uncontrollable fashion. This is, of course, quite a common experience. It happens, for example, if one tries to go on reading much after the normal time for going to bed. The printed page swims in front of the eyes, and it is completely consistent with Pavlovian theory that if the reader shakes his head, or gets up and walks a little, thereby adding new sources of excitation, the instability disappears. It soon returns, however, and continues to return with increasing frequency until the reader is compelled to yield to sleep.

Similar phenomena occur when inhibition is artificially induced by drugs such as alcohol, or by general anesthetics. Disturbances of perception are frequently reported by patients recovering from general anesthesia. For example, if the oculomotor nuclei are active, so that the eyes can move readily, but the afferents from the extrinsic muscles of the eyes are blocked, the patient may perceive the face of a nurse as appearing in a succession of different positions in space but without appearing to move from one position to the next. The translation appears to be instantaneous and there is no evidence of the phi-phenomenon, although the conditions are apparently exactly what, according to gestalt theory, is required for this.

11.11. The discussion up to this point has enabled us to deduce the existence of three forms of conscious experience—pain, hunger, and fatigue—that are not commonly regarded as belonging to the field of perception. They are usually included among the "sensations," which in classical psychology have been rigidly demarcated from perception. Nevertheless the demonstration, brief as it is, that these forms of experience can be explained in terms of conditioning of adaptive responses strongly suggests that they are in fact forms of perception, and that there is no need to postulate primary sensations of pain, hunger, and fatigue as the foundations on which they are built.

It is precisely here that the distinction between sensation and perception reaches its *reductio ad absurdum.* It is possible to argue that the sensation of green I have when I look at the tree outside my window is independent of my perception of the position of the tree and the shape of its leaves, because I can produce a sensation of green by fixating a point on a red object and then shutting my eyes. In the latter case there is no perceived object to carry the green sensation. Or I can look at the tree by moonlight, in which case I can still perceive its position and shape, but there is no sensation of green. This seems to mean that sensation and perception are basically different phenomena. In the case of pain, hunger, and fatigue there is no possibility of abstracting the sensations from the relative perception of the state of the body. Sensation and perception are one and the same experience, and no amount of introspective analysis can establish a difference between them.

The error, it would seem, arises from the implicit assumption that sensation is the raw material out of which perception is fashioned. But this, as we have seen, still leaves us with the unsolved problem of explaining how nerve impulses arriving at different parts of the cortex can generate sensory experiences that differ in quality. The only way to avoid this dilemma, I submit, is to deny the validity of the distinction between sensation and perception, and assume that all forms of conscious experience have a behavioral basis.

11.12. We turn now to the exteroceptors. If our hypothesis is sound, the differences between the traditional five senses, vision, hearing, touch, taste, and smell, should be associated with different modes of behavioral adjustment to the environment, and it is at once obvious that they are. It is quite unnecessary to present an exhaustive catalogue of the differences; it is sufficient to show that in the case of each exteroceptor there are some forms of behavior that cannot be conditioned to any pattern of stimulation not containing components mediated by the given exteroceptor. For example, if a mosquito buzzes round my head and lands on the back of my neck, I may see and hear it before it lands, but the blow I aim at it could not be directed with any accuracy were it not for the tactile stimuli generated by its bite. This is even more obvious when the enemy is a flea that attacks with neither visible nor audible declaration of war. The fact that there is a large class of responses that cannot be evoked unless tactile components are included in the pattern of stimulation means that the resulting perception must be qualitatively different from other forms.

Auditory and visual stimuli are both conditioned to responses directed to the position of the sources, but there are some important differences. An auditory stimulus from a source behind the head can evoke the response of turning the body around in preparation for a more detailed reaction. Such a response can never be conditioned to visual stimuli for the simple reason that there are no eyes in the back of the head. The rear-view mirror enables a motorist to respond to events taking place behind his back, but that is a sophisticated mode of behavior that comes into operation only long after the modalities have been firmly established.

On the other hand visual stimuli are capable of being conditioned to responses directed to points in space with a degree of accuracy that is completely impossible if the stimulus is auditory. No doubt the accuracy of the localization of a source of sound could be greatly increased, as it is in the blind, but in people with a normal equipment of receptors localization of sound is quite crude, and can be modified with great ease. Thus the voices of the actors in a cinema are perceived as coming from the actors and moving with them, although the actual source of the sound is stationary.

Blind people, as we have seen, can perceive the positions of objects in their environment by acquiring appropriate responses to the echoes of their own voices, but the minimum size of the objects that can be located in this way is determined by the upper limit of hearing and the maximum frequency of the sound waves they can produce. Even if a blind man could produce tones at a frequency of 20,000 cycles per second, he could not detect the presence of objects of less than about 8 mm. in diameter. The bat, which makes use of essentially the same technique as the blind man, can detect much smaller objects because the tones it produces are much higher in pitch and it can respond to reflected waves with a very much higher frequency. If man were equipped with the voice and ears of a bat he could learn to detect, as the bat does, objects as little as half a millimeter in diameter, but this would not make visual and auditory perception identical, because reflected sound waves are not affected by variations in molecular structure within an object, as light waves are, and because there are responses that can be conditioned to visual but not auditory stimuli, and others that can be conditioned to auditory but not visual stimuli.

Among the former the most important are the oculomotor responses that, as we saw in 2.19, are conditioned to patterns of stimulation in which the visual component arises from the periphery of the retina. Responses of this kind cannot be conditioned to stimuli in which the exteroceptive components are due to reflected sound waves, since there is no means of reinforcing them. Oculomotor responses do of course occur in response to auditory stimuli, but this is explainable in terms of interpenetration of the visual and auditory subsystems. When so evoked they are not directly reinforced if the source of the sound is invisible, as in darkness, whereas they are almost invariably reinforced when they are evoked by a peripheral retinal stimulus. (An obvious exception is that when a faint star is fixated it becomes invisible, but this is of no importance, since perception is not commonly acquired under conditions of dark adaptation.)

Among responses that can be conditioned to auditory but not visual stimuli is that, already mentioned, of turning around in response to a sound coming from behind the head. However, the infant is not likely to acquire this before he has achieved some control over his movements, so that it is probably not decisive in establishing the distinction between auditory and visual perception. But there is another group of responses that can be conditioned quite early in life. When the baby cries, from whatever cause, the mother almost invariably utters comforting sounds as she approaches. She continues to talk while lifting the baby and attending to his needs, whether by relieving some local irritation or by giving the breast. The tactile and other stimuli incidental to being picked up can, particularly if the mother is quick and efficient in relieving the distress, become conditioned to the inhibition of crying, and the sound of the mother's voice then becomes a conditioned stimulus for the same response. This generalizes to other similar auditory stimuli, such as the father's voice, but as he does not usually relieve the distress, and of course cannot satisfy the infant's hunger if he is breast fed, the response is extinguished. That is, the baby learns to respond to his mother's but not to his father's voice. Since the eyes are usually shut during crying, it is evident that this differential conditioning is not based on visual stimuli. In the same manner the response of turning the head toward the mother's breast can be conditioned to the tones of her voice but is subject to extinction when evoked by the father's voice. In this way a primitive differentiation of pitch is established.

The further elaboration of this theme must be left for a later work, but in the meantime enough has been said to show that even in the earliest stage of life the modes of behavior conditioned to visual and auditory stimuli are sufficiently different to warrant the deduction that the resulting forms of perceptual experience must differ qualitatively from each other.

11.13. The modalities of taste and smell have so much in common that most people fail to realize that what they call the taste of a substance is the resultant of the stimulation of both gestatory and olfactory receptors. Nevertheless the two modalities are quite distinct, in the sense that the odor of a substance that is about to be put in the mouth is not commonly recognized as being a component of its taste when it is in the mouth. This curious phenomenon is completely at variance with any doctrine that seeks to explain the modalities in terms of specific energies in the projection areas, since the olfactory receptors are presumably stimulated in the same way whether the particles reach them from the external atmosphere or from the mouth; but the facts are very easily explained in terms of the behavioral theory of perception.

At first the process of feeding involves a chain of unconditioned reflexes. Contact of the nipple with the cheek evokes a rotation of the head that brings the mouth to the nipple. Contact with the lips evokes the sucking reflex, and finally the milk in the mouth evokes the swallowing reflex. It seems highly improbable that the first two of those reflexes can be conditioned to either olfactory or gustatory stimuli during the period when the diet is confined to milk. Since the milk is not exposed to air before being taken into the mouth, the stimulation of the chemical receptors occurs simultaneously with the unconditioned stimulus for the swallowing reflex and after the stimuli for the other reflexes in the chain. In these circumstances the combined chemical stimuli can be conditioned to swallowing but not to the preceding reflexes. It is only when the diet is supplemented by other foods that can stimulate the olfactory receptor before entering the mouth that the range of conditioning can be extended. Olfactory stimuli can then be conditioned to the response of putting the substance in the mouth, and of course to the subsequent responses of mastication and swallowing. For obvious reasons gustatory stimuli cannot be conditioned to the first response.

The swallowing reflex is inhibited when the stomach is full, so that the resulting interoceptive stimuli in conjunction with olfactory and gustatory stimuli become conditioned to inhibition of mastication, and in conjunction with the olfactory stimuli alone to inhibition of the response of putting the food in the mouth.

We have here a behavioral basis for both the affinity between taste and smell, and for the distinction between them. They are distinct because only olfactory stimuli can be conditioned to putting a substance in the mouth; they are closely allied because both types of stimuli are jointly conditioned to the subsequent responses. At the same time the participation of interoceptive stimuli in the process provides a basis for the addition of the dimension of pleasant-unpleasant to both taste and smell. When the responses are inhibited, the taste and smell of food are unpleasant. They become progressively more pleasant as the inhibition decreases.

The development of different qualities within the modalities of taste and smell is too large a subject to be dealt with in this brief summary, but it should be evident that by reason of the great variety of substances that are required for the maintenance of the body in good health, and the great variety of the proportions in which those substances occur in common foods, there must be a great deal of differential conditioning of eating responses to the odors and tastes of different foods. Given this conditioning, taste and smell must necessarily be differentiated into a variety of qualities.

11.14. In the course of our discussion we have seen that the classical distinction between sensation and perception cannot be maintained. An even more striking discovery is that the classical distinction between cognitive and affective consciousness is equally questionable. Introspective psychologists used to say that all conscious processes had three aspects, cognitive, conative, and affective; and it was natural enough to assume that those components of experience depended on different and mutually independent physiological structures. The conative component was the most difficult to assign to any specific physiological basis, and this difficulty was usually circumvented by the assumption, explicit or implicit, that conation could be explained only by the activities of a "ghost in the machine." (When Freud realized that there were a great many actions that could not be attributed to this ghost, the correct scientific procedure would have been to reject the ghost hypothesis; but what he did in fact was to retain the classical ghost as an explanation of consciously intended actions and to invent an excommunicated ghost called the "Unconscious" to account for the rest.) Nowadays psychologists have much to say about motivation, but the problem of the origin of conative *experience* is quietly shelved.

The search for a physiological basis of affective experience appeared to be more successful. Near the end of the nineteenth century James and Lange suggested, independently of one another, that emotions were essentially sensory experiences, the stimuli being the interoceptive and proprioceptive impulses that arise in consequence of emotional behavior. The theory was *not*, it must be observed, a behavioral theory, since it implied specific energies in some part of the brain, presumably the postcentral gyrus. The subsequent researches of Cannon, Head, and others led to the theory that the real center, both for emotional behavior and affective experience, is the thalamus. But the doctrine of specific energy still remained as part of the axiomatic basis of this theory. The energy was merely given a more accurate address.

One of the most effective criticisms leveled against the James-Lange theory was that emotion can be experienced before the viscera have had time to generate the impulses postulated by James. Little less damaging were the results of experiments in which the viscera were stirred up by injections of adrenalin. Some subjects reported no emotions at all, others said they felt as if they were about to be emotionally disturbed, and a few reported real emotions, mostly unpleasant. It does not seem to have been generally recognized that these two criticisms apply with equal force to the thalamic theory. The evidence on which this theory rests includes the reports of patients with unilateral thalamic lesions, which show that somesthetic stimuli do in fact contribute to affective experience. The theory does not deny the role of stimuli originating in the viscera, and is consequently vulnerable.

It would seem that there is only one way to meet these criticisms, and that is by postulating that the emotional experience is dependent on neural events that include the efferent processes that give rise to emotional behavior. But this behavior, as J. B. Watson demonstrated long ago, is subject to conditioning, so that in the vast majority of cases the efferent processes that initiate it make use of conditioned reflex arcs, or engrams. Thus the facts that disprove the James-Lange theory are completely consistent with an interpretation of emotional experience in terms of the same kind of mechanism that we have already postulated as the basis of perceptual experience.

11.15. Although it is a perfectly obvious fact that emotional behavior includes overt actions as well as internal activities controlled by the autonomic nervous system, it is notorious that investigators of emotion have almost invariably confined their attention to the internal components. Elaborate experiments have been carried out, for example, with the object of discovering whether the different emotional experiences are characterized by distinctive patterns of facial expression, but the results have invariably been disappointing. Similarly no clear-cut distinctions between the patterns of visceral activity accompanying the several emotions have been found. In short, the system was found to be irregular, and consequently no scientific laws could be deduced from it.

When a system proves to be irregular the appropriate procedure is to change it, usually by the addition of other variables, and in the present case the most obvious thing to do is to include the subject's overt behavior. It may be argued that there is no point in doing this because the overt behavior is the direct consequence of the emotion. Certainly that is how it appears to be in our conscious experience, but since it is precisely that experience that we are seeking to explain, the argument carries no weight.

In this connection it is instructive to recall Watson's early investigation of the stimuli that evoke emotional responses in infants. It will be remembered that he described the response to a sudden loud noise or to loss of support as "fear" and the response to inhibition of the infant's movements as "rage"; but subsequent careful examination of those two responses revealed not the slightest trace of difference between them. It is evident that Watson, despite his vigorous denial of the scientific respectability of conscious phenomena, was interpreting the infant's behavior in the light of his own experience, thereby violating one of the principles on which he proposed to build his scientific system. At the same time this error prevented him from recognizing that the response of the infant to colic or to local irritation of the skin is equally indistinguishable from the responses he called fear and rage.

The position then is that a single response involving the entire skeletal musculature and the sympathetic nervous system is evoked unconditionally by a relatively small number of stimuli but can be conditioned to a very much larger range of stimuli. However, as the infant grows and acquires the immensely complex system of behavior on which perception depends, it becomes increasingly possible for him to escape from the critical state by taking further action relative to the situation that is responsible for the disturbance. At the same time the skeletal muscles are playing an increasingly important part in the maintenance of posture and other activities, with the result that the thrashing movements that are so prominent in the early chaotic emotional behavior become less evident, being replaced by a general stiffening of the sinews and an increased muscular energy. The autonomic components of the response are likely to remain largely unchanged, to begin with at any rate.

It is evident that the kind of action that will succeed in terminating the critical state depends on the source of the disturbance. In some cases attack will succeed, and this kind of response will therefore become conditioned to any stimuli that regularly precede the unconditioned stimulus. For example, if the disturbance is caused by an action of another person, his features and gestures will become conditioned stimuli for the attacking response. In other cases attack will merely prolong the disturbance, and some form of evasive action, such as flight, or going into hiding, or remaining still to avoid attracting attention, may prove more effective, and such responses will become conditioned to stimuli presented by the disturbing agency. Finally, if the disturbance is due to bodily injury neither of these actions will suffice to relieve it, and the child is likely to revert to the primitive response of crying, since that commonly secures the intervention of an adult.

Here then we have three types of situation, all of them conditioned to responses that have as a common component a vigorous activity of the sympathetic nervous system but differ markedly with respect to their other components. We can therefore conclude that the relative conscious experiences will have some features in common and also some differentiating features. Pain, fear, and rage are all recognized as unpleasant experiences, but they are nevertheless clearly distinguishable from one another. The hypothesis that fear and rage are distinguished in consciousness because the stimuli are conditioned to different modes of behavior provides a simple explanation of the fact that emotion is experienced before the viscera have had time to act. It is the activity of the engrams mediating the overt responses that is responsible for the distinctive quality of the emotion, whereas it is the action of the viscera that is responsible for the common quality of unpleasantness.

This discussion, brief and inadequate as it is, should make it clear that a person's emotional life is very much an individual matter, depending on his own history, as Freud long ago recognized. However, the mechanism turns out to be very different from that envisaged by Freud. It is both simpler and more concrete. From this we may deduce that the crippling anxieties of neurotics are more likely to be removed by procedures based on the theory of conditioning than by methods based on Freudian theory. The remarkable success achieved by Wolpe (1958) in relieving anxiety by methods derived from Hullian theory provide a striking confirmation of this deduction.

11.16. We consider finally those receptors that do not generate any kind of "sensation," such as the semicircular canals. Much of the afferent energy originating in the vestibule goes to the cerebellum, but some goes to the cortex and should, according to the doctrine of specific energy, give rise to some kind of sensory experience. No vestibular sense has ever been reported. We cannot count the giddiness that follows the sudden stoppage of prolonged rotation, since this disappears completely in ballet dancers. A "sense" that vanishes so readily has surely no claim to recognition.

The absence of a vestibular sense does not of course mean that vestibular stimuli are of no importance. What it does mean is that it makes nonsense of the theory that stimuli cannot contribute to perception unless they first come into consciousness in the form of sensation. There is no vestibular sense, but there *is* perception of rotation, and this perception is determined by the conditioning of appropriate responses to vestibular stimuli.

To understand what kind of perception this must be we can appeal once more to the principle of interpenetration. Vestibular stimuli collaborate with other proprioceptive stimuli and with retinal stimuli to determine perception of the spatial ordering of the environment. They also collaborate with other proprioceptive stimuli and with auditory stimuli to determine the perception of the directions from which sounds are perceived as coming. And finally they collaborate with pressure stimuli as determined by gravity to generate perception of the posture of the body and its position relative to the gravitational axis. The participation of vestibular stimuli in all these fields of perception implies that the properties of each field are incorporated in the others. Thus the perceived rotation that results from vestibular stimulation is not just an abstract rotation but is rotation within the same space that is perceived visually and auditorily. In particular, it is measurable in relation to a reference frame that has no representation in the vestibular stimuli themselves.

Now visual stimuli, as we have seen in Chapter 10, are conditioned not only to responses that are adapted to space but also to responses that are essentially nonspatial, and this is even more obvious in the case of responses to auditory stimuli. Even the responses conditioned to somesthetic stimuli have nonspatial components. For example, when one is carrying a weight, behavior is adapted not only to the direction in which the weight is pulling but also to its magnitude, and to the internal state of the organism as determined by fatigue. Vestibular stimuli are not directly implicated in any of those additional responses. Their function is apparently limited to the control of behavior adapted to space, and we may therefore deduce that the perceptual experience mediated by vestibular stimuli has a purely spatial quality. There is no vestibular sense precisely because there are no nonspatial responses conditioned to vestibular stimuli. In short, what I am suggesting now is that the distinction between sensation and perception is in essence the distinction between the activity of engrams mediating nonspatial behavior and that of engrams mediating spatial behavior. Because there are no nonspatial responses conditioned to vestibular stimuli the resulting perceptual experience is nonsensory.

11.17. These last statements may appear to be nothing but wild fantasy, invented for the purpose of filling up an awkward gap in the theory. But in fact they can be fully substantiated. Throughout this book I have assumed without question that there are proprioceptive afferents from the extrinsic muscles of the eyes. There has been a great deal of argument about this question, and it is only quite recently that the existence of such afferents has been established by physiological research (Cooper, Daniel, and Whitteridge, 1955). But long before this evidence came to light I had proved the existence of the disputed afferents, and, although I did not recognize it at the time, provided experimental evidence in support of the statements at the end of the previous section.

Having reached the conviction that the perception of space could not be explained without assuming proprioceptive afferents from the ocular muscles I decided to search for introspective evidence of their existence. My argument was that if we can detect the activities of the skeletal muscles we should also be able to detect the activities of the ocular muscles. Accordingly I shut my eyes and directed my attention to the space behind my eyeballs. For about ten minutes nothing happened, and then quite suddenly I became aware of a very lively but apparently chaotic succession of muscle twitches. Presently the chaos disappeared and I was able to identify the twitches as being located in the eight rectus muscles. In order to satisfy myself that I was not just imagining the twitches I gave myself a number of verbal stimuli and observed the consequent oculomotor activity. The first stimulus was "the Eiffel Tower," and almost before I had finished pronouncing the words I observed a rapid succession of twitches such as would have been produced by scanning the tower, starting at the base and moving upward in a series of lateral zigzags of diminishing amplitude. When I thought of my hands and then of the moon, the twitches were located in the positions occupied by the internal recti in the first case and by the external recti in the second, while there was a distinct relaxation of tension in the internal recti.

Some years later, while I was engaged with the second experiment described in Chapter 9, I wished to compare the movements of my eyes in walking, climbing stairs, and the like, with and without the distorting spectacles. At first I found it difficult to detect the twitches, but after turning the eyes as far as possible to right, left, up, and down, thereby producing afferent stimuli of maximum strength, the smaller stimuli could be detected with ease. I then made a discovery that proves beyond all reasonable doubt that the twitches I was observing were real and not imagined. When I thought of myself climbing stairs my eyes executed a rhythmical up and down movement, keeping time with my leg movements. The upward movement was rapid, indicating a saccadic movement, while the downward movement was slow, as when the eyes are following a moving object. The range of movement was about equal to the visual angle subtended by one step. Since I habitually look at each step before putting a foot on it, the observed sequence of twitches was consistent with the hypothesis that in imagining myself climbing stairs I was actually reproducing the oculomotor component of this activity and observing it introspectively.

When I imagined myself walking down stairs the observed twitches differed in two respects from those described above. First, the range of the movement was distinctly narrower. This of course is consistent with the fact that the visual angle subtended by a step beyond the feet is narrower in descending than in ascending. Second, the slow downward movement of the eyes alternated between two markedly different speeds. One speed was approximately the same as that observed when I imagined myself climbing, while the other was at least twice as slow. This finding was so completely unexpected that I repeated the observations several times, but always with the same results—regular rhythm when ascending, irregular when descending.

Being completely at a loss to account for the observed difference I went to a staircase in the hope of solving the riddle and discovered that my right foot takes more than twice as long to descend a step as my left foot, but there is no such difference in ascending. As I had not previously been aware of this fact about myself, it is evident that the observed twitches could not have been a figment of my imagination. On the contrary, the twitches gave me accurate information about myself that was subsequently confirmed by independent observation.

In all these observations there was never any evidence of activity of the oblique muscles, but a later experiment enabled me to detect these as well. With the object of testing the hypothesis proposed by Bates (1944) that accommodation is effected by the oblique muscles and not by the ciliary bodies, I read a single volume edition of Motley's *Rise of the Dutch Republic* without my glasses. Apart from a troublesome diplopia that I could eliminate only by half closing my eyes, I had no difficulty in securing perfectly clear definition of the small type. Introspective observation of oculomotor activity while I imagined myself to be reading without my glasses revealed tensions in the region of the oblique muscles. There was no evidence of such tensions when I repeated the observations with my glasses on.

11.18. These observations prove the existence of proprioceptive afferents from the ocular muscles, and this proof would retain its validity even if physiological research had not yet succeeded in demonstrating them. But it is not primarily for this purpose that I have reported my observations. They show that afferents whose existence was for a long time denied on the ground that there was no evidence of them, either physiological or psychological, can actually be made to generate sensory impressions of a very definite and precise character. This naturally prompts us to ask by what mechanism these sensory impressions come into existence. It is obviously fruitless to say that they have been there all the time, but that normally we do not notice them because we do not attend to them. The essence of a sensory experience is that it is conscious, and if we do not "notice" it, it simply does not exist as a sensory experience, regardless of what afferent events there may be. The notion of an unnoticed sensory or perceptual experience is a contradiction in terms, but it is a contradiction that is implicit in a great deal of psychological thinking. The assumption seems to be that stimulation of the receptors automatically generates such experience, but that much of it remains latent until it is brought into the full blaze of consciousness by attention. This type of theory seems to imply not one ghost in the machine but two, the second one—attention—being required to whip the first one into some semblance of life.

To answer our question we must consider the events that led to the emergence of the new sensory experience. It is at once obvious that it was not "attention" that brought it to light, since concentrated attention produced no results for some ten minutes. Judging by what happened on the second occasion, when I deliberately turned my eyes as far as possible in four different directions, the events can be reconstructed as follows. The extreme tension generated inhibition, resulting in the relaxation of the muscles. This made it possible for a symbolic response, which we may represent by the words "there is tension here," to be conditioned to the afferent impulses generated by the contracted muscles. Reinforcement was provided by recognition that this was precisely what I was looking for. As soon as a symbolic response was conditioned to the strongest stimuli it generalized to the weaker stimuli generated by less extensive contractions. But this is a new kind of response, altogether different from those that have previously been conditioned to compound patterns of stimulation including the afferents from the ocular muscles. It differs in two respects. First, the stimuli are the proprioceptive afferents alone, and not those afferents in conjunction with a variety of other stimuli. And second, the responses are nonspatial in character, while those conditioned to the compound stimuli are essentially spatial. Our theory then leads to the deduction that the activation of the engrams mediating these new responses must give rise to a new form of perceptual experience.

This, then, is the final piece of evidence I have to offer in support of the behavioral theory of perception. The evidence that perception can be changed by conditioning a new set of responses to existing patterns of stimulation may conceivably have left the reader unconvinced that the pre-experimental forms of perception are generated by conditioning. He may have argued that to demonstrate how a phenomenon can be changed is not equivalent to demonstrating how it originally came into being. Unquestionably this is a weighty argument, and the only convincing way to answer it is to demonstrate that in fact new forms of perceptual experience can be generated by the postulated mechanism. The experiment described above provides the necessary demonstration, but it is by no means the only one. Every worker who acquires skill in the selection and handling of the materials of his trade generates forms of perception that are unknown to others.

CHAPTER 12

Other Theories

12.1. The theory expounded in the preceding chapters was developed almost entirely without reference to the contributions of other workers in the field of perception. This policy was adopted quite deliberately, partly with the object of avoiding polemics that would tend to obscure the argument, but chiefly because the goal I had set myself seemed to be radically different from that of most other writers. If two or more scientists, ostensibly concerned with the same sector of nature, differ from each other not only with respect to the explanatory principles they seek to establish but also with respect to what they are trying to explain, it is evident that there can be little or no common ground between them. If A and B espouse different principles and at the same time aim at different goals, there is no point in A attacking B's principles: he might as well attack quantum theory for its failure to account for hysterical anesthesia. The only kind of scientific quarrel that is likely to have fruitful results is one between workers who are in basic agreement as to what they are trying to explain.

Now that I have presented my own problem and offered a tentative solution, a brief comparison with a representative sample of contemporary theories may be of some value. There is no question here of attempting a comprehensive survey: that has already been admirably done by F. H. Allport. My purpose in this chapter is to clarify my own theory by showing how it differs from other theories, and since these spring from a limited number of clearly distinguishable tendencies, it will be sufficient to deal with one example of each. It goes without saying that few authors exhibit one and only one tendency. On the contrary, good ideas offered by one author tend to be accepted by others, often with some modification, so that many contemporary theories are markedly eclectic in character. A well-known example is Tolman's attempt to combine gestalt principles with learning theory, and there are many others. I shall not attempt to deal with any eclectic theory taken as a whole, since my primary concern is with the basic elements that are incorporated in such theories.

12.2. The most fundamental differences between theories of perception are ultimately philosophical in origin. The rise of behaviorism in the early decades of the twentieth century focused attention on those differences, and a vigorous controversy arose between the advocates of nativism and empiricism. The essence of nativism is that conscious experiences are directly generated by brain processes without the mediation of any intervening variable; that consciousness, to put it crudely, is a kind of secretion of the brain. This implies that consciousness comes into existence as soon as the afferent paths and the neurons of the cortical projection areas have reached maturity. The gradual development observed in certain aspects of consciousness would then be explained by an appeal to maturation. In its most thoroughgoing form empiricism claims that the neurons are physiological structures, operating entirely in accordance with the laws of physics and chemistry. Their structure is such that they can receive and transmit impulses more readily than the cells of other tissues, but they cannot generate any nonmaterial essence such as consciousness. If, in spite of this, the intact organism develops what we call consciousness, this is to be interpreted as a system of relations between the organism and its environment, and the gradual development of this system, attributed by nativists to maturation, is explained in terms of the laws of learning. Since the neurons play a vital part in the process, neuronal activity is a necessary condition of consciousness, but is not in itself sufficient. Nativism, on the contrary, holds neuronal activity to be sufficient.

Today the sharp line of distinction between those opposing views has been so blurred that it almost appears as if the controversy has been settled. But in fact the settlement is illusory. What has happened is that nativists have been compelled, by experimental evidence, to make certain concessions to their opponents, while most empiricists, faced with the formidable difficulties that stand in the way of explaining the most primitive forms of conscious experience, have tended to concede that territory to the nativists.

The result of this compromise is that today there are hardly any authors who aim at writing a completely general theory of perception, that is, at writing a single set of mutually consistent principles that will suffice to account for all perceptual phenomena without exception. Those who lean toward nativism ignore those aspects of perception that must be explained in terms of learning, but in doing so they are virtually admitting that two entirely different sets of principles are required to explain the whole realm. Similarly, those who are philosophically inclined to empiricism make the same tacit admission whenever they admit the validity of the distinction between sensation and perception, and elect to leave the study of sensation to the psychophysicists. The theory presented in this work differs from all those in that it starts from the assumption that there are not two realms but one inclusive realm. It rejects the assumption that the principles that account for one part of this realm are inapplicable to the rest, and for two reasons. First, it is impossible to determine an exact boundary between two parts of the realm, so that one can say with certainty that this phenomenon belongs to one of the regions and that to the other. And second, even if such a division were possible, it is contrary to the spirit of science to assume that there is absolutely no common ground between the two regions. Yet that is precisely what we must maintain if we hold that some forms of perception are explainable in terms of nativism and others in terms of empiricism, since the two doctrines not only have nothing in common but are mutually incompatible.

The present state of eclecticism in perceptual theory is in some ways similar to the state of chemistry before the atomic theory was developed. It was assumed that dead matter and the constituents of living bodies required different explanatory principles, until it was discovered that the essential difference between organic and inorganic compounds is that the former are all compounds of carbon. Although the distinction between organic and inorganic chemistry continues to be maintained, chiefly for reasons of practical convenience, it is now universally recognized that exactly the same set of basic principles is applicable to both realms.

12.3. Having rejected the concept of two realms, each with its own basic principles, there was no alternative to the rejection of nativism, since numerous experiments had demonstrated that there were at least some perceptual phenomena that could not be explained in terms of nativism. Hence the theory presented here differs from contemporary theories not only in rejecting eclecticism but in rejecting its nativist component. It is therefore fitting that this survey should begin with the theory of Gibson, the most distinguished of present-day exponents of nativism.[1]

Every scientific theory rests on an axiomatic basis which is its philosophical foundation. The axioms are not always explicitly stated, and it is not always easy to discover what they are. But Gibson leaves us in no doubt that one of his axioms is that perception is innate. That being so, the task of the perceptionist, as he sees it, is to demonstrate that the proximal stimuli in themselves contain sufficient information to account for all the forms and properties of perception without having to appeal to empiricist principles. In particular, he must show that those properties emphasized by gestaltists, such as the continuity of surfaces and the segregation of figure from ground, have their exact counterparts in the stimulus.

The essence of his theory is that in order to account for the facts of perception, we need a new kind of psychophysics, in which the emphasis is not on isolated or punctate stimuli varying in quality or intensity, but on the patterning, or ordinal arrangement, of stimuli encountered in the everyday world. Thus we cannot understand the perception of distance without recognizing that surfaces present gradients of texture to the eye, and that the different elements of such a gradient are always ordered in the same manner in the retinal stimulus no matter what the direction of the eye may be. Again, those gradients change in a completely determinate manner when the subject moves through the environment, so that the changing pattern of stimulation always contains the information that is necessary to generate perception both of the spatial ordering of the environment and of the subject's position in it. All this I

1. The gap between our theories is aptly expressed in a remark Gibson once made to me in conversation: "You are more wrong than anyone else I know." Presumably what he meant was that whereas his other opponents make some concession to nativism, I make none. Others are wrong in part, in that they claim a larger share of the territory than Gibson is willing to concede to empiricism; I am the most wrong because I claim the whole territory and would leave none to him.

concede, and I gladly admit that I am heavily indebted to Gibson for his admirable exposition of those hitherto neglected aspects of the stimulus.

In a later publication (Gibson, 1958) he investigates more fully the changes that result from locomotion, and notes the "explosive" expansion of the retinal image as the distance of an object diminishes to zero. This expansion, he believes, is not only innately perceived, but its perception automatically stops the forward progression of the animal. Thus his axioms include the one that was explicitly stated by Michotte, as quoted in 3.6, that the function of perception is to control behavior.

Gibson seems to hold that the information contained in light is not only necessary but *sufficient* to account for perception, but on the question how this information, which is not itself perception, gets translated into perception, he has nothing to say, except that perception is innate. But this is not a theory in the ordinary sense of the word. It is no more than an axiom. We may say that the capacity of the flea genes to mold the body of a flea and not that of a shrimp is innate; but no biologist would honor such a statement by calling it a theory.

In any case the statement is not, strictly speaking, true. Before the Darwinian revolution in biology it was widely accepted (although nothing was then known about the genes), and it was assumed that the flea had long ago come into sudden existence as a result of a special act of creation, and had gone on reproducing its kind ever since. Today we know that the flea, like other organisms, owes its present shape to the combined operation of mutation, natural selection, and the property of the nucleic acid molecule (the main constituent of the gene) that enables it to assemble other molecules of the same form from simpler substances in its environment. The old creationist dogma has given way to a doctrine in which the emphasis is not on forms but on processes. Linnaeus thought he was starting a new era in biology when he constructed a scientific method for the classification of species, but in fact his work was the final flowering of a tendency that was already doomed.

There seems to be a close analogy between the belief that perception is innate and the creationist explanation of species. Both have the effect of restricting investigation to the description and classification of forms, and excluding questions concerning origins. Both also imply that there are mysteries in nature that will never be revealed to the probing eye of science. Although nativists do not openly postulate a specific act of creation, as pre-Darwinian biologists did, it is difficult to shake off the suspicion that this is an implicit part of their belief. For nativism implies that certain groups of neurons have the specific property that they can generate conscious experiences such as sensations; but biochemistry and neurophysiology have not shown that these neurons are essentially different from others for which no such claims have been made. So it would seem that intellectual honesty requires the nativist either to state boldly that the sensory neurons have been specially created (in a manner calculated to baffle research within the framework of the physical sciences) to act as what Fechner called "der Sitz der Seele im Körper," or to admit openly that he has no theory regarding the origin of consciousness. If he adopts neither of these courses, and still remains a nativist, there is some justification for describing nativism as the modern counterpart of pre-Darwinian creationism.

12.4. Nativists do not as a rule go around proclaiming that they are nativists: they reveal themselves rather by the kind of questions they ask, and more particularly by the kind of questions they refrain from asking. Thus the gestalt school of psychology has asked many penetrating and necessary questions about the structure of perception, but never any questions as to how that structure comes to be built up. They have formulated hypotheses concerning the physiological structures underlying perceptual structures, but have never asked the vital question how the leap from the physiological to the mental realm is effected. It is one thing to claim that there are electrical field forces in the brain with properties analogous to the properties of perception, but it is quite another matter to claim that those forces at the same time generate events of a kind that are completely unknown to physics.

The chief difference between Gibson's theory and that of the gestalt school is that they search in different places for the structural analogues of perception. But this difference, striking as it may seem at first sight, is in reality quite superficial in comparison with the basic similarity between them. The similarity is that both are concerned primarily with structure, both seem to be content that they have solved the problem of perception when they have discovered a physical analogue of perceptual structure, both recognize the importance of simultaneity, and both avoid coming to grips with the vital question of the leap from the physical to the psychological realm.

Gestalt psychologists are not unmindful of perceptual change, as witness their extensive investigations of figural aftereffects, but their explanations of such changes are invariably in terms of structural neural changes of a temporary character brought about by prolonged fixation. They have no explanation in such terms of the more lasting changes discussed in Chapters 8, 9, and 10, or of the developmental changes described by Piaget in his numerous publications. In short, gestalt psychology is another form of creationism.

12.5. The influence of gestalt theory has been very widespread, and understandably so, since it has brought to light a great many previously unsuspected facts about perception. It is therefore not surprising that Erismann and Kohler have attempted to explain some of the more permanent changes they have induced experimentally by postulating structural changes of a more lasting character than those that account for after-images or figural aftereffects. They were prompted to suggest this solution by the observation that a subject wearing wedge prisms reports a slight straightening of the curved image of a vertical straight line even when he does nothing more than look at it. Erismann had originally assumed that straightening could occur only if the subject took some action relative to the stimulus-object and corrected his mistakes, and he thought of this action as being primarily manual. Since the change occurred, although on a small scale, in the absence of such action, he felt compelled to look for an explanation in other terms.

The theory held by Erismann and Kohler is essentially an eclectic one. The perceptual changes that occur in an experiment are divided into two main classes, which may be called structural and situational respectively. The situational changes are those that depend on the action taken by the subject to correct errors in manipulating objects. For example, the changes that occurred in Experiment II (Chapter 9) were described by Kohler as situational. Structural changes are those that occur apparently in the absence of behavioral errors or of any opportunity to correct them. These are attributed to some kind of long-term physiological adaptation brought about by simple exposure to the distorted image. Apparently this involves an extension of the gestalt principle that a perceived shape will take the simplest form consistent with the field forces that are supposed to be operating in the brain. Now if the retinal image is permanently transformed so that all vertical straight lines appear as curves, the field forces tend to produce the simpler perceptual form of the straight line. Prolonged activities of this kind ultimately result in a permanent change in the structure of the brain, having the effect that the simpler perceptual structure is more readily induced. When the spectacles are removed, this new structure has the effect that vertical straight lines are now curved in the opposite direction, and to the same extent as the straightening of the curved lines seen through the spectacles.

Apart from the fact that no direct test of this physiological hypothesis is available, the theory rests on the assumption that "passive" contemplation involves no action on the part of the subject. It is, in fact, an active process directed toward the external field, and if we treat it as such we can arrive at a more parsimonious explanation of the perceptual changes than that offered by Erismann and Kohler. We need only one set of principles and not two.

The final test of the theory is experimental. If passive contemplation produces a slow physiological change, and if this change, as they maintain, never reaches completion, then it is impossible to account for the rapid adaptation of the aphakic patient to distortion that is much more severe than that produced by wedge prisms. As shown in 9.30, the curvature and instability of the perceptual field are *completely* eliminated by the simple process of scanning outlines. Since the change occurs in the absence of manipulation of objects, it would seem that this is precisely the kind of situation where the physiological adaptation postulated by Erismann and Kohler must operate. But the change is neither slow nor incomplete, so that some other mechanism must be invoked.

Since Erismann actually started his researches from the point of view of the behavioral theory, we can now understand that his deviation into nativism springs not from a philosophical predilection but from a formulation of the theory that was too crude and restrictive. To him behavior meant actions that involved making contact with objects or moving in such a way as to avoid contact.

He could not appreciate that ocular movements are also behavior, and that they also involve "contacts" with objects. As soon as this is recognized, the behavioral theory can be seen to explain equally well both the slow and incomplete adaptation under passive contemplation of an object through wedge prism spectacles, and the rapid and complete adaptation of the aphakic patient.

12.6. Erismann's eclecticism has its roots partly in the incompleteness of his theory as originally formulated, and partly in the vitality and energy of his own personality, which prompted him to test his theory experimentally before it had been subjected to a rigorous logical scrutiny. And this, I believe, is true of many eclectics whose sympathies are on the side of empiricism. They are often vigorous and inventive experimentalists, who are so apt to see the experimental possibilities of a new idea that they are eager to test it at once, and are impatient of the apparent idleness involved in the necessarily lengthy process of checking the logical validity and sufficiency of the idea. And in this attitude they are encouraged by the ready availability of an impressive panoply of instruments (collectively known as "Experimental Design") that will enable them to estimate the probable truth of virtually any kind of incomplete hypothesis they may choose to invent.

If we are dealing with a system whose regularity is assured only if we include n variables, but we have no immediate means of knowing what those variables are, two types of procedure are open to us. We may aim at regularity from the beginning, or we may be content with an irregular system and employ statistical methods to determine whether the included variables are essential to the system or not. The first procedure is not likely to succeed until a substantial body of knowledge about the various parts of the system has been accumulated, and even when the knowledge is available, it requires an act of creative intelligence to assemble the independent variables in such an order that it is possible to predict with reasonable accuracy the values of the dependent variables.

In the course of the search the active experimentalist, whose creative imagination has suggested to him that this or that independent variable is essential to the system, is likely to devise an experimental program at once without waiting to ask whether his selected variable is both necessary and sufficient to determine the dependent variable. He cannot answer the question of sufficiency without adopting the first procedure, which is irksome to his active disposition; but there are plenty of statistical methods that will enable him to answer the question whether the selected variable is necessary or not. It goes without saying that a positive answer to this question adds to our knowledge and increases the likelihood of a successful outcome when the first procedure is adopted. It does this in two ways. First, if statistical criteria are satisfied at a high level of significance, we have proof that the relevant variable, or at least something closely associated with it, is a necessary component of the regular system we are seeking to construct. And second, if correlations significantly less than unity are obtained (and this is invariably the case when the method under review is adopted), this establishes that the system assembled by the investigator is an irregular one that needs to be enlarged by the inclusion of other variables. Thus even an incomplete or inadequate theory makes an important contribution to the final solution of the problem.

12.7. As an example of a theory arising out of the second type of procedure we may select the sensory-tonic field theory proposed by Wapner and Werner. The independent variables incorporated in the system constructed by these writers include sensory variables, by which they mean exteroceptive stimuli, and tonic variables, which are the efferent impulses that are required to maintain bodily posture. The dependent variables include certain selected aspects of perception, such as perception of the vertical. The authors thus set themselves at the outset a strictly limited goal, in the apparently reasonable expectation that if this is attained, their theory can be generalized to the whole range of perceptual phenomena.

They recognize that the perception of the vertical cannot be explained in terms of retinal stimuli alone, since tilting the head to right or left changes the direction of the retinal image of a vertical line. Evidently a second input variable is required, and this must be functionally related to the angle of tilt of the head, if the rotation of the retinal image is to be compensated for in perception. We can easily form a regular system with one parameter, the objective direction of a straight line that stimulates the retina, and two variables, the direction of the retinal image of the line and the angle of tilt of the head. But if this system is to generate perception of the direction of the line as invariant, two other conditions must be satisfied. First, the two variables must have their values registered in some way: they must be real variables of the system that generates the perception, and not just numerical values written down by an outside observer. And second, there must be some mechanism whereby the values of the variables are processed so as to yield an invariant answer so long as the parameter remains unchanged. Let us see how Wapner and Werner propose to meet these demands.

The most striking feature of their handling of the first requirement is the fundamentally different status they accord to the two variables. The retinal variable is treated as if it were capable of generating perception of direction quite independently of the second variable. In their book on *Perceptual Development* (1957) they put forward the hypothesis that early in life a vertical line is perceived as being vertical only when the head is erect and the proximal stimulus is therefore parallel to the retinal Y axis, and that it is perceived as being tilted through the angle $-\theta$ when the head is tilted through the angle θ. No explanation of this supposed fact is offered, and indeed the proposition is presented as if it were self-evident and required no proof. So, despite the fact that the authors are philosophically predisposed to favor empiricism, there is a nativist doctrine at the very heart of their theory.

For their second variable they have a choice between the proprioceptive afferents incidental to the position in which the head is held, and the efferent processes by which the posture is maintained. If the body is erect and motionless, it may be assumed that each of these variables is a single-valued function of the position of the head, so that either of them will serve the purpose. Wapner and Werner choose the efferent, or tonic, variable. This variable, it would seem, has no intrinsic or independent power to generate perception, and at first it has no power to influence the inherently unstable perception that is assumed to be native to the retinal variable. However, it gradually acquires this power over a period of years, and may even go too far and overcompensate for the errors of the primitive system. Learning is thus implied, but no attempt is made to specify precisely what is learned.

12.8. This brings us to the authors' solution of the problem how the system meets the demand for a mechanism that will process the values of the two variables to generate perceptual stability. Their answer is that the organismic state, as represented by the tonic variable, is capable of establishing what they call an "equilibrial axis" whose direction varies relative to the head but remains constant relative to the gravitational axis. When the tonic forces operating on the two sides of the head are equally balanced, the head is erect and the equilibrial axis is in line with the vertical axis of the head. With the head tilted to an angle θ, the tonic forces are unequal, but since the difference between them is assumed to be a function of the angle of tilt, it can establish that the equilibrial axis is at the angle $-\theta$ relative to the vertical axis of the head and therefore in an invariant position relative to the objective vertical.

It seems then that the values of the two main variables cannot be fed directly into the computer to generate the expected invariant answer; but the tonic variable must first be converted into another variable whose essential character is not clearly stated. It is not very easy to discover whether or not it involves consciousness of the position of the equilibrial axis relative to the position of the head, and to avoid the risk of misinterpreting the authors, I shall merely say that it carries this information.

Now this transformation to a new variable makes the computational process so delightfully simple that one wonders why it should take as many years to build the machinery as the authors claim. Assuming the objective line to be vertical and the angle of the head to be θ, then the retinal variable is at $-\theta$, and the organismic variable carries the information that the equilibrial axis is also at $-\theta$ relative to the direction of the head. If we subtract the latter value from the former we get $-\theta - (-\theta) = 0$, which is the perceived position of the line relative to the vertical. This can easily be generalized to lines at any angle. Let the line be at an angle ϕ to the vertical, and the head, as before, at θ. Then the values of the two variables are $\phi - \theta$ and $-\theta$, and subtraction gives ϕ as the perceived direction. Actually the authors do not say anything about subtraction. They limit their exposition to the case of the vertical line, and content themselves with showing that no matter what value the sensory variable may take, the organismic variable has that same value, so that the two are always balanced. It is this balancing that they take to be the necessary condition for constancy. If they had attempted to generalize to oblique lines they could not have failed to recognize that the true condition for constancy is not equality of the two variables, but invariance of the difference between them.

This means therefore that if the system is to generate perceptual constancy it must contain machinery that is capable of carrying out a process analogous to subtraction. But we look in vain for any hint as to what sort of organic machinery could perform this operation, and we must therefore conclude that Wapner and Werner have failed to solve not only the general problem of perception but also the strictly limited problem to which they confined themselves.

12.9. Their failure is even more strikingly demonstrated when they try to show how normal perception is restored in a subject who wears distorting spectacles. They consider a hypothetical case of a subject who wears prisms that rotate the proximal stimulus produced by a vertical line through an angle of 30°, and (to judge by the diagrams on pp. 59 f., Wapner and Werner, 1957) maintain this proximal stimulus in a constant direction relative to an external frame of reference no matter what the direction of the head may be. Now a total reflecting prism mounted in a spectacle frame, and carried on the nose in the usual way, will rotate the image of any line, whether vertical or oblique, through 30° whenever its base is set at 15° to the horizontal (or vertical). If it is to do this when the head is erect, the base must be at 15° to either the horizontal or the vertical axis of the frame. But in that case any tilting of the head to right or left will change the direction of the proximal stimulus relative to the external frame of reference. The only way to produce the kind of results envisaged by the authors is to mount the prism in a ball bearing and attach a weight to it, so that its base remains at a constant angle with the horizontal.

Assuming then that the subject is actually carrying this cumbersome machinery on his face, we must recognize that there is one perceptual inconstancy that he escapes. The direction of any line in a plane at right angles to the optic axis remains constant, as it does when one is wearing no spectacles at all or when one is wearing Stratton lenses. Inconstancy is produced by backward or forward tilting of the head, or by rotation about the vertical axis, but not by tilting to right or left. Yet it is precisely by this nonexistent inconstancy that Wapner and Werner propose to illustrate how their theory can explain the restoration of constancy.

Actually what they try to explain is not the restoration of constancy but the elimination of a constant error. They do this by supposing that a new equilibrial axis is established by some mechanism they do not attempt to specify. The scale of the organismic variable is provided with a new origin, so that the operation of subtraction once more yields a zero answer when the objective line is vertical. Thus the reprograming of the analogue computer involves nothing more complex than the addition of a constant to all results. It is evident that other instructions must be fed into the machine if the prisms are *fixed* in the spectacle frame and planted firmly on the nose, since in that case tilting the head through the angle θ does not leave the proximal stimulus in a constant direction relative to an external frame of reference but rotates it through the angle 2θ, so that its direction on the retina is θ instead of $-\theta$. Subtraction then yields the answer 2θ instead of zero. And generally, if the objective direction of the line is ϕ, the answer is $\phi + 2\theta$. (No new principle is involved if the prisms are mounted obliquely, so that this case need not be considered separately.) The obvious way to deal with this situation is to program the machine to add the values of the variables instead of subtracting, but if we retain the concept of an equilibrial axis whose position relative to the head must be subtracted from the position of the proximal stimulus relative to the retinal Y axis, then the objective direction of this equilibrial axis is no longer constant but variable. Its objective direction is 2θ when θ is the direction of the head.

12.10. The model proposed by Wapner and Werner fails, not because it is a mathematical model, but because it does not disclose any real mechanism having the properties of the mathematical model. This is just another way of saying that it omits some of the essential variables that are necessary if the system is to generate a dependent variable that looks reasonably like perception as we know it. The need for a real mechanism, located somewhere within the central nervous system, has been recognized by several writers, and the rapidly growing discipline of neurophysiology has raised hopes that it might reveal the shape of the required mechanism. Needless to say, the mechanism, when it is found, must be consistent with the established principles of neurophysiology. This is a necessary condition, but it is not sufficient. One can construct numerous models, all consistent with neurophysiology, to account for isolated behavioral phenomena, but if other essential variables are omitted from the system, it will not suffice to explain perception.

The best known model of this kind is that proposed by Hebb (1949). The problem he sets himself is not the construction of a general theory of perception but the limited problem of explaining the visual perception of shape. This has been discussed at great length by the gestalt school, and Hebb begins by showing that their field theory is inconsistent with the findings of neurophysiology. The brain, he argues very convincingly, is incapable of generating perception of shape without some kind of learning process, and here, of course, I am in complete agreement with him. I agree with him, too, that the learning must necessarily be slow because of the very large number of detailed learnings that have to be accomplished. We disagree, however, in our speculations as to the *kind* of learning that is involved. Whereas I am disposed to assume that all learning is essentially of the same kind, Hebb maintains that there are two basically different kinds, his second variety being more akin to biotaxis than to conditioning. His theory of perception also differs from mine in that it contains a residual element of nativism, although he is just as firmly opposed to animism as I am.

12.11. The first thing to be noted is that the machinery proposed by Hebb does not actually generate perception. All that he claims for it is that it adds the property of shape to a primitive core of conscious experience that initially lacks that property. We are thus faced at the outset with a philosophical dilemma. Some forms of stimulation can produce conscious experience immediately, whereas others can do so only through the mediation of a learning process. In other words, some neurons are born with the mystical property that they can secrete consciousness, while others have it thrust upon them by the formation of new links with their neighbors.

The evidence on which Hebb relies for the hypothesis of the primitive core is drawn largely from Senden's monograph on operated cases of congenital cataract. He himself warns against placing too much reliance on such evidence, since the cataract patient is not an infant at the very beginning of the developmental process;

but he does not heed his own warning. Thus he assumes that because the patient, on opening his eyes after the operation, reports a rich glow of color, color is one of the properties of the primitive unmediated consciousness. This conclusion would be incontestable if no light whatsoever reached the patient's retina during the period of his blindness. But in fact light does reach his retina, and its wave composition varies with the environment he is in, just as it does for people with normal eyes. Consequently there is no lack of opportunity for him to acquire differential responses to lights of different composition. Thus if he walks from a green lawn onto a red gravel path, there is a change in retinal stimulation, and at the same time a slightly different technique of walking is required. Here we have all the elements that are needed for differential conditioning; and the blaze of color on opening the eyes is therefore no proof that color vision is innate.

Senden's evidence shows further that the cataract patient cannot distinguish a triangle from a square until he has counted the corners several times, and Hebb therefore concludes that a fixated corner produces some kind of primitive unmediated perception in its own right. This he attributes to the distinctive ridge of excitation produced in the striate area, and its sudden termination and change of direction. What the patient sees, in fact, is a blur, with little resemblance to the sharply defined ridge in the cortex. But we have no right to infer from this that the infant, looking at an angular object for the first time, has a similar perceptual experience. The patient is already living in a world that is spatially ordered, and retinal stimulation may well have made a small contribution to this ordering. But the infant's world, as presented through his receptors, is totally devoid of order, and we cannot assume, in the absence of direct evidence (which is unobtainable), that he perceives even a blur. For even a blur, it should be noted, implies some order, although it is sadly lacking in precision. Even a blur has a position, not absolute perhaps, but at least relative to some other blur.

This raises an important philosophical question that has direct relevance to Hebb's theory. Let us accept that when an infant fixates one corner of a triangular figure he does not perceive the triangle as a whole. This means that if he perceives the fixated corner as a vague blur, he does not perceive the other corners at all, even as the vaguest of blurs. For if he did perceive them as blurs they would be perceived as having positions relative to one another and to the fixated corner. But if the positions of the three corners relative to one another are perceived, the triangle is perceived, and the proposition from which we started is contradicted. We must accept, therefore, that there is no perception of the other two corners. But in that case there is no frame of reference by which the position of the fixated corner can be perceived. An object that has no determinate position in space can only be either everywhere, like the air around us, or nowhere at all; and in neither case can it be perceived as having a position. The axiomatic basis of Hebb's theory is thus self-contradictory, and therefore no system having such a basis can exist.

12.12. This discussion incidentally brings to light a gap in my own theory. I have been assuming throughout that the perception of shape is primarily dependent on the perception of position, and that nothing else is required. But since an object that stands out from its background presents a steep gradient of luminosity at its boundary, it follows that the perception of its position in space implies perception of a difference between the lighter and darker areas. If it can be shown that there is a behavioral basis for this discrimination, then it can be accepted as forming part of the axiomatic basis of the whole argument from Chapter 2 onward.

Without attempting a systematic discussion of the problem, it can be said that in principle the solution is very simple. When the environment is illuminated there is continuous, if chaotic, activity in the optical afferent system, and an endless succession of unlearned responses can be evoked. A small proportion of these are reinforced. On the other hand, when the environment is in darkness, unlearned responses of the type included in the set U defined in (3.4.23), are not accompanied by the retinal stimuli specified by the elements of that set, and accordingly, any chance reinforcement of such responses does not establish any conditioned response to light. It follows that light, no matter what its distribution, becomes a conditioned stimulus for a generalized activity of the organism, and darkness for the cessation of such activity. But if there is even a primitive differentiation of learned behavior in response to light and darkness, our theory implies that there is a primitive perceptual distinction between light and darkness.

This primitive perceived light will at first be almost completely undifferentiated within itself, as if the subject were in a thick fog. But the structure of the retina is beautifully adapted to allow the process of differentiation to begin at once. There is a high concentration of receptors in the macular region, and particularly the fovea; but more important than that is the fact that each cone in the fovea has its own ganglion cell, whereas in the periphery there is one ganglion cell to two or more receptors. The result of this arrangement is that the total volume of afferent energy reaching the striate area is not a simple function of the total energy of light falling on the retina. Even if the total light is held constant, the volume of afferent energy varies according to whether the eyes are directed toward an area of low or high luminosity.

The immediate result of this structure is that, by Hulls' principle of stimulus intensity dynamism, manual conditioned responses are more likely to be established if the object to which the action is directed is in a well-lit area; and by secondary conditioning the infant then learns to turn his eyes in the direction of this area. But this conditioning implies that the original undifferentiated fog begins to be differentiated into areas of varying brightness. The high concentration of ganglion cells in the macular region has the effect that, once the process of differentiation has begun, progressively finer differentiations can be made within the center of the visual field, so that ultimately steep gradients of luminosity give rise to the perception of sharp lines between brighter and darker areas.

This hypothesis is supported by the experience of congenital cataract patients. Given adequate training and motivation, the patient's initially blurred visual field gradually sharpens until normal visual acuity is attained. With poor training or none at all, the patient may get so discouraged that he abandons the effort to improve his vision, and continues to rely on the system of habits that enabled him to live through his period of blindness.

Other evidence is found in the treatment of the condition known as *amblyopia*, in which there is a low level of visual acuity, often in one eye only, and often accompanied by a narrowing of the visual field, in the absence of physiological defects or errors of refraction. Stutterheim (1937) reports that this condition is frequently associated with inadequate control of ocular convergence. Apparently what happens is that if the patient cannot converge accurately on near objects, he uses one eye only and becomes virtually monocular. This means that accurate oculomotor responses are not conditioned to stimuli applied to the neglected eye, and its field is consequently blurred and restricted in range. Stutterheim has found that amblyopia is often completely cured when the patient is given intensive training in convergence. The effect of this training is that ocular responses that were originally conditioned to stimuli applied to one retina only are now extended to the other, with a resulting increase in acuity and range.

12.13 Since no system of the kind envisaged by Hebb can exist, it would seem superfluous to subject his theory to further analysis. But in case the reader is not convinced by the argument of 12.11, on the ground that we may have omitted some essential property of the system that would make it internally consistent, let us assume that some such feature does in fact exist, making the system viable, and proceed to inquire whether the proposed mechanism can generate perception of shape.

Hebb begins by assuming that when one corner of a triangle is fixated, each of the other corners activates a reflex arc that tends to evoke an ocular movement bringing the peripheral stimulus to the fovea. The result is that the eyes tend to move from corner to corner in a random order, thus permitting certain changes in neural organization that make possible the perception of the triangle as a whole.[2] Now it is known that the optic tract contains a small proportion of fibers, all originating from the periphery of the retina, that bypass the lateral geniculate and run directly to the superior colliculi, where they synapse with fibers to the oculomotor nuclei. But the evidence seems to show that the adequate stimulus for these reflex arcs is a light of relatively high intensity, such as is produced by a source of light, and certainly much higher than that produced by a corner of a triangle. There is no evidence that the light reflected by common substances in the infant's environment comes up to the threshold.

There is no reason why a stimulus that is subliminal for the unconditioned reflex should not become a conditioned stimulus for the

2. It is interesting to note that Lotze, in his *Mikrokosmos* (1856–64), appealed to exactly the same mechanism to account for what he called "local signature." In his view, a sensation aroused by stimulating a peripheral point on the retina acquires a local significance after it has evoked a reflex ocular movement of a specific direction and extent. Thus Lotze's theory implies that the perception of space is learned.

same response, in which case the circuit includes the lateral geniculates, the occipital cortex, and the superior colliculi, with afferents from the ocular muscles to give the necessary precision to the response. Were it not for this kind of conditioning it would be impossible for the aphakic patient to iron out the distortions and instability of his visual field. The fact that this process is accomplished in a relatively short time suggests that the conditioned reflex circuit must be one of the simplest in the whole system. The adjustment could hardly be effected so quickly if the relevant reflexes were unconditioned. It seems therefore that the reflexes on which Hebb relies are conditioned. But in that case they cannot serve his purpose unless they are already in existence before the process he describes can begin. In other words, a behavioral basis for the perception of shape is already being laid, and his mechanism is therefore superfluous.

Let us suppose, however, that oculomotor conditioned reflexes are not sufficient, and that Hebb's mechanism is necessary as well. We must now ask whether, given the ocular reflexes, conditioned or unconditioned, the proposed mechanism can generate perception of shape. Hebb uses a triangle, ABC, to illustrate his argument. When fixation is on A there is direct perception of the corner A, but no perception of the triangle as a whole. However, during this fixation there is an activity, due to the rest of the triangle, in a group, a, of cortical cells in areas 17 (the primary projection area) and the neighboring area 18. Reverberating circuits in the system may remain active long enough to allow the formation of new synaptic junctions between the cells of a. Repeated fixation of A strengthens these connections and adds to them, so that ultimately a becomes a linked assembly of cells. In like manner, repeated fixations of B and C result in cell assemblies b and c.

It is important to observe that Hebb does not claim that the arousal of activity in assembly a when A is fixated is enough to generate perception of the triangle as a whole. The perceptual experience is still apparently much the same as it was before the new links were forged. That is, the subject perceives two lines radiating from their point of intersection and, presumably, gradually fading out. What, then, is the function of the assemblies? Hebb's answer is that with repeated and random transfer of fixation from corner to corner, links are now established between the three assemblies, with the result that when one is aroused the others tend to be aroused also. Now, since the arousal of assembly a, whether by direct stimulation or by induction from b or c, involves the perception of two lines radiating from A, and similarly, b and c give perception of two lines radiating from B and C respectively, the arousal of all three, one by direct stimulation and the other two by induction, should generate perception of two lines radiating from A, two from B, and two from C; and with luck one of the pair from A will extend far enough to meet one from B and the other to meet one from C, and similarly one from B will meet one from C, so that at last the triangle will be perceived as a whole.

There is a very serious error in this reasoning. Hebb insists that the three assemblies lie within the same tissue, but this cannot be true. The triangle occupies three completely different positions relative to the optic axis when the three corners are fixated, and therefore the three groups of cells it arouses lie in three quite distinct portions of area 17. The same presumably applies to the cells of area 18 that are incorporated in the assemblies. There is, however, one small group of cells common to the three assemblies—in the cortical projection of the fovea. These cells are aroused to activity whether fixation is on A, B, or C. Hence the three assemblies radiate outward from a common origin. If, therefore, we make the assumption that the figure as perceived is topologically equivalent to the distribution of cortical cells that are active in producing the perception, we must conclude that what the subject would perceive is not a triangle but three lines with a common point of intersection.

It may be argued that I have done an injustice to the theory by neglecting Hebb's statement that the total activity that gives rise to the perception of the triangle is not identical with the sum of the activities in a, b, and c, and also his insistence that eye movements, actual or incipient, play an important part in the process. Actually I have not neglected these points, but have devoted some thought to the question whether they could rescue the theory from the absurdity revealed above. Unfortunately it is just here that Hebb deviates from the high standard of precision that characterizes his exposition. He does not point to any particular feature of the total activity, differing from the sum of the three activities, that would enable one to deduce that the three perceived pairs of lines have different points of intersection when the total activity includes induced activity in two of the assemblies, and a common intersection when the three assemblies are all aroused by direct stimulation. The statement about eye movements is equally unhelpful. With the best will in the world, the theory cannot be made to work.

12.14 It is not possible to study perception without observing that the perceptual field is changed by movements of the body as a whole, and to a lesser extent by movements of the head and eyes, but few writers have recognized the central role that movement plays in the development of perception. Erismann's first impulse was to place the burden of explanation on movement, but he subsequently modified his view when, as he thought, perceptual changes occurred without movement. Gibson discusses at length the changes in stimulation brought about by movement, and argues that because they are completely determined by the structure of the environment and the path followed by the subject, in a word, because they conform to the laws of geometry, they are sufficient to generate, innately of course, perception of the environment and of the subject's own movement in it. It is significant that this part of his theory is illustrated by the changes in retinal stimulation induced by flying in an aircraft, which, of course, are not accompanied by the proprioceptive stimuli that occur when the movement is effected by the subject's own efforts.

Eye movements play an important part in Hebb's theory, but chiefly as a means of transferring fixation from point to point of a figure, so that several cell assemblies can be formed, and links can be established between them. Thus in his theory the role of movement is not primary but secondary.

The first writer to state clearly the primary importance of movement in the development of the perception of space was not a psychologist but the mathematician Henri Poincaré. In *La Science et l'hypothèse* (1902), he demonstrates that the concept of space cannot be generated except by a being who is able to move about in his environment, and whose movements are registered by his kinesthetic sense. A completely immobile organism, he points out, would have no possible means of distinguishing between what he calls changes of state and changes of position, and therefore could not form any concept of space. He defines a change of position as a change in the pattern of sensory data that can be "corrected" by a movement of the observer. Such a change can be brought about by a change in the position of an object, and the pattern of stimulation presented before the change took place can be restored by a movement that brings the subject into the same position relative to the object. A change of state is a change in stimulation that cannot be reversed by taking up a different position. Since voluntary movement gives rise to kinesthetic sensations, it is possible to distinguish between changes of stimulation that are due to the movements of external objects and those that are due to our own movements. But changes of stimulation, without movement on our part, can be effected by a change in the state of an object, such as a change in color, while the object remains stationary. Such changes cannot be reversed by any movement we may make. Mobility therefore gives us the means of distinguishing between changes of state and changes of position.

The question then arises: how do these discriminations enable us to arrive at a concept of geometric space, or at a representation of geometric space in consciousness? A geometrician, Poincaré tells us, would answer this question in his own way, but since we all arrive at a representation of space, whether or not we have been trained in geometry, there must be another answer. That is to say, Poincaré recognizes that there is a psychological as well as a mathematical problem.

As a preliminary to answering the psychological question Poincaré examines visual space, tactile space, and motor space, and concludes that not one of them in itself carries enough information to generate a representation of geometric space. It is only by combining the information from the three realms that this result can be achieved. This implies "association of ideas," which must of necessity be extremely complex, since the contraction of the same muscle can give rise to different movements according to the relative positions of the limbs.

Without attempting to specify the details of the process (which, after all, is a task for a psychologist rather than a mathematician), Poincaré roundly declares that the association is acquired by learning, like any other association of ideas. And the course of this learning is determined by a multitude of experiences that in turn are dependent on the properties of the world in which we live. A being living in a different kind of world (for example, a non-Euclidean world), would acquire a different set of associations between his sensory data, and would arrive at a satisfactory representation of his own space.

Poincaré's analysis, then, shows that the perception of space is not innate but acquired by learning, and that bodily movement is an essential condition for this learning. But we can go further. In *La Valeur de la science* (1905) he states clearly that the only unvarying meaning that can be given to the statement that an object is perceived as occupying such-and-such a position in space, is that such-and-such a movement must be executed in order to make contact with it. To localize an object means to represent to oneself the kinesthetic sensations that accompany this movement. Thus his theory implies not only that learning is involved, but that what is learned is a movement that makes contact with the object. And since it is difficult to understand how we can represent to ourselves the kinesthetic sensations that a particular movement would induce without being in a state of readiness to perform that movement, it is evident that there is nothing in Poincaré's theory that is at variance with the theory presented in this volume. The details are not elaborated, but the essential members of the conceptual framework are there.

12.15. Having outlined the process by which geometric space comes to be represented in consciousness, Poincaré goes on to describe the mathematical properties of the system. To do this he first draws a distinction between what he calls *external* and *internal* changes. An external change is a change in the sensory input brought about by a change in an external object while no change occurs in the position or posture of the subject; an internal change is likewise a change in sensory input, but it is brought about by a change in the position of the subject and therefore includes kinesthetic components. In order to avoid the complications induced by changes in bodily posture, Poincaré assumes posture, including orientation of head and eyes, to be held constant throughout. (In this work the difficulty has been met by the definition of the functional equivalence classes, $\Phi(\delta)$.)

Among the external changes there are some that can be annulled by correlative internal changes, and similarly, among the internal changes there are some that can be reversed by external changes. Poincaré applies the term "displacement" (déplacement) to any change, whether internal or external, that is capable of being annulled by a correlative change of the other category. "Thus this reciprocity serves to define a particular class of phenomena that we call displacements. *It is the laws of these phenomena that constitute the subject matter of geometry.*" [3] The sentence italicized by Poincaré makes it clear that the primary purpose of his discussion was to find a rational foundation for the science of geometry. In the course of his search he has found it necessary to consider the problem of the perception of space—not the problem of perception in general—and having reached a satisfactory solution of this problem he goes on to discuss the mathematical properties of the phenomena he calls displacements, so that the rest of his argument is a contribution not to psychology but to mathematics. It is necessary to emphasize this point because Piaget, as we shall see presently, has taken the mathematical structure to have a basic psychological significance. For this reason we must give some attention to this structure.

Poincaré first deduces that the space defined by displacements is homogeneous. Suppose that an external change α has the effect that a set of impressions A is transformed to another set B, and that a voluntary movement β serves to correct α by restoring A. On another occasion A is transformed to B by another external change α'. Experience shows that α', like α, can be corrected by another voluntary movement β', having exactly the same kinesthetic components as β, and restoring A. In other words, the sequence of events can be repeated indefinitely, and always with the same results. This property of the displacements is expressed in mathematical language by saying that the continuum is homogeneous and isotropic.

It is the fact that operations can be repeated indefinitely that makes mathematical reasoning possible, and what Poincaré has succeeded in doing here is to demonstrate that this condition is satisfied by operations that involve complex sets of sensory data. To make the demonstration complete, he adds, it would be necessary to show that displacements, as defined by him, conform to a multitude of other laws which he refrains from enumerating, but which mathematicians sum up by saying that the displacements form "a group."

3. *Ce sont les lois de ces phénomènes qui font l'objet de la géométrie. La Science et l'hypothèse*, p. 82.

The "continuum or group of displacements" is further investigated in *La Valeur de la science*, but there is no need to pursue the matter further, except to note that the continuum is found to have six dimensions.

12.16. Since the concept of the group plays an important part in Piaget's theory of perception and intelligence, we should first have a clear understanding of what it means. It is defined by Kershner and Wilcox as follows.

If G is a set, and o is an operation on $G \times G$ to G, then (G,o) is a group if the following axioms are satisfied:

I. For every $a,b,c \varepsilon G$
$(a o b) o c = a o (b o c)$.
II. For every $a,b \varepsilon G$ there is an $x \varepsilon G$ such that
$a o x = b$.
III. For every $a,b \varepsilon G$ there is a $y \varepsilon G$ such that
$y o a = b$.

The reader can easily verify that the axioms are satisfied by the set of positive and negative integers, including zero, together with the operation +. On the other hand the same set with the operation $\times$ does not form a group, since, although axiom I is satisfied ($ab \times c = a \times bc$), axioms II and III are not. For example, if for a,b we choose 4,5, there is no integer x such that $4x = 5$.

Let us see how Poincaré's group of displacements fits into this scheme. Recall that a displacement is defined as a change of stimulation effected by a movement either of an external object or of the observer's body, of such a kind that it can be annulled by a correlative movement of the other category. This means that the set on which the operations are performed is a set whose elements are patterns of afferent events in the visual apparatus. Our first problem is to specify the elements of this set. Since for every external change α there is an internal change β which reverses α, and both changes involve movement in space (but without changes in orientation or posture), it is evident that the afferent event varies as a function of the position of the external object relative to the observer. Let $p = (x,y,z)$ be the position of the object relative to the frame of reference $R(\Omega)$, defined in 4.2. If S is the set of afferent events, and $s = f(p)$, it follows that s is adequately specified if we specify p. Consequently the set involved in the group may be represented by P, the set of positions relative to $R(\Omega)$.

The internal change β that serves to reverse the external change α includes both exteroceptive and proprioceptive afferents, and the latter are assumed to be a function of the direction and distance through which the body moves. If with Poincaré, we simplify matters by assuming that $R(\Omega)$ is translated to a new position without rotation of the axes, the proprioceptive afferents can be adequately specified by specifying the translation of $R(\Omega)$ in terms of an element of P. This enables us to define an operation on $P \times P$ to P, such that $p_1 \circ p_2 = p_3$, where p_1 and p_3 are the positions, relative to $R(\Omega)$, of an object that determines visual patterns s_1 and s_3, and p_2 specifies the new position of $R(\Omega)$ relative to its initial position, and determines the proprioceptive events.

Our next problem is to define the operation o in such a manner that it can be applied directly to the elements of P, considered as positions. If we write $p_1 = (x_1, y_1, z_1)$ and $p_2 = (x_2, y_2, z_2)$ we can define an operation + by writing

$$p_1 + p_2 = (x_1 + x_2, y_1 + y_2, z_1 + z_2) = p_3.$$

In terms of geometry this simply means that if the coordinates of a point p_1 are augmented by (x_2, y_2, z_2), it takes the new position p_3. If p_1 specifies the position of a point relative to $R(\Omega)$ and p_2 specifies a movement of $R(\Omega)$, the coordinates of p_2 must be considered as negative if $R(\Omega)$ moves nearer to p_1, and positive if the distance is increased. We can now test whether the structure $(P,+)$ is a group. In applying the test we must always remember that the element following the + sign specifies a movement of the frame of reference, or, of course, a movement of the object.

Axiom I states that $(p_1 + p_2) + p_3 = p_1 + (p_2 + p_3)$. In the left-hand side of this equation p_1 is the position of a point and p_2 and p_3 are movements, while in the right-hand side p_1 and p_2 are positions and p_3 is a movement, but $(p_2 + p_3)$ is also a movement. But this is of no importance, since every element of P, whether it refers to a position or a movement, is represented by three numbers, x, y, and z. Applying the rule defining the operation, we get

$$\begin{aligned}(p_1 + p_2) + p_3 &= (x_1 + x_2, y_1 + y_2, z_1 + z_2) + (x_3, y_3, z_3) \\ &= (x_1 + x_2 + x_3, y_1 + y_2 + y_3, z_1 + z_2 + \\ &\quad z_3),\end{aligned}$$

and $p_1 + (p_2 + p_3) = (x_1,y_1,z_1) + (x_2 + x_3, y_2 + y_3, z_2 + z_3)$
$= (x_1 + x_2 + x_3, y_1 + y_2 + y_3, z_1 + z_2 + z_3)$.

Hence $(p_1 + p_2) + p_3 = p_1 + (p_2 + p_3)$, and axiom I is satisfied.

It is easy to see that axioms II and III are also satisfied, and hence that $(P,+)$ is a group.

Let us recall now that the elements of P are the values of an independent variable which give rise to certain afferent events, exteroceptive when p represents the position of an object, and both exteroceptive and proprioceptive when it represents a movement of the subject; and that these afferent functions constitute the only information at our disposal. This means that we are begging the question when we argue that $(P,+)$ is a group, since the elements of P on which we have been operating are the values of the independent variable, to which we have no direct access. (On the other hand it is quite lawful to postulate a group structure $(P,+)$ as an explanation of the regularities found in the afferent system.)

The proof that the group axioms are satisfied must come from direct observation of the afferent functions themselves. It was this that Poincaré recognized when he noted that the same sequence of afferent events could be repeated indefinitely. This is one of the properties of group structure. Another is reversibility of operations. Experience shows that there are operations, changing afferent events from A to B, of such a kind that another operation changes B back to A. But the process can be reversed. That is, if the change from A to B is effected without proprioception and from B to A with proprioception, there is another displacement in which the change from A to B is effected with proprioception and from B to A without it. It is because the system of displacements conforms to all the properties of the group that Poincaré can speak of the continuum or group of displacements.

The fact that this system of exteroceptive and proprioceptive afferent events behaves in the orderly manner that is characteristic of a group means for Poincaré that our sense data provide an adequate foundation for a science of geometry. Its significance for psychology is that it provides a basis for the development of perception of a stable environment. Hence it is to be expected that group properties will be displayed both by geometric space and by perceived space. The exact sense in which this is to be understood will be made clear when we examine Piaget's theory.

12.17. A rapid reading of Piaget's works might suggest that his theory comes closer to that presented in this book than that of any other contemporary writer, since in his view perception in its mature form does not exist from the beginning of life, but is built up by gradual stages through the intervention of movement; but in fact there are two fundamental differences.

First, although Piaget is opposed to the extreme nativist view that the perception of space is innate, he is in complete agreement with nativism in assuming that from birth the sensory apparatus is capable of generating conscious experiences. This is not stated explicitly, but is simply taken for granted as if it required no proof. These conscious experiences follow one another in a manner that is fully determined by what Poincaré calls external and internal changes, but at first the child is not in possession of a code enabling him to translate this consciousness of primitive, disembodied qualities into the sophisticated consciousness of a stable environment that does not move when he moves in it.

The second difference is directly dependent on the first. If the basic ingredients of perception are all present from birth, then the function of movement is not, as in my theory, to generate those ingredients, but to organize them into distinctive classes. Both views carry the implication that the perception of the external world is built up by a long and gradual process, and both are supported by the careful observations and ingenious experiments that Piaget made on his own children.

Piaget's view implies that the primitive ingredients of perception initially constitute a completely internal world of experience; and, in fact, he has stated this explicitly. Referring to the first months of life, he writes:

> Far from consisting of objects, the universe depends on personal action; far from being externalized, it is not dissociated from subjective elements; and far from knowing himself and placing himself in relation to things, the subject does not know himself and is absorbed into things [Piaget, 1955, pp. 104 f.].

One of the main functions of movement, then, is to externalize this inner world of experience.

For my theory this problem does not exist, since the internal events are physiological events and not conscious experiences. The linking of those events, through conditioning, to efferent processes that result in establishing contact with objects, means that perception is externalized from the moment it comes into existence. The object is perceived as being at the end of the path prescribed by the conditioned reflex arc.

12.18. Strange as it may seem to those who are familiar with Piaget's discussion of Poincaré (ibid., pp. 102 ff.), his theory is in many ways quite similar to Poincaré's. The differences that he emphasizes spring largely from the meaning that Piaget originally gave to the word "group." Whereas in *The Psychology of Intelligence* (1950) he presents an orthodox mathematical definition of the group, it had a completely different meaning in *The Child's Construction of Reality*, originally published in 1937. Thus, on page 61, we find the following statement:

> Surely, if he saw the object uninterruptedly, nothing would be easier for him than to form the two following groups (we shall designate by M the positions of the object when it is at rest in the child's hand and by A and B the other positions of the same object):
>
> (1) $M \rightarrow A$; $A \rightarrow B$; $B \rightarrow M$, or
> (2) $M \rightarrow A$; $A \rightarrow M$; $M \rightarrow B$; $B \rightarrow M$.

Again, on p. 105, he writes:

> A group is a closed circle of operations that return to the point of departure through an operation of the group as a whole.

It is evident that Piaget has departed very radically from the mathematical concept of the group. In the group $(P,+)$, defined in 12.16, $+$ is an operation on $P \times P$ to P, which means that any element of P may be the terminus of the operation. The axioms imply, of course, that a sequence of two or more operations can result in a return to the point of departure, but they also imply that there are many more sequences that do not terminate in this way. It is also contrary to mathematical usage to speak of a series of operations as being a group, and still more so to speak of two series, involving the same elements, as being *two* groups.

To any reader who is familiar with group theory, Piaget's unorthodox use of the term is likely to have the effect that his meaning is obscured or even distorted. Similarly, anyone who has accepted Piaget's meaning is likely to misunderstand Poincaré's analysis: and that is what Piaget himself appears to have done. He criticizes Poincaré for statements that are mathematically irreproachable, because he reads into them the meanings that he himself attaches to the terms. Thus he assumes that when Poincaré speaks of displacements he is referring to a simple translocation of objects in three-dimensional space instead of changes in a six-dimensional afferent space. And when Poincaré speaks of the group of displacements, Piaget assumes that he is implying some kind of awareness of the orderliness of the world.

But in fact the continuum of displacements, as defined by Poincaré, satisfies the group axioms from the beginning, independently of whether we assume primitive consciousness or not; and it is precisely because it does so, precisely because it is an orderly, regular system, that the perception of three-dimensional space can be developed out of it.

For Piaget, on the other hand, the group seems to be not a particular kind of order in itself, but an *awareness* of order, and that is why he can speak of groups in the plural where mathematical usage would prescribe the singular. He feels compelled to use the plural because his observations on children show that the order is grasped bit by bit. These observations show that the infant's behavior is at first disorderly, but stage by stage it becomes more effectively adapted to the properties of the environment. Each new achievement is interpreted by Piaget as signifying the formation of a new group, the addition of a new element of order to the child's consciousness of his environment.

Assuming that Poincaré is speaking the same scientific language as himself, Piaget reads into his analysis the belief that the child is from the beginning aware of the distinction between changes of state and changes of position.

> By stating that the distinction between changes of position and changes of state is present at the very first, Poincaré seems

> to have reconstructed the elementary stages of spatial concepts more logically than psychologically, which is tantamount to saying that he has endowed primitive consciousness with postulates presupposing an already refined mental elaboration [p. 103].

Piaget goes on to show that this refinement can arise only as a result of a long process of development, which of course is precisely what Poincaré maintained. Without movement and an enormous wealth of experiences, including numerous reversals of external changes by the appropriate internal changes, the distinction remains a property of the system but cannot be apprehended in consciousness.

It is clear, then, that the two views are essentially the same. Poincaré has described the mathematical properties of the system that are necessary and sufficient for the development of perceived space, but has not worked out the details of this process; Piaget has neglected the initial properties of the system, but has devoted a great deal of attention to the developmental process. Although Poincaré says nothing about primitive consciousness, it seems reasonable to suppose that he assumed the afferent events defined by his continuum of displacements to produce immediate effects in consciousness. Here too, therefore, there is no opposition between the two views.

12.19. It is precisely on this latter point that Piaget's theory differs most radically from mine. For him the raw material from which the perception of space is elaborated is from the beginning *conscious*. Thus, at the outset of his discussion, he writes: "Among all the impressions which assail his consciousness, the child distinguishes and quickly recognizes certain stable groups which we shall call pictures" (p. 4).

My objection to this statement is, first, that it is intrinsically unverifiable, whether by direct or indirect means, and second, that, when considered in conjunction with Piaget's main theory, it offends against the principle of parsimony by postulating two entirely different mechanisms to account for the class of phenomena that we call conscious. It is as if a biologist were to maintain that some species were specially created and the rest evolved.

Finally, if we interpret the word "picture" in the ordinary sense as referring to a two-dimensional structure, we must reject Piaget's statement because it attributes stability to a constantly changing two-dimensional substructure of a multidimensional structure. As Poincaré has shown, the multidimensional structure satisfies the group axioms, but this does nót mean that they are satisfied by two of its dimensions abstracted from the whole. If a person who knows nothing of the laws of perspective were to examine a number of photographs of the same building taken from different angles, he might easily conclude that the shape of the building was unstable. And similarly, when an object is projected on different parts of the retina it arouses a wide variety of patterns of activity in the brain. This pattern is very far from satisfying the group axioms, so that if we assume a primitive consciousness at birth, we cannot attribute to it any group properties, even in Piaget's sense of the term.

This means that the inherent order of the multidimensional structure cannot represent itself in consciousness as an orderly three-dimensional or two-dimensional structure unless there is, first, an orderly three-dimensional world, including both the external world and mobile subject, that is responsible for the multidimensional structure, and second, a mechanism by which the elements of the multidimensional structure can be related to the properties of the three-dimensional world. Piaget recognizes this, but only to a limited extent. The argument of this book is that the most likely mechanism is the conditioning of responses adapted to the spatial ordering of the world; but since the afferent structure is multidimensional from the beginning, there can be no such thing as a primitive consciousness already possessing rudiments of group order before the conditioning process has begun.

12.20. Finally, we may consider Piaget's contention, in *The Psychology of Intelligence*, that intelligence conforms to the axioms of the group but perception does not. It is with the latter part of this statement that we are concerned.

Part of the evidence is derived from the geometric illusions, and particularly Delboeuf's illusion. If two circles of equal radius are placed side by side, and one of them is inscribed in a circle of larger radius, the inscribed circle is perceived as being smaller than the isolated circle. As the radius of the circumscribed circle increases, starting from that of the inscribed circle, the illusion increases to a maximum and then diminishes, reaching zero when the radius is three times that of the inscribed circle.

Piaget deduces from this that perceived space does not conform to the axioms of the group; but what he has done, in fact, is to construct an ideal space by assembling a number of perceived spaces, each determined by a different objective situation, and superimposing them one on another. We can at once concede that this ideal space does not satisfy the group axioms, but it remains an ideal space and tells us nothing about real perceived space. If, as we have argued, an essential feature of perception is the simultaneous existence of its elements, this condition is not satisfied by Piaget's ideal space, which is derived from a *succession* of perceptual spaces.

Let us satisfy the condition of simultaneity by drawing a number of Delboeuf figures in different positions on one sheet of paper, each one having a different radius of the circumscribed circle. If the illusion works in the same way in these circumstances as it does when the figures are presented separately, some of the inscribed circles will appear to differ from one another. But this does not mean that the total perceived space does not satisfy the group axioms. It certainly differs from the geometric space established by measurement with compass and ruler, but that would be true even if there were no illusion.

Here it is pertinent to refer to Poincaré's distinction between a mathematical and a physical continuum (Poincaré, 1902, ch. 2), which, it is interesting to note, he was prompted to make by Fechner's work on the differential threshold. A mathematical continuum has the property that no matter how small the interval between two of its elements, we can always intercalate between them another element such that $A < B < C$. A physical continuum, on the other hand, has the property that, no matter how refined our instruments of measurement, it is always possible to find two elements, A and C, such that $A < C$, and to interpose between them a third element, B, such that $A = B$, $B = C$, and $A < C$. This basic contradiction is an ineluctable property of all physical continua, and it must always be recognized when we are considering whether a given continuum satisfies the group axioms.

Now suppose that we examine an object with the naked eye, and find three distances, A,B,C, such that $A = B$, $B = C$ and $A < C$; and then examine these same distances with a magnifying lens, finding that $A < B < C$. Thus the operation of comparing A and B yields different results on the two occasions. But it would be manifestly false to conclude that perceived space does not possess group properties, on the ground that the operation is not indefinitely repeatable. The reason is that we have not repeated the same operation but performed two different operations by adding magnification to the second one.

In the same way, when we establish the existence of a geometric illusion by comparing perceived magnitudes with measured magnitudes, we do not thereby establish that perceived space does not satisfy the group axioms.[4]

Returning now to our hypothetical case where several Delboeuf figures are presented simultaneously, comparisons may show that circle A is less than B, B less than C, and so forth; but this does not mean that the same operation, performed on the same two elements of the continuum, is being repeated with different results. The operation is performed on a different pair of elements each time. If it were repeated on the same two elements a number of times it would always yield the same result—$A < B$. That is to say, the figure as a whole remains perceptually stable, but if this is true when the several figures are presented simultaneously, it is also true when they are presented singly. What Piaget has done is to switch from one operation (comparison of sizes by direct observation) to another (comparison by measurement with a ruler) in the midst of the argument without giving notice of his intention to

4. What happens when a geometric illusion is induced is not that perceived space ceases to conform to the group axioms, but that the response we are ready to make to a simple figure is modified when that figure is complicated by additions to it. Thus the response to a diagonal line with a gap in it is altered when a vertical structure fills the gap, as in Poggendorf's figure. The vertical lines induce a readiness to move from one to the other through the shortest distance, that is, horizontally. A vertical movement is then required to catch the beginning of the continuation of the diagonal line, which is therefore perceived as being out of alignment with the portion on the other side of the vertical structure. When the existence of an illusion is revealed by measurement, the situation is still further complicated by the addition of a measuring device such as a ruler. The ruler introduces two constancies: its edge is always straight, and its scale divisions are equal to one another and invariant. Those constancies dominate perception when the ruler is applied to the illusory figure; and perception in the absence of the ruler can thereupon be recorded as being erroneous.

do so. These operations are not identical, and his conclusion is therefore unwarranted. Analogously, if I is the set of integers, we cannot determine whether (I,+) is a group if we occasionally substitute × for +, or if we include in the set some numbers that are not integers.

12.21. The rebuttal of Piaget's argument is not equivalent to proving that perceived space satisfies the group axioms. To establish this proof we must consider a single perceptual structure and not a sequence of different structures. That is, we must recognize the simultaneity that is an essential feature of perception.

We may begin by considering a situation that offers a minimum of complications. The night sky presents a two-dimensional projection of a four-dimensional structure, and its distance is so great that no measurable change in the positions of its points relative to one another can be produced by the movements of an observer on the earth. The only changes that can take place in the retinal image of the stars are those effected by movements of the eyes. We can therefore neglect all proprioception except that associated with such movements. We can also neglect the slow change due to the rotation of the earth, since we are concerned with perception as a simultaneous process.

The position of a star may be specified by two angles relative to a frame of reference. In astronomical usage the frame may be defined by the earth's polar axis and a great circle from pole to pole through an agreed point in the celestial sphere, and the angles are known as the *declination* and *right ascension* of the star. For practical observational purposes a constant, depending on the latitude of the observatory, must be added to the declination, and a variable, depending on the sidereal time at which the observation is to be made, must be added to the right ascension. These operations have the effect that the position of the star is now related to a frame of reference defined by the zenith and meridian at the observatory, and the telescope can be directed accordingly.

We can define a mathematical continuum, Γ, by saying that each of its elements specifies two angles, x and y; and an operation, +, by saying that

$$\gamma_1 + \gamma_2 = (x_1,y_1) + (x_2,y_2) = (x_1 + x_2, y_1 + y_2) = \gamma_3.$$

We now give a physical interpretation to Γ by saying that γ_1 specifies the declination and right ascension of a fixed star, γ_2 specifies an angle, x_2, determined by the latitude of an observatory, and an angle, y_2, determined by the sidereal time at which an observation is to be made, and γ_3 specifies the position of a star relative to the zenith and meridian at the observatory. Then for any specific γ_1, the operation $\gamma_1 + \gamma_2 = \gamma_3$ always results in the telescope being trained on the same part of the celestial sphere. That is, γ_1 and γ_3 always refer to one and the same star; and this is true no matter where the observatory may be or at what time the observation is made. We know that γ_1 and γ_3 refer to the same star because, when the telescope is directed to it, a sequence of specific operations applied to the telescope will always bring into its field the same sequence of stars with the same sequence of magnitudes. These operations are indefinitely repeatable, and always with the same results.

It is evident that when we give this physical interpretation to $(\Gamma,+)$, and find that the group axioms are satisfied, what we have achieved is a demonstration that there are certain constancies and regularities in the physical continuum. The operation $\gamma_1 + \gamma_2 = \gamma_3$, defined above, establishes that the position of the observatory relative to the polar axis is constant, and that the earth revolves with a uniform angular velocity. And the subsequent train of operations reveals that the stars have fixed positions relative to one another in the celestial sphere. If more refined operations reveal that the group axioms are not exactly satisfied, this means that the system constructed by the scientist is not regular and must be enlarged by the inclusion of additional variables. This is precisely what astronomers have done.

12.22. The ordinary observer knows nothing of the sophisticated frames of reference employed by the astronomer, but he has his own frames of reference, $R(\Delta)$ and $R(\Omega)$. For convenience let us choose as our observer the author of a poem in the *Greek Anthology*, who describes how, while reclining at a feast, he watched the pageantry of the moving constellations. His reclining position means that $R(\Delta)$ will suffice for our purpose. We define Δ as a set whose elements specify the magnitudes of the stars and their polar coordinates relative to $R(\Delta)$. If we neglect the magnitudes, the positions of the stars may be represented by elements of a set Γ, which is defined as including, in addition, elements that specify the direction of the optic axis relative to $R(\Delta)$, and still other elements that specify the direction of the light from each star relative to the optic axis. It will be seen that elements of the first type are analogous to the declination and right ascension of a star, those of the second type are analogous to the angles determined by the latitude of the observatory and the reading on the sidereal clock, and those of the third type are analogous to the position of a star relative to the observatory's own frame of reference.

We now define an operation, $\gamma_1 + \gamma_2 = \gamma_3$, by saying that γ_1 specifies the position of a star relative to $R(\Delta)$, γ_2 is the direction of the optic axis relative to $R(\Delta)$, and γ_3 is the position of the retinal image of the same star. If the stars occupy fixed positions on the celestial sphere, and if the period of observation is held short enough to avoid any appreciable change in γ_1, due to rotation of the earth, or to a change in the position of the observer's body, $(\Gamma,+)$ satisfies the group axioms.

$(\Gamma, +)$ is not yet a perceptual structure. It is what Piaget would call an objective and not a subjective group. To find whether the corresponding perceptual structure has group properties we must examine the elements of Π. Let us select any three stars, 1, 2, and 3, and specify that the first one is fixated, giving the eye the direction γ_1, and the star the position (0,0) in the retinal field. Now Π contains, *inter alia*, two elements, ϕ_2 and ϕ_3, specifying patterns of stimulation, q_2 and q_3, which include common proprioceptive components due to γ_1, and exteroceptive components due to γ_2 and γ_3, the retinal positions of stars 2 and 3. In addition, ϕ_2 specifies an engram, $e_{1.2}$, which prepares for the response of moving the eye through the angle γ_4 from the position γ_1 to γ_2, which will bring star 2 to the retinal position (0,0); and similarly, ϕ_3 specifies an engram, $e_{1.3}$, that would move the eye through the angle γ_5 from γ_1 to γ_3, giving star 3 the retinal position (0,0). These engrams constitute operations on $\Gamma \times \Gamma$ to Γ. They are, if you like, symbolic operations, but they are nevertheless real events in the brain.

But that is not all. By short trace conditioning, q_2 and q_3 also activate an engram, $e_{2.3}$, mediating the response of moving the eye through the angle γ_6 from γ_2 to γ_3, and an engram, $e_{3.2}$, mediating the moving of the eye through the angle $-\gamma_6$ from γ_3 to γ_2. Generalizing to the whole of Π, we can say that all the operations specified by $(\Gamma,+)$ are simultaneously represented in Π, which is therefore a group. And what an astonishing phenomenon it is. It is, so to speak, a group that has ceased to be a mathematical abstraction and has become a living reality. The operations that establish it as a group are performed not serially but in a single moment of time. At the same time, although the simultaneity of its operations confers on it the unique property of subjectivity, it is nevertheless unmistakably a physical continuum, since it satisfies Poincaré's criterion that it is always possible to find three elements, A,B,C, such that $A = B$, $B = C$, and $A < C$.

12.23. Piaget states, in *The Psychology of Intelligence,* that the one feature of perception that might persuade him to consider perception as conforming to group structure is the constancies. He should have listened to this persuasive voice, and examined anew his grounds for concluding that perception has not all the group properties; for it is, in fact, decisive.

Consider first the simplified situation discussed in 12.19. No matter what the initial direction of the eye may be, the operation of fixating star 1 always brings the optic axis to the direction γ_1, and the retinal image of the star to (0,0). That is to say, the engrams, $e_{2.1}$, $e_{3.1}$, . . . $e_{n.1}$, all prepare for responses that terminate in exactly the same way, and therefore generate perception of the star occupying a constant position. Similarly, engrams of the form $e_{2.3}$, $e_{2.4}$, $e_{3.4}$, and the like, retain their identity through all directions of the optic axis, so that no matter what part of the retina stars 2, 3, and 4 stimulate, their perceived relative positions remain invariant. The shape of a constellation is not changed by changing the line of regard. These constancies could not arise unless the group axioms were satisfied, nor could they arise unless the material environment were stable. Their existence therefore testifies both to the group character of perception and to the existence of certain stabilities in the external world.

If for the starry heavens above us we substitute the accessible world around us, so that patterns of exteroceptive stimulation are altered by all manner of changes of posture and position, we must increase the complexity of the operations that can be performed on the afferent patterns, but no new principles are thereby introduced. Poincaré succeeded in reducing his continuum of displacements to six dimensions by assuming that movements were to be made without changes of bodily posture, but he was fully aware that the real continuum has many more dimensions. In fact he wonders whether the total number should not be equal to the number of muscles in the body. That is of course unnecessary, since muscular activity is coordinated by the action of the nervous system. Recognizing this, we may say that a continuum of 17 dimensions suffices to generate visual space with all its constances.

The operation is multidimensional, but that does not exclude specific operations with zero components in all but one of the dimensions, as when the eyes are moved horizontally while the rest of the body is inactive. This multidimensional operation, when applied to the multidimensional afferent continuum, serves to define a group. But just because it is multidimensional, the process of building into the cortex the machinery for carrying out the necessary operations must proceed by stages. In this respect, at least, Piaget and I are in complete agreement.

CHAPTER 13

Philosophical Implications

13.1. The theory presented in the foregoing chapters has obvious bearings on philosophy, and particularly on epistemology and ontology. I have neither erudition nor skill in the field of philosophy, and should therefore leave the task of investigating the philosophical implications to others better qualified; nevertheless I feel that my own reflections on the subject may not be wholly irrelevant or without interest. But there is another and more powerful motive for undertaking the task. Hayek (1952) has formulated a theory that is similar to mine in the sense that he considers the main work of the nervous system to be the classification of impulses, and this classification to be the essence of the sensory order, although he does not postulate any mechanism for determining the class to which any impulse is to be assigned. He ends his book with a chapter devoted to a discussion of the philosophical consequences of his theory. Some of his conclusions are irreconcilable with those that flow from the theory presented here, and one of them goes so far as to deny the possibility of ever constructing such a theory. If for no other reason than to defend myself against the implication that all I have done in this book is worthless, it is necessary to show that the conclusions drawn by Hayek from his incomplete theory are no longer valid when the theory is extended by the inclusion of a mechanism of classification.

13.2. It follows from the definition of the set Π, and the proposition that Π is identifiable with perception, that there is no justification for the disjunction of subject and object that has been a basic axiom for all writers on the theory of knowledge, with a few notable exceptions such as Spinoza. This disjunction implies that "mind" exists prior to any knowledge that it may acquire; and this is independent of any theory the philosopher may hold regarding the nature of mind. If, like Descartes, he thinks of mind as being an essence that has no properties in common with matter, the prior existence of mind is of course a basic axiom of his doctrine. But if he rejects the theory of an independent mind-stuff, which he can scarcely avoid doing after Ryle's brilliant exposure (1949) of the contradictions inherent in the "dogma of the ghost in the machine," he may still maintain the priority of mind on the ground that the sense-data upon which all knowledge depends are immediate and unanalysable experiences. That is, despite the rejection of the Cartesian dogma, mind is still held to be a realm that is distinct from the order of nature. Thus the doctrine of the immediacy of sense-data actually reasserts the dogma of the ghost in the machine even if the philosopher nominally rejects it.

Now the set Π describes a collection of "sense-data" that are in operation simultaneously, and the belief in their immediacy can therefore be tested by examining the definition of Π. Let us to begin with assume that the word "immediate" is defined in such a manner as to admit the mediation of the electrochemical processes in the receptor organs and afferent nerves, and possibly also in the cells of the primary projection areas of the cortex. This would imply that any element of Q, as defined in (3.4.20), is sufficient to generate a sense-datum. But that is precisely what it cannot do until it has been linked by conditioning to some response that has been reinforced through the mediation of an encounter between the organism and the object that is responsible for the exteroceptive components of the element of Q. It is equally impossible for the exteroceptive components alone to determine a sense-datum, since there is no set of responses that can be functionally related to those components. For if we set up a system in which the variables include A, exteroceptive functions of stimulus energies from the external environment, and B, responses directed to the objects in the environment, but proprioceptive functions of the orientation of the receptor organs are excluded, and we define $R \subset A \times B$ as a set with elements of the form (a,b) such that b is the response evoked by a; then it is evident that R is not a function. But if an element of A cannot evoke a unique response, it is impossible that it can generate a unique sense-datum.

We can conclude, therefore, that if a philosopher defines sense-data as being not only immediate but generated by afferent events aroused by single receptors, he is doubly handicapped in his efforts to write a satisfactory theory of knowledge.

13.3. If we define sense-data as being elements of Π, it is at once evident that these are not merely the raw material from which knowledge is derived, but *they are themselves knowledge.* For an element of Π specifies a piece of matter occupying a position in space and reflecting light into the eyes; it specifies further that the light from this object generates afferent impulses which, in conjunction with proprioceptive afferents determined by the orientation of the eyes and head, activate an engram mediating a response directed to the object, whether the response be actually evoked or not. Now this engram is not something that was there from the beginning but has been built up by a process of conditioning, and it is important to observe that the reinforcement of the conditioned response was not random but was determined by some property of the object, such as its position relative to the subject. The engram, so to speak, represents a portion of the history of the organism's commerce with the environment, written in the form of temporary connections built into the brain.

The activation of an engram puts the subject into a state of readiness for the appropriate response. We have seen that the hypothesis that this state of readiness is identical with an element of perception is sustained by the confirmation of a substantial number of deductions, and particularly by the experiments described in Chapter 9. But we may equally well identify the state of readiness with *knowledge* that the object has such-and-such a property. But in that case knowledge is not something *derived from* a mysterious and undefined subject-object relation and involving some equally mysterious entities known as sense-data. *Knowledge is itself a subject-object relation* that can be defined with precision, and sense-data are simply the form that knowledge takes at its lowest level. We shall take up the question of higher levels of knowledge presently, but first it is necessary to consider the important question of the validity of the lowest level of knowledge, since knowledge even at the highest level is always tested in the end by an appeal to sense-data. If they are false, knowledge of any kind is impossible.

13.4. The doctrine of the immediacy of sense-data has given rise to a serious difficulty for those philosophers who accept it. If knowledge is to be derived from sense-data conceived in this way, how can we ever be certain of its validity in view of the fact that illusory experiences such as mirages can occur? If some sense-data give us false information, how can we be certain that other sense-data are not equally unreliable? Actually there is no real answer to this question, since the doctrine of immediacy precludes the possibility of the alteration and correction of sense-data through interaction between organism and environment. If sense-data are unalterable, the only thing that is open to us when their validity is under suspicion is to reinterpret them in the light of their consequents. But the consequents themselves are simply other sense-data, and we have no right to attach more validity to them than to those that are suspect. Thus the various criteria that have been proposed for testing the reliability of sense-data, such as observing whether the same sequence is repeated every time we scan a scene, leave us in the same quandary as before, since the appeal is always from sense-data to sense-data.

The dilemma vanishes if we interpret sense-data as mediated events reflecting the history of the subject's interaction with his environment. For if a particular set of sense-data should be false, any behavior that may be evoked by such data will fail to be reinforced, and if this happens often enough the relevant sense-data will simply cease to exist, or will be replaced by others that are valid. If, on the other hand, no behavior is evoked by the fallacious data, error will remain. These points are fully illustrated by the second experiment described in Chapter 9. When I put my distorting spectacles on for the first time, the resulting sense-data were fallacious, since the patterns of stimulation were conditioned to responses that were no longer consistent with the actual positions of objects in the environment. However, the design of the experiment was such that only limited classes of those prepared-for responses were actually evoked, with the result that only certain limited classes of sense-data were transformed so as to reflect the true properties of the environment, while others remained fallacious to the end. Thus I had true knowledge of the configuration of the narrow strip of ground on which I proposed to walk, but erroneous knowledge of the rest. This is because the narrow strip evoked actual behavior that was subject to correction, while the rest evoked only scanning behavior which was mostly reinforced.

Again, while I sat at the table I had true knowledge of its dimensions and of the fact that it had a plane surface, but erroneous knowledge of its orientation to the gravitational axis. Here again the dimensions and shape of the table evoked actual responses that were misdirected at first but were subject to correction, whereas no adjustment of behavior relative to gravity was called for.

13.5. However, it is a mistake to assume that the erroneous sense-data were erroneous in every respect. They were not. Although shapes were distorted, and in a manner that varied with the orientation of the head, the spatial *ordering* of the perceived environment was not destroyed. Thus if I kept my head in a fixed position and scanned the scene in front of me, movements of the eyes designed to fixate particular points were always successful. My knowledge of the positions of those points was true knowledge in the sense that they always turned out to be where I expected them to be. It was only when the fixation response included a movement of the head, or when a manual or bodily response was evoked, that expectation was falsified. If I had gone to a shooting gallery there is no reason to suppose it would have been more difficult to hit the target with the spectacles on than without them, since in both cases success depends upon aligning the sights of the gun with the target. If the perceived position of the target is erroneous so are the perceived positions of the sights. Consequently, if the three points are collinear within this distorted field, a hit will testify to the validity of the knowledge. It is evident that no amount of practice at shooting would have affected the erroneous components of the knowledge. If I had observed another marksman it would have seemed to me that he must inevitably miss, since his rifle would be perceived as pointing in the wrong direction. When his bullet nevertheless hit the target, apparently following a curved path, it would become evident that in fact his sights were in the geodesic from eye to target.

If, on the other hand, I had attempted to play a game of table tennis, I would certainly have failed at first, since success depends upon knowing the position of the ball relative to a frame of reference in the player's own body, and also the position of the point on the table to which he proposes to direct the ball. Initially these positions are erroneously perceived, because the sense-data involve readiness for responses directed to positions other than those actually occupied by the ball and the aimed-at point. However, the game demands that many of the prepared-for responses be actually evoked, and the resulting negative reinforcement will have the effect that the player will immediately begin to modify his behavior, and will thereby acquire sense-data that will reflect the true positions in space.

13.6. The process of acquiring this true knowledge involves a principle that seems to me to be of primary importance for epistemology. This is that the limited truthfulness of the erroneous sense-data plays a vital part in the correction of the errors. Although the normal Euclidean space of everyday life is transformed into a non-Euclidean space, with numerous translations and transformations arising from movements of the head, it is nevertheless a metric space, which implies, among other things, that the ordinal arrangement of its points is not changed by the transformations and is in fact identical with that of the Euclidean space. From this it follows that when the player makes an ineffective stroke, the direction of his error, although not at first its exact extent, is known, and by virtue of the limited truthfulness of his sense-data. For example, if the ball approaches him on his left side, it will be perceived as being nearer to the median plane of his head than it actually is, and his stroke will fall short. But he will then see the ball passing beyond his bat. If it approaches him on the right it will be perceived as being farther away than it is, but then it will be seen passing his bat on the near side. That is, it is precisely the truthful component of his fallacious sense-data that enables him to eliminate the erroneous component.

It is at once evident that this simple principle is in continuous operation throughout the whole realm of science. No matter what conclusions a scientist may reach regarding the physical order, the test of their validity invariably involves an appeal to sense-data. There are many sectors of the physical order that cannot yield sense-data, because there are no appropriate receptor organs, but they can always be made to produce effects in other physical systems that do yield sense-data. Thus small electric potentials can be made to move the needle of a galvanometer, and the conjunction of the needle with a specific division on the scale gives a sense-datum that is universally accepted as valid. This sense-datum constitutes true knowledge of the behavior of the needle, but not of the forces that caused it to move. Nevertheless it is precisely this truthful knowledge that enables us to reach higher levels of knowledge.

There is thus no ground whatsoever for the notion that the sensory order or phenomenal world is an entirely fallacious and unreliable guide to knowledge of the physical order. It is, on the contrary, the final court of appeal, and without it scientific knowledge of any kind would be absolutely impossible.

13.7. Probably no aspect of the sensory order has contributed more to philosophical confusion than color, since it bears no obvious relation to the physical stimulus, that is, the wave length of the light. The confusion arises primarily from the erroneous assumption that what we are reacting to when we see a color is the wave length of light. It is nothing of the kind. The wave length of the light is a matter of no consequence to us until we begin studying physics. Prior to that we learn to react to some property of the object reflecting the light, and that is invariably a property that is directly relevant to our own needs as living organisms. When we pick the red tomatoes from the plant and leave the green ones, it is not longer wave lengths that we are selecting but tomatoes that will be good to eat. When a child selects the blue toothbrush rather than the yellow, what he is selecting is not a shorter wave but the approval of his mother and, at a later stage, freedom from contamination by the germs from somebody else's mouth. Thus the knowledge embodied in the sense-data we call colors has nothing whatever to do with wave lengths. It is knowledge about certain relevant properties of the objects we encounter in our everyday lives. Needless to say, this is not equivalent to denying that it is the composition of the light that determines the physiological responses of the retina and the events in the optic tract and optic radiation.

It is necessary to stress that color is by no means unique in this respect. All visual perception is mediated by light, but when a bird flies overhead we do not say that the flux of light is interrupted in a particular manner, and with certain rhythmical fluctuations; we say that a bird is flying overhead. Surely nobody in his senses would claim that this knowledge is misleading on the ground that it is knowledge not about light, the medium through which it is conveyed, but about a bird. Why then should we reject as illusory the knowledge embodied in experiences of color, on the ground that it is not knowledge about wave length, the medium through which it is conveyed?

There is an even more powerful reason why we should not reject as illusory the knowledge embodied in color. This is that it was precisely through the medium of this supposedly fallacious knowledge that physicists arrived at their knowledge of the composition of light. When Newton passed a narrow ray of sunlight through a prism and saw the solar spectrum for the first time, the knowledge he thereby obtained was expressed in terms of a spatial ordering of colors, that is, in terms of ordinary sense-data. But just because those sense-data were arranged in a particular and invariant order it was possible to suspect that beneath this there was some other kind of order that had nothing of the property of color in it. Thus the sense-data that are despised on the ground that they reveal nothing of the "true" character of the physical world turn out to be an essential tool in the hands of the scientist who is seeking to discover the real properties of the physical order. Those amateur philosophers, chiefly physicists, who would tell us that the phenomenal world is an illusion, and the "real" physical order is something of an altogether different character, can surely be convicted of base ingratitude, since without the phenomenal world they would be unable to learn anything further about the physical order.

But that is not all. Once the relation between color and wave length in the spectrum has been established, the color scale, which primarily embodied knowledge of certain properties of objects and substances, acquires the additional character that it embodies knowledge about light. To say that a particular band of the spectrum has such-and-such a hue is equivalent to saying that the light at that point has such-and-such a wave length. The words in which the information is conveyed are different, but for certain purposes the two statements say the same thing. Moreover, there is a formal similarity between the scale of colors and the set of numbers used to specify the wave length. Both scales are qualitatively discontinuous. The sense-data red, yellow, green, and blue are qualitatively not more different from one another than the words one, two, three, and four, or the symbols 1, 2, 3, and 4, used to designate points on a quantitative scale. Since the colors do not repeat themselves in the spectrum, it is evident that a color and a number can refer to the same ray. Thus to say that Fraunhofer line C is in the bright red and to say that its wave length is 6564 Angström units are two equivalent statements, although the latter has a higher degree of precision.

It must be understood, of course, that it is only when we look at an actual spectrum that our sense-data embody knowledge about light. In all other circumstances they carry no specific information about light, since two or more different mixtures of light can produce one and the same color. In that case the sense-data continue to embody knowledge of certain properties of the objects that reflect the light. Considered as knowledge about light they are fallacious, but as knowledge about the properties of objects they are truthful; and it is precisely through the agency of this truthful component that they can be made to give true knowledge about the light dispersed by a prism.

13.8. Since the whole fabric of knowledge rests on a foundation of sense-data, it is evident that the most important task for epistemology is to establish that those sense-data represent true knowledge, in however limited a sense. Whether or not they are a true guide to higher levels of knowledge is immaterial as long as they can be shown to be truthful in some respect, since experiments can always be designed in such a way that an appeal can be made to this truthful aspect of sense-data.

To answer this question we must consider the way in which sense-data are acquired. We have assumed Ashby's theory of the multistable system and have sought to give concrete meaning to it by setting up an initially unstable system including A, variables that are functions of certain selected features of the environment; B, variables that are afferent functions of the variables included under A; C, afferent functions of the orientation of the receptor organs and the posture of the body; D, efferent step-functions of variables that are not specified; E, drive functions that come into operation when the system gets into a critical state; and F, a mechanism of conditioning whereby values of the step-functions that happen to carry the system out of a critical state are linked to those values of the functions included under B, C, and E that are active in the system at the moment when the successful efferent event occurs. It is assumed that the organic system, considered in isolation, is incapable of terminating a critical state, and that this can be done only by establishing some relation between organism and environment. This implies that the variables listed under A must be functions of properties of the environment that can contribute to the stabilizing of the system. Thus the light entering the eyes from any object is a joint function of the position of the object and its molecular structure. The light itself contributes nothing directly to the stabilizing of the system, but the molecular structure of the object does, provided that the position of the hand can be changed to make it coincide with that of the object.

The variables listed under B are joint functions of the A variables and of the orientation of the body and the receptor organs. That is, when specific values are assigned to the A variables and the orientation variables, the values of the B variables are exactly determined. So also are the values of the C variables, since they are functions of the orientation variables. It is evident then that when the elements of the compound set including both B and C variables are conditioned to responses that establish adaptive relations between the organism and the objects that are responsible for the values taken by the A variables, the organism has thereby achieved knowledge about those objects. It is, however, a strictly limited knowledge, since it is confined to those properties of the external world that contribute directly to the adaptation of the system. Thus it includes knowledge about the positions of objects but not about their chemical constitution or their microscopic structure, or about the stimulus energies that generate the B variables.

We come now to the crucial question, whether this limited knowledge is true knowledge. We can answer with the utmost confidence that it is. For although the relation between the A and B variables is a one-many relation, and similarly there is a one-many relation between the afferent variables B and C taken together, and the D variables, yet the conditioning process has the effect that this one-many relation is transformed into a function. And since the source of the reinforcement of the conditioned responses is the properties of the external environment of which the A variables are functions, it follows that the effect of the adaptation is to establish a one-to-one correspondence between those properties and the conditioned responses. Thus to each element of knowledge there corresponds one and only one value of some independent objective variable, and to each value of such a variable there corresponds one and only one element of knowledge. One can surely not ask for a more rigorous criterion of the validity of knowledge.

13.9. We can go further. Not only does the existence of this one-to-one correspondence guarantee the validity of the knowledge that is embodied in perception, but the manner in which it is built up guarantees the independent existence of both the perceiver and the objective properties he perceives. For unless the properties of the environment that serve to reinforce the subject's responses were real and stable, there would be no possibility of consistent reinforcement of only the responses that terminate in establishing the appropriate relations between subject and object. And similarly, unless the subject were a real organism and not an already formed "mind," there would be no possibility of all the elements of a single equivalence class of patterns of stimulation being conditioned to one and the same response, or to responses that all terminate in the same way. Obviously a "mind" consisting of an immaterial or ghostly essence, confronted with the innumerable elements in each of a large number of equivalence classes, would have to go through the same process of learning that is demanded of an organism unencumbered with a useless ghost, and as the organism is fully equipped for the task, the principle of parsimony requires that the existence of the ghost be denied.

Descartes' doubting led him to the conclusion that the only statement he could make with conviction was *Cogito ergo sum*. The existence of the external world was thus apparently left to be deduced from his cogitation. On the other hand my doubting, which was chiefly occasioned by the remnants of the Cartesian philosophy still to be found in psychological thinking, has led to a conviction that may be summed up in the words *Percipio ergo ego perceptaque sumus*. The *ego* in this case, however, refers not to an immaterial subject or mind but to a living organism.

13.10. This at once raises the important question of the validity of the commonly accepted distinction between the phenomenal order and the "real" or physical order. It was this distinction that prompted Hayek to undertake his bold and interesting excursion into the realm of theoretical psychology; but whereas his speculations have led him to assert that the gulf between the phenomenal and physical orders is unbridgeable, and that it will always be necessary to adopt what he calls a "practical dualism," the theory presented here leads to the conclusion that the phenomenal order and knowledge of the physical order constitute a continuous whole, since the phenomenal order is itself *knowledge* of a limited sector of the physical order.

Moreover, it must be observed that the method of acquiring scientific knowledge is not essentially different from that of acquiring the knowledge embodied in sense-data. Always we have something in the form of the set U defined in (3.4.23), or preferably the set $_2U$ defined in (4.5.2). That is, the scientist is confronted with certain patterns of stimulation to which he has as yet no conditioned response, but those patterns include components to which there are responses that have been reinforced by past experience. These include not only the responses that have generated the body of knowledge we call the sensory order but also a large number of responses acquired by the scientist in the course of his training and research. For the vast majority of purposes this knowledge is adequate: the scientist can satisfy his everyday needs, physiological, social, esthetic, and the like, and he can answer most of the scientific questions put to him. But there are always some questions he cannot answer; that is, there are always some complex patterns of stimulation to which no ready-made response is available. We may say that the system consisting of the scientist and the sector of nature in which he is interested is in a critical state. He will lose his self-respect and the esteem of his colleagues if he cannot find the answer.

Now just as the set U includes unlearned responses that are evoked when the system is in a critical state, so the system in which the scientist is involved includes unlearned responses. They are, however, of a very much more complex character than those of the set U. Typically such a response takes the form of a tentative answer to the question that is puzzling the scientist: he formulates a hypothesis. But this response, unlike those incorporated in U, is not subject to direct reinforcement or extinction, because it does not in itself establish contact with the objects or processes to which it refers. Consequently the logical implications of the hypothesis must be worked out, and those implications must be tested by setting up experiments that will establish the required kind of contacts with the objects and processes concerned. If the experimental results are in agreement with the calculated results, the response expressed in the hypothesis is reinforced and the scientist has acquired a new element of knowledge. If the experimental results do not agree, the initial response is extinguished and the scientist tries another. Thus there is no essential difference between the two methods of acquiring knowledge. In both cases there are unlearned responses that are either extinguished or reinforced, and in both cases the extinguishing or reinforcing agency is some property of the physical order. Furthermore, in both cases an element of knowledge becomes active whether actual contact with the known object be established or not. That is, in both cases knowledge is a state of readiness for action. Both perceiver and scientist know that if certain operations are performed on the environment certain quite specific results will follow. Hence the validity of both types of knowledge is guaranteed.

13.11. The chief difference between the two types of knowledge lies in the apparent immediacy of sense-data as opposed to the obviously mediated character of scientific knowledge. Actually this apparent immediacy is a necessary and inevitable property of the knowledge embodied in sense-data. It is inevitable for the simple reason that the mediating process, by its very nature, lies outside the field of consciousness. There are good grounds for supposing that an afferent process, starting at a receptor surface and terminating in a primary projection area, is nothing more than a physiological event, comparable to any other event such as the secretion of digestive enzymes in response to the presence of food in the stomach. In itself such an event does not and cannot generate anything in the nature of knowledge, since knowledge implies ability to take some action relative to the thing that is known. It should be evident even to the most casual observer that afferent impulses give the newborn infant no ability to control anything whatsoever. It is equally evident that the efferent impulses that determine the movements made by the infant cannot be the carriers of knowledge. Indeed it is impossible to see how knowledge of any kind can come into existence until afferent neurons have been linked with efferent neurons in such a way that something quite specific can be done about the source of the afferent impulses. When such knowledge does come into existence it must necessarily do so unheralded.

This is still not quite enough to account for the apparent immediacy. If the action to be taken relative to the source of the afferent impulses produced its effect only through the medium of a long and complicated chain of intermediate events—the customary condition for the acquisition of scientific knowledge—there could be no knowledge in the form of sense-data at all, for the simple reason that during the first stages of life no responses would ever be reinforced under such conditions. To become conditioned responses it is essential that they be reinforced with a minimum of delay, and they can do that only if they are related to some simple property of the source of the afferent impulses, such as its position in space. If this condition is satisfied, the knowledge that is generated is knowledge that can be tested at once by a simple and direct act of the organism. This directness, together with the fact that the mediating processes are events at a purely physiological level, has the effect that the knowledge must of necessity have the quality of apparent immediacy. All that immediacy means, then, is that the mediating processes are not conscious events.

13.12. Another and no less important difference between sensory and scientific knowledge concerns the character of the systems that generate the two types. Sensory knowledge is generated by a multistable system consisting of a living organism in an environment. The system that generates scientific knowledge is also a multistable system, but it consists of a constantly changing set of individuals all of whom have achieved adaptation not only to the normal environment but also, in varying degrees, to that sector of nature which is their common field of inquiry and which also supplies the relevant environmental variables of the system. Although the several subsystems of this higher order system, that is, the individual scientists confronted with their own particular problems, are to some extent independent of one another, there is yet constant interaction between them, and successful adaptations made in one of them commonly have far-reaching effects throughout the whole system, especially when some fundamental piece of knowledge is acquired. Thus scientific knowledge is not the private property of one person inaccessible to all others, as the sensory order apparently is, but is the common property of all.

It is the adaptation of the system as a whole that generates knowledge rather than that of the individual subsystems, since the contributions of individual scientists may be false, and indeed frequently are. There are several reasons for this that are well known to scientists, and they need not be enumerated here. But if a false response made by one scientist should be reinforced, thereby convincing him that he has discovered some truth, it will sooner or later be extinguished in the system as a whole.

Thus the process of acquiring knowledge, which begins in the simplest way in each individual, goes on continuously expanding in the community of scientists as a whole.

13.13. The private character of the knowledge embodied in sense-data has been the source of an enormous amount of confusion among both philosophers and psychologists. This confusion, it seems to me, springs directly from the dogma of the ghost in the machine. For as long as we think of mind as being an independent realm rather than a set of acquired relations between an organism and its environment, we must of necessity think of it as being not just one realm but as many realms as there are sentient beings in the universe, each one completely enclosed in itself, each one incapable of peeping inside any of the others, like the Leibnizian "monads." But the most extraordinary thing that must be postulated about this immaterial mind is that it is capable of peeping at its own corporal cage and the wider world around it, and at the same time of peeping at itself while engaged in the act of peeping at the material world. It is not surprising that the behaviorists scornfully rejected introspection as a method of psychological investigation.

The mystery disappears as soon as we think of a sense-datum as an act of knowing, or as the realization of a potential relation between the organism and a detail of the environment. The act of knowing is a private event, and nobody but the person in whom it takes place can report its occurrence; but what is known is public and is open to be known by anyone else who may be present. From this point of view there is no essential difference between the knowledge embodied in sense-data and that which is derived from scientific investigation. In both cases the things that are known or to be known are open to public scrutiny, and in both cases the act of knowing is a private event that cannot be directly observed by anyone else.

This does not mean, however, that those private events do not constitute a legitimate subject for scientific inquiry. On the contrary, it is most important that they should be studied. The history of science shows that there have been innumerable acts of knowing that have turned out to be unjustified, and even in the field of sense-data illusory and hallucinatory experiences occur with sufficient frequency to warrant an inquiry into the genesis of this kind of knowledge. For this purpose it is necessary to get subjects to report their acts of knowing as they occur, thereby making their private events public. This does not involve introspection in the sense in which Wundt and Titchener understood it. The subjects are asked to report not on what is going on in their minds simultaneously with the act of knowing, but simply on what they perceive at the moment. That such inquiries can be fruitful is amply demonstrated by the experiments discussed in Chapters 8, 9, and 10.

The status of reports of this kind is not essentially different from, say, that of the demonstration of the movements of subatomic particles with the aid of the Wilson cloud chamber. We do not see the actual particles, but their passage through the vapor-laden gas converts some of the vapor into visible droplets which constitute pointer-readings from which the passage of the particles may be known. In the same way the language in which the subject of an experiment on perception reports his acts of knowing is a set of pointer-readings by which those acts may be publicly known. There is no more mystery in the one case than in the other.

It may be objected that the two cases are not comparable, because the cloud chamber cannot lie whereas the human subject can. Actually this is a distinction without a difference. Any piece of scientific apparatus can "lie" if it develops a fault unknown to the investigator. A good scientist tests his apparatus from time to time by subjecting it to a series of standard operations. If the results deviate significantly from what is expected, the apparatus is overhauled or replaced. Similarly a psychologist does not employ subjects whose capacity for reporting is defective, for whatever reason. A good psychologist will test the reliability of his experimental subjects by exposing them to certain standard situations. For example, he will not use color-blind subjects for experiments on color vision. If any report deviates markedly from the norm the subject is rejected, and it is of no consequence whether the deviation be due to inadequate vocabulary, a defect of character, a bias against the experimenter, unwillingness to submit to the discipline of the experiment, or anything else. A psychologist is not more likely to be led astray by false reports from his subjects than any other scientist is by defects in his material or apparatus. His errors are much more likely to arise from defects in his theoretical constructs.

13.14. We turn now to the question to which Hayek returns a pessimistic answer, that is, the question whether it is ever possible to arrive at a full understanding of the processes of mind, or even of the limited class of them that are included in the sensory order. We shall consider first the reasoning that led Hayek to his negative answer. He thinks of the brain as being a classifying machine. It receives primary impulses from the receptor organs, but those impulses have no significance in themselves. It is only what happens after they reach the projection areas that can give them any meaning. In Hayek's terminology, the class to which a primary impulse belongs depends upon its "following," that is, the subsequent impulses to which it gives rise in other parts of the brain. Thus if two impulses, however similar they may be initially, have different followings, they generate different qualities in the sensory order; and if two impulses have the same following, they generate identical sensory qualities, no matter how dissimilar they may be originally. Clearly there is a close affinity between this and the argument that the elements of $\Phi(\delta)$, defined in (3.9.1), determine an invariant of perception because the engrams they specify prepare for responses that have one and the same terminus.

The most important difference between Hayek's theory and mine is that he has not addressed himself to the question what determines the following of any primary impulse. He seems to recognize that the following is not predetermined by the structure of the nervous system, since he quotes the Innsbruck experiments as evidence that the following may be changed by "experience," but, unless I have completely misunderstood him, this "experience" is confined to the sensory order itself. It has lost its internal consistency and somehow it sets itself right. But how a misclassification can correct itself without some mechanism for redirecting the misclassified items is a mystery. It is difficult to avoid the conclusion that Hayek's machine, despite his disclaimers, has a ghost in it after all.[1]

The lack of a mechanism for determining what the followings of the primary impulses are to be implies that the followings are predetermined by the structure of the brain. That is, the brain must be considered as a kind of sorting machine with built-in instructions for sorting. The fact that a diminutive ghost must be installed to smooth out discrepancies and correct any errors that may arise, as when somebody is misguided enough to twist the input channels by wearing distorting spectacles, is sufficient to condemn the theory. Strictly speaking, therefore, nothing more need be said about it. But it cannot be left at that, because in his philosophical chapter Hayek has deduced from his conception of the brain as a ready-made classifier the conclusion that it can never classify its own classificatory activities, and therefore it is forever impossible to write a full explanation of the mental order in terms of physical events.

His argument, briefly, is that the number of different questions a classifying machine can answer is very much greater than the number of distinct answers it can give. If, therefore, it were required to classify its own classificatory activities, it would have to be capable of giving as many different answers as the number of different questions it can handle. It would therefore have to be a very much bigger machine than in fact it is. He then goes on:

> Applying the same general principle to the human brain as an apparatus of classification it would appear to mean that, even though we may understand its *modus operandi* in general terms, or, in other words, possess an explanation of the principle on which it operates, we shall never, by means of the same brain, be able to arrive at a detailed explanation of its working in particular circumstances, or be able to predict what the results of its operations will be [Hayek, 1952, pp. 188 f.].

This would be a valid argument if it could be shown that the rules of classification were built into the brain from the start. But this is not so. The function of the cortex, as Pavlov never ceased

1. I am happy to report that in a recent conversation with me Professor Hayek wholeheartedly accepted the proposition that a mechanism for determining the following of an impulse is required.

to insist, is the formation of temporary connections mediating adaptive reactions to the environment, and, as I have tried to show in this book, the classification of primary impulses is a by-product of this activity, resulting in the emergence of the sensory order. It is thus completely misleading to describe the brain as an "apparatus of classification." It *becomes* such an apparatus by virtue of performing its proper function as the instrument through which the multistable system—organism in environment—achieves stability.

It is equally misleading to say that the brain cannot classify its own classificatory activities. Of course if we think of the brain as a self-contained instrument the statement is true, but it is vacuously true, since the brain considered in this manner is incapable of doing anything at all. It is precisely this important fact that is overlooked by those writers who have been so busy looking for parallels between the working of an electronic computer and that of the brain. The truth is that neither instrument can be properly understood apart from the setting in which it operates. The working of a computer is not to be understood by a simple consideration of its construction and of the scientific principles underlying the action of its several parts. Its operation requires the intervention of someone who knows how to set it going to carry out a particular program; that in turn requires a scientist who has formulated a problem that is capable of being translated into terms of a computer program; and finally this implies that the scientist has been confronted with some natural phenomena that he is as yet unable to explain. It is only within this context that the operation of the computer is intelligible; apart from this the machine is just a complicated and meaningless assemblage of hardware. In like manner the brain cannot be understood except by considering the behavior of the whole system of which it is a part, that is, an organism living in an environment to which it must learn to respond in various appropriates ways if it is to survive.

The matter may be expressed in a different way by saying that neither the brain nor the electronic computer can, of its own initiative, *ask* any question. Questions arise only within an ultrastable system. In fact we can define a question as an area of instability within the behavioral field of a multistable system; and it is the system as a whole that finds the answer through the process of achieving stability. The brain by itself neither asks nor answers the question, although it is actively involved in both processes, but it records the answer when found. In a system that includes an electronic computer, the computer does not ask the question, nor is it actively involved in the asking. It is, however, actively involved in the process of finding the answer. Indeed, this process includes the activities of designing and constructing the computer as well as the actions of preparing a program for it and translating this program into a series of concrete operations performed on its input channels. Needless to say, the people who perform those operations are not necessarily involved in the asking of the question. This is just another aspect of the fact, mentioned earlier, that the multistable system that generates scientific knowledge includes a multitude of people.

13.15. It is now evident that Hayek's pessimistic answer to his question springs directly from the erroneous notion that the brain itself is the sole author of its own classifications. It is this same error that causes him to see the gulf between the sensory order and the physical order as being unbridgeable, and prompts him to propose a practical dualism that recognizes and emphasizes this gulf. I believe we shall arrive at a more optimistic answer if we recognize that the classifying machine is not the brain itself but the whole multistable system of which it forms a part.

The first problem we have to consider is whether this system can generate questions about itself. In general the answer is no. A man seldom has occasion to question the veracity of his own senses, and when he does he usually finds an objective explanation of the error. In any case the adaptations to which errors of this kind give rise are such as to reduce the probability of their recurrence. As a rule, sensory errors raise questions about the environment and not about the system that generates knowledge of the environment. In this sense the isolated multistable system cannot classify its own classificatory actions because it cannot generate the kind of question that leads to such higher order classification.

It is a different matter with a larger system consisting of an environment containing a number of individuals who can communicate with one another, and in particular can report their knowledge. Let us call this larger system a *community system*, and each of the multistable subsystems contained in it an *individual system*. Often enough mutually incompatible reports about some objective event are given, and sometimes this will create a critical state in the community system. This gives rise to a search which we may describe as elements of a set $_cU$, defined as the unlearned behavior of the community system. This will commonly generate knowledge in the form that the facts were as A reported them and not as B reported them. In such a case the knowledge generated by the community system is of the same order as that generated by the individual system. That is, it is knowledge about the environment and not about the process of knowing. Most scientific knowledge is of this kind.

It may happen that the discordant reports are unimportant in themselves and give rise to no critical state in the community system, but they may easily give rise to a critical state in some individual system by generating the question: if one and the same event gives rise to two discordant reports, what reliance can we place on knowledge, and how does knowledge come into being? The man in whom this question arises has started on a career as a philosopher, and of course he can start others on the same career by communicating his question to them. Now it is important to observe that the individual system in which this question is generated includes among its environmental components two other individual systems that have arrived at different adaptations relative to an element of the environment that is common to them, and this implies that the search on which our philosopher now embarks is similar in form to any other scientific inquiry. Thus he is not seeking to classify the classificatory activities of his own brain, but to understand the different classifications arrived at by two other brains.

Nevertheless, since he himself is the central component of a system that is similar in form to the two systems that have generated the question, it is natural that the inquiry should be extended to include himself. And because his own behavior and experience are more available for observation than that of any other person, it is not surprising that the method of introspection should so frequently have been employed in efforts to solve the problem of knowledge. But the thinker who chooses this method has in fact entered a blind alley. He is trying to do what Hayek rightly says cannot be done, to make his brain classify its own actions. After a fair trial the method of introspection is today almost completely abandoned, because the results it has yielded have proved to be of no scientific value.

13.16. It is clear now that the failure of introspection to produce worthwhile results is attributable to the fact that it attempts to find within a restricted system an answer to a question that can only be generated by a wider system in which the environmental elements include other persons. Obviously knowledge cannot be born out of a system that is incapable of generating a question. Now the question about the origin and nature of knowledge arises, as we have seen, only because knowledge about one and the same object or event is found to vary from person to person, and it is clear that the answer cannot be generated by any system from which those other persons are excluded. In particular, since knowledge is nonexistent at birth and accumulates throughout life, the system that generates the answer must include among its environmental elements persons covering a wide range of ages.

The answer is generated in essentially the same way as the answer to any other scientific question. The community system including all the people who are looking for the answer produces a long succession of unlearned responses, each in the form of a hypothesis together with its logical implications and a series of manipulations of the environment, which in this case means manipulation of individual systems in which knowledge occurs. It will be seen that there is no reason why the author of a hypothesis should not include his own individual system among those to be manipulated. Each scientist communicates his response to his colleagues, some of whom may repeat it, with or without modifications. A large proportion of the hypotheses are extinguished because the results of the manipulations do not reinforce them. Some of them get limited reinforcement, and thereafter new unlearned responses are likely to involve some modification of these partly successful ones. In the end this complex system, including a multitude of brains, will generate knowledge of how knowledge is generated in an individual multistable system.

True knowledge about the way in which the kind of knowledge we call sense-data is generated will come into existence when the manipulations arising out of some scientific guess succeed in generating the predicted sense-data.

13.17. It will be seen that, even if an investigator includes himself among his experimental subjects, there is nothing in common between the process described here and Hayek's notion of a brain classifying its own actions. The essence of the matter is that although neither the question nor the answer could be generated if there were no brains in the system, it would be equally impossible to generate either if there were nothing but brains in the system. Moreover, when the question is properly formulated, we can see that it is not really a question about brains at all. It is a question about an organism having certain properties, including a brain, living in an environment having certain other properties, and surviving because the properties of organism and environment are brought into certain specific relations with one another. The establishment of these relations, in which the brain plays a very important part, implies that the *organism*, and not just its brain alone, has acquired knowledge of those properties of the environment that are material to its survival.

Now this system in which knowledge is generated is an integral part of the system of nature, and therefore forms part of the environment in which other organisms live. Consequently if knowledge is not limited to the sensory order but can, in principle, be extended indefinitely to include any aspect of the order of nature, there is no inherent obstacle to the acquisition of knowledge of the details of the mechanism by which the first elements of knowledge are generated. Moreover, the system that generates this higher knowledge is likewise an integral part of the natural order, and is therefore itself capable of entering into a still more complex system that can generate a question concerning the manner in which higher knowledge is reached, and has within itself the means of answering this question.

Needless to say, this goal will not be reached without much labor, but when it is reached it is clear that nothing more is needed, since the solution of this problem is at the same time the solution of the problem how we generate knowledge of the way in which higher knowledge is generated. In other words, the solution of the problem how higher knowledge is generated must of necessity be reached by the same kind of process as that whereby any other piece of higher knowledge comes into being. There is therefore no need to suppose that there must be an infinite series of brains of ever expanding complexity, each one able to comprehend the one immediately below it but not itself. In short, if we have knowledge of how knowledge is generated, we have, *ipso facto*, knowledge of how *knowledge of how knowledge is generated* is generated.

13.18. Finally, the theory enables us to arrive at an understanding of the nature of consciousness. For a long time the majority of psychologists and philosophers have thought of consciousness as being the product of some special kind of energy generated by the brain. This view is briefly summed up by Tyndall's (1874) famous statement that the brain secretes thought as the liver secretes bile. We only need to substitute consciousness for thought. Of course nobody would dream of suggesting that consciousness can be extracted from the cells of the brain and subjected to chemical analysis: the "secretion" is thought of as being some particularly subtle kind of energy that so far has eluded all efforts to define it in physical terms.

The reason for this elusiveness is not that it is impossible to define consciousness in physical terms but that most of the people who have attempted to solve the problem have confined their attention to events taking place within the nervous system. They have, quite understandably, assumed that since it is abolished by damage to the nervous system, or by the application of a general anesthetic, consciousness is something that is generated by the brain itself, just as various hormones are generated by the glands of internal secretion. But whereas it is a comparatively simple matter to observe an isolated endocrine gland secreting its hormones, nobody has yet been able to detect an isolated brain in the act of generating consciousness. There is a large and growing body of knowledge about the electro chemical processes in the brain, but none of this tells us anything at all about consciousness. In fact the more we know about the action of the brain, the more difficult it is to understand how it can produce anything but neural action.

Now one of the important properties of Π is that its elements are simultaneously active. If, therefore, we consider an element of Π to be a piece of knowledge about the environment, then the whole set describes the simultaneous knowing of a large number of facts about the environment. But this is precisely what is meant by being conscious. There is no such thing as an abstract state of consciousness without content. When we are conscious we are always conscious of something, and that something is always in a setting that forms part of the content of consciousness. In short, I suggest that the essence of consciousness is simultaneity of knowing.

But, the reader may object, this does not tell us anything about what consciousness *is*, since each of the simultaneous acts of knowing is itself characterized by the property of consciousness. It is as if one were to say that H_2O does not become water until millions of molecules of the stuff are assembled in one place. The answer is that while it is quite true that each molecule of H_2O is a molecule of water, and that its character is not changed by its being united with other molecules, nevertheless the assemblage of molecules has certain properties not possessed by the isolated components. For example, if they are distributed through the air in the form of water vapor we cannot quench our thirst or wash with them. Analogously, there is no reason why elements of Φ should not, when united in the set Π, generate a new property that is not evident when they are acting in isolation.

One way of testing this hypothesis is to inquire whether isolated elements of Φ can operate without the accompaniment of consciousness. They can. An obvious example is somnambulism. This may be accompanied by a rudimentary consciousness in the form of a dream, and the dream may be forgotten before the sleeper awakes. This example is therefore not very convincing. But there are many others. Here is one that I witnessed in part. A young man was knocked off his bicycle and suffered a concussion. He lost consciousness, but he was able to pick himself up and walk home with his bicycle, following an unfrequented road, a distance of two or three miles. He was still unconscious when he reached home. Evidently the need to get home provided a drive that was strong enough to activate the engrams mediating the choice of the correct path, but not enough to generate readiness for responses to other stimuli encountered along the way. Here then we have clear evidence that consciousness is not a necessary accompaniment of the operation of isolated elements of Φ.

Even more convincing are the innumerable phenomena of the type that prompted Freud to propose his theory of the Unconscious, that is, the so-called unconscious actions. The essence of the matter is that while one subsystem is in action, determining readiness for a restricted range of responses, an isolated engram belonging to another subsystem is by chance aroused to activity, resulting in an action that is at variance with the general stream of behavior. Although the subject is conscious all the time, his unpremeditated action is not accompanied by consciousness because it is an isolated element of a subset of Φ that is not generally active at the moment. It represents an intrusion into the existing behavioral field of a response that belongs to another behavioral field of the same multistable system.

We can conclude therefore that there is no need to postulate some mysterious form of neural energy that cannot be described in ordinary scientific terms, some ghostly essence distilled by certain selected neurons that contrive to perform their scientifically illicit activities in the most impenetrable and frustrating secrecy. And if consciousness can be explained without requiring any neurons to violate the laws of their own nature, we may at last register a claim for the recognition of the study of conscious experience as a legitimate branch of natural science. Thus the revolt of the early behaviorists against the "mentalist" assumptions of classical psychology has led, through the assiduous investigation of the laws of behavior, to a new assertion of the scientific respectability of the once despised phenomena of consciousness.

References

Am. J. Ophthalmology, Editorial, 1952. The adjustment to aphakia. 35, 118–22.

ASHBY, W. ROSS, 1952. *Design for a brain*. London, Chapman and Hall.

—— 1956. *An introduction to cybernetics*. London, Chapman and Hall.

BATES, W. H., 1944. *Good sight without glasses*. London, Faber and Faber.

BERLYNE, D. E., 1960. *Conflict, arousal and curiosity*. New York, McGraw-Hill.

COOPER, SYBIL; DANIEL, P. M.; and WHITTERIDGE, D., 1955. Muscle spindles and other sensory endings in the extrinsic eye muscles, the physiology and anatomy of these receptors and of their connexions with the brainstem. *Brain*, 78, 564–83.

EWERT, P. H., 1930. A study of the effect of inverted retinal stimulation upon spatially coordinated behavior. *Genetic Psychol. Monogr.*, 8.

GIBSON, J. J., 1950. *Perception of the visual world*. Boston, Houghton Mifflin.

——— 1958. Visually controlled locomotion and visual orientation in animals. *Brit. J. Psychol.*, 49, 182–94.

GRAHAM, C. H., 1951. Visual perception. In *Handbook of experimental psychology*, ed. S. S. Stevens. New York, John Wiley and Sons.

HAYEK, F. A., 1952. *The sensory order*. London, Routledge and Kegan Paul.

HEBB, D. O., 1949. *The organization of behavior*. New York, John Wiley and Sons.

HOWELLS, T. H., 1944. The experimental development of color-tone synesthesia. *J. exp. Psychol.*, 34, 87–103.

HULL, C. L., 1943. *Principles of behavior*. New York, Appleton–Century.

JAMESON, WILLIAM, 1959. *The wandering albatross*. New York, William Morrow.

KERSHNER, R. B. and WILCOX, L. R., 1950. *The anatomy of mathematics*. New York, Ronald Press.

KOFFKA, K., 1936. *Principles of gestalt psychology*. New York, Harcourt, Brace.

KOHLER, I., 1951. Über Aufbau und Wandlungen der Wahrnehmungswelt. *Öster. Ak. Wiss.* Proceedings 227, vol. 1.

LAND, EDWIN H., 1959. Experiments in color vision. *Sci. Am.*, May 1959.

LASHLEY, K. S. and RUSSELL, J. T., 1934. The Mechanism of vision: XI. A preliminary test of innate organization. *J. Genet. Psychol.*, 45, 136–44.

LOTZE, H., 1856–64. *Mikrokosmos.* 3 vols. Leipzig, Verlag von S. Hirzel.

MELZACK, R. and SCOTT, T. H., 1957. The effects of early experience on the response to pain. *J. Comp. Physiol. Psychol.*, 50, 155–61.

METZGER, WOLFGANG, 1953. *Gesetze des Sehens.* 2nd ed. Frankfurt am Main, Kramer.

MICHOTTE, A., 1954. *La perception de la causalité.* Louvain, Presses Universitaires.

PAVLOV, J. P., 1955. *Selected works.* Moscow, Foreign Languages Publishing House.

PETTIGREW, T. F.; ALLPORT, G. W.; and BARNETT, E. O., 1958. Binocular resolution and perception of race in South Africa. *Brit. J. Psychol.*, 49, 265–78.

PIAGET, JEAN, 1955. *The child's construction of reality.* London, Routledge and Kegan Paul. Originally, *La construction du réel chez l'enfant,* 1937. Neuchatel, Delachaux et Niestlé.

——— 1950. *The psychology of intelligence.* London, Routledge and Kegan Paul. Originally, *La psychologie de l'intelligence,* 1947. Collèction Armand Colin, Paris.

POINCARÉ, HENRI, 1902. *La science et l'hypothèse.* Paris. Flammarion.

——— 1905. *La valeur de la science.* Paris, Flammarion.

RILEY, D. A. and ROSENZWEIG, M. R., 1957. Echolocation in Rats. *J. Comp. Physiol. Psychol.*, 50, 323–28.

RYLE, G., 1949. *The concept of mind.* London, Hutchinson.

SENDEN, M. VON, 1932. *Raum- und Gestaltauffassung bei operierten Blindgeborenen vor und nach der Operation.* Leipzig, Barth.

SHERRINGTON, CHARLES S., 1911. *The integrative action of the nervous system.* New Haven, Yale University Press.

STRATTON, G. M., 1897. Vision without inversion of the retinal image. *Psychol. Rev.*, 4, 341–60, 463–81.

STUTTERHEIM, N. A., 1937. *Eyestrain and convergence,* London, H. K. Lewis.

TAYLOR, J. G. and PAPERT, S., 1956. A theory of perceptual constancy. *Brit. J. Psychol.*, 47, 216–24.

TYNDALL, JOHN, 1874. Fragments of science. *Brit. Assoc. Advance. Sci. Rep.* 44.

WAPNER, SEYMOUR, and WERNER, HEINZ, 1957. *Perceptual development: An investigation within the framework of sensory-tonic field theory.* Worcester, Mass, Clark University Press.

WATSON, J. B., 1924. *Psychology from the standpoint of a behaviorist.* 2nd ed. Philadelphia, Lippincott.

WITKIN, H. A., 1949. Perception of body position and of the position of the visual field. *Psychol. Monogr. Gen. and App.*, No. 302.

——— 1960. The problem of individuality in development. In *Perspectives in psychological theory.* New York, International Universities Press.

WOLPE, JOSEPH, 1958. *Psychotherapy by reciprocal inhibition.* Stanford, Stanford University Press.

Index

A, a: A_1, A_2, defined, 19, 40; A_3–A_{11} defined, 16, 40; A_{12}–A_{14}, defined, 55
Above-below relationships in perception, 153
Accommodation, ocular, 134; effected by oblique muscles, 296
Achromatism. *See* Color blindness
Action, not defined by terminus alone, 38
Acuity. *See* Visual acuity
Adaptation: transformation of system, 4–5; analysis of development in infancy, 14 ff.; mechanism in infant, 25 ff.; acceleration through generalization, 34; generates invariant states of readiness, 45; effect of gravity, 70 ff.; mutual independence of subsystems of multistable system, 199 f. *See also* Reaching responses
Aerial perspective, 134
Affection, conscious experience: and cognition, distinction queried, 288 f.; theories, 289 f.
Afferent functions in process of adaptation, 14 ff.; definition, 16 ff.; values in reaching response, 16 ff.; neural processes lie outside field of consciousness, 350
After-images, color perception, 253
Aircraft piloting, gravitation and perception, 88–89
Alcoholic intoxication, effect on horizontal-vertical frame of reference, 89
Alexander, S., 51, 60
Allport, G. W., 161 f., 366
Ambiguous figure, Schröder staircase, 173
Amblyopia, 315–16
Angles determining position of eyes in sockets and head relative to trunk (A_3–A_9), defined, 16, 40
Angles subtended by distances along floor, role of locomotion in perception, 109–11
Aphakia, 229–30, 305–06, 317
Ashby, W. R., 4, 5, 22, 24, 25, 34, 99, 131, 163, 197, 205, 214, 226, 346, 365
Association areas, cortex, 38
Attention: misleading concepts of, 139; fringe and focus of, 139–40; ghost-in-the-machine concept, 296–97
Auditory perception: and visual perception, distinctions on behavioral grounds, 285–86; "sixth sense" of blind reported as pressure stimuli on face, 272
Autokinesis, 34; explanation, 152; incidental conditioning, 153
Automatic interpolation device, 31; perception of texture, 114
Autonomic nervous system, role in emotions, 290

B, b: B_3, proprioceptive afferent function in reaching response, defined, 16
B, b, afferent function specifying forces acting on semicircular canals, defined, 75
Backward conditioning, reaching response, 104–05
Balance, postural, 72 ff.; loss of in infancy, 23
Barnett, E. O., 161 f., 366
Bates, W. H., 296, 365
Behavioral theory of perception: basic principles, 3, 298–337 passim; experimental predictions, 163–88, 194–231
Berkeley, G., 113, 166
Berlyne, D. E., 138 n., 365
Bicycle riding, adaptation, 125

Binet-Simon Scale, color-naming test, 248
Binocular vision: parallax, 135; doctrine of corresponding points, 140 ff.; fusion, 145, 161–62; behavioral theory of, 146; depth perception, 149 f.; perception of depth through telescope, 155–56; rivalry, 151 ff.; singularity of field due to independence of subsystems, 226
Biotaxis, 312
Blind, perception of objects in environment, 272–75
Body movements, (M(T)), making contact with object, 103
Bounded nature of visual field (Gibson), 47
Brain as a classifying machine (Hayek), 354 f.; notion rejected, 356, 359–60. *See also* Cortex
Brain "secretion" (Tyndall), 361
Brain stem reticular activating system (BSRAS), function, 138–39, 276
Burt, C., 248

C, c: C_1–C_8, defined, 74–75
Cannon, W., 289
Cannon-Bard theory of emotions, 289 f.
Cartesian dualism. *See* Dualism
Cartesian product, set theory, 9, 16, 22
Cataract, congenital, 82; effect of removal, 165, 229; perception of color on removal, 313; development of acuity on removal, 315
Cell assemblies (Hebb), 317
Center of rotation, moving field experiment, 67–69
Cerebral cortex. *See* Cortex
Channels of information. *See* Information theory
Child-rearing, effect of differences on development of perception, 73
Ciliary bodies, 296
Cognition and affection, classical distinction questionable, 288 f.
Color bands, wedge prism experiments, 260 ff.
Color blindness and deficiency: misnaming of colors by young children, 245; genesis in restriction of choice in early childhood, 249. *See also* Color discrimination
Color constancy, 234 ff., 239; analysis of, 249–52; simultaneous color contrast, 251 f.; large individual differences, 252
Color contrast, simultaneous, 232 f.; Hering's window, 251; successive, 253
Color discrimination, failure in intelligent children, 245; development related to group's color vocabulary, 248; develops with social maturity, 249
Color indeterminacy, new dyes, 252
Color naming: verbal responses to different wave lengths, 239 ff., 246 ff.; role of language in refinement of color perception, 247; interpersonal agreement in, 248. *See also* Color blindness
Color-odor synesthesia, 247
Color perception, 232–69; binocular rivalry, 160; nature of, 244; source of philosophical confusion, 344; not innate, 313; not directly related to wave length, 233, 245, 344; dependent on variety of environmental stimuli, 233 ff.; same formal properties as space perception, 236 ff., 247; not fully determined by retinal processes, 237, 245; and molecular structure of matter, 238, 242; role of language, 239 ff., 246 ff.; function of nonverbal responses, 239, 240 ff., 247; origin related to selecting responses, 240 f., 244, 344; differential conditioning with choice and eating of different foods, 241 ff.; role of interoceptive stimuli, 242; role of olfactory responses, 241 f.; definition of ${}_4\Pi$, 244; function of engram mediating conditioned response, 247; cultural and individual differences, 248–49; no useful information from after-images, 253–54; changes with tinted spectacles, 255; in cataract-operated patient, 313
Color-scale, embodies knowledge about light, 345–46
Color-tone synesthesia, 246–47
"Community system," interindividual communication, 357–58
Complementary colors, 249 f.; symbolic representation, 250
Complexity of system expressed in new simplicity (Alexander), 51

Compound readiness for sets of responses (Π), 42, 64
Computer, analogy with brain, 356
Conation, classical distinction from cognition and affection, 289 f.
Conative experience, 289
Conceptual nervous system, requirements of, 311–12
Conditioned responses, mediated by engrams, 39
Conditioned stimuli, traces acting as, 45
Conditioning: mechanism of adaptation, 6; classical and instrumental, 6; gives rise to ultrastability, 34; differential, 35, 197 f.; as a principle of learning, vindication of, 37; of stimulus to its unconditioned response, 279
Cones and rods, retina, 232
Congenital cataract. *See* Cataract, congenital
Consciousness: nature of, 361 ff.; private character of, 1–2; behavioral basis of, 284; system of relations between organism and environment, 299 f.; distinction between cognition and affection questioned, 288 f.; and conation, 289 f.; nativist and empiricist viewpoints, 299 ff.; Hebb's theory of, 312; primitive (Piaget), 326, 329; not a function of brain alone, 361; identified with simultaneity of knowing, 361 f.; open to scientific study, 1 2, 363. *See also* Mind; Perception; Phenomenal order; Sense-data
Constancy. *See* Color constancy; Object constancy; Perceptual constancies
Contact lens. *See* Prismatic contact lens
Continuum: isotropic, 322; distinction between mathematic and physical, 331
Convergence, ocular, 315–16
Cooper, S., 294, 365
Coordination, hand-and-eye, 14 ff.
Corresponding points, binocular vision, 140 ff.; doctrine examined, 142 ff.
Cortex: function of, 355–56; striate area, 19, 38; association areas, 38; motor area, 56; projection area, 56; inhibition and fatigue, 281. *See also* Brain
Crawling: not a result of maturation only, 70–71; acquisition of responses to gravity, 85–86; regression to, in ambulatory child, 117–18; transition to walking, revolutionary effect on perception, 118. *See also* Locomotion; Walking
Critical state of a system (Ashby), 4, 6; in infancy, 22 ff.; minor, 23, 25, 60, 83; major, 23, 25
Crying: primitive response in instrumental behavior, 292; response to hunger and pain, 278–79; conditioning of interoceptive impulses, 280

Δ, δ (delta), defined, 17, 39; redefined to include color stimuli, 236
D, d, drive stimuli, defined, 23, 41
Daniel, P. M., 294, 365
Darwin, C., 302–03
Definitions of symbols leading up to Π summarized, 39–41
Delboeuf's illusion, 330–32
Depth perception, 99–100, 105 ff., 118 ff., 134 ff.; role of parallax, 134 ff.; role of locomotion, 99 ff., 106, 109–11; effect of limitation of child's movements, 107–08; disruption in adult, 108–09; development with growth in size, 118–20; distance of vertical barriers, 120 f.; doctrine of corresponding points refuted, 145 ff.; binocular vision, 149 f.
Descartes, R., 3, 81, 339, 348
Diplopia, 140; subject's lack of awareness of, 148–49
Displacement, parallactic. *See* Parallax
Distance perception. *See* Depth perception
Distorting spectacles. *See* Spectacles, distorting
Domain of a relation, set theory, 10
Dot experiment crucial to theory of perception, 51–52
Double vision. *See* Diplopia
Drive, critical state of system, 4, 23, 56
Drive reduction (Hull), 6
Drive stimuli (Hull), 6, 22; defined, 23, 24, 41
Drowsiness, causing loss of positional constancy, 283
Dualism: Cartesian, 81, 339, 348; "practical" (Hayek), 349, 357

E, e, defined, 39, 41; E′, e′, defined, 39, 41; E″, e″, defined, 39, 41
Eating and color perception, 241 f.
Echolocation: in blind, 273, 285–86; in rats, 273 n.; in bats, 285–86
Eclecticism, theories of perception, 1, 299; rejected, 167 f., 301 ff.
Effective reaction potential (Hull), 30
Electronic computer, analogy with brain, 356
Elements, set theory, 7–8, 10–11
Emotion: theories, 289 ff.; autonomic and behavioral components, 290 f.; experience unique for each individual, 292
Empiricism and nativism, theories of perception, 167 f., 299 ff.
Engram: concept revived, 38 f.; defined as set of neural structures (E′), 39, 41
Environment: adaptation to, 14 ff.; spatial ordering of, 12, 79 ff., 96; change in perceived position of, 57–58; perceived by infant without corresponding perception of his own position in it, 60; manipulation excluded in prismatic contact lens experiment, 222 f.
Environmental functions: Γ, γ, defined, 17; Ψ, ψ, defined, 17; Δ, δ, defined, 17, 39; Ω, ω, defined, 55
Epistemology, behavioral theory of perception, 338 f. *See also* Knowledge
Equilibrial axis (Wapner and Werner), 309
Equivalence class, set theory, 11, 26, 63
Erect posture, acquisition of, 72 ff.
Erismann, T., 170, 171 f., 180, 206, 220, 227, 304 f., 319
Euclidean space, gradual approximation to perception of, 155 f. *See also* Geometric space
Ewert, P. H., 169 f., 365
Experience. *See* Affection; Cognition; Conation; Consciousness; Emotion; Mind; Perception; Phenomenal order; Sensation; Sense-data
Experiment, analogous to acquisition of sense-data, 349
Experimental design, possibly misleading in testing of hypotheses, 306
Experimental evidence, behavioral theory of perception, 163 ff.; caution in interpretation, 165–66; specific predictions tested, 194 ff.
External (real) world, stability of, 336
Exteroceptive components of stimulation in motor acts, 24
Exteroceptors. *See* Receptor organs
Eye: afferent processes (V_1 and V_2), defined, 40; afferent impulses (V_3–V_8), defined, 16, 17, 40; angles giving position in sockets (A_3–A_8), 16, 18, 21–22, defined, 40; movements (M and M(E)), defined, 22 f., 36, 41; orientations (O), 16 ff., 18, 21, defined, 40; set of positions (Z and Z(E)), 22, defined, 40; proprioceptive connections in extrinsic muscles, 294 f.; role of oblique muscles in accommodation, 296; pupillary aperture, 19; refracting media, 19; saccadic movements, 48–49, 294–95. *See also* Retina

F, f, defined, 36–37, 41; ${}_2F$, defined, 61, 63; ${}_3F$, 128 f.; F(G), defined, 78
Falling movements, infancy, 23
Fatigue: perception of, 278, 281; not primary sensation but learned perception, 284
Fear: in infancy (Watson), 23, 290–91; behavioral components in experience of, 292
Fechner, G. T., 303, 331
Field, (Ashby), 4. *See also* Multistable system
Field dependency (Witkin), 93
Fixation, visual, 33–34; joint movement of head and eyes, 36; effect on perception, 50–51; responses to goal-objects, 62; effect of inverting spectacles, 177 ff.; wedge prism experiment, 220; eye movements acquired by conditioning, 222 ff.
Flying in birds, not a result of maturation only, 71
Focus of attention, 139–40
"Following," brain impulses (Hayek), 354
Food, choice of and development of color perception, 241–43
Formal equivalence class, 26
Frame of reference: with origin in neck, 55; spinal, 54; objective, 65; gravita-

tional, 74; horizontal-vertical, 80; perceptual, 65, 129–30
Freud, S., 61, 289, 292, 362
Function, set theory, 11
Functional equivalence classes, 26, 37, 48

Γ, γ (gamma), defined, 17
G(H), defined, 76
Generalization, 26 f.; principle, 35, 61; of inhibition, 35; perception of texture, 114
Geometric space: representation in consciousness, 320 f.; Poincaré's principles, 322
Gestalt theories of perception, 303 ff.
Ghost in the machine, 296–97, 339, 348, 352
Gibson, J. J., 47, 49, 50, 57, 111, 117, 140, 301 f., 319, 365
Goal-directed responses in infancy, 25 f., 28 f.
Goal gradient hypothesis (Hull), 104, 216
Gradient of reinforcement, 104
Gradients of texture (Gibson), 111 f.; in floor, 115 f.; in walls, 120 ff.
Graham, C. H., 142, 365
Grasping: reflex in infant, 25 ff.; movements making contact with object (M(S)), 103
Gravitational axis, adaptive responses, 80–81
Gravitational frame of reference, 74
Gravitational pressures in body, 56
Gravity: effect on perception, 70 ff.; response variables, 70 ff.; role in experiments on retinal inversion, 178 f.; horizontal-vertical framework, wedge-prism experiment, 218–19
Group structure: definition, 323; Piaget's concept, 327; group theory, 328; perception of night sky, 335
Growth in size of child, effect on depth perception, 118–19
Gustation. *See* Taste perception

H, h, defined, 19, 40
Hand-and-eye coordination: prerequisites for development, 14; afferent variables necessary for, 15 f.
Hand movements (M): necessary variables, 15 ff., 21 f.; conditioning in infancy, 25 f.; single stage and two-stage, 29 f.; defined, 36, 41
Hand position, proprioceptive afferent functions, (V_9–V_{11}), 15; defined, 20, 21, 40
Hayek, F. A., 338, 348–49, 354 f., 365
Head: angles determining position relative to trunk (A_3–A_8), 16 ff., defined, 40; orientations (O), 16 ff., together with eye, definition, 40; movements (M and M(H)), 22, 24, defined, 36, 41; rolling movements in infancy, 73 ff., 78; pressure stimuli, 76; immobilization, 83; undulations during locomotion, 135
Head, H., 163, 289–90
Hebb, D. O., 165, 312 f., 365
Hering, E., 232, 234
Hering's window, 251, 270
Horizontal, perception of, 94–95
Horizontal-vertical frame of reference: perceptual field, 80–81; artificial distortion, 88–89; effect of alcoholic intoxication, 89; private to each individual, 130
Howard-Dolman apparatus, 141
Howard-Dolman threshold, 143
Howells, T. H., 246 f., 264, 365
Hull, C. L., 6, 22, 25, 27, 30, 33 n., 104, 177, 199, 262, 263, 292, 315, 365
Hunger: perception of, 278 f.; not primary sensation but learned perception, 284; and pain, similarities and differences, 279
Hunger reduction, nipple as conditioned stimulus, 23
Hypothesis in science, analogy with unlearned response, 359

Ideal space (Piaget), 331
Immediacy of sense-data, 232, 339; obstacle to scientific approach to problem of modalities, 271; difficulty for epistemologists, 341; explanation of, 350–51
Indeterminacy, principle of, 25
Individual differences, adaptation to experimental interference with perception, 164–65

"Individual system," single multistable system contrasted with "community system," 357–58
Information theory, 99; channels of communication, 134
Inhibition: generalization, 35; Pavlovian theory, 281 f.
Innsbruck experiments, 171 ff.
Intelligence, conforms to axioms of group (Piaget), 330
Intermodality perception. *See* Synesthesia
Interoceptive stimuli: conditioning to eating responses, color perception, 242; conditioning to crying response, 280–81
Interpenetration, principle of, 81, 82, 84; horizontal-vertical frame of reference, 96–97; readaptation of disrupted systems, 195; experimental acceleration, 199–200; visual and gravitational systems (reversing spectacles), 201; wedge prism spectacles, different subsystems, 210; perception of rotation, 293
Interpolated responses: process of adaptation to environment, 30–31; perception of texture, 114
Intoxication, effect on horizontal-vertical frame of reference, 89
Introspection: rejection by early behaviorists, 352; not different from any other kind of observation, 353; fruitless concept in epistemology and structural psychology, 358–59
Inverting spectacles, experiments, 166, 167 ff.; analysis of transformations, 173–75; prediction of perceptual changes, 176; anomalies in experimental evidence, 180–81; perceptual instabilities, 181 f.; adaptation to instability, 183 f.; effect of removal, 185. *See also* Reversing spectacles; Spectacles, distorting
Irradiation, principle of (Pavlov), 26
Irradiation hypothesis, color contrast, 233, 251 f.
Isotropic continuum (Poincaré), 322

J, j, defined, 75
James, W., 289–90
James-Lange theory of emotions, 289–90
Jameson, Sir W., 71, 365

K, k (gravitational stimulation), 76
K, k (retinal stimulation), defined, 18, 40
Kershner, R. B., 7, 12, 323, 365
Kinesthesia, role in space perception, 319 f. *See also* Proprioceptive afferent functions
Knee jerk, elicited conditionally by originally inadequate tensions, 279–80
Knowledge: defined behaviorally, 340 ff., role of sense-data in acquisition of, 343; state of readiness for action, analogous to perception, 349–50; depends on afferent-efferent connections, 350–51; a function of whole organism, 360; of knowledge, 360; of knowledge of knowledge, 360
Koffka, K., 19, 233, 365
Kohler, I., 170, 172, 180, 187, 198, 206, 207, 210, 212, 220, 227, 255 f., 258, 263, 266, 275, 304 f., 365

Λ, λ (lambda), positions of R(Δ) relative to R(G), defined, 74; wave lengths of reflected light, defined, 235
Land, E. H., 233 f., 254 f., 365
Lange, C., 289 f.
Language: role in perception, 165 f., 178, 185, 201; role in perception of color, 246–47
Lashley, K. S., 38, 273 n., 365
Learning: process of adaptation to environment in infancy, 14 ff.; one-factor and two-factor theories, 312. *See also* Conditioning
Left-right relationships in perception, 153
Leibniz, G. W., 352
Lens, distorting. *See* Spectacles
Light: wave length and color, 232–33, 245, 344; wave length and overt responses, 239; origin of physicist's knowledge of wave composition of, 345. *See also* Color; Eye; Retina
Line of behavior (Ashby), 4
Linear perspective, locomotion, 99
Linnaeus, C., 302
Local signature (Lotze), 316 n.
Locomotion, 70 ff., 98 ff.; effect on in-

fant's perception, 66, 70 ff., 98 ff.; roles of maturation and learning, 70–72; retinal functions, 98 f.; proprioceptive and pressure stimuli, 98; distance perception, 99 ff., 106, 109–11; multiple channels of information, 99; Gibson's theory of perception, 302. *See also* Crawling; Walking
Locomoter conditioning, perception of slope and texture, 115 f.
Locomotor instability of alcoholic, 89
Lotze, H., 316 n., 366

M, m, defined, 22, 41, redefined, 36; ₂M, defined, 62; ₃M, defined, 103; M(γ), defined, 36; M(A), defined, 22, 41; M(E), defined, 22, 41; M(G), defined, 74; M(H), defined, 22, 41; M(L), defined, 103; M(S), defined, 103; M(T), defined, 58, 103
Mass action (Lashley), 38
Maternal intervention, critical states in infancy, 22–23
Maternal overprotection and field dependency, 93–94
Mathematical models in psychology, 12 f.
Major cirtical states, infancy, 23, 25
Maturation, nativist explanation of development of consciousness, 299 f.
Melzack, R., 278, 366
Mental events, reality and determinacy of, 1–2. *See also* Consciousness; Experience; Mind; Perception; Phenomenal order; Sense-data
Mentalism, rejection by early behaviorists, 363
Metzger, W., 145, 366
Michotte, A., 42, 302, 366
Mind: concept of, 339; set of acquired relations between organism and environment, 352; can its processes be understood? 354
Mind-stuff, 339
Minor critical states, 23, 25, 60, 74, 83
Modalities, sensory, 271 ff.; distinctions due to learning, 271 ff.; behavioral hypothesis of genesis, 275 f.
Molecular structure of matter, color equivalence, 238, 242
Monads (Leibniz), 352
Motion, perception of as a result of trunk movements in infancy, 67
Movement: eye, head, and hand, 22 f., 36, 41; making contact with object, 103; of field, effect of inverting spectacles, 186–87; central role in development of perception, 319; role in Piaget's theory, 326
Moving environment, effect of inverting spectacles, 168–69
Moving field experiment, center of rotation in area that can be reached, 67
Müller, J., 140
Multiple states of readiness for responses, 42 ff.
Multistable system (Ashby), 4, 5, 34, 356; illustrated by experiment with reversing spectacles, 188; mutual independence of subsystems of U, 34–35; experimental disruption of subsystems, 194 f., 199 f., 226; relevancy in human adaptation, 205–06; how set up, 346 f.

N, n, changes in position of body and resulting changes in pressure stimuli related to R(G), defined, 76
N, n, neural processes equivalent to R, r, defined, 19, 40
Nativism and empiricism, theories of perception, 167 f., 299 f.
Nearer-farther relationships in perception, 153
Neck: pressure stimuli, 76; contraction of muscles to prevent rolling of head, 76
Need-state, 6
Negative after-images, 253
Neurosis, treatment by conditioning, 292
Newton, I., 1, 345
Night sky, perception of, 333 f.
Noise. *See* Information theory
Nonmetric space of child, 109
Notation, set theory, 6; illustrated by game of chess, 8 ff.; definitions leading up to Π summarized, 39–41
Null-functions (Ashby), 34, 77

Ω, ω (omega), defined, 55
O, o, defined, 18, 40
Object constancy, 26 ff., 45, 48, 65; role of locomotion, 106–07

Object fixation, joint movements of head and eyes, 36
Object-subject, independent existence of each, 348
Objective frame of reference, 65
Objects in environment: adaptation in infancy, 14 ff., 25 ff.; position and light energies, 17 ff., 39; grasping reflex, 25 ff.; change in position, 30 ff.; constancy of perception, 26 ff., 45, 48, 65, 106–07
Ocular. *See* Eye; Retina
Ocular convergence, 315–16
Ocular responses: goal-object fixation, 33 f., 226; behavioral nature of, 306
Olfaction. *See* Smell
One-to-one correspondence: set theory, 11; between reaching movement and goal-object, 37
Optic. *See* Eye; Retina
Optic axis, 18; deviations of light rays from, 19, 40
Optic nerve, afferent processes, 16, 18–21, 40
Optic radiation, 19
Ordered pairs, set theory, 8, 38
Ordered 3-tuples, 17
Ordinal stimulation in similar patterns, (refutation of) Gibson's explanation for different positions of same environment, 57–58
Organismic field. *See* Multistable system
Orientation: eye, 16 f., 18, 21, 40; head, 16 f., 21, 40
Overdetermination of system. *See* Information theory
Overprotection, maternal, 93–94

Φ, ϕ (phi): defined, 39, 41; ${}_2\Phi$, defined, 63; ${}_3\Phi$, defined, 131; ${}_4\Phi$, defined, 244; $\Phi(G)$, defined, 79
Π(pi): defined, 39, 41; ${}_1\Pi$, restated, 129; ${}_2\Pi$, defined, 63, 129; ${}_3\Pi$, derivation traced, 128–31; ${}_4\Pi$, defined, 244
Ψ, ψ (psi), defined, 17
P, p, pairs of objects or points in environment, defined, 153
P, p, patterns of pressure stimuli in head and neck, defined, 76
Pain: genesis of experience, 277–78, 291; not primary sensation but learned perception, 284, 292; pathological insensitivity to, 278; and hunger, similarities and differences, 279
Palmar reflex in infant, 25
Papert, S., 84, 189–93, 198, 201, 267, 366
Parallax, 134–62; and locomotion, 134 ff.; binocular, 135–62; displacements as conditioned stimuli for locomotor responses, 137, 138; displacements, redefined, 323; not observed during locomotion toward a goal, 139; doctrine of corresponding points, 140–48
Parallel arrangements, adaptation of subsystems (Ashby), 5
Parameter to reacting system, 197, 263
Part-functions (Ashby), 34–35
Partitioning, set theory, 11
Patellar reflex, elicited by originally inadequate tensions, 279–80
Pavlov, I. P., 24, 26, 35, 45, 107, 271, 276, 279, 281, 282, 283, 355, 366
Perceived stimulus $(q \in {}_2Q)$, defined, 59–60
Perceiver, reality of, 348
Perception: current theories, 1, 220, 298–337; natural phenomenon open to scientific investigation, 1, 361–63; reliability of reports, 2, 352–54; and unconscious motivation, 3; identified with Π, 39, 41, 42; identified with ${}_2\Pi$, 63, 129; development traced from ${}_1\Pi$ to ${}_3\Pi$, 128–31; identified with ${}_4\Pi$, 244; spatial ordering of environment, 36–69; temporal priority over action questioned, 42–43; a function of learned behavior rather than mere stimulation, 47–48, 138, 167, 214; 297; complexity of Π as opposed to simplicity of percept, 51; change of position of environment in infancy, 57–58; of infant's environment but not his own position in it, 60; role of gravity, 70–97; effect of child-rearing practices on development of, 73; gravitational world and visual world, 88; horizontal-vertical frame of reference, 88–97, 307 f.; role of locomotion, 97–133; role of parallax, 134–62; experimental transformation of afferent functions, 163–88,

194–231; current views of function, 220; color, 232–69; and sensation, distinction queried and rejected, 232 ff., 284; synesthetic, 246–47; role of receptor organs, 270–97; monistic point of view, 300; eclectic and nativistic theories rejected, 167 f., 301 ff.; gestalt theories, 303 f.; Hebb's theory of vision, 314 f.; night sky, 333–36; philosophical implications, 338–63. *See also* Consciousness; Mind; Phenomenal order; Sense-data; Vision
Perceptual constancies, 26, 45, 48; size, 106–07, 127 f.; role of locomotion, 106–07, 110–11, 131, 215; perception of vertical barriers (walls) 126 f.; development in child from 1 to 3, 131; color, 239, 244 ff.; and group structure, 336. *See also* Color constancy; Object constancy; Positional constancy
Perceptual frames of reference, 65, 130
Perceptual field, impossibility of interindividual comparison, 130
Perspective, linear, 99
Pettigrew, T. F., 161, 366
Phenomenal order, 1–2; essential in scientific enquiry, 345; and physical order, 348
Phi-phenomenon, 283
Philosophical implications, behavioral theory of perception, 338–63
Physical and sensory order (Hayek), 357
Physiological models, requirements of, 311–12
Piaget, J., 155, 304, 322, 323, 326 ff., 335, 336, 366
Piloting of aircraft, gravitation and perception, 88–89
Pitch discrimination, genesis in infant, 286–87
Poggendorf's figure, 332 n.
Poincaré, H., 319 f., 321 f., 327, 328, 331, 336, 366
Pointer readings, analogy with subject's verbal report, 353
Position: of environment, perceived change, 57–58; of body, perception, 88
Positional constancy, 65, 69; a relative attribute of perception, 67; loss during states of drowsiness, 283
"Practical dualism" (Hayek), 349
Pre-Copernican universe, analogy with infant's space perception, 66
Predictions from behavioral theory tested, 194–231
Pressure stimuli: on head and neck (P), defined, 76; on face, "sixth sense" of blind, 272
Primary operation (Ashby), 4
Primitive consciousness (Piaget), 326, 329
Printed matter, mirrored perception with reversing spectacles, 188
Prismatic contact lens experiment, 222–31; mutual independence of distortions in different parts of the field, 227. *See also* Spectacles, distorting; Wedge prism experiment
Proper subsets, set theory, 8
Proprioceptive afferent functions: hand position (V_9–V_{11}), 20, 21, 40; extrinsic eye muscles, 294
Proximal stimuli: applied to retina (R), 19, 40; corresponding neural processes in retina (N), 19
Pseudofovea, 146
Pseudomacula, 145–46, 148
Pseudophone, 163
Psychotherapy, conditioning procedures, 292
Ptolemaic cosmology, analogy with infant's space perception, 66, 69, 105–06

Q, q, defined, 24, 41; ${}_2Q$, defined, 56, 129; ${}_3Q$, defined, 102, 130; ${}_4Q$, defined, 237; ${}_4\bar{Q}$, defined, 256; $Q(\delta)$, defined, 26, 41; Q(G), defined, 76; Q(w), defined, 238; ${}_2Q(y)$, defined, 57; Q(z), defined, 27, 41

R, r (proximal stimuli, retina), defined, 19, 40; $R(\Delta)$, 55; $R(\Omega)$, 55; $R\ ({}_1\Pi)$, defined, 129–30; $R({}_2\Pi)$, defined, 65, 129; R(G), defined, 74
Race, perception of, 161–62
Rage: in infancy (Watson), 23, 290–91; behavioral components in experience, 292
Range of a relation, set theory, 10

Reaching responses: infant's adaptation to environment, 15 ff., 60–62; afferent variables required, 15 ff.; hand movements, 15 ff., 36; roundabout paths, 28–29; one-to-one correspondence with goal-object, 37; conditioned, 58, 103 f.; compensatory movements in execution of, 62; backward conditioning, 104–05; theory of binocular vision, 146, 149; effect of distorting lenses, 177 f., 185 f., 199, 217–19; color perception, 240 f.
Reaction potential, effective, 30
Reactive inhibition (Hull), 262–63
Readiness for response: definition of state of system, 41–42; independent of specific pattern of stimulation, 45; identified with knowledge, 340 f.
Real (external) world, stability of, 336
Receptor organs: role in perception, 270 f.; processes lie outside field of consciousness, 350; differences in perception due to differing modes of behavioral adjustment, 284
Reciprocal inhibition, treatment of neuroses, 292
Reflexes, conditioned and unconditioned, 24; palmar, 25 ff.
Regression to more primitive and complex levels of organization, 61
Regular system (Ashby), 22
Reinforcement: of reaching response, 36, 61–62; delay in, increment in habit strength, 199; of perceptual responses, criterion of true knowledge, 341 f.
Relation, set theory, 9, 11
Response, fallacious definition solely in terms of terminus, 38
Restriction of movement, infancy, 23
Reticular activating system, brain stem function (BSRAS), 138–39
Retina: variables in infant, 5; hand-and-eye coordination, 15 ff.; functions in proximal stimuli and neural events, 19, 40; rectangular coordinates, 19; rods and cones, 232; structure adapted for light-dark discrimination, 315
Retinal disparity. *See* Parallax, binocular
Retinal image, 49; locomotion and depth perception, 99 ff.; object size constancy, 107
Retinal impulses, no physiological congruence between pair, 146
Retinal inversion. *See* Inverting spectacles
Retinal irradiation, unnecessary concept for simultaneous color contrast, 251
Retinal points, positions defined (H), 19, 20, 40
Retinal processes, not sole determiner of color perception, 245
Retinal rivalry. *See* Binocular vision, rivalry
Retinal stimulation: in infant, 5; of periphery, 49–50; not sole determiner of visual perception, 167, 214
Reversing spectacles, experiments, 172 f., 195 ff.; intermittent wearing, 198 f.; anomalous perceptions, 201–02, 206–07; subvocal repetition of instructions, 201; mathematical analysis of effects, 189–93. *See also* Inverting spectacles; Spectacles, distorting
Riley, D. H., 273 n., 366
Rivalry, binocular, 157 f.
Rods and cones, retina, 232
Rosenzweig, M. R., 273 n., 366
Russell, J. T., 273 n., 365
Ryle, G., 339, 366

Σ (sigma), defined, 21, 40; $\Sigma(G)$, 90; $\overline{\Sigma}(G)$, 90
S, s, defined, 20, 40
Saccadic eye movements, 48–49, 294–95
Scanning movements of eyes, prismatic contact lens experiment, 222 f., 227; independence of different parts of environment, 228
Schermann, A., 198, 199, 200
Schröder staircase, ambiguous figure, 173
Science of mind, 2, 363
Scientific experiment, analogous to acquisition of sense-data, 349 f.
Scientific knowledge, distinguished from sensory knowledge by interpersonal agreement, 351–52
Scott, T. H., 278, 366
Seizing movements, M(S), making contact with object, 103
Semicircular canals, perception of rotation, etc., 74–75, 292 f.

Senden, M. von, 82, 312, 366
Sensation and perception: historical distinction, 232; distinction rejected, 284, 293; distinction related to spatial and nonspatial behavior, 293–94
Sense-data: conditions necessary for their generation, 339; interpreted as mediated events reflecting history of subject's interaction with environment, 341; importance of role in acquisition of true knowledge, 343–44; essential in scientific enquiry, 345–46; conceived as act of knowing, 352
Sensory and physical order (Hayek), 357
Sensory modalities, 270 f.
Sensory experience: immediacy, 232, 271; permanence, 271; role of receptors, 270 f.
Sensory-tonic field theory (Wapner and Werner), 370 f.; failure as a perceptual theory, 310
Serial adaptation of subsystems (Ashby), 5
Set theory, conventions and notation, 6–12
Shannon, C. E., 99
Shape: constancies, 127 f.; perception of (Hebb), 312 f., 316 f.
Sherrington, C. S., 145, 366
Short-trace conditioned reflexes (Pavlov), 24
Shrinkage of distance with growth of subject, 119–20
"Silent" areas, cortex, 38
Simultaneous readiness for set of responses (Π), 65
Single-valued function, set theory, 11
Singular perception. *See* Binocular vision
Sitting, not a result of maturation only, 70–71
Sitting and walking two independent subsystems, wedge prism experiment, 210
Situational changes in perception, gestalt theory, 304
"Sixth sense" of blind, single sense organ mediates two different modalities, 272
Size constancy. *See* Perceptual constancies
Skeletal musculature, role in emotions, 290
Sleep, 56; spreading of inhibition, 281–82
Slope of ground, perceptual adaptation in locomotion, 115 f.
Smell, 287–88; and food colors, 241
Sodium light test, wedge prism experiment, 266–67
Space perception, 36 ff., 53 ff.; non-Euclidean and nonmetric in child, 109; gradual approximation to Euclidean, 155; role of ocular fixation, 222 f.; role of retinal and proprioceptive stimuli, 229; and color perception, 236; Hebb's theory, 312 f.; central role of movement, 319 f.; displacement (Poincaré), 321; 17-dimensional continuum, 337. *See also* Depth perception; Geometric space; Spatial ordering of environment
Spatial ordering of environment, 12; complex relationship with organism, 42; effect of adaptation to gravity, 79 ff., 96; role of locomotion, 105; autokinesis, 154; topological equivalence, 154–55; color perception, 237; perception by blind, 272–75; distortion through drowsiness, drugs, alcohol, 283
Specific nerve energies, 270 f.; doctrine rejected, 275
Spectacles, distorting: use of to transform afferent functions, 163 f.; explanation of constancy in terms of sensory-tonic field theory, 310. *See also* Inverting spectacles; Prismatic contact lens; Reversing spectacles; Squint glasses; Tinted spectacles; Wedge prism spectacles
Spectrum, 234; observation yields knowledge about light, 346
Spherical aberration, removal of cataracts, 229–30
Spine as frame of reference (in sitting posture), 54
Spinoza, B. de, 339
Squint glasses, depth perception, 155. *See also* Spectacles, distorting
Squinting, binocular vision with singular perception explained, 145–48
Stable system (Ashby), 4
Standing: not a result of maturation only,

Standing (*continued*)
70–71; acquisition of responses to gravity, 86
Stairs, perception of, 333 f.
State of system (Ashby), 4
Steady state, system in infancy, 23
Step-functions (Ashby), 4, 24, 25; interpreted as unlearned behavior, 24
Stereoscopic vision. *See* Depth perception
Stimulus intensity dynamism (Hull), 33 n., 315
Stimulus variables, hand-eye coordination, 14 ff.
Stratton, G. M., 167, 168 ff., 170, 179, 183, 185, 195, 196, 310, 366
Striate area, cortex, 19, 38
Structural theories of perception, 303 f.
Stutterheim, N. A., 315, 316, 366
Subject-object relationship: no justification for disjunction, 338–39; definition of knowledge, 340; independent existence of each, 348
Subsets, set theory, 7; empty, 7; proper, 8
Subsystems (Ashby), 5; disruption of, importance in testing behavioral theory, 194–95
Successive color contrast, 253
Synesthesia: color-tone, 246; color-odor, 247
Sympathetic nervous system, role in emotions, 271–72
System (Ashby), 4; absolute, 4; regular, 4; stable, 4; state determined, 4; ultrastable, 4, 77; multistable, 5; unstable, 77

T, t, defined, 16–17, 75
Tactile perception, 285
Taste perception: influence of olfaction, 287–88; and food color, 241
Taylor, J. G., 160, 207, 366
Terman-Merrill Scale, color-naming test, 248
Texture gradients, Gibson's theory of space perception, 111 ff.
Texture of walls, 120 f.
Thalamic theory of emotions, 289
Theories of perception, 298 f.
Thinghood of objects, 18
Threshold, differentiation, 331
Throwing of missiles, depth perception, 151
Tilted room experiments (Witkin), 73, 89–94
Tinted spectacles, change in color perception, 255 f. *See also* Spectacles, distorting
Titchener, E. B., 353
Tolman, E. C., 299
Tonic variables (Wapner and Werner), 301
Topology, spatial ordering of environment, 154–55
Trace conditioned reflexes (Pavlov), 24
Traces, acting as conditioned stimuli, 45
Trial-and-error in development of perception, 128
Triangle, Hebb's analysis of perception, 316 f.
Trunk: angles of tilt and twist, 55; mobility, 53–54; afferent functions, 55–56; movements, 58
Truth, empirical criterion, 344
Two-toned spectacles. *See also* Tinted spectacles
Tyndall, J., 361, 366

U, defined, 41; $_2$U, defined, 59; $_3$U, defined, 103, 128; U(G), defined, 77
Ultrastable system, 4, 25, 38, 77, 356; brought about by conditioning, 34; mutual independence of subsystems before learning begins, 34–35
Unbounded nature of visual world (Gibson), 46–47
Unconditioned reflexes, 24
Unconscious, Freud's theory of, 362; role in Freudian account of conation, 289; motivation and perception, 3
Undulations of head during locomotion, 135
"Unity of the mind," principle of interpenetration, 81–82
Unlearned behavior, 6, 25
Unstable system (Ashby), 25, 77; adaptation in infancy, 14 ff.; summary of variables included, 346
Unpleasant emotions, roles of visceral and overt responses, 292

V: V_1 and V_2, defined, 40; V_3–V_{11}, defined, 16–17, 40; V_{12}–V_{14}, defined, 56; V_0, defined, 20; V(A,B), defined, 144
Verbal responses. *See* Language
Verification principle in science, criterion of sense-data, 343–44
Vertical, perception of: in tilted rooms, 73, 89–94; constancy of direction, 84–85; sensory-tone field theory, 301 f.
Vertical barriers: perception of distance through texture, 120 f.; arrest in child's locomotion, 120
Vertical frame of reference, perceptual field, 80, 81
Vestibule: stimulation, 74, 76; no specific "sensation," 292, 294; perception of rotation, etc., 292
Vision. *See* Binocular vision; Perception; Visual acuity, development of in cataract-operated patients, 315; Visual angles, distance perception, 100 f.
Visual acuity, development of in cataract-operated patients, 315
Visual angles, distance perception, 100 f.
Visual field: Gibson's contrast with visual world, 47, 49; contrast refuted, 50; expansion of, 98 ff.
Visual fixation. *See* Fixation, visual
Visual perception: not a function of retinal stimulation alone, 47–48, 138, 167, 214, 297; and perception of body position, 88; and auditory perception, distinction on behavioral grounds, 285–86; of space (Hebb), 312 f.
Visual world. *See* Visual field

W, defined, 238
Walking: not a result of maturation only, 70–72; acquisition of responses to gravity, 86–87; revolutionary transition from crawling, 118; and sitting, two independent systems, 210. *See also* Crawling; Locomotion
Wall: of null-functions (Ashby), 34, 77; of part-functions, 35; of inactive part-functions, wedge prism experiment, 214
Walls, arrest in child's locomotion, 120 f.
Wapner, S., 307 f., 366
Watson, J. B., 23, 78, 290, 291, 366
Wave length of light: no one-to-one correspondence with color perception, 233, 245, 345; verbal and qualitative responses to, 239; nonverbal responses to, 240
Wedge prism spectacles, experiment, 207 ff.; perceptual distortions produced, 210–11; fixation experiment, 220; physiological explanation refuted, 220–27; color-band experiments, 259 ff., 267; after-effect colors, 266. *See also* Prismatic contact lens; Spectacles, distorting
Werner, H., 307 f., 366
Whitteridge, D., 294, 365
Wilcox, L. R., 7, 12, 323, 365
Witkin, H. A., 73, 89, 90, 93, 94, 95, 96, 97, 365
Wolpe, J., 292, 365
Wundt, W., 353

Y, y, defined, 55

Z, z, defined, 22; Z(A), defined, 22, 40; Z(E), defined, 22, 40; Z(H), defined, 22, 40; $z(q_1)$, defined, 27, 41

www.ingramcontent.com/pod-product-compliance
Ingram Content Group UK Ltd.
Pitfield, Milton Keynes, MK11 3LW, UK
UKHW041623031026
15587UKWH00001B/13

9 780837 169576